Revolutionary Patriots

of

Talbot County

Maryland

1775–1783

Henry C. Peden, Jr.

HERITAGE BOOKS
2024

HERITAGE BOOKS
AN IMPRINT OF HERITAGE BOOKS, INC.

Books, CDs, and more—Worldwide

For our listing of thousands of titles see our website at
www.HeritageBooks.com

Published 2024 by
HERITAGE BOOKS, INC.
Publishing Division
5810 Ruatan Street
Berwyn Heights, MD 20740

Copyright © 1998 Henry C. Peden, Jr.

All rights reserved. No part of this book may be reproduced or transmitted in any form or by any means, electronic or mechanical, including photocopying, recording or by any information storage and retrieval system without written permission from the author, except for the inclusion of brief quotations in a review.

International Standard Book Number
Paperbound: 978-1-58549-501-6

INTRODUCTION

This book has been compiled for the purpose of serving as a research tool for locating the men and women of Talbot County, Maryland who served in the military, rendered material aid to the army or navy, took the Oath of Allegiance and Fidelity, served in an office or on a committee at the town, county or state level, or in some fashion contributed and supported the fight for freedom by the American colonies from the rule of Great Britain during the Revolutionary War, 1775-1783.

It is hoped that this book, which is the fourteenth in a series on Revolutionary War patriots and soldiers in Maryland, will encourage and enable interested persons to become members of such patriotic organizations as The Sons of the American Revolution, The Daughters of the American Revolution, The Sons of the Revolution, and The Society of the Cincinnati.

Information for this book has been gleaned from many primary and secondary sources, which makes this book far more than just a listing of names and ranks. Many of the approximately 3,000 persons named herein have genealogical data included with their respective entries, such as places of residence and dates of birth, death, and marriage, names of wives, husbands, children and other relatives, plus descriptions, occupations, and other information gleaned from church registers, military lists, pension files, probate accounts, and marriage records.

Each entry in this book has been documented and a key to that documentation has been implemented within the text to enable the reader to review the cited source. A letter followed by a number is the code used for a source and the page within that source. For example, [Ref: D-555] would indicate that the information can be found on page 555 of Reference D, which is *Archives of Maryland, Volume 18*. The coded sources cited herein are as follows:

A = *Archives of Maryland, Volume XI*. "Journal of the Maryland Conventions, July 26 - August 14, 1775, and Journal and Correspondence of the Maryland Council of Safety, August 29, 1775 - July 6, 1776" (Baltimore: Maryland Historical Society, 1892)

B = *Archives of Maryland, Volume XII*. "Journal and Correspondence of the Maryland Council of Safety, July 7, 1776 - December 31, 1776" (Baltimore: Maryland Historical Society, 1893)

C = *Archives of Maryland, Volume XVI*. "Journal and Correspondence of the Council of Safety, January 1, 1777 - March 20, 1777" and "Journal and Correspondence of the State Council, March 20, 1777 - March 28, 1778"

(Baltimore: Maryland Historical Society, 1897)

D = *Archives of Maryland, Volume XVIII.* "Muster Rolls and Other Records of Service of Maryland Troops in the American Revolution, 1775-1783" (Baltimore: Maryland Historical Society, 1900)

E = *Archives of Maryland, Volume XXI.* "Journal and Correspondence of the Council of Maryland, April 1, 1778 - October 26, 1779" (Baltimore: Maryland Historical Society, 1901)

F = *Archives of Maryland, Volume XLIII.* "Journal and Correspondence of the State Council of Maryland, 1779-1780" (Baltimore: Maryland Historical Society, 1924)

G = *Archives of Maryland, Volume XLV.* "Journal and Correspondence of the State Council of Maryland, 1780-1781" (Baltimore: Maryland Historical Society, 1927)

H = *Archives of Maryland, Volume XLVII.* "Journal and Correspondence of the State Council of Maryland, 1781" (Baltimore: Maryland Historical Society, 1930)

I = *Archives of Maryland, Volume XLVIII.* "Journal and Correspondence of the State Council of Maryland, 1781-1784" (Baltimore: Maryland Historical Society, 1931)

J = *Revolutionary War Military Collection, Manuscript MS.1814, Box 5* (Baltimore: Maryland Historical Society, Manuscript Division)

K = Wright, F. Edward. *Maryland Eastern Shore Vital Records, 1751-1775* (Westminster, Maryland: Family Line Publications, 1984)

L = Miller, Richard B. "Some Little Known Data Regarding Maryland Signers of the Oath of Fidelity," *Maryland Genealogical Society Bulletin*, Volume 27, No. 1, pp. 101-124 (Winter, 1986)

M = Clements, S. Eugene and Wright, F. Edward. *The Maryland Militia in the Revolutionary War* (Westminster, Maryland: Family Line Publications, 1987)

N = Richardson, Albert Levin. "Revolutionary Militia: Some Names of the Officers and Privates in the Talbot County Forces" and "The Oath of Fidelity in Talbot County." *Maryland Original Research Society of Baltimore* (Baltimore: Genealogical Publishing Company, 1913, pp. 86-105, 106-114)

O = *Calendar of Maryland State Papers, The Red Books, No. 4, Part 1* (Annapolis: The Hall of Records Commission, 1950)

P = Papenfuse, Edward C., et al. *An Inventory of Maryland State Papers, Volume I*, "The Era of the American Revolution, 1775-1789" (Annapolis: The Hall of Records Commission, 1977)

Q = *Maryland Genealogical Society Bulletin* (as cited)

R = Papenfuse, Edward C., et al. *A Biographical Dictionary of the Maryland Legislature, 1635-1789* (Baltimore: The Johns Hopkins University Press, 1979), 2 volumes

S = *Maryland Genealogies: A Consolidation of Articles from the Maryland Historical Magazine* (Baltimore: Genealogical Publishing Company, 1980), 2 volumes

T = Brumbaugh, Gaius M. *Maryland Records: Colonial, Revolutionary,, County and Church From Original Sources, Volume II* (Baltimore: Genealogical Publishing Company, 1985, reprint).

U = *National Genealogical Society Quarterly* (as cited)

V = Wright, F. Edward. *Maryland Eastern Shore Vital Records, 1726-1750* (Westminster, Maryland: Family Line Publications, 1983)

W = White, Virgil D. *Genealogical Abstracts of Revolutionary War Pension Files* (Waynesboro, Tennessee: The National Historical Publishing Company, 1990), 4 volumes

X = *Maryland Pension Rolls of 1835: Report from the Secretary of War in Relation to the Pension Establishment of the United States* (Baltimore: Genealogical Publishing Company, 1968, reprint)

Y = *DAR Patriot Index, Centennial Edition* (Washington, D. C.: Daughters of the American Revolution, 1990), 3 volumes

Z = *Roster of Captain Thomas Bullen's Militia Company* (Maryland Historical Society, Revolutionary War Collection MS.1814, Box 3)

      It must be noted that it is not possible to know who all of the patriots were who served in or from Talbot County during the entire Revolutionary War period. This is especially true for those who joined the Maryland Line and served in the Continental Army. Due to the constant reorganization of the Maryland troops during the war, it is not easily determinable which soldier served from which county. It appears, however, that many men from Talbot County served in the 5th

Maryland Continental Line.

Finally, as may be the case in works such as this, it is possible that some patriots and soldiers may have been omitted inadvertently. Therefore, one should see *Archives of Maryland, Volume 18* (Muster Rolls of Maryland Troops During the American Revolution, 1775-1783) for perhaps other soldiers who served from Talbot County in the Maryland Continental Line.

            Henry C. Peden, Jr.
            Bel Air, Maryland
            November 4, 1998

REVOLUTIONARY PATRIOTS OF TALBOT COUNTY, MARYLAND, 1775-1783

ABBOTT, Ezekiel. Private, 4th Independent Company of Maryland Regular Troops, Capt. James Hindman's Company, September, 1776 muster roll; enlisted January 23, 1776; reportedly "deserted" on August 3, 1776, but returned ["taken again"] on August 5, 1776 [Ref: D-25].

ABBOTT, James. Private, Militia, Capt. Thomas Bullen's Company; no date was given; possibly late 1775 or early 1776 [Ref: Z-3].

ABBOTT, John. Private, Militia, Capt. Thomas Bullen's Company; no date was given; possibly late 1775 or early 1776 [Ref: Z-3]. See "Thomas Abbott," q.v.

ABBOTT, Mercey. See "Thomas Abbott," q.v.

ABBOTT, Samuel. Captain, Militia, 4th Battalion, May 13, 1776. Captain, Bullinbrook Company, April 9, 1778. Captain, 38th Battalion, December 3, 1779; succeeded [Ref: M-47, E-24, F-28].

ABBOTT (ABOTT, ABBET), Samuel. Steward on the barge *Fearnought* under Capt. Levin Spedden; enlisted June 1, 1782; 5'11" tall; fair complexion; born in Talbot County [Ref: D-612, D-613]. Took the Oath of Allegiance and Fidelity on or about March 1, 1778 [Ref: J-1814, N-106/114].

ABBOTT, Samuel Jr. Private, Militia, Capt. Thomas Bullen's Company; no date was given; possibly late 1775 or early 1776 [Ref: Z-3]. Private, Militia, Bullin Brook Company, 4th Battalion, 1777-1778 [Ref: N-86/105, M-224]. Private, Militia, Bullinbrook Company, 4th Battalion, 1780-1781 [Ref: N-86/105, M-231].

ABBOTT, Samuel Sr. Private, Militia, Bullinbrook Company, 4th Battalion, 1780-1781 [Ref: N-86/105, M-231].

ABBOTT, Thomas (1738-   ). Born in St. Peter's Parish, Talbot County, on January 26, 1738, son of John and Mercey Abbott [Ref: V-79]. Private, Militia, Capt. Thomas Bullen's Company; no date was given; possibly late 1775 or early 1776 [Ref: Z-3]. Private, 7th Maryland Line, enlisted on May 30, 1778 and honorably discharged on March 6, 1779 [Ref: D-184].

ABELL (ABEL), Jonathan. First Lieutenant, 38th Battalion, May 23, 1776. Captain, Miles River Company, April 9, 1778 [Ref: M-47, A-438, E-25]. Took the Oath of Allegiance and Fidelity on or about March 1, 1778 [Ref: J-1814, N-106/114]. County Court Justice, 1778 [Ref: E-250]. Captain, Militia, 38th Battalion, 1778; succeeded April 12, 1780 [Ref: N-92, M-47, F-139].

ACRES, James. See "James Akers," q.v.

ACRES, John. See "John Akers," q.v.

ADAMS, Eusebeus. Private, Militia, Third Haven Company, 4th Battalion, 1777-1778 [Ref: N-86/105, M-225].

ADAMS, Moses. Private, Militia, Third Haven Company, 4th Battalion, 1777-1778 [Ref: N-86/105, M-225]. Private, Militia, Third Haven Company, 4th Battalion, 1780-1781 [Ref: N-86/105, M-232].

ADLEY, Richard. Private in the militia who was draughted on August 30, 1781 to reinforce the American Army and to serve in the Maryland Continental Troops until December 10, 1781 [Ref: D-387]. Took the Oath of Allegiance and Fidelity on or after March 1, 1778 [Ref: J-1814, N-106/114].

AKERS, Elizabeth. See "John Akers," q.v.

AKERS (ACRES), James. Private, Militia, Capt. Thomas Bullen's Company; no date was given; possibly late 1775 or early 1776 [Ref: Z-3]. Private, Militia, Third Haven Company, 4th Battalion, 1777-1778 [Ref: N-86/105, M-225]. Private, Militia, Bullinbrook Company, 4th Battalion, 1780-1781 [Ref: N-86/105, M-231]. Private in the militia who was draughted on August 30, 1781 to reinforce the American Army and to serve in the Maryland Continental Troops until December 10, 1781 [Ref: D-387]. See "John Akers," q.v.

AKERS (ACRES), John. Private, Militia, Bullinbrook Company, 4th Battalion, 1780-1781 [Ref: N-86/105, M-231]. Took the Oath of Allegiance and Fidelity on or after March 1, 1778 [Ref: J-1814, N-106/114]. John Acres, son of James and Elizabeth, was born in St. Peter's Parish, Talbot County, on January 23, 1729 [Ref: V-67].

AKERS (ACKERS), William. Took the Oath of Allegiance and Fidelity on or about March 1, 1778 [Ref: J-1814, N-106/114].

AKERS, William Jr. Private, Militia, Volunteer Company, 4th Battalion, 1777-1778 [Ref: N-86/105, M-223].

AKIN, Thomas. Private, Militia, Union Company, 4th Battalion, 1777-1778 [Ref: N-86/105, M-223].

ALDERN, Margaret. See "Foster Maynard," q.v.

ALDRICE, Elisabeth. Rendered patriotic service by supplying bacon for the use of the Army in May, 1778 [Ref: P-172].

ALEXANDER, Hannah. Rendered patriotic service by supplying bacon for the use of the Army in June, 1778 [Ref: P-175].

ALEXANDER, James. Private, Militia, Volunteer Company, 4th Battalion, 1777-1778 [Ref: N-86/105, M-223]. Private, Militia, Volunteer Company, 4th Battalion, 1780-1781; name listed twice [Ref: N-86/105, M-230].

ALEXANDER, John. Private, Militia, Volunteer Company, 4th Battalion, 1777-1778 [Ref: N-86/105, M-223].

ALEXANDER, William. First Lieutenant, [72nd?] Volunteer Company, 4th Battalion, April 9, 1778 [Ref: M-48, E-24].

ALEXANDER, William. Private, Militia, Volunteer Company, 4th Battalion, 1780-1781 [Ref: N-86/105, M-230].

ALL, William. Private, 4th Independent Company of Maryland Regular Troops, Capt. James Hindman's Company, September, 1776 muster roll; enlisted February 3, 1776 [Ref: D-23].

ALLEN (ALLIN), Charles. Private, Militia, Sword in Hand Company, 4th Battalion, 1777-1778 [Ref: N-86/105, M-224]. Private, Militia, Sword in Hand Company, 4th Battalion, 1780-1781 [Ref: N-86/105, M-231]. Private in the militia who was draughted on August 30, 1781 to reinforce the American Army and to serve in the Maryland Continental Troops until December 10, 1781 [Ref: D-387].

ALLEN, Elizabeth. See "Nicholas Thomas," q.v.

ALLEN (ALLIN), Emanuel. Private, Militia, 2nd Volunteer Company, 4th Battalion, 1777-1778 [Ref: N-86/105, M-225]. Took the Oath of Allegiance and Fidelity on or about March 1, 1778 [Ref: J-1814, N-106/114]. "Emanual Allen" was a lieutenant in the 5th Maryland Line; enlisted May 6, 1778; reported missing after the Battle of Camden, S. C. on August 16, 1780 [Ref: D-183].

ALLEN, Gilbert. Private, 5th Maryland Line; enlisted December 10, 1776; reported missing after the Battle of Camden, S. C. on August 16, 1780 [Ref: D-182].

ALLEN, James. Private, 5th Maryland Line; enlisted July 8, 1777 and still in service in November, 1780 [Ref: D-182].

ALLEN (ALLIN), John. Private, Militia, Volunteer Company, 4th Battalion, 1780-1781 [Ref: N-86/105, M-229].

ALLEN (ALLIN), Moses. Took the Oath of Allegiance and Fidelity on or about March 1, 1778 [Ref: J-1814, N-106/114]. Appointed a Justice of the Peace on December 4, 1779 [Ref: F-31].

ALLEN (ALLIN), Nathan. Private, Militia, Volunteer Company, 4th Battalion, 1780-1781 [Ref: N-86/105, M-229].

ALLEN (ALLIN), Ruebin. Private, Militia, Volunteer Company, 4th Battalion, 1777-1778 [Ref: N-86/105, M-223].

ALLEN (ALLIN), William. Private, Militia, Volunteer Company, 4th Battalion, 1777-1778 [Ref: N-86/105, M-223]. Private, Militia, Volunteer Company, 4th Battalion, 1780-1781 [Ref: N-86/105, M-230]. Took the Oath of Allegiance and Fidelity on or after March 1, 1778 [Ref: J-1814, N-106/114].

ALLINGHAM, Joseph. Private, Militia, Oxford Company, 38th Battalion, 1777-1778 [Ref: N-86/105, M-228]. Took the Oath of Allegiance and Fidelity on or about March 1, 1778 [Ref: J-1814, N-106/114].

ALLOWAY, William. Ensign, Militia, Wye Company, 4th Battalion, 1780-1781 [Ref: N-96, M-228]. Took the Oath of Allegiance and Fidelity on or about March 1, 1778 [Ref: J-1814, N-106/114]. Rendered patriotic service by supplying corn for the use of the Army in March, 1780 [Ref: P-273].

ANDERSON, Alexander. Private, Militia, Volunteer Company, 4th Battalion, 1780-1781 [Ref: N-86/105, M-229]. Took the Oath of Allegiance and Fidelity on or about March 1, 1778 [Ref: J-1814, N-106/114]. Draughted on May 1, 1781 to serve until December 10, 1781 in the Maryland Continental Troops [Ref: D-371].

ANDERSON, Archibald. First Lieutenant, 4th Independent Company of Maryland Regular Troops, September, 1776 muster roll; commissioned January 5, 1776 or February 14, 1776, both dates were given [Ref: D-23, A-159].

ANDERSON, Marion. See "James Hindman," q.v.

ANDERSON, Perry. Private, Militia, Sword in Hand Company, 4th Battalion, 1777-1778 [Ref: N-86/105, M-224]. Private, Militia, Volunteer Company, 4th Battalion, 1780-1781 [Ref: N-86/105, M-229]. Took the Oath of Allegiance and Fidelity on or about March 1, 1778 [Ref: J-1814, N-106/114].

ANDERSON, Thomas. Private, Militia, Volunteer Company, 4th Battalion, 1780-1781 [Ref: N-86/105, M-230]. Took the Oath of Allegiance and Fidelity on or about March 1, 1778 [Ref: J-1814, N-106/114]. Ensign, 4th Battalion, Capt. William Stevens' Company; no date was given [Ref: M-48].

ANDERSON, William. Private, Militia, Volunteer Company, 4th Battalion, 1777-1778 [Ref: N-86/105, M-223]. Private, Militia, Volunteer Company, 4th Battalion, 1780-1781 [Ref: N-86/105, M-230].

ANDERSON, William (Miles Creek). Private, Militia, Capt. Thomas Bullen's Company; no date was given; possibly late 1775 or early 1776 [Ref: Z-3].

ANDREWS, James. Private, Militia, Hand & Hand Company, 4th Battalion, 1777-1778 [Ref: N-86/105, M-226].

ANTHONY, James. Private, Militia, Union Company, 4th Battalion, 1777-1778 [Ref: N-86/105, M-223].

ANTHONY, Joseph. Private, Militia, Hand & Hand Company, 4th Battalion, 1777-1778 [Ref: N-86/105, M-225].

ANTHONY, William. Private, Militia, Hand & Hand Company, 4th Battalion, 1777-1778 [Ref: N-86/105, M-226].

APPLEGARTH (APPLEGIRTH), George. Took the Oath of Allegiance and Fidelity on or after March 1, 1778 [Ref: J-1814, N-106/114]. Private, Militia, Bayside Company, 38th Battalion, 1780-1781 [Ref: N-86/105, M-233].

APPLEGARTH (APPLEGIRTH), George Jr. Private, Militia, Bayside Company, 38th Battalion, 1777-1778 [Ref: N-86/105, M-228]. Took the Oath of Allegiance and Fidelity on or after March 1, 1778 [Ref: J-1814, N-106/114].

APPLEGARTH (APPLEGIRTH), Nathaniel. Private, Militia, Broad Creek Company, 38th Battalion, 1777-1778 [Ref: N-86/105, M-227]. Private, Militia, Broad Creek Company, 38th Battalion, 1780-1781 [Ref: N-86/105, M-234]. Took the Oath of Allegiance and Fidelity on or after March 1, 1778 [Ref: J-1814, N-106/114].

APPLEGARTH (APPLEGIRTH), Robert Jr. Private, Militia, Bayside Company, 38th Battalion, 1780-1781 [Ref: N-86/105, M-233]. Took the Oath of Allegiance and Fidelity on or after March 1, 1778 [Ref: J-1814, N-106/114].

APPLEGARTH (APPLEGIRTH), Robert Sr. Private, Militia, Bayside Company, 38th Battalion, 1777-1778 [Ref: N-86/105, M-228]. Took the Oath of Allegiance and Fidelity on or after March 1, 1778 [Ref: J-1814, N-106/114].

APPLEGARTH (APPLEGERTH, APPLEGIRTH), Thomas. Private, Militia, Hearts of Oak Company, 38th Battalion, 1777-1778 [Ref: N-86/105, M-226]. Private, Militia, Hearts of Oak Company, 38th Battalion, 1780-1781 [Ref: N-

86/105, M-235]. Took the Oath of Allegiance and Fidelity on or after March 1, 1778 [Ref: J-1814, N-106/114].
APPLEGARTH, William. Private, Militia, Broad Creek Company, 38th Battalion, 1780-1781 [Ref: N-86/105, M-234].
ARDERY (ARDRY), John. Private, Militia, Bullin Brook Company, 4th Battalion, 1777-1778 [Ref: N-86/105, M-224]. Private, Militia, Bullinbrook Company, 4th Battalion, 1780-1781 [Ref: N-86/105, M-231].
ARMSTRONG, Foster. Private, Militia, Capt. Thomas Bullen's Company; no date was given; possibly late 1775 or early 1776 [Ref: Z-3]. Private, Militia, Volunteer Company, 4th Battalion, 1777-1778 [Ref: N-86/105, M-223]. Private, Militia, Volunteer Company, 4th Battalion, 1780-1781 [Ref: N-86/105, M-230]. Took the Oath of Allegiance and Fidelity on or about March 1, 1778 [Ref: J-1814, N-106/114].
ARMSTRONG, Francis. Private, Militia, Sword in Hand Company, 4th Battalion, 1777-1778 [Ref: N-86/105, M-224]. Private, Militia, Sword in Hand Company, 4th Battalion, 1780-1781 [Ref: N-86/105, M-231].
ARMSTRONG, Francis. Private, Militia, Third Haven Company, 4th Battalion, 1780-1781 [Ref: N-86/105, M-232].
ARMSTRONG, Francis. Private, Militia, Wye Company, 4th Battalion, 1780-1781 [Ref: N-86/105, M-229].
ARMSTRONG, Francis. Took the Oath of Allegiance and Fidelity on or about March 1, 1778 [Ref: J-1814, N-106/114].
ARMSTRONG, John. Private, Militia, Volunteer Company, 4th Battalion, 1777-1778; name listed three times [Ref: N-86/105, M-223].
ARMSTRONG, John. Private, Militia, Volunteer Company, 4th Battalion, 1780-1781 [Ref: N-86/105, M-230].
ARMSTRONG, Russel. Private, 4th Independent Company of Maryland Regular Troops, Capt. James Hindman's Company, September, 1776 muster roll; enlisted January 25, 1776 [Ref: D-24].
ARRINGTON, James. Private, Militia, Bullin Brook Company, 4th Battalion, 1777-1778 [Ref: N-86/105, M-224].
ARRINGTON, Lodman. Took the Oath of Allegiance and Fidelity on or about March 1, 1778 [Ref: J-1814, N-106/114].
ARRINGTON, William. Private, Militia, Bullin Brook Company, 4th Battalion, 1777-1778 [Ref: N-86/105, M-224]. Took the Oath of Allegiance and Fidelity on or about March 1, 1778 [Ref: J-1814, N-106/114].
ARUNDEL, William. See "William Aurundle," q.v.
ASHCRAFT (ASHCROFT), Thomas. Private, Militia, United Company, 38th Battalion, 1777-1778 [Ref: N-86/105, M-227]. Private, Militia, United Company, 38th Battalion, 1780-1781 [Ref: N-86/105, M-233]. Took the Oath of Allegiance and Fidelity on or after March 1, 1778 [Ref: J-1814, N-106/114].

ASHCROFT (ASHCRAFT), James. Private, Militia, 4th Battalion, Capt. Greenbury Goldsborough's Company, reviewed and passed July 27, 1776 [Ref: D-68].
ATKINS, John. Private, Militia, 4th Battalion, Capt. Greenbury Goldsborough's Company, reviewed and passed July 27, 1776 [Ref: D-68].
ATKINSON, Aaron Jr. Private, Militia, Union Company, 4th Battalion, 1777-1778 [Ref: N-86/105, M-223]. Private, Militia, Union Company, 4th Battalion, 1780-1781 [Ref: N-86/105, M-230].
ATKINSON, Aaron Sr. Private, Militia, Union Company, 4th Battalion, 1777-1778 [Ref: N-86/105, M-223]. Private, Militia, Union Company, 4th Battalion, 1780-1781 [Ref: N-86/105, M-230].
ATKINSON, Joseph. Private, Militia, Volunteer Company, 4th Battalion, 1780-1781 [Ref: N-86/105, M-229].
ATKINSON (ARTKINSON), Soloman. Private, Militia, Union Company, 4th Battalion, 1780-1781 [Ref: N-86/105, M-230].
AUKIN, Thomas. Private, Militia, Sword in Hand Company, 4th Battalion, 1777-1778 [Ref: N-86/105, M-224].
AULD, Daniel. Son of John Auld and Mary Sherwood, he served as a private in the militia, Broad Creek Company, 38th Battalion, 1780-1781 [Ref: S-I:26, N-86/105, and M-234, which listed the name as "Daniel Auld, Jr."]. On March 9, 1826 the Treasurer of the Western Shore was directed to pay to Daniel Auld, of Talbot County, half pay of a private for his services during the Revolutionary War. On February 17, 1832 the Treasurer was directed to pay to Sarah Auld, of Talbot County, widow of Daniel, a soldier of the revolution, such sum as may be due her said husband at time of his death. On March 9, 1832 the Treasurer was directed to pay to Sarah Auld, of Talbot County, widow of Daniel Auld, a soldier of the Revolutionary War, during widowhood, half yearly, half pay of a private, for services rendered by her husband during said war. On January 19, 1848, the Treasurer of the State was directed to pay to Philip Pasterfield, of Talbot County, surviving brother and legal representative of Sarah Auld, widow of Daniel Auld, a soldier of the Revolutionary War, balance of any pension due to Sarah Auld, on June 28, 1847, at time of her death. [Ref: T-316].
AULD, Edward (1734-1777). Son of John Auld and Mary Sherwood, he married Sarah Haddaway, daughter of Col. William Webb Haddaway, in 1757, and died in the Revolutionary War [Ref: S-I:26].
AULD, Elizabeth. See "James Lowe," q.v.
AULD, Hugh (1745-1813). Son of John Auld and Mary Sherwood, he served as a first lieutenant in the militia, United Company, 38th Battalion, April 9, 1778 through 1781 [Ref: S-I:26, N-93, N-102, M-233, M-108, E-25, which listed the name as "Hugh Odd" and "Hugh Old"]. Took the Oath of Allegiance and Fidelity on or about March 1, 1778 [Ref: J-1814, N-106/114]. "Hugh Auld, Sr." was born on May 23, 1745, married Frances Harrison, served as a first

lieutenant in the revolution, died on December 7, 1813, and is buried in Arlington Cemetery [Ref: Y-94, S-I:26].
AULD, John. Son of John Auld and Mary Sherwood, he served as a private in the militia, United Company, 38th Battalion, 1777-1778 [Ref: S-I:26, N-93, M-227]. See "Daniel Auld" and "Edward Auld" and "Hugh Auld" and "Philemon Auld," q.v.
AULD, Philemon (Philimon). Son of John Auld and Mary Sherwood, he served as a private in the militia, Broad Creek Company, 38th Battalion, 1777-1778 [Ref: S-I:26, N-86/105, M-227]. Private, Militia, Broad Creek Company, 38th Battalion, 1780-1781 [Ref: N-86/105, M-234]. Took the Oath of Allegiance and Fidelity on or about March 1, 1778 [Ref: J-1814, N-106/114].
AULD, Samuel. Private, Militia, Broad Creek Company, 38th Battalion, 1777-1778 [Ref: N-86/105, M-227]. Private, Militia, Broad Creek Company, 38th Battalion, 1780-1781 [Ref: N-86/105, M-234].
AULD, Sarah. See "Daniel Auld, Jr.," q.v.
AULD, Thomas (1758-1798). Son of Edward Auld and Sarah Haddaway, Thomas was born on August 24 or 29, 1758, married Elizabeth Dawson, and died on or before July 4, 1798 [Ref: S-I:27, Y-94]. Private, Militia, Miles River Company, 38th Battalion, 1777-1778 [Ref: N-86/105, M-227]. Sergeant, Militia, Bayside Company, 38th Battalion, 1780-1781 [Ref: N-102, M-233]. Took the Oath of Allegiance and Fidelity on or about March 1, 1778 [Ref: J-1814, N-106/114].
AURUNDLE, John. Private, Militia, Hand & Hand Company, 4th Battalion, 1777-1778 [Ref: N-86/105, M-225].
AURUNDLE (AURANDLE, AURENDAL), Lodman. Private, Militia, Hand & Hand Company, 4th Battalion, 1777-1778 [Ref: N-86/105, M-225]. Private, Militia, Hand in Hand Company, 4th Battalion, 1780-1781 [Ref: N-86/105, M-232].
AURUNDLE (ARUNDAL), Lodman. Private, Militia, Sword in Hand Company, 4th Battalion, 1780-1781 [Ref: N-86/105, M-231].
AURUNDLE (AURUNDAL), Truman(?). Private, Militia, Sword in Hand Company, 4th Battalion, 1777-1778 [Ref: N-86/105, M-224].
AURUNDLE (AURUNDLE), William. Private, Militia, Hand & Hand Company, 4th Battalion, 1777-1778 [Ref: N-86/105, M-226]. Private, Militia, Hand in Hand Company, 4th Battalion, 1780-1781 [Ref: N-86/105, M-232]. Took the Oath of Allegiance and Fidelity on or about March 1, 1778 [Ref: J-1814, N-106/114].
AUSMAN, Jonathan. See "Jonathan Osmond," q.v.
AUSTIN, Cloudsberry (Cloudsbury). Private, Militia, Sword in Hand Company, 4th Battalion, 1777-1778 [Ref: N-86/105, M-224]. Private, Militia, Sword in Hand Company, 4th Battalion, 1780-1781 [Ref: N-86/105, M-231]. Private in the militia who was draughted on August 30, 1781 to reinforce the American Army and to serve in the Maryland Continental Troops until December 10, 1781 [Ref: D-387].

AUSTIN, James. Private, Militia, 4th Battalion, Capt. Greenbury Goldsborough's Company, reviewed and passed July 27, 1776 [Ref: D-67]. Private, Militia, Sword in Hand Company, 4th Battalion, 1777-1778 [Ref: N-86/105, M-224]. Took the Oath of Allegiance and Fidelity on or about March 1, 1778 [Ref: J-1814, N-106/114]. Private, Militia, Sword in Hand Company, 4th Battalion, 1780-1781 [Ref: N-86/105, M-231].

AUSTIN, John. Private, Militia, 2nd Volunteer Company, 4th Battalion, 1777-1778 [Ref: N-86/105, M-225]. Private, Militia, Volunteer Company, 4th Battalion, 1780-1781 [Ref: N-86/105, M-229]. Took the Oath of Allegiance and Fidelity on or about March 1, 1778 [Ref: J-1814, N-106/114].

AUSTIN, Richard. Took the Oath of Allegiance and Fidelity on or about March 1, 1778; name listed twice [Ref: J-1814, N-106/114].

AUSTIN, Richard Jr. Took the Oath of Allegiance and Fidelity on or about March 1, 1778; name listed twice [Ref: J-1814, N-106/114]. Private, Militia, Sword in Hand Company, 4th Battalion, 1780-1781 [Ref: N-86/105, M-231].

AUSTIN, Thomas. Private, Militia, Third Haven Company, 4th Battalion, 1777-1778 [Ref: N-86/105, M-225]. Private, Militia, Third Haven Company, 4th Battalion, 1780-1781 [Ref: N-86/105, M-232]. Took the Oath of Allegiance and Fidelity on or after March 1, 1778 [Ref: J-1814, N-106/114].

AUSTIN, William. Took the Oath of Allegiance and Fidelity on or about March 1, 1778; name listed twice [Ref: J-1814, N-106/114].

AYERS (AYRS), James. Private, Militia, Miles River Company, 38th Battalion, 1777-1778 [Ref: N-86/105, M-227]. Took the Oath of Allegiance and Fidelity on or about March 1, 1778 [Ref: J-1814, N-106/114]. Private, Militia, Miles River Company, 38th Battalion, 1780-1781 [Ref: N-86/105, M-235].

BACON, Thomas. See "Samuel Chamberlaine," q.v.

BADSY (BADSAY), Richard. Private, Militia, Bayside Company, 38th Battalion, 1777-1778 [Ref: N-86/105, M-228]. Private, Militia, Bayside Company, 38th Battalion, 1780-1781 [Ref: N-86/105, M-233].

BAILEY (BAILY, BALEY), William. Private, Militia, Third Haven Company, 4th Battalion, 1777-1778 [Ref: N-86/105, M-225, which listed the name as "William Baley"]. Took the Oath of Allegiance and Fidelity on or after March 1, 1778 [Ref: J-1814, N-106/114]. Private, Militia, Third Haven Company, 4th Battalion, 1780-1781 [Ref: N-86/105, M-232].

BAKER, Elizabeth. See "Francis Baker," q.v.

BAKER, Francis. Private, Militia, Wye Company, 4th Battalion, 1777-1778 [Ref: N-86/105, M-222]. Private, Militia, Wye Company, 4th Battalion, 1780-1781 [Ref: N-86/105, M-229].

BAKER, Francis (c1735-c1789). A son of Henry and Elizabeth Baker, he married by 1765 to Frances Clayland (only child of Harris Clayland) and had at least two children, Samuel Baker and Henry Clayland Baker. Francis served on the Committee of Observation in 1775. He attended the Maryland Convention, but was discharged on December 11, 1775 for a "breach of the continental association" by violating the non-importation agreements. Though his name was not published as an enemy, he was barred from holding any future office of trust. By June, 1776, however, this part of the sentence had been rescinded [Ref: A-4, R-70, R-71, R-72, R-109, O-1]. First Lieutenant, Militia, 4th Battalion, commissioned May 16, 1776; resigned August 13, 1776 [Ref: M-49, A-428]. Took the Oath of Allegiance and Fidelity on or about March 1, 1778 [Ref: J-1814, N-106/114]. Draughted on August 30, 1781 to reinforce the American Army and serve in the Maryland Continental Troops until December 10, 1781 [Ref: D-387, R-109]. Francis Baker was born circa 1735, lived in Cecil County, Talbot County, and Harford County, Maryland, and possibly York County, Pennsylvania with his son Henry, and died in debt sometime after 1789 [Ref: R-109].

BAKER, Henry. Private, Militia, Wye Company, 4th Battalion, 1777-1778 [Ref: N-86/105, M-222]. Private, Militia, Wye Company, 4th Battalion, 1780-1781 [Ref: N-86/105, M-229]. See "Francis Baker," q.v.

BAKER, Samuel. Private, Militia, Wye Company, 4th Battalion, 1780-1781 [Ref: N-86/105, M-229]. See "Francis Baker," q.v.

BAKER, Thomas. Private, Militia, Oxford Company, 38th Battalion, 1777-1778 [Ref: N-86/105, M-227]. Private, Militia, Oxford Company, 38th Battalion, 1780-1781 [Ref: N-86/105, M-235]. Took the Oath of Allegiance and Fidelity on or after March 1, 1778 [Ref: J-1814, N-106/114].

BALL, James (1731-1808). Son of James and Mary Ball, born on February 23, 1731 in Talbot County, James was a Quaker who built ships before, during and after the American Revolution at his yard in Broad Creek on the Great Choptank River. He married his cousin Elizabeth Kemp (1732-1814) in August, 1756, and their children were John (1757-1787), Susannah (1759-1842), James (born 1763), Rachel (1766-1857), and Thomas (born 1769). [Ref: S-I:12-15]. Took the Oath of Allegiance and Fidelity on or about March 1, 1778 [Ref: J-1814, N-106/114].

BALL, James (1757-1787). Son of James Ball and Elizabeth Kemp, he was born on October 16, 1757 and died on December 21, 1787 [Ref: S-I:13]. Private, Militia, Broad Creek Company, 38th Battalion, 1777-1778 [Ref: N-86/105, M-226, which listed the name as "James Baul (Basil?)"]. Private, Militia, Broad Creek Company, 38th Battalion, 1780-1781 [Ref: N-86/105, M-234].

BALL, John. Private, Militia, Bayside Company, 38th Battalion, 1777-1778 [Ref: N-86/105, M-228]. Private, Militia, Bayside Company, 38th Battalion, 1780-1781 [Ref: N-86/105, M-233]. One John Ball was a lieutenant on the barge *Terable* in 1781 [Ref: D-610]. See "James Ball," q.v.

BALL, Levin. Private, Militia, Bullinbrook Company, 4th Battalion, 1780-1781 [Ref: N-86/105, M-231].

BALL, Mary. See "James Ball," q.v.

BALL, Rachel. See "James Ball," q.v.

BALL, Susannah. See "James Ball," q.v.

BALL, Thomas. Corporal, Militia, Broad Creek Company, 38th Battalion, 1780-1781 [Ref: N-103, M-234]. See "James Ball," q.v.

BALL, William. Took the Oath of Allegiance and Fidelity on or about March 1, 1778 [Ref: J-1814, N-106/114].

BANDY, James. Took the Oath of Allegiance and Fidelity on or about March 1, 1778 [Ref: J-1814, N-106/114].

BANDY, John. Private, Militia, 2nd Volunteer Company, 4th Battalion, 1777-1778 [Ref: N-86/105, M-225]. Private, Militia, 2nd Volunteer Company, 4th Battalion, 1777-1778 [Ref: N-86/105, M-224].

BANDY, Thomas. Private, Militia, Capt. Thomas Bullen's Company; no date was given; possibly late 1775 or early 1776 [Ref: Z-3].

BANNING, Ann. See "Henry Banning," q.v.

BANNING, Anthony. See "Henry Banning," q.v.

BANNING, Araminta. See "Henry Banning," q.v.

BANNING, Henry (c1736-1818). Son of William and Jane Banning, he married twice: first wife unknown; second wife was Araminta ----. His children were: Anthony, Thomas, John Wesley, Jane (married a Parrott), Ann (married James Earle Denny), and a daughter (name unknown) married John Kersey [Ref: R-113]. Captain, Militia, May 13, 1776. Attended the Maryland Convention on July 3, 1776 for the purpose of forming a new government [Ref: O-35, R-113, R-76]. Lieutenant Colonel, Militia, 38th Battalion, September 8, 1776; resigned February 26, 1777 [Ref: M-51, R-114]. Captain, Militia, Hearts of Oak Company, 38th Battalion, 1778-1781 [Ref: N-94, N-104, M-234, M-50, E-25]. Justice, Talbot County, 1774-1778; Justice of the Orphans Court, appointed June 4, 1777; Justice of the Peace, appointed November 20, 1779; Judge, Second Election District, appointed in 1800 [Ref: R-113, R-114, C-264, E-163, F-22]. On January 9, 1778 the Maryland Council issued a Special Commission of Oyer & Terminer & Goal Delivery for the Eastern Shore according to the late Act of Assembly and directed in Talbot County" to Henry Banning and four others to be Judges of the Special Court [Ref: C-463, C-538].

BANNING, Jane. See "Henry Banning," q.v.

BANNING, Jeremiah. Captain, Militia, Hearts of Oak Company, November 21, 1775. First Major, 4th Battalion, January 12, 1776. Colonel, 38th Battalion, April 9, 1778 [Ref: M-51, E-24]. Took the Oath of Allegiance and Fidelity on or about March 1, 1778 [Ref: J-1814, N-106/114]. Justice of the Peace, appointed on November 21, 1778 and November 20, 1779 and January 17, 1782, at which time he was also appointed a Judge of the Orphans Court [Ref: E-250, F-22, I-46]. "Jeremiah Banning, Esqr." was Naval Officer, 7th District, before December 4, 1779 [Ref: F-31].

BANNING, John. See "Henry Banning," q.v.

BANNING, Susan. See "Hugh Sherwood, of Huntington," q.v.

BANNING, Thomas. Se "Henry Banning," q.v.

BANNING, William. See "Henry Banning," q.v.
BARBER, James. Private, Militia, 4th Battalion, Capt. Greenbury Goldsborough's Company, reviewed and passed July 27, 1776 [Ref: D-68].
BARKER, Thomas. Private, 4th Independent Company of Maryland Regular Troops, Capt. James Hindman's Company; enlisted February 5, 1776; he was "left on Long Island, August 29, 1776." [Ref: D-24].
BARNABY, John. Private, Militia, Volunteer Company, 4th Battalion, 1780-1781 [Ref: N-86/105, M-230].
BARNABY, Richard. Took the Oath of Allegiance and Fidelity on or about March 1, 1778 [Ref: J-1814, N-106/114]. On August 8, 1780, James Hindman, Purchasing Agent for Talbot County, advised Governor Lee and the Maryland Council, in part, that he had "purchased of Mr. Richard Barnaby a hundred barrels of flour at £67.10, which I shall send forward to the Head of Elk as soon as possible..." [Ref: G-44].
BARNES, James Sr. Took the Oath of Allegiance and Fidelity on or about March 1, 1778 [Ref: J-1814, N-106/114].
BARNES, Job. Private, 4th Independent Company of Maryland Regular Troops, Capt. James Hindman's Company, September, 1776 muster roll; enlisted January 20, 1776 [Ref: D-24].
BARNES, William. Private, Militia, Broad Creek Company, 38th Battalion, 1777-1778 [Ref: N-86/105, M-226]. Took the Oath of Allegiance and Fidelity on or about March 1, 1778 [Ref: J-1814, N-106/114].
BARNETT, Matthew Lewis. Paid £7 by the Maryland Council of Safety on October 12, 1776, "for collecting & ascertaining the number of souls in Talbot County." [Ref: B-337]. See "Matthew Lewes Barrett," q.v.
BARNETT, Lewis. Private, Militia, Capt. Thomas Bullen's Company; no date was given; possibly late 1775 or early 1776 [Ref: Z-3].
BARNETT, Noble. Private, Militia, Volunteer Company, 4th Battalion, 1777-1778 [Ref: N-86/105, M-223]. Private, Militia, Volunteer Company, 4th Battalion, 1780-1781 [Ref: N-86/105, M-230]. Took the Oath of Allegiance and Fidelity on or about March 1, 1778 [Ref: J-1814, N-106/114].
BARNETT, Peter. Private, Militia, Union Company, 4th Battalion, 1777-1778 [Ref: N-86/105, M-223]. Private, Militia, Third Haven Company, 4th Battalion, 1780-1781 [Ref: N-86/105, M-232]. Took the Oath of Allegiance and Fidelity on or after March 1, 1778 [Ref: J-1814, N-106/114].
BARNETT, Richard. Private, Militia, Volunteer Company, 4th Battalion, 1777-1778 [Ref: N-86/105, M-223]. Private, Militia, Volunteer Company, 4th Battalion, 1780-1781 [Ref: N-86/105, M-230]. Took the Oath of Allegiance and Fidelity on or after March 1, 1778 [Ref: J-1814, N-106/114].
BARNETT, Thomas. Private, Militia, Volunteer Company, 4th Battalion, 1777-1778 [Ref: N-86/105, M-223]. Took the Oath of Allegiance and Fidelity on or after March 1, 1778 [Ref: J-1814, N-106/114].

BARNETT, Thomas. Private, Militia, Bullin Brook Company, 4th Battalion, 1777-1778 [Ref: N-86/105, M-224]. Took the Oath of Allegiance and Fidelity on or about March 1, 1778 [Ref: J-1814, N-106/114].

BARNETT, Thomas. Private, Militia, Volunteer Company, 4th Battalion, 1780-1781 [Ref: N-86/105, M-230]. Took the Oath of Allegiance and Fidelity on or about March 1, 1778 [Ref: J-1814, N-106/114].

BARNETT, Thomas. Rendered patriotic service by supplying bacon and pork for the use of the Army in July, 1778 [Ref: P-183].

BARNETT, Thomas (Island Creek). Took the Oath of Allegiance and Fidelity on or after March 1, 1778 [Ref: J-1814, N-106/114].

BARNETT, Thomas Jr. Ensign, Militia, Capt. Thomas Bullen's Company; no date was given; possibly late 1775 or early 1776 [Ref: Z-3]. Took the Oath of Allegiance and Fidelity on or about March 1, 1778 [Ref: J-1814, N-106/114].

BARNETT, Thomas 3rd. Private, Militia, Bullinbrook Company, 4th Battalion, 1780-1781 [Ref: N-86/105, M-231].

BARNETT, William. Private, Militia, Capt. Thomas Bullen's Company; no date was given; possibly late 1775 or early 1776 [Ref: Z-3].

BARNEY, William. Private, Militia, Hearts of Oak Company, 38th Battalion, 1777-1778 [Ref: N-86/105, M-226]. Private, Militia, Hearts of Oak Company, 38th Battalion, 1780-1781 [Ref: N-86/105, M-234]. Took the Oath of Allegiance and Fidelity on or about March 1, 1778 [Ref: J-1814, N-106/114].

BARNS, James. Ensign, Militia, Broad Creek Company, 38th Battalion, April 9, 1778 through 1781 [Ref: N-94, N-103, M-234, M-51, E-25].

BARNS, William. Lieutenant on the barge *Intrepid* on June 1, 1781 [Ref: D-609].

BARNWELL, James. Private, Militia, Union Company, 4th Battalion, 1780-1781 [Ref: N-86/105, M-230]. Took the Oath of Allegiance and Fidelity on or about March 1, 1778 [Ref: J-1814, N-106/114]. Rendered patriotic service by supplying bacon for the use of the Army in May, 1778 [Ref: P-169]. Appointed as Inspector of Tobacco at Kingstown on August 30, 1780 and resigned before October 9, 1780 [Ref: F-271, and F-320, which listed the name as "Jr."]. Refused a commission from the Maryland Council on September 23, 1780 [Ref: P-319, which listed the name as "James Barnwell, J.P."].

BARNWELL, John. Private, Militia, Union Company, 4th Battalion, 1777-1778 [Ref: N-86/105, M-223].

BARNWELL, John James Jr. Took the Oath of Allegiance and Fidelity on or about March 1, 1778 [Ref: J-1814, N-106/114].

BARRETT, Edward. See "Solomon Barrett," q.v.

BARRETT, Elizabeth. See "Solomon Barrett," q.v.

BARRETT, Matthew Lewes. Took the Oath of Allegiance and Fidelity on or about March 1, 1778 [Ref: J-1814, N-106/114]. See "Matthew Lewis Barnett," q.v.

BARRETT, Nicholas. Private, 5th Maryland Line; enlisted February 10, 1777; discharged February 7, 1780 [Ref: D-185].

BARRETT, Solomon. Private, 5th Maryland Line; enlisted June 19, 1779 and served through 1782 [Ref: D-186, D-463]. Placed on the pension rolls as a musician in the Maryland Line on June 30, 1818, aged 70, with an annual allowance of $96 effective April 30, 1818 [Ref: X-41/514, which listed the name as "Solomon Barrett"]. Revolutionary War pensioner and head of household in 1840 Census of Maryland (Talbot County, 1st District); age 76 [Ref: Q-442, which listed the name as "Solomon Barrot"]. Pension application W-703 states that Solomon Barrett or Barrott was married first to Elizabeth ---- and had three children, viz., Tristram, Solomon, and Edward. He married second to Mrs. Susan Pritchett in Easton on March 25, 1834. She was age 47 in 1853. See "John L. Elbert," q.v.

BARRETT (BARROTT), Nicholas. Private, Militia, Union Company, 4th Battalion, 1780-1781 [Ref: N-86/105, M-230].

BARRETT, Tristram. See "Solomon Barrett," q.v.

BARRON (BARON), James. Private, Militia, Union Company, 4th Battalion, 1777-1778 [Ref: N-86/105, M-223]. Took the Oath of Allegiance and Fidelity on or about March 1, 1778 [Ref: J-1814, N-106/114].

BARROW, Andrew. Private, Militia, Union Company, 4th Battalion, 1777-1778 [Ref: N-86/105, M-223]. Private, Militia, Union Company, 4th Battalion, 1780-1781 [Ref: N-86/105, M-230]. Took the Oath of Allegiance and Fidelity on or about March 1, 1778 [Ref: J-1814, N-106/114].

BARROW, David Davis. Private, Militia, Union Company, 4th Battalion, 1777-1778 [Ref: N-86/105, M-223]. Private, Militia, Union Company, 4th Battalion, 1780-1781 [Ref: N-86/105, M-230]. Took the Oath of Allegiance and Fidelity on or about March 1, 1778 [Ref: J-1814, N-106/114, which listed the name as "D. Davis Barrow"].

BARROW, James. Private, Militia, Union Company, 4th Battalion, 1780-1781 [Ref: N-86/105, M-230]. Took the Oath of Allegiance and Fidelity on or about March 1, 1778 [Ref: J-1814, N-106/114]. One James Barrow was a private in the 5th Maryland Line who enlisted on June 16, 1778 and was reported missing after the Battle of Camden, S. C. on August 16, 1780 [Ref: D-186]. Additional research may be necessary before drawing conclusions.

BARROW, James. Private, Militia, Bayside Company, 38th Battalion, 1777-1778 [Ref: N-86/105, M-228]. Private, Militia, Bayside Company, 38th Battalion, 1780-1781 [Ref: N-86/105, M-233]. Took the Oath of Allegiance and Fidelity on or about March 1, 1778 [Ref: J-1814, N-106/114].

BARROW, John. Private, Militia, Union Company, 4th Battalion, 1777-1778 [Ref: N-86/105, M-223]. Sergeant, Militia, Union Company, 4th Battalion, 1780-1781 [Ref: N-97, M-229]. Took the Oath of Allegiance and Fidelity on or about March 1, 1778 [Ref: J-1814, N-106/114].

BARROW, Richard. Private, Militia, Union Company, 4th Battalion, 1777-1778 [Ref: N-86/105, M-223]. Private, Militia, Union Company, 4th Battalion, 1780-

1781 [Ref: N-86/105, M-229]. Took the Oath of Allegiance and Fidelity on or about March 1, 1778 [Ref: J-1814, N-106/114].

BARROW, Samuel. Ensign, Militia, Union Company, 4th Battalion, April 12, 1780 through 1781 [Ref: N-97, M-229, M-51, F-139]. Took the Oath of Allegiance and Fidelity on or about March 1, 1778 [Ref: J-1814, N-106/114]. Deputy Assistant Purchasing Agent, 1778 [Ref: P-170, P-173]. Paid £7 10s. for services rendered on March 11, 1779, by Col. Christopher Birkhead [Ref: E-319].

BARROW, Thomas. Took the Oath of Allegiance and Fidelity on or about March 1, 1778 [Ref: J-1814, N-106/114]. Rendered patriotic service by transporting bacon for the use of the Army in June, 1778 [Ref: P-173].

BARTLETT, Daniel. Private, Militia, Oxford Company, 38th Battalion, 1777-1778 [Ref: N-86/105, M-228]. Private, Militia, Oxford Company, 38th Battalion, 1780-1781 [Ref: N-86/105, M-235].

BARTLETT, James. Private, Militia, Hearts of Oak Company, 38th Battalion, 1780-1781 [Ref: N-86/105, M-234].

BARTLETT, John (1742-1783). Son of Joseph Bartlett (1707-1772) and Martha Milton, John married Susannah Thatcher and their son Robert Bartlett (1782-1832) married Sarah Fairbanks, daughter of James Fairbanks [Ref: S-1:20]. Private, Militia, Hearts of Oak Company, 38th Battalion, 1777-1778 [Ref: N-86/105, M-226]. Private, Militia, Hearts of Oak Company, 38th Battalion, 1780-1781 [Ref: N-86/105, M-234].

BARTLETT, Joseph. See "John Bartlett," q.v.

BARTLETT, Richard. Private, Militia, Hearts of Oak Company, 38th Battalion, 1777-1778 [Ref: N-86/105, M-226]. Private, Militia, Hearts of Oak Company, 38th Battalion, 1780-1781 [Ref: N-86/105, M-234].

BARTLETT, Robert. See "John Bartlett," q.v.

BARWICK, John. Private, Militia, Sword in Hand Company, 4th Battalion, 1777-1778 [Ref: N-86/105, M-224]. Private, Militia, Sword in Hand Company, 4th Battalion, 1780-1781 [Ref: N-86/105, M-231]. Took the Oath of Allegiance and Fidelity on or about March 1, 1778 [Ref: J-1814, N-106/114].

BARWICK, William. Private, Militia, Hand & Hand Company, 4th Battalion, 1777-1778 [Ref: N-86/105, M-225]. Took the Oath of Allegiance and Fidelity on or about March 1, 1778 [Ref: J-1814, N-106/114].

BAUL, James. See "James Ball," q.v.

BAXTER, Robert. Private, Militia, Union Company, 4th Battalion, 1777-1778 [Ref: N-86/105, M-223]. Took the Oath of Allegiance and Fidelity on or about March 1, 1778 [Ref: J-1814, N-106/114].

BEALL, Elizabeth. See "John Bracco," q.v.

BEALL, Nathaniel. See "John Bracco," q.v.

BEAUVER, William. Private, 4th Independent Company of Maryland Regular Troops, Capt. James Hindman's Company, September, 1776 muster roll; enlisted February 2, 1776 [Ref: D-24].

BELL, John. Took the Oath of Allegiance and Fidelity on or about March 1, 1778 [Ref: J-1814, N-106/114].
BELL, Joseph. Private, Militia, Hand in Hand Company, 4th Battalion, 1780-1781 [Ref: N-86/105, M-232].
BELL, Josephus. Private, Militia, Third Haven Company, 4th Battalion, 1777-1778 [Ref: N-86/105, M-225].
BENDON, William. Private, Militia, Capt. Thomas Bullen's Company; no date was given; possibly late 1775 or early 1776 [Ref: Z-3].
BENNY, Benjamin. Took the Oath of Allegiance and Fidelity on or about March 1, 1778 [Ref: J-1814, N-106/114, which listed the name as "Benja. Benney"]. Private, Militia, Volunteer Company, 4th Battalion, 1780-1781 [Ref: N-86/105, M-229].
BENNY, Charles Walker. Private, Militia, Sword in Hand Company, 4th Battalion, 1780-1781 [Ref: N-86/105, M-231]. Second Lieutenant, 4th Battalion, November 4, 1782 [Ref: M-52, I-298].
BENNY, James. Private, Militia, Wye Company, 4th Battalion, 1777-1778 [Ref: N-86/105, M-222].
BENNY, John. Private, 5th Maryland Line; enlisted on April 2, 1778 and died in August, 1778 [Ref: D-185].
BENNY, Thomas. Private, Militia, Volunteer Company, 4th Battalion, 1780-1781 [Ref: N-86/105, M-229]. Took the Oath of Allegiance and Fidelity on or about March 1, 1778 [Ref: J-1814, N-106/114].
BENNY, William. Ensign, Militia, Sword in Hand Company, 4th Battalion, April 9, 1778 through 1781 [Ref: N-86, N-99, M-230, M-53, E-24]. Took the Oath of Allegiance and Fidelity on or about March 1, 1778 [Ref: J-1814, N-106/114]. One William Benny married Mary Hart in St. Peter's Parish, Talbot County, on September 1, 1760 [Ref: K-55].
BENSON, Anne. See "James Benson," q.v.
BENSON, Charlotte. See "James Benson," q.v.
BENSON, Elizabeth. See "James Benson," q.v.
BENSON, James (c1725-1792). Son of Perry Benson (1694-1751) and Rebecca ----, he married Hannah Ratcliffe in 1748 and had these children: Perry, James, William, Robert, Margaret (married Dr. Edward White), Rebecca, Elizabeth, Charlotte, and Anne. James attended the Maryland Convention in 1775 and 1777-1778 [Ref: A-3, O-4, R-71, R-76, R-78, R-130, R-131]. Captain, Militia, Miles Neck Company, 38th Battalion, January 1, 1776 [Ref: M-53]. Took the Oath of Allegiance and Fidelity on or about March 1, 1778 [Ref: J-1814, N-106/114]. County Court Justice, 1778 [Ref: E-250]. Commissioner of the Tax, 1779-1782 [Ref: R-131]. See "Joseph Benson," q.v.
BENSON, James. Private, Militia, Miles River Company, 38th Battalion, 1780-1781 [Ref: N-86/105, M-235].
BENSON, James. Private, Militia, Hearts of Oak Company, 38th Battalion, 1780-1781 [Ref: N-86/105, M-235]. See "Joseph Benson," q.v.

BENSON, Joseph. Private, Militia, Hearts of Oak Company, 38th Battalion, 1780-1781 [Ref: N-86/105, M-234]. He applied for a pension (S12989) in Baltimore City on January 30, 1846, aged 82, stating he had enlisted at age 16 in Talbot County where he was born. He mentioned the following Bensons who served in the war: Capt. James Benson, Gen. Perry Benson, Adjutant Nicholas Benson (his uncle), Ensign Perry Benson (his father), James Benson (his brother), and Perry Benson (his brother). All of these men were related to him and all were deceased before 1846. He also applied for bounty land (#46942-160-55) on October 30, 1855, aged 93. He stated he lived for a short time in Dorchester County and Caroline County and in 1798 moved to Baltimore City. His daughter, Mrs. Samuel Lucas, lived in Baltimore in 1853 and his son, S. E. Benson, lived in Washington, D. C. in 1858 [Ref: W-241].

BENSON, Margaret. See "James Benson," q.v.

BENSON, Nicholas. Took the Oath of Allegiance and Fidelity on or about March 1, 1778 [Ref: J-1814, N-106/114]. Adjutant during the war [Ref: W-241]. See "Joseph Benson," q.v.

BENSON, Perry. Ensign, Militia, Hearts of Oak Company, February 7, 1776. Second Lieutenant, 38th Battalion, May 23, 1776 [Ref: M-53, A-140, A-438]. Took the Oath of Allegiance and Fidelity on or about March 1, 1778 [Ref: J-1814, N-106/114]. Received bounty land (#236-300-25) in May, 1789 for service as a captain in 5th Maryland Line; placed on the pension rolls (S10087) as a captain on October 26, 1810 with an annual allowance of $240 effective January 1, 1803; lived in Talbot County in 1819; died October 2, 1827 [Ref: X-18/514, W-241]. It should be noted that there was also a Perry Benson who was a first lieutenant in the 5th battalion of militia in Queen Anne's County on June 13, 1777 [Ref: M-53]. See "Joseph Dawson" and "James Benson" and "Joseph Benson," q.v.

BENSON, Perry (of James). Ensign, Militia, 4th Battalion, July 1, 1776 [Ref: M-53, A-539, D-67]. Ensign, Militia, Hearts of Oak Company, 38th Battalion, December 3, 1779 through 1781 [Ref: N-104, M-234, M-53, F-28, which listed the name without the "of James"]. One Perry Benson (1751-1814) married Anne Bromwell and was an ensign in the revolution [Ref: Y-234]. See "James Benson" and "Joseph Benson," q.v.

BENSON, Rebecca. See "James Benson," q.v.

BENSON, Robert. See "James Benson," q.v.

BENSON, S. E. See "Joseph Benson," q.v.

BENSON, William. See "James Benson," q.v.

BENT, William. Private, Militia, 4th Battalion, Capt. Greenbury Goldsborough's Company, reviewed and passed July 27, 1776 [Ref: D-67]. Private, Militia, Volunteer Company, 4th Battalion, 1777-1778 [Ref: N-86/105, M-223]. Took the Oath of Allegiance and Fidelity on or about March 1, 1778 [Ref: J-1814, N-106/114]. Private, Militia, Volunteer Company, 4th Battalion, 1780-1781 [Ref: N-86/105, M-230].

BERKHORN(?), John. Private, Militia, 2nd Volunteer Company, 4th Battalion, 1777-1778 [Ref: N-86/105, M-224].
BERRIDGE, William (1744-   ). Son of William and Elizabeth Berridge of Gainsborough in Lincolnshire, Great Britain, was born April 15, 1744, baptized in infancy, and married Grace Macmahan on December 30, 1773 in St. Peter's Parish, Talbot County [Ref: K-56, K-57]. Took the Oath of Allegiance and Fidelity on or about March 1, 1778 [Ref: J-1814, N-106/114].
BERRIDGE, William. Drummer, Militia, Bullinbrook Company, 4th Battalion, 1780-1781 [Ref: N-99, M-231].
BERRY, Daniel. Private, Militia, Capt. Thomas Bullen's Company; no date was given; possibly late 1775 or early 1776 [Ref: Z-3]. Took the Oath of Allegiance and Fidelity on or about March 1, 1778 [Ref: J-1814, N-106/114].
BERRY, Daniel. Private, Militia, Volunteer Company, 4th Battalion, 1777-1778 [Ref: N-86/105, M-223]. Private, Militia, Volunteer Company, 4th Battalion, 1780-1781 [Ref: N-86/105, M-230]. Took the Oath of Allegiance and Fidelity on or about March 1, 1778 [Ref: J-1814, N-106/114].
BERRY, James (of Daniel). Took the Oath of Allegiance and Fidelity on or after March 1, 1778 [Ref: J-1814, N-106/114].
BERRY, James Jr. Private, Militia, Third Haven Company, 4th Battalion, 1777-1778 [Ref: N-86/105, M-225]. Private, Militia, Third Haven Company, 4th Battalion, 1780-1781 [Ref: N-86/105, M-232].
BERRY, James Jr. Private, Militia, Sword in Hand Company, 4th Battalion, 1777-1778 [Ref: N-86/105, M-224]. Private, Militia, Sword in Hand Company, 4th Battalion, 1780-1781 [Ref: N-86/105, M-231]. Private in the militia who was draughted on August 30, 1781 to reinforce the American Army and to serve in the Maryland Continental Troops until December 10, 1781 [Ref: D-387].
BERRY, James Sr. Private, Militia, Third Haven Company, 4th Battalion, 1777-1778 [Ref: N-86/105, M-225]. Private, Militia, Third Haven Company, 4th Battalion, 1780-1781 [Ref: N-86/105, M-232].
BERRY, John. Private, Militia, Union Company, 4th Battalion, 1777-1778 [Ref: N-86/105, M-223]. Private, Militia, Union Company, 4th Battalion, 1780-1781 [Ref: N-86/105, M-229].
BERRY, John. Private, Militia, Volunteer Company, 4th Battalion, 1777-1778 [Ref: N-86/105, M-223].
BERRY, John. Took the Oath of Allegiance and Fidelity on or after March 1, 1778 [Ref: J-1814, N-106/114].
BERRY, Joseph. Private, Militia, Sword in Hand Company, 4th Battalion, 1777-1778 [Ref: N-86/105, M-224]. Private, Militia, Sword in Hand Company, 4th Battalion, 1780-1781 [Ref: N-86/105, M-231].
BERRY, Mary. See "Christopher Bruff," q.v.
BERRY, William. Ensign, Militia, Third Haven Company, 4th Battalion, May 11, 1778 [Ref: N-100, M-232, M-53, E-73]. Paid £9 for services rendered on March 11, 1779, by Col. Christopher Birkhead [Ref: E-319].

BESWICK (BESSWICK, BESWICKS), George. Private, Militia, Wye Company, 4th Battalion, 1777-1778 [Ref: N-86/105, M-222]. Private, Militia, Wye Company, 4th Battalion, 1780-1781 [Ref: N-86/105, M-228]. Took the Oath of Allegiance and Fidelity on or about March 1, 1778 [Ref: J-1814, N-106/114]. Rendered patriotic service by supplying bacon for the use of the Army in June, 1778 and also by hauling provisions [Ref: P-176].

BESWICK (BESWICKS), Nathan. Private, Militia, Wye Company, 4th Battalion, 1777-1778 [Ref: N-86/105, M-222]. Private, Militia, Wye Company, 4th Battalion, 1780-1781 [Ref: N-86/105, M-228].

BESWICK (BESSWICK, BESWICKS), Richard. Private, 4th Independent Company of Maryland Regular Troops, Capt. James Hindman's Company, September, 1776 muster roll; enlisted January 25, 1776 [Ref: D-24]. Private, Militia, 2nd Volunteer Company, 4th Battalion, 1777-1778 [Ref: N-86/105, M-225]. Private, Militia, Wye Company, 4th Battalion, 1780-1781 [Ref: N-86/105, M-228]. Private in the militia who was draughted on August 30, 1781 to reinforce the American Army and to serve in the Maryland Continental Troops until December 10, 1781 [Ref: D-387]. Took the Oath of Allegiance and Fidelity on or about March 1, 1778 [Ref: J-1814, N-106/114].

BETTS, John (Clerk). Provided a receipt for wheat from Peregrine Tilghman, Purchasing Agent, on April 7, 1780 and May 3, 1780 [Ref: P-282, P-288].

BEVERAGE, Mary Ann. See "Thomas Barnett Sewell," q.v.

BIGG (BIGGS), John. Took the Oath of Allegiance and Fidelity on or after March 1, 1778 [Ref: J-1814, N-106/114]. Private, Militia, Oxford Company, 38th Battalion, 1777-1778 [Ref: N-86/105, M-228].

BEWLEY (BEWLY), Joseph. On January 9, 1778 the Maryland Council issued a Special Commission of Oyer & Terminer & Goal Delivery for the Eastern Shore according to the late Act of Assembly and directed in Talbot County" to Joseph Bewley and four others to be Judges of the Special Court [Ref: C-463, C-538]. Appointed a Justice of the Peace on November 20, 1779 [Ref: F-22]. See "Joseph Buley," q.v.

BIRCKHEAD, Ann. See "Christopher Birckhead," q.v.

BIRCKHEAD (BIRKHEAD, BURKHEAD), Christopher (c1730-1788). Son of Christopher Birckhead and Ann Harrison, he married first to Ann Edmondson (daughter of Pollard Edmondson) and second to Henrietta Trippe. His children were: Solomon (physician in Cambridge); Christopher (died in 1799); James (died circa 1800); John Trippe (died in 1796); William; Levin; Edward; Henry; and, Ann (never married, died in 1791). [Ref: Y-258, R-133]. Colonel, Militia, 4th Battalion, January 12, 1776 [Ref: M-53]. Justice of the Orphans Court (appointed June 4, 1777). [Ref: C-274]. Took the Oath of Allegiance and Fidelity on or about March 1, 1778 [Ref: J-1814, N-106/114]. County Lieutenant from July 1, 1777 to 1781 [Ref: N-86/105, M-228, M-236, M-53, C-304, C-507, P-175]. Justice of the Peace (appointed November 20, 1779). [Ref: F-22].

BIRCKHEAD, Edward. See "Christopher Birckhead," q.v.
BIRCKHEAD, Henry. See "Christopher Birckhead," q.v.
BIRCKHEAD, James and John. See "Christopher Birckhead," q.v.
BIRCKHEAD, Levin. See "Christopher Birckhead," q.v.
BIRCKHEAD, Solomon. Private, Militia, Bullin Brook Company, 4th Battalion, 1777-1778 [Ref: N-86/105, M-224]. See "Christopher Birckhead," q.v.
BIRCKHEAD, William. See "Christopher Birckhead," q.v.
BIRKHAM, John. Took the Oath of Allegiance and Fidelity on or about March 1, 1778 [Ref: J-1814, N-106/114]. See "John Burkham," q.v.
BISCOE, Jonathan. Private, Militia, Miles River Company, 38th Battalion, 1780-1781 [Ref: N-86/105, M-235].
BISCOE, William. Private, Militia, Miles River Company, 38th Battalion, 1777-1778 [Ref: N-86/105, M-227]. Private, Militia, Miles River Company, 38th Battalion, 1780-1781 [Ref: N-86/105, M-235]. Took the Oath of Allegiance and Fidelity on or about March 1, 1778 [Ref: J-1814, N-106/114].
BLACKWELL, John. Took the Oath of Allegiance and Fidelity on or about March 1, 1778 [Ref: J-1814, N-106/114].
BLADES, Benjamin. Private, Militia, United Company, 38th Battalion, 1777-1778 [Ref: N-86/105, M-227].
BLADES, Benjamin Jr. Private, Militia, United Company, 38th Battalion, 1780-1781 [Ref: N-86/105, M-233]. Took the Oath of Allegiance and Fidelity on or after March 1, 1778 [Ref: J-1814, N-106/114].
BLADES, Edmond. Private, Militia, Miles River Company, 38th Battalion, 1777-1778 [Ref: N-86/105, M-227]. Took the Oath of Allegiance and Fidelity on or about March 1, 1778 [Ref: J-1814, N-106/114]. Corporal, Militia, United Company, 38th Battalion, 1780-1781 [Ref: N-102, M-233].
BLADES, Edmond (Edmund) Jr. Private, Militia, Miles River Company, 38th Battalion, 1777-1778 [Ref: N-86/105, M-227]. Private, Militia, Miles River Company, 38th Battalion, 1780-1781 [Ref: N-86/105, M-235]. Took the Oath of Allegiance and Fidelity on or about March 1, 1778; listed the name twice [Ref: J-1814, N-106/114].
BLADES, Ezekiel. Private, Militia, United Company, 38th Battalion, 1780-1781 [Ref: N-86/105, M-233].
BLADES, Isaiah. Private, Militia, United Company, 38th Battalion, 1780-1781 [Ref: N-86/105, M-233].
BLADES, James. Private, 5th Maryland Line; enlisted March 31, 1777; reported missing after the Battle of Camden, S. C. on August 16, 1780 [Ref: D-185].
BLADES, John. Corporal, Militia, United Company, 38th Battalion, 1780-1781 [Ref: N-102, M-233]. Draughted on August 30, 1781 to reinforce the American Army and to serve in the Maryland Continental Troops until December 10, 1781 [Ref: D-387]. Took the Oath of Allegiance and Fidelity on or after March 1, 1778 [Ref: J-1814, N-106/114].

BLADES, Levi. Private, Militia, United Company, 38th Battalion, 1780-1781 [Ref: N-86/105, M-233].
BLADES, Thomas. Private, Militia, United Company, 38th Battalion, 1780-1781 [Ref: N-86/105, M-233]. Private in the militia who was draughted on August 30, 1781 to reinforce the American Army and to serve in the Maryland Continental Troops until December 10, 1781 [Ref: D-387].
BLADES, William. Private, Militia, Miles River Company, 38th Battalion, 1777-1778 [Ref: N-86/105, M-227]. Private, Militia, Miles River Company, 38th Battalion, 1780-1781 [Ref: N-86/105, M-235].
BLAKE, John. Private, Militia, 2nd Volunteer Company, 4th Battalion, 1777-1778 [Ref: N-86/105, M-224]. Took the Oath of Allegiance and Fidelity on or about March 1, 1778 [Ref: J-1814, N-106/114]. Private, Militia, Miles River Company, 38th Battalion, 1780-1781 [Ref: N-86/105, M-235].
BLAKE, John (of Peter). Private, Militia, Miles River Company, 38th Battalion, 1780-1781 [Ref: N-86/105, M-235].
BLAKE, John (of William). Private, Militia, Volunteer Company, 4th Battalion, 1780-1781 [Ref: N-86/105, M-229].
BLAKE, Peter. Took the Oath of Allegiance and Fidelity on or about March 1, 1778 [Ref: J-1814, N-106/114].
BLAKE, Sikes (Syke). Private, Militia, Miles River Company, 38th Battalion, 1777-1778 [Ref: N-86/105, M-227]. Took the Oath of Allegiance and Fidelity on or about March 1, 1778 [Ref: J-1814, N-106/114]. Private, Militia, Miles River Company, 38th Battalion, 1780-1781 [Ref: N-86/105, M-235].
BLAKE, William. Private, Militia, Miles River Company, 38th Battalion, 1777-1778 [Ref: N-86/105, M-227]. Took the Oath of Allegiance and Fidelity on or about March 1, 1778; name listed twice [Ref: J-1814, N-106/114]. One William Blake appears on "a list of men blown up in the barges" in 1782 [Ref: D-615]. See "John Blake," q.v.
BLANCH, Thomas. Private, Militia, Oxford Company, 38th Battalion, 1777-1778 [Ref: N-86/105, M-228]. Private, Militia, Oxford Company, 38th Battalion, 1780-1781 [Ref: N-86/105, M-235].
BLANCH, William. Private, 4th Independent Company of Maryland Regular Troops, Capt. James Hindman's Company, September, 1776 muster roll; enlisted February 4, 1776 [Ref: D-24].
BODFIELD, Zadock. See "Zadock Botfield," q.v.
BOE(?), John. Private, Militia, Hand & Hand Company, 4th Battalion, 1777-1778 [Ref: N-86/105, M-225].
BOND, Francis. Took the Oath of Allegiance and Fidelity on or about March 1, 1778 [Ref: J-1814, N-106/114].
BOND, Robert. Private, Militia, 4th Battalion, Capt. Greenbury Goldsborough's Company, reviewed and passed July 27, 1776 [Ref: D-67]. Private, Militia, Union Company, 4th Battalion, 1777-1778 [Ref: N-86/105, M-223]. Took the Oath of Allegiance and Fidelity on or about March 1, 1778 [Ref: J-1814, N-

106/114]. Private, Militia, Union Company, 4th Battalion, 1780-1781 [Ref: N-86/105, M-230].

BOND(?), William. Private, Militia, Volunteer Company, 4th Battalion, 1780-1781 [Ref: N-86/105, M-230].

BOOKER, James. See "John Bracco," q.v.

BOOKER, John. Took the Oath of Allegiance and Fidelity on or about March 1, 1778 [Ref: J-1814, N-106/114].

BOOKER, Lambeth (Lambert). Private, Militia, Union Company, 4th Battalion, 1777-1778 [Ref: N-86/105, M-223]. Took the Oath of Allegiance and Fidelity on or about March 1, 1778 [Ref: J-1814, N-106/114]. Private, Militia, Union Company, 4th Battalion, 1780-1781 [Ref: N-86/105, M-229].

BOOTH, Anthony. Took the Oath of Allegiance and Fidelity on or about March 1, 1778; name listed twice [Ref: J-1814, N-106/114].

BOOTH, William. Private, Militia, Capt. Thomas Bullen's Company; no date was given; possibly late 1775 or early 1776 [Ref: Z-3].

BOOTMAN, John. Private, Militia, Bayside Company, 38th Battalion, 1780-1781 [Ref: N-86/105, M-233].

BORDLY, William. Private, Militia, Wye Company, 4th Battalion, 1777-1778 [Ref: N-86/105, M-222].

BOTFIELD (BODFIELD), Zadock (1746-   ). Born in St. Peter's Parish, Talbot County, on March 3, 1746, son of Zadock Bodfield [Ref: V-91]. Took the Oath of Allegiance and Fidelity on or about March 1, 1778 [Ref: J-1814, N-106/114]. First Lieutenant on the barge *Fearnought* under Capt. Levin Spedden in 1782 [Ref: D-613].

BOWDLE, Henry. Took the Oath of Allegiance and Fidelity on or about March 1, 1778 [Ref: J-1814, N-106/114].

BOWDLE, Henry Jr. (1756-1816). Private, Militia, Volunteer Company, 4th Battalion, 1777-1778 [Ref: N-86/105, M-223, which listed the name without the "Jr."]. Took the Oath of Allegiance and Fidelity on or about March 1, 1778 [Ref: J-1814, N-106/114]. Private, Militia, Volunteer Company, 4th Battalion, 1780-1781 [Ref: N-86/105, M-230]. Henry Bowdle, Jr. was born in Maryland in 1756, married Ruth Mullikin, was a private in the revolution, and died in 1816 [Ref: Y-318].

BOWDLE, John. Private, Militia, Union Company, 4th Battalion, 1777-1778 [Ref: N-86/105, M-223]. Private, Militia, Third Haven Company, 4th Battalion, 1780-1781 [Ref: N-86/105, M-232].

BOWDLE, Joseph. Private, Militia, Oxford Company, 38th Battalion, 1777-1778 [Ref: N-86/105, M-227].

BOWDLE, Loftus. Private, Militia, Capt. Thomas Bullen's Company; no date was given; possibly late 1775 or early 1776 [Ref: Z-3].

BOWDLE, Phebe. See "Nicholas Martin," q.v.

BOWDLE, Stephen. Took the Oath of Allegiance and Fidelity on or about March 1, 1778 [Ref: J-1814, N-106/114]. Rendered patriotic service by supplying bacon for the use of the Army in April, 1778 [Ref: P-161].

BOWDLE, Thomas. Private, Militia, Capt. Thomas Bullen's Company; no date was given; possibly late 1775 or early 1776 [Ref: Z-3].

BOWDLE, Tristram. Private, Militia, Bullin Brook Company, 4th Battalion, 1777-1778 [Ref: N-86/105, M-224]. Private, Militia, Bullinbrook Company, 4th Battalion, 1780-1781 [Ref: N-86/105, M-231]. Took the Oath of Allegiance and Fidelity on or about March 1, 1778 [Ref: J-1814, N-106/114]. Appointed as Inspector of Tobacco at Parson's Landing on August 30, 1780 [Ref: F-271].

BOWDLE, William. Private, Militia, 2nd Volunteer Company, 4th Battalion, 1777-1778 [Ref: N-86/105, M-225]. Took the Oath of Allegiance and Fidelity on or about March 1, 1778 [Ref: J-1814, N-106/114]. Private, Militia, Volunteer Company, 4th Battalion, 1780-1781 [Ref: N-86/105, M-229].

BOWEN, Abraham. Private, Militia, 2nd Volunteer Company, 4th Battalion, 1777-1778 [Ref: N-86/105, M-225].

BOWMAN, Ann. See "James Bowman" and "Joseph Bowman," q.v.

BOWMAN, James (1759-   ). Born in St. Peter's Parish, Talbot County, on June 12, 1759, a son of Samuel and Ann Bowman [Ref: K-56]. Private, Militia, Union Company, 4th Battalion, 1777-1778 [Ref: N-86/105, M-223]. Took the Oath of Allegiance and Fidelity on or about March 1, 1778 [Ref: J-1814, N-106/114]. Private, Militia, Union Company, 4th Battalion, 1780-1781 [Ref: N-86/105, M-230].

BOWMAN, Joseph (1760-   ). Born in St. Peter's Parish, Talbot County, on November 18, 1760, a son of Samuel and Ann Bowman [Ref: K-56]. Private, Militia, Sword in Hand Company, 4th Battalion, 1777-1778 [Ref: N-86/105, M-224].

BOWMAN, Samuel (1758-   ). Born in St. Peter's Parish, Talbot County, on January 17, 1758, a son of Samuel and Ann Bowman [Ref: K-56]. Private, Militia, Sword in Hand Company, 4th Battalion, 1777-1778 [Ref: N-86/105, M-224]. Took the Oath of Allegiance and Fidelity on or about March 1, 1778 [Ref: J-1814, N-106/114]. Private, Militia, Sword in Hand Company, 4th Battalion, 1780-1781 [Ref: N-86/105, M-231]. See "James Bowman" and "Joseph Bowman," q.v.

BOYCE, Alexander. Private, Militia, Capt. Thomas Bullen's Company; no date was given; possibly late 1775 or early 1776 [Ref: Z-3].

BOYD, Robert. Private, Militia, Miles River Company, 38th Battalion, 1777-1778 [Ref: N-86/105, M-227]. Took the Oath of Allegiance and Fidelity on or about March 1, 1778 [Ref: J-1814, N-106/114].

BOZMAN, John. Private, Militia, Union Company, 4th Battalion, 1777-1778 [Ref: N-86/105, M-223]. Private, Militia, Oxford Company, 38th Battalion, 1780-1781 [Ref: N-86/105, M-235]. John Leeds Bozman, son of John and Lucretia

Bozman, was born in St. Peter's Parish, Talbot County, on August 25, 1757. John Bozman and Lucretia Leeds were married in June, 1754 [Ref: K-56].

BOZMAN, Lucretia. See "John Bozman," q.v.

BRACCO, Ann. See "James Bracco" and "John Bracco," q.v.

BRACCO, James. Private, Militia, 4th Battalion, Capt. Greenbury Goldsborough's Company, reviewed and passed July 27, 1776 [Ref: D-67]. Ensign, 7th Maryland Line, commissioned February 10, 1777; Lieutenant, December 28, 1777; resigned January 3, 1780 [Ref: D-189]. James married Ann ----, became the Register of Wills in 1785 after his father John Bracco resigned, and died by 1794 [Ref: R-158]. See "John Bracco," q.v.

BRACCO, James. Private, Militia, Miles River Company, 38th Battalion, 1780-1781 [Ref: N-86/105, M-235].

BRACCO, John (c1725-1794). He married Elizabeth Beall (daughter of Nathaniel Beall and Elizabeth Brooke) by 1753 and their children were: John (physician in Queen Anne's County, married Henrietta Nicholson, and died in 1794); James (married Ann ----, became Register of Wills in Talbot County in 1785, and died by 1794); and, Priscilla (married James Booker). John moved from Queen Anne's County to Talbot County by 1761 and held public office in both counties. In Queen Anne's County he served in the Maryland Lower House, 1754-1758. From Talbot County he attended the Maryland Convention in 1776 and was selected one of the judges of elections for Talbot County on November 8, 1776. He also served in the following capacities: Deputy Commissary, 1771-1777; Committee of Observation (elected 1774); Loan Officer in the Continental Loan Office (appointed 1777); Commissioner of the Tax (appointed 1777); Register of Wills, 1777-1785 (resigned); Justice of the Court of Oyer and Terminer and Gaol Delivery (commissioned 1778); Judge, Court of Appeals (appointed 1778); Justice of the Orphans Court, 1789 to at least 1791 [Ref: E-22, E-112, I-46, O-55, R-76, R-90, R-158]. On January 9, 1778 the Maryland Council issued a Special Commission of Oyer & Terminer & Goal Delivery for the Eastern Shore according to the late Act of Assembly and directed in Talbot County" to John Bracco and four others to be Judges of the Special Court [Ref: C-463, C-538].

BRACCO, Priscilla. See "John Bracco," q.v.

BRACKNELL, James. Private, Militia, Wye Company, 4th Battalion, 1780-1781 [Ref: N-86/105, M-229].

BRADDOCK, James. Private, Militia, United Company, 38th Battalion, 1777-1778 [Ref: N-86/105, M-227]. Took the Oath of Allegiance and Fidelity on or about March 1, 1778 [Ref: J-1814, N-106/114].

BRADFORD, James. Private, Militia, Capt. Thomas Bullen's Company; no date was given; possibly late 1775 or early 1776 [Ref: Z-3].

BRADSHAW, Edith. See "John Bradshaw," q.v.

BRADSHAW, John (1729-). Born in St. Peter's Parish, Talbot County, on May 17, 1729, a son of Thomas and Edith Bradshaw [Ref: V-89]. Took the Oath of Allegiance and Fidelity on or after March 1, 1778 [Ref: J-1814, N-106/114].

BRADSHAW, John. Private, Militia, Capt. Thomas Bullen's Company; no date was given; possibly late 1775 or early 1776 [Ref: Z-3]. Private, Militia, Oxford Company, 38th Battalion, 1777-1778 [Ref: N-86/105, M-227, which listed the name as "John Bradsha"].

BRADSHAW, Thomas. See "John Bradshaw," q.v.

BRASCUP (BRASSCUP), Thomas. Private, Militia, 2nd Volunteer Company, 4th Battalion, 1777-1778 [Ref: N-86/105, M-224]. Took the Oath of Allegiance and Fidelity on or after March 1, 1778 [Ref: J-1814, N-106/114]. Private, Militia, Volunteer Company, 4th Battalion, 1780-1781 [Ref: N-86/105, M-229].

BRATCHEE, William. Private, 4th Independent Company of Maryland Regular Troops, Capt. James Hindman's Company, September, 1776 muster roll; enlisted February 12, 1776 [Ref: D-24].

BRERELY, Allen (Allin). Private, Militia, Bayside Company, 38th Battalion, 1777-1778 [Ref: N-86/105, M-228]. Private, Militia, Bayside Company, 38th Battalion, 1780-1781 [Ref: N-86/105, M-233].

BRICE, Nicholas. Private, Militia, Bayside Company, 38th Battalion, 1777-1778 [Ref: N-86/105, M-228].

BRIDGES, Daniel. Sergeant, Militia, Broad Creek Company, 38th Battalion, 1780-1781 [Ref: N-103, M-234]. Took the Oath of Allegiance and Fidelity on or after March 1, 1778 [Ref: J-1814, N-106/114].

BRIDGES, John. Private, Militia, Hand & Hand Company, 4th Battalion, 1777-1778 [Ref: N-86/105, M-226]. Took the Oath of Allegiance and Fidelity on or about March 1, 1778 [Ref: J-1814, N-106/114]. Private, Militia, Hand in Hand Company, 4th Battalion, 1780-1781 [Ref: N-86/105, M-232].

BRIDGES, William. Private, Militia, Oxford Company, 38th Battalion, 1777-1778 [Ref: N-86/105, M-227]. Private, Militia, Oxford Company, 38th Battalion, 1780-1781 [Ref: N-86/105, M-235].

BRIGHT, Ebenezer. Took the Oath of Allegiance and Fidelity on or about March 1, 1778 [Ref: J-1814, N-106/114].

BRIGHT, James. Private, 5th Maryland Line; enlisted June 14, 1777; discharged by Col. Forrest on May 14, 1780 [Ref: D-185].

BRINING, Edward. Sergeant, Militia, Capt. Thomas Bullen's Company; no date was given; possibly late 1775 or early 1776 [Ref: Z-3].

BRINN (BRIN), John. Private, Militia, Third Haven Company, 4th Battalion, 1777-1778 [Ref: N-86/105, M-225]. Sergeant, Militia, Third Haven Company, 4th Battalion, 1780-1781 [Ref: N-100, M-232]. Took the Oath of Allegiance and Fidelity on or after March 1, 1778 [Ref: J-1814, N-106/114].

BRINN, William. Private, Militia, Third Haven Company, 4th Battalion, 1777-1778 [Ref: N-86/105, M-225]. Private, Militia, Third Haven Company, 4th

Battalion, 1780-1781 [Ref: N-86/105, M-232]. Private in the militia who was draughted on August 30, 1781 to reinforce the American Army and to serve in the Maryland Continental Troops until December 10, 1781 [Ref: D-387]. See "William Bryn," q.v.

BRINSFIELD, George. Private, 5th Maryland Line; enlisted August 5, 1777; discharged October 13, 1778 [Ref: D-185].

BRINSFIELD, George Jr. Private, Militia, Capt. Thomas Bullen's Company; no date was given; possibly late 1775 or early 1776 [Ref: Z-3].

BRINSFIELD, James. Private, Militia, Capt. Thomas Bullen's Company; no date was given; possibly late 1775 or early 1776 [Ref: Z-3].

BRINSFIELD, Moses. Private, Militia, Bullin Brook Company, 4th Battalion, 1777-1778 [Ref: N-86/105, M-224]. Private, Militia, Bullinbrook Company, 4th Battalion, 1780-1781 [Ref: N-86/105, M-231].

BRINSFIELD, Perry. Private, Militia, Bullinbrook Company, 4th Battalion, 1780-1781 [Ref: N-86/105, M-231].

BRINSFIELD (BRINCEFIELD), Solomon. Private, Militia, Bullin Brook Company, 4th Battalion, 1777-1778 [Ref: N-86/105, M-224]. Took the Oath of Allegiance and Fidelity on or about March 1, 1778; name listed twice [Ref: J-1814, N-106/114]. Private, Militia, Bullinbrook Company, 4th Battalion, 1780-1781 [Ref: N-86/105, M-231].

BRINSFIELD, William. Took the Oath of Allegiance and Fidelity on or about March 1, 1778 [Ref: J-1814, N-106/114]. On April 9, 1778, William Maynadier was paid £6 5s. per certificate of John Bracco, Register of the Orphans Court, on account of William Brinsfield, a wounded soldier (private) in the 1st Class of the 4th Battalion of militia in Talbot County [Ref: E-22, E-77].

BRISTOL, Negro (a free man). Private in the militia who was draughted on August 30, 1781 to reinforce the American Army and to serve in the Maryland Continental Troops until December 10, 1781 [Ref: D-387].

BROADWAY (BROADAWAY), Robert. Private, Militia, Sword in Hand Company, 4th Battalion, 1777-1778 [Ref: N-86/105, M-224]. Took the Oath of Allegiance and Fidelity on or about March 1, 1778 [Ref: J-1814, N-106/114].

BROMWELL, Abraham (Abram). Private, Militia, Hearts of Oak Company, 38th Battalion, 1777-1778 [Ref: N-86/105, M-226]. Took the Oath of Allegiance and Fidelity on or about March 1, 1778 [Ref: J-1814, N-106/114]. Private, Militia, United Company, 38th Battalion, 1780-1781 [Ref: N-86/105, M-233].

BROMWELL, Anne. See "Perry Benson (of James)," q.v.

BROMWELL, Edward. Private, Militia, Third Haven Company, 4th Battalion, 1777-1778 [Ref: N-86/105, M-225]. Private (substitute), Militia, Third Haven Company, 4th Battalion, 1780-1781 [Ref: N-86/105, M-232].

BROMWELL (BRUMWELL), Edward. Private, Militia, Oxford Company, 38th Battalion, 1777-1778 [Ref: N-86/105, M-228]. Private, Militia, Oxford Company, 38th Battalion, 1780-1781 [Ref: N-86/105, M-235].

BROMWELL, Edward. Took the Oath of Allegiance and Fidelity on or about March 1, 1778 [Ref: J-1814, N-106/114].

BROMWELL, Edward Jr. Took the Oath of Allegiance and Fidelity on or after March 1, 1778 [Ref: J-1814, N-106/114].

BROMWELL (BRUMWELL), George. Seaman whose name appears on "a list of men blown up in the barges" in 1782 [Ref: D-615].

BROMWELL (BRUMWELL), Jacob. Private, Militia, Oxford Company, 38th Battalion, 1777-1778 [Ref: N-86/105, M-227]. Private, Militia, Oxford Company, 38th Battalion, 1780-1781 [Ref: N-86/105, M-235].

BROMWELL, Peter. Private, 4th Independent Company of Maryland Regular Troops, Capt. James Hindman's Company, September, 1776 muster roll; enlisted January 22, 1776 [Ref: D-24].

BROMWELL, Spedden. Took the Oath of Allegiance and Fidelity on or about March 1, 1778 [Ref: J-1814, N-106/114].

BROOKE, Elizabeth. See "John Bracco," q.v.

BROOME, John. See "Jonathan Hopkins," q.v.

BROWN, Catherine. See "William Maynadier," q.v.

BROWN, George. Private, Militia, Hand in Hand Company, 4th Battalion, 1780-1781 [Ref: N-86/105, M-232]. Private in the militia who was draughted on August 30, 1781 to reinforce the American Army and to serve in the Maryland Continental Troops until December 10, 1781 [Ref: D-387].

BROWN, John. Second Lieutenant, Militia, Third Haven Company, 4th Battalion, 1780-1781 [Ref: N-100, M-232].

BROWN, John. Private, Militia, Oxford Company, 38th Battalion, 1780-1781 [Ref: N-86/105, M-235]. Private who enlisted on March 30, 1781 to serve 3 years in the Maryland Continental Troops [Ref: D-371].

BROWN, John. Private, Militia, Bullin Brook Company, 4th Battalion, 1777-1778 [Ref: N-86/105, M-224]. Private, Militia, Bullinbrook Company, 4th Battalion, 1780-1781 [Ref: N-86/105, M-231].

BROWN, John. Took the Oath of Allegiance and Fidelity on or about March 1, 1778 [Ref: J-1814, N-106/114].

BROWN, Robert. Private, Militia, Bullin Brook Company, 4th Battalion, 1777-1778 [Ref: N-86/105, M-224]. Took the Oath of Allegiance and Fidelity on or about March 1, 1778 [Ref: J-1814, N-106/114].

BROWN, Sarah Scott. See "William Maynadier," q.v.

BROWN, Thomas. Private, 4th Independent Company of Maryland Regular Troops, Capt. James Hindman's Company, September, 1776 muster roll; enlisted January 20, 1776 [Ref: D-24].

BROWNE, Robert. See "James Tilghman, Jr.," q.v.

BROWNE, William. Took the Oath of Allegiance and Fidelity on or after March 1, 1778 [Ref: J-1814, N-106/114].

BROWNING, Peter. Private, Militia, Volunteer Company, 4th Battalion, 1780-1781 [Ref: N-86/105, M-230].

BRUFF, Christopher (1760-1805). Private, Militia, 4th Battalion, Capt. Greenbury Goldsborough's Company, reviewed and passed July 27, 1776 [Ref: D-67]. Private, Militia, Union Company, 4th Battalion, 1777-1778 [Ref: N-86/105, M-223]. Private, Militia, Union Company, 4th Battalion, 1780-1781 [Ref: N-86/105, M-230]. Took the Oath of Allegiance and Fidelity on or about March 1, 1778 [Ref: J-1814, N-106/114]. Christopher Bruff was born in Maryland in 1760, served as a private in the revolution, married Mary Berry, and died on November 17, 1805 [Ref: Y-407].

BRUFF, Edward. Private, 6th Maryland Line, enlisted July 24, 1777; transferred to Marines on October 15, 1777 [Ref: D-275].

BRUFF, Henrietta. See "James Bruff," q.v.

BRUFF, James (1734-1815). Captain, Maryland troops; married Henrietta Bruff; died November 15, 1815 [Ref: Y-407].

BRUFF, John (1740-1819). Private, Militia, United Company, 38th Battalion, 1777-1778 [Ref: N-86/105, M-227]. Private, Militia, United Company, 38th Battalion, 1780-1781 [Ref: N-86/105, M-233]. John Bruff was born in Maryland on December 4, 1740, married Lucy Hopkins, served as a private in the revolution, and died on November 12, 1819 [Ref: Y-407].

BRUFF, Joseph. Captain, Militia, May 13, 1776. Major, Militia, 4th Battalion, April 9, 1778 [Ref: N-90, M-57, E-24]. Took the Oath of Allegiance and Fidelity on or about March 1, 1778 [Ref: J-1814, N-106/114]. Appointed by the Council of Maryland as Collector of Cloathing in Talbot County on January 27, 1778, and Purchaser of Cloathing (Commissary) on June 5, 1781 [Ref: C-474, E-300, G-462, G-593]. Appointed a Court Justice and a Judge of the Orphans Court on November 21, 1778 [Ref: E-250]. See "Jonathan Hopkins," q.v.

BRUFF, Richard. Captain, Militia, Union Company, 4th Battalion, May 11, 1778 through 1781 [Ref: N-97, M-229, M-57, E-73]. Captain, Union Company, who was "draughted" on May 1, 1781 to serve until December 10, 1781 in the Maryland Continental Troops [Ref: D-371].

BRUFF, Richard. Private, Militia, Union Company, 4th Battalion, 1777-1778 [Ref: N-86/105, M-223]. Took the Oath of Allegiance and Fidelity on or about March 1, 1778 [Ref: J-1814, N-106/114].

BRUMWELL, George. See "George Bromwell," q.v.

BRYAN, Arthur. Private, Militia, Miles River Company, 38th Battalion, 1777-1778 [Ref: N-86/105, M-227]. Took the Oath of Allegiance and Fidelity on or about March 1, 1778 [Ref: J-1814, N-106/114]. Private, Militia, Miles River Company, 38th Battalion, 1780-1781 [Ref: N-86/105, M-235].

BRYAN, John. Private, Militia, Bayside Company, 38th Battalion, 1780-1781 [Ref: N-86/105, M-233]. Took the Oath of Allegiance and Fidelity on or about March 1, 1778 [Ref: J-1814, N-106/114].

BRYAN, Stephen. Private, 4th Independent Company of Maryland Regular Troops, Capt. James Hindman's Company, September, 1776 muster roll; enlisted February 4(?), 1776 [Ref: D-24].

BRYAN, William. Private, Militia, 4th Battalion, Capt. Greenbury Goldsborough's Company, reviewed and passed July 27, 1776 [Ref: D-68].

BRYN, William. Private, Militia, Capt. Thomas Bullen's Company; no date was given; possibly late 1775 or early 1776 [Ref: Z-3]. See "William Brinn," q.v.

BUCKLEY, Arnold. Private, Militia, Bullin Brook Company, 4th Battalion, 1777-1778 [Ref: N-86/105, M-224]. Took the Oath of Allegiance and Fidelity on or after March 1, 1778 [Ref: J-1814, N-106/114]. Private, Militia, Bullinbrook Company, 4th Battalion, 1780-1781 [Ref: N-86/105, M-231].

BUCKLEY (BUCKLY), Henry. Private, Militia, Volunteer Company, 4th Battalion, 1777-1778 [Ref: N-86/105, M-223]. Took the Oath of Allegiance and Fidelity on or after March 1, 1778 [Ref: J-1814, N-106/114]. Private, Militia, Volunteer Company, 4th Battalion, 1780-1781 [Ref: N-86/105, M-230]. Private aboard the barge *Fearnought* under Capt. Levin Spedden; enlisted May 28, 1782; 5'9" tall; fair complexion; born in Talbot County [Ref: D-611].

BUCKLEY, James. Private, Militia, Volunteer Company, 4th Battalion, 1777-1778 [Ref: N-86/105, M-223]. Private, Militia, Volunteer Company, 4th Battalion, 1780-1781 [Ref: N-86/105, M-230].

BUCKLEY, John. Private, 4th Independent Company of Maryland Regular Troops, Capt. James Hindman's Company, September, 1776 muster roll; enlisted January 24, 1776 [Ref: D-25]. Private, 5th Maryland Line; enlisted November 3, 1777; reportedly "deserted" on November 20, 1778 [Ref: D-184].

BUCKLEY, Mary. See "William Buckley," q.v.

BUCKLEY, Samuel. Private, Militia, Volunteer Company, 4th Battalion, 1777-1778 [Ref: N-86/105, M-223]. Private, Militia, Volunteer Company, 4th Battalion, 1780-1781; name listed twice [Ref: N-86/105, M-230].

BUCKLEY, Thomas. Private, 4th Independent Company of Maryland Regular Troops, Capt. James Hindman's Company, September, 1776 muster roll; enlisted January 24, 1776 [Ref: D-24]. Private, Militia, Volunteer Company, 4th Battalion, 1777-1778; name listed twice [Ref: N-86/105, M-223]. Private, Militia, Volunteer Company, 4th Battalion, 1780-1781 [Ref: N-86/105, M-230]. One Thomas Buckley married Rachel Flemming on January 14, 1759 in St. Peter's Parish, Talbot County [Ref: K-55].

BUCKLEY, William (1726-   ). Born in St. Peter's Parish, Talbot County, on October 8, 1726, son of William and Mary Buckley [Ref: V-84]. Took the Oath of Allegiance and Fidelity on or after March 1, 1778 [Ref: J-1814, N-106/114, which listed the name as "William Buckby?"].

BULEY, Elizabeth. See "James Tilghman, Jr.," q.v.

BULEY (BEWLY), Joseph. Private, Militia, Wye Company, 4th Battalion, 1777-1778 [Ref: N-86/105, M-222]. Private, Militia, Wye Company, 4th Battalion, 1780-1781 [Ref: N-86/105, M-229].

BULLEN (BULLING), Henry. Private, Militia, Hearts of Oak Company, 38th Battalion, 1780-1781 [Ref: N-86/105, M-235].

BULLEN, James. Private, Militia, Union Company, 4th Battalion, 1777-1778 [Ref: N-86/105, M-223]. Private, Militia, Union Company, 4th Battalion, 1780-1781 [Ref: N-86/105, M-230].
BULLEN, John. Private, Militia, Wye Company, 4th Battalion, 1780-1781 [Ref: N-86/105, M-228]. Private, Militia, Bullinbrook Company, 4th Battalion, 1780-1781 [Ref: N-86/105, M-231]. One John Bullen, eldest son of Thomas and Rachel Bullen, was born in St. Peter's Parish, Talbot County, on April 26, 1740 "on Saturday between the hours of eleven and twelve of clock in the forenoon." [Ref: V-80].
BULLEN (BULLIN), Thomas. Private, Militia, Bullin Brook Company, 4th Battalion, 1777-1778 [Ref: N-86/105, M-224]. Private, Militia, Bullinbrook Company, 4th Battalion, 1780-1781 [Ref: N-86/105, M-231].
BULLEN, Thomas. Captain, Militia; no date was given; possibly late 1775 or early 1776 [Ref: Z-3]. Took the Oath of Allegiance and Fidelity on or after March 1, 1778 [Ref: J-1814, N-106/114]. See "John Bullen," q.v.
BULLEN, Thomas Jr. Private, Militia, Capt. Thomas Bullen's Company; no date was given; possibly late 1775 or early 1776 [Ref: Z-3]. Private, Militia, Bullinbrook Company, 4th Battalion, 1780-1781 [Ref: M-231, N-86/105, which listed the name without the "Jr."].
BULLEN, Rachel. See "John Bullen," q.v.
BULLEN (BULLIN), William. Private, Militia, Union Company, 4th Battalion, 1777-1778 [Ref: N-86/105, M-223]. Private, Militia, Union Company, 4th Battalion, 1780-1781 [Ref: N-86/105, M-229]. Took the Oath of Allegiance and Fidelity on or about March 1, 1778 [Ref: J-1814, N-106/114]. Rendered patriotic service by supplying bacon for the use of the Army in May, 1778 [Ref: P-169].
BUNTON, Joseph. Private, Militia, Third Haven Company, 4th Battalion, 1780-1781 [Ref: N-86/105, M-232]. Paid £9 for services rendered on March 11, 1779, by Col. Christopher Birkhead [Ref: E-319].
BURCH, Robert. Private, Militia, Union Company, 4th Battalion, 1780-1781 [Ref: N-86/105, M-230]. Waterman on the barge *Intrepid* in 1781 [Ref: D-610]. Private aboard the barge *Fearnought* under Capt. Levin Spedden; enlisted May 27, 1782; 5'5" tall; dark complexion; born in Talbot County [Ref: D-611].
BURGESS, Allen (Allin). Private, Militia, Bullin Brook Company, 4th Battalion, 1777-1778 [Ref: N-86/105, M-224]. Private, Militia, Bullinbrook Company, 4th Battalion, 1780-1781 [Ref: N-86/105, M-231]. Rendered patriotic service by supplying bacon for the use of the Army in April, 1778 and also by hauling provisions [Ref: P-163].
BURGESS, George. Private, Militia, Hand in Hand Company, 4th Battalion, 1780-1781 [Ref: N-86/105, M-232]. Took the Oath of Allegiance and Fidelity on or about March 1, 1778 [Ref: J-1814, N-106/114].

BURGESS, Gilbert. Private, 4th Independent Company of Maryland Regular Troops, Capt. James Hindman's Company, September, 1776 muster roll; enlisted February 12, 1776 [Ref: D-24].
BURGESS, Henry. Ensign, Militia, 2nd Volunteer Company, June 17, 1777 [Ref: M-58].
BURGESS, James. Private, 4th Independent Company of Maryland Regular Troops, Capt. James Hindman's Company, September, 1776 muster roll; enlisted January 24, 1776 [Ref: D-24].
BURGESS, John. Private, Militia, Hand in Hand Company, 4th Battalion, 1780-1781 [Ref: N-86/105, M-232].
BURGESS, Thomas. Private, 4th Independent Company of Maryland Regular Troops, Capt. James Hindman's Company, September, 1776 muster roll; enlisted January 26(?), 1776 [Ref: D-24].
BURGESS, William. Private, 4th Independent Company of Maryland Regular Troops, Capt. James Hindman's Company, September, 1776 muster roll; enlisted January 25, 1776 [Ref: D-25].
BURGESS, William. Private, Militia, 2nd Volunteer Company, 4th Battalion, 1777-1778 [Ref: N-86/105, M-225].
BURGESS, William. Private, Militia, Union Company, 4th Battalion, 1777-1778 [Ref: N-86/105, M-223].
BURGESS, William. Took the Oath of Allegiance and Fidelity on or about March 1, 1778 [Ref: J-1814, N-106/114].
BURKE, James. Took the Oath of Allegiance and Fidelity on or about March 1, 1778 [Ref: J-1814, N-106/114].
BURKETT, Jesse. Waterman on the barge *Intrepid* in 1781 [Ref: D-610].
BURKETT, John. Took the Oath of Allegiance and Fidelity on or after March 1, 1778 [Ref: J-1814, N-106/114].
BURKHAM, John. Rendered patriotic service by supplying bacon for the use of the Army in May, 1778 [Ref: P-169]. See "John Birkham," q.v.
BURTON, Ann. See "John Stevens," q.v.
BURTT, John. Took the Oath of Allegiance and Fidelity on or about March 1, 1778 [Ref: J-1814, N-106/114].
BUSH, Joseph. Private, Militia, Volunteer Company, 4th Battalion, 1780-1781 [Ref: N-86/105, M-229]. Private aboard the barge *Fearnought* under Capt. Levin Spedden; enlisted June 1, 1782; 5'10 1/2" tall; dark complexion; born in Talbot County [Ref: D-612].
BUTLER, Moses. Private, Militia, Wye Company, 4th Battalion, 1777-1778 [Ref: N-86/105, M-222].
BYRAM, Stephen. Private, 4th Independent Company of Maryland Regular Troops, Capt. James Hindman's Company, September, 1776 muster roll; enlisted February 6, 1776 [Ref: D-25].
CADE, Jarman (Jerman). Private, Militia, 4th Battalion, Capt. Greenbury Goldsborough's Company, reviewed and passed July 27, 1776 [Ref: D-67].

Private, Militia, Sword in Hand Company, 4th Battalion, 1777-1778 [Ref: N-86/105, M-224]. Private, Militia, Sword in Hand Company, 4th Battalion, 1780-1781 [Ref: N-86/105, M-231]. Took the Oath of Allegiance and Fidelity on or about March 1, 1778 [Ref: J-1814, N-106/114].
CADNER, Thomas. Private, Militia, Wye Company, 4th Battalion, 1777-1778 [Ref: N-86/105, M-222].
CAILE, Michael. Private, Militia, Union Company, 4th Battalion, 1777-1778 [Ref: N-86/105, M-223].
CAIN (CANE), John. Private, Militia, Third Haven Company, 4th Battalion, 1777-1778 [Ref: N-86/105, M-225]. Took the Oath of Allegiance and Fidelity on or after March 1, 1778 [Ref: J-1814, N-106/114]. Private, Militia, Third Haven Company, 4th Battalion, 1780-1781 [Ref: N-86/105, M-232].
CALDWELL, David. Took the Oath of Allegiance and Fidelity on or about March 1, 1778 [Ref: J-1814, N-106/114].
CALLAHAN, Joseph. Took the Oath of Allegiance and Fidelity on or about March 1, 1778 [Ref: J-1814, N-106/114].
CALLAHAN, Michael. Private, Militia, Bullin Brook Company, 4th Battalion, 1777-1778 [Ref: N-86/105, M-224].
CALLENDAR, Andrew (1740-   ). Born in St. Peter's Parish, Talbot County, on November 7, 1740, a son of William and Rebecca Callendar [Ref: V-81]. Private, Militia, Third Haven Company, 4th Battalion, 1777-1778 [Ref: N-86/105, M-225]. Private, Militia, Third Haven Company, 4th Battalion, 1780-1781 [Ref: N-86/105, M-232]. Took the Oath of Allegiance and Fidelity on or after March 1, 1778 [Ref: J-1814, N-106/114].
CALLENDAR, John (1735-   ). Born in St. Peter's Parish, Talbot County, on June 22, 1735, a son of William and Rebecca Callendar [Ref: V-81]. Private, 4th Maryland Line, Rawlings' Regiment, enlisted July 17, 1776 and honorably discharged on July 11, 1779 [Ref: D-99, D-301].
CALLENDAR, Rebecca. See "Andrew Callendar" and "John Callendar" and "William Callendar," q.v.
CALLENDAR, William (1737-   ). Born in St. Peter's Parish, Talbot County, on October 27, 1737, a son of William and Rebecca Callendar [Ref: V-81]. Private, Militia, Third Haven Company, 4th Battalion, 1780-1781 [Ref: N-86/105, M-232].
CALLENDAR, William Jr. Private, Militia, Capt. Thomas Bullen's Company; no date was given; possibly late 1775 or early 1776 [Ref: Z-3].
CALLIGHAN (CALLIGHANE), Griffin. Private, Militia, Wye Company, 4th Battalion, 1777-1778 [Ref: N-86/105, M-223]. Private, Militia, Wye Company, 4th Battalion, 1780-1781 [Ref: N-86/105, M-229].
CALLIGHAN, Joseph. Private, Militia, Wye Company, 4th Battalion, 1777-1778 [Ref: N-86/105, M-222]. Private, Militia, Wye Company, 4th Battalion, 1780-1781 [Ref: N-86/105, M-228].

CALLUM, William Glin. Private, Militia, Union Company, 4th Battalion, 1780-1781 [Ref: N-86/105, M-229].
CALVERT, John. Took the Oath of Allegiance and Fidelity on or about March 1, 1778 [Ref: J-1814, N-106/114].
CAMPBELL (CAMBELL), Duncan (Dunken, Dunkin). Private, Militia, United Company, 38th Battalion, 1777-1778 [Ref: N-86/105, M-227]. Took the Oath of Allegiance and Fidelity on or about March 1, 1778 [Ref: J-1814, N-106/114]. Private, Militia, United Company, 38th Battalion, 1780-1781 [Ref: N-86/105, M-233].
CAMPBELL (CAMBELL), John. Private, Militia, 2nd Volunteer Company, 4th Battalion, 1777-1778 [Ref: N-86/105, M-225]. Took the Oath of Allegiance and Fidelity on or about March 1, 1778 [Ref: J-1814, N-106/114]. Private, Militia, Volunteer Company, 4th Battalion, 1780-1781 [Ref: N-86/105, M-229].
CAMPER, Abraham. Private, Militia, Broad Creek Company, 38th Battalion, 1780-1781 [Ref: N-86/105, M-234].
CAMPER, Adam. Private, Militia, Broad Creek Company, 38th Battalion, 1777-1778 [Ref: N-86/105, M-227].
CAMPER, Charles. Private, Militia, Wye Company, 4th Battalion, 1780-1781 [Ref: N-86/105, M-229].
CAMPER, James. Took the Oath of Allegiance and Fidelity on or about March 1, 1778 [Ref: J-1814, N-106/114].
CAMPER, John. Private, Militia, Broad Creek Company, 38th Battalion, 1777-1778 [Ref: N-86/105, M-226]. Private, Militia, Broad Creek Company, 38th Battalion, 1780-1781 [Ref: N-86/105, M-234].
CAMPER, Thomas. Private, 4th Independent Company of Maryland Regular Troops, Capt. James Hindman's Company, September, 1776 muster roll; enlisted January 26, 1776 [Ref: D-24]. Private, Militia, Broad Creek Company, 38th Battalion, 1777-1778 [Ref: N-86/105, M-227]. Private, Militia, Broad Creek Company, 38th Battalion, 1780-1781 [Ref: N-86/105, M-234].
CAMPER, William. Private, Militia, Broad Creek Company, 38th Battalion, 1777-1778 [Ref: N-86/105, M-226]. Took the Oath of Allegiance and Fidelity on or after March 1, 1778 [Ref: J-1814, N-106/114]. Private, Militia, Broad Creek Company, 38th Battalion, 1780-1781 [Ref: N-86/105, M-234].
CANAHAN, John. Private, Militia, Hand & Hand Company, 4th Battalion, 1777-1778 [Ref: N-86/105, M-225].
CANNON, Clement. Corporal, 4th Independent Company of Maryland Regular Troops, September, 1776 muster roll; enlisted as a private on January 23, 1776 [Ref: D-23].
CANNON, Sales (Sails). Private, Militia, Bullin Brook Company, 4th Battalion, 1777-1778 [Ref: N-86/105, M-224]. Took the Oath of Allegiance and Fidelity on or about March 1, 1778 [Ref: J-1814, N-106/114, which listed the name as "Sailes Cannar"]. Private, Militia, Bullinbrook Company, 4th Battalion, 1780-

1781 [Ref: N-86/105, M-231]. Private aboard the barge *Fearnought* under Capt. Levin Spedden; enlisted June 1, 1782; 5'10" tall; dark complexion; born in Talbot County [Ref: D-612, which listed the name as "Sails Canner"].

CANNON, Thomas. Private, 5th Maryland Line, enlisted August 28, 1777 and "left out" in April, 1778 [Ref: D-191]. Took the Oath of Allegiance and Fidelity on or about March 1, 1778 [Ref: J-1814, N-106/114].

CARDIFF, William. Private, Militia, Bayside Company, 38th Battalion, 1780-1781 [Ref: N-86/105, M-233].

CARDIFFE, Robert. Took the Oath of Allegiance and Fidelity on or about March 1, 1778 [Ref: J-1814, N-106/114].

CAREY (CAIRY), Dennis. Took the Oath of Allegiance and Fidelity on or about March 1, 1778 [Ref: J-1814, N-106/114]. Private, Militia, Volunteer Company, 4th Battalion, 1777-1778 [Ref: N-86/105, M-223]. Private, Militia, Volunteer Company, 4th Battalion, 1780-1781 [Ref: N-86/105, M-230].

CAREY, Henry. Took the Oath of Allegiance and Fidelity on or about March 1, 1778 [Ref: J-1814, N-106/114].

CAREY, Joseph. Took the Oath of Allegiance and Fidelity on or about March 1, 1778 [Ref: J-1814, N-106/114].

CARLISLE, Norman. Took the Oath of Allegiance and Fidelity on or about March 1, 1778 [Ref: J-1814, N-106/114].

CARNER, Noah. See "Noah Corner," q.v.

CARNEY, Solomon Jr. Private, Militia, Third Haven Company, 4th Battalion, 1780-1781 [Ref: N-86/105, M-232].

CARNEY, William. Private, Militia, Bullinbrook Company, 4th Battalion, 1780-1781 [Ref: N-86/105, M-231].

CARR, Henry (1739-   ). Born in St. Peter's Parish, Talbot County, on July 26, 1739, son of John and Judith Carr [Ref: V-80]. Took the Oath of Allegiance and Fidelity on or about March 1, 1778 [Ref: J-1814, N-106/114].

CARR, John. See "Henry Carr," q.v.

CARR, John Jr. Private, Militia, Capt. Thomas Bullen's Company; no date was given; possibly late 1775 or early 1776 [Ref: Z-3].

CARR, Joseph. Private, Militia, Bullin Brook Company, 4th Battalion, 1777-1778 [Ref: N-86/105, M-224]. Private, Militia, Bullinbrook Company, 4th Battalion, 1780-1781 [Ref: N-86/105, M-231]. Took the Oath of Allegiance and Fidelity on or after March 1, 1778 [Ref: J-1814, N-106/114].

CARR, Judith. See "Henry Carr," q.v.

CARR, Mathew. Private, 5th Maryland Line; enlisted on June 6, 1778 and reportedly "deserted" on July 2, 1779 [Ref: D-193].

CARR, Moses. Private, Militia, Bullin Brook Company, 4th Battalion, 1777-1778 [Ref: N-86/105, M-224]. Took the Oath of Allegiance and Fidelity on or about March 1, 1778 [Ref: J-1814, N-106/114]. Private, Militia, Bullinbrook Company, 4th Battalion, 1780-1781 [Ref: N-86/105, M-231].

CARR, William. Private, Militia, Capt. Thomas Bullen's Company; no date was given; possibly late 1775 or early 1776 [Ref: Z-3].
CARRIDINE, James. Private, Militia, Wye Company, 4th Battalion, 1777-1778 [Ref: N-86/105, M-222].
CARROLL, Charles. See "Matthew Tilghman," q.v.
CARROLL (CAROL), Denton. Took the Oath of Allegiance and Fidelity on or about March 1, 1778 [Ref: J-1814, N-106/114]. Private, Militia, Miles River Company, 38th Battalion, 1777-1778 [Ref: N-86/105, M-227].
CARSLAKE, Edward. Private, Militia, Union Company, 4th Battalion, 1777-1778 [Ref: N-86/105, M-223]. Took the Oath of Allegiance and Fidelity on or about March 1, 1778 [Ref: J-1814, N-106/114].
CARSLICK, John. Private, Militia, Wye Company, 4th Battalion, 1777-1778 [Ref: N-86/105, M-222].
CARTER, John. Private, Militia, Broad Creek Company, 38th Battalion, 1780-1781 [Ref: N-86/105, M-234].
CARTER, Mary Ann. See "Philip Horney," q.v.
CATON, Richard. Private, 4th Independent Company of Maryland Regular Troops, Capt. James Hindman's Company, September, 1776 muster roll; enlisted January 29, 1776 [Ref: D-24].
CATROP, John. Private, Militia, Union Company, 4th Battalion, 1777-1778 [Ref: N-86/105, M-223]. Took the Oath of Allegiance and Fidelity on or about March 1, 1778 [Ref: J-1814, N-106/114]. Private, Militia, Union Company, 4th Battalion, 1780-1781 [Ref: N-86/105, M-230].
CATROP, Lambert. Rendered patriotic service by supplying bacon for the use of the Army in May, 1778 [Ref: P-165].
CATROP, Lemon (Lemmon) John. Private, Militia, Union Company, 4th Battalion, 1777-1778 [Ref: N-86/105, M-223]. Took the Oath of Allegiance and Fidelity on or about March 1, 1778 [Ref: J-1814, N-106/114]. Private, Militia, Union Company, 4th Battalion, 1780-1781 [Ref: N-86/105, M-230].
CATROP, Stephen. Private, Militia, Union Company, 4th Battalion, 1780-1781 [Ref: N-86/105, M-230].
CATROP, Thomas. Private, Militia, Union Company, 4th Battalion, 1777-1778 [Ref: N-86/105, M-223]. Private, Militia, Union Company, 4th Battalion, 1780-1781 [Ref: N-86/105, M-229].
CATROP, William. Private, Militia, Union Company, 4th Battalion, 1777-1778 [Ref: N-86/105, M-223]. Private, Militia, Union Company, 4th Battalion, 1780-1781 [Ref: N-86/105, M-230]. Private in the militia who was draughted on August 30, 1781 to reinforce the American Army and to serve in the Maryland Continental Troops until December 10, 1781 [Ref: D-387].
CATROP, William Marsh. Second Lieutenant, Militia, 4th Battalion, April 9, 1778 [Ref: N-87, N-89, M--60, E-24]. Took the Oath of Allegiance and Fidelity on or about March 1, 1778 [Ref: J-1814, N-106/114]. Private(?), Militia, Union Company, 4th Battalion, 1780-1781 [Ref: M-229].

CAULK, Daniel. Private, Militia, Broad Creek Company, 38th Battalion, 1777-1778 [Ref: N-86/105, M-226]. Seaman on the barge *Terable* in 1781 [Ref: D-610]. See "Daniel Cork," q.v.
CAULK, John. Private, Militia, Bayside Company, 38th Battalion, 1777-1778 [Ref: N-86/105, M-228].
CAULK, John. Private, Militia, Hearts of Oak Company, 38th Battalion, 1777-1778 [Ref: N-86/105, M-226].
CAULK, John. Took the Oath of Allegiance and Fidelity on or about March 1, 1778 [Ref: J-1814, N-106/114]. Appointed as Inspector of Tobaaco at Sherwood's Landing on August 30, 1780 [Ref: F-271]. See "John Cork," q.v.
CAULK, John Jr. Private, Militia, Broad Creek Company, 38th Battalion, 1777-1778 [Ref: N-86/105, M-226].
CAULK, John (of James). Private, Militia, Bayside Company, 38th Battalion, 1780-1781 [Ref: N-86/105, M-233].
CAULK, Joseph. Private, Militia, Broad Creek Company, 38th Battalion, 1777-1778 [Ref: N-86/105, M-227]. Private, Militia, Broad Creek Company, 38th Battalion, 1780-1781 [Ref: N-86/105, M-234].
CAULK, Michael. See "Michael Cork," q.v.
CAULK, Peter. Private, Militia, Broad Creek Company, 38th Battalion, 1780-1781 [Ref: N-86/105, M-234].
CECILL (CECIL, CEACIL), John. Private, Militia, Hand & Hand Company, 4th Battalion, 1777-1778 [Ref: N-86/105, M-225]. Took the Oath of Allegiance and Fidelity on or about March 1, 1778 [Ref: J-1814, N-106/114]. Private, Militia, Hand in Hand Company, 4th Battalion, 1780-1781 [Ref: N-86/105, M-232].
CECILL (CACILL), Thomas. Took the Oath of Allegiance and Fidelity on or about March 1, 1778 [Ref: J-1814, N-106/114].
CECILL, Thomas Jr. Private, Militia, Hand in Hand Company, 4th Battalion, 1780-1781 [Ref: N-86/105, M-232].
CECILL (CEACIL), William. Private, Militia, Hand & Hand Company, 4th Battalion, 1777-1778 [Ref: N-86/105, M-225]. Took the Oath of Allegiance and Fidelity on or about March 1, 1778 [Ref: J-1814, N-106/114]. Private, Militia, Hand in Hand Company, 4th Battalion, 1780-1781 [Ref: N-86/105, M-232].
CHAMBERLAINE, Anna Maria. See "Samuel Chamberlaine," q.v.
CHAMBERLAINE, Harriet. See "Samuel Chamberlaine," q.v.
CHAMBERLAINE, Henrietta. See "James Lloyd Chamberlaine" and "William Nicols," q.v.
CHAMBERLAINE, Henry. See "Samuel Chamberlaine," q.v.
CHAMBERLAINE, James Lloyd (1732-1783). Son of Samuel Chamberlaine and Henrietta Maria Lloyd, he married Henrietta Maria Robins on May 16, 1757 and they had these children: Samuel (died 1784); Robins (died young); Robins (1773-1808); Henrietta Maria (married William Hayward, Jr.); and, Margaret

(married Col. John Hughes). James served in the Lower House of the Maryland Legislature, 1771-1781, attended the Maryland Convention, 1775-1776, served on the Fifth Maryland Council of Safety in November, 1776, and was replaced on February 3, 1777, since he "declined to act." [Ref: A-3, O-1, O-4, O-28, R-70, R-71, R-72, R-74, R-206, R-207, C-109]. Brigadier General, Militia, January 6, 1776; resigned on December 26, 1776, stating his reasons in a letter to the Maryland Council of Safety, as follows: "A sincear desire to render my country every service in my power, induced me to accept of the enclosed commission, but finding myself disappointed that many of us rather disposed to quarrell with his neighbour than face the enemy, that a general discontent prevails and unwillingness in the people to do any duty or even attend musters, and a disregard to any sort of order, several battalions without field officers and others absolutely refusing to obey the commands of those appointed over them, has determined me to resign that commission with which I was honored by the Convention and wish be that succeeds me may give general satisfaction." [Ref: A-431, M-61, B-552, B-553]. Chairman, Talbot County Committee of Safety, 1776 [Ref: A-240]. Appointed by the Maryland Council of Safety on January 27, 1776 to collect gold and silver coin in Talbot County to comply with the Resolve of Congress [Ref: A-132]. Took the Oath of Allegiance and Fidelity on or about March 1, 1778 [Ref: J-1814, N-106/114, J-1814, which listed the name as "Jas. Lloyd Chamberlain, Coms. Tax"]. Rendered patriotic service by supplying wheat for the use of the Army in March, 1780 [Ref: P-276]. See "Samuel Chamberlaine" and "William Milward," q.v.

CHAMBERLAINE, James Lloyd. Private, Militia, Union Company, 4th Battalion, 1777-1778 [Ref: N-86/105, M-223]. Private (substitute), Militia, Union Company, 4th Battalion, 1780-1781 [Ref: N-86/105, M-230].

CHAMBERLAINE, Margaret. See "James Lloyd Chamberlaine," q.v.

CHAMBERLAINE, Marion. See "Samuel Chamberlaine," q.v.

CHAMBERLAINE, Martha. See "William C. Seth," q.v.

CHAMBERLAINE, Richard. See "Samuel Chamberlaine," q.v.

CHAMBERLAINE, Robins. See "James Lloyd Chamberlaine," q.v.

CHAMBERLAINE, Samuel (1742-1811). Son of Samuel Chamberlaine and Henrietta Maria Lloyd, he married Henrietta Maria Hollyday on January 15, 1772 and they had these children: Anna Maria (1774-1836); Henrietta Maria (1776-1804); Marion (1778-1820); Sarah Hollyday (1781-1820); Harriet Rebecca (born 1783); James Lloyd (1785-1844); Henry (born 1787); Samuel (1790-1828); and, Richard Lloyd (1792-1831). Samuel was a Judge of the Court Appeals in 1778, Justice of the Peace in 1778, Commissioner of the Tax in 1779-1798, Trustee of the Poor in 1787-1793, Naval Officer at Oxford, Talbot County, 1768-1777 (succeeded his father who resigned in his favor), and served in the Maryland Lower House in 1778 [Ref: R-78, R-208, R-209, E-112, E-250]. "Samuel Chamberlaine, 3rd son of Samuel Chamberlain, Esq., late of St. Michaels, Talbot County, who was youngest son of Thomas Chamberlaine of Langhall near West Chester in Great Britain, by his first wife, was born August 23, 1742, baptized by Henry Nicols, Rector, St. Michaels, confirmed by Bishop Claggett on May 26, 1793, married January 15, 1772 to Henrietta Maria Hollyday, died May 30, 1811, and buried June 1, 1811. Henrietta Maria Chamberlaine, eldest daughter of Henry and Anna Maria Hollyday of St. Michael's Parish, was born December 5, 1750, baptized by Rev. Thomas Bacon, confirmed by Bishop Claggett on May 26, 1793, married January 15, 1772 to Samuel Chamberlaine, died January 9, 1832, and buried January 11, 1832." [Ref: K-57].

CHAMBERLAINE, Samuel. Private, Militia, Oxford Company, 38th Battalion, 1777-1778 [Ref: N-86/105, M-228]. Took the Oath of Allegiance and Fidelity on or about March 1, 1778 [Ref: J-1814, N-106/114]. Private (substitute), Militia, Oxford Company, 38th Battalion, 1780-1781 [Ref: N-86/105, M-235]. Rendered patriotic service by supplying wheat for the use of the Army in March, 1780 [Ref: P-278]. See "James Lloyd Chamberlaine," q.v.

CHAMBERLAINE, Sarah. See "Samuel Chamberlaine," q.v.

CHAMBERLAINE, Thomas. See "Samuel Chamberlaine," q.v.

CHAMBERLAINE, Tommy. See "William Milward," q.v.

CHAMBERS, Griffin. Private, Militia, 2nd Volunteer Company, 4th Battalion, 1777-1778 [Ref: N-86/105, M-224]. Took the Oath of Allegiance and Fidelity on or about March 1, 1778; name listed twice [Ref: J-1814, N-106/114].

CHAMBERS, Isaac. Private, Militia, Sword in Hand Company, 4th Battalion, 1777-1778 [Ref: N-86/105, M-224]. Took the Oath of Allegiance and Fidelity on or about March 1, 1778; name listed twice [Ref: J-1814, N-106/114]. Private, Militia, Sword in Hand Company, 4th Battalion, 1780-1781 [Ref: N-86/105, M-231].

CHAMBERS, John. Private, Militia, Wye Company, 4th Battalion, 1777-1778 [Ref: N-86/105, M-223]. Private, Militia, Wye Company, 4th Battalion, 1780-1781 [Ref: N-86/105, M-229]. Took the Oath of Allegiance and Fidelity on or about March 1, 1778 [Ref: J-1814, N-106/114].

CHAPLAIN (CHAPLAINE, CHAPLIN), Francis. Private, Militia, Volunteer Company, 4th Battalion, 1777-1778 [Ref: N-86/105, M-223]. Took the Oath of Allegiance and Fidelity on or after March 1, 1778 [Ref: J-1814, N-106/114]. Private, Militia, Volunteer Company, 4th Battalion, 1780-1781 [Ref: N-86/105, M-230].

CHAPLAIN (CHAPLAINE, CHAPLIN), James. Private, Militia, Volunteer Company, 4th Battalion, 1777-1778 [Ref: N-86/105, M-223]. Private, Militia, Volunteer Company, 4th Battalion, 1780-1781; name listed twice [Ref: N-86/105, M-230].

CHAPLAIN (CHAPLAINE), John. Private, Militia, Volunteer Company, 4th Battalion, 1777-1778 [Ref: N-86/105, M-223]. Took the Oath of Allegiance and Fidelity on or after March 1, 1778 [Ref: J-1814, N-106/114]. Private,

Militia, Volunteer Company, 4th Battalion, 1780-1781 [Ref: N-86/105, M-230].
CHAPLAIN (CHAPLAINE, CHAPLIN), Thomas. Private, Militia, Volunteer Company, 4th Battalion, 1777-1778 [Ref: N-86/105, M-223]. Took the Oath of Allegiance and Fidelity on or after March 1, 1778 [Ref: J-1814, N-106/114]. Private, Militia, Volunteer Company, 4th Battalion, 1780-1781 [Ref: N-86/105, M-230]. Rendered patriotic service by supplying bacon for the use of the Army in June, 1778 [Ref: P-175].
CHAPLAIN (CHAPLAINE, CHAPLIN), William. Private, Militia, Volunteer Company, 4th Battalion, 1777-1778 [Ref: N-86/105, M-223]. Private, Militia, Volunteer Company, 4th Battalion, 1780-1781 [Ref: N-86/105, M-230]. Private in the militia who was draughted on August 30, 1781 to reinforce the American Army and to serve in the Maryland Continental Troops until December 10, 1781 [Ref: D-387].
CHAPLIN, Francis. Sergeant, Militia, Capt. Thomas Bullen's Company; no date was given; possibly late 1775 or early 1776 [Ref: Z-3].
CHAPMAN, Daniel. Private, Militia, Sword in Hand Company, 4th Battalion, 1777-1778 [Ref: N-86/105, M-224]. Took the Oath of Allegiance and Fidelity on or about March 1, 1778; name listed twice [Ref: J-1814, N-106/114]. Private, Militia, Sword in Hand Company, 4th Battalion, 1780-1781 [Ref: N-86/105, M-231].
CHAPMAN, John. Private, Militia, Union Company, 4th Battalion, 1777-1778 [Ref: N-86/105, M-223]. Took the Oath of Allegiance and Fidelity on or about March 1, 1778 [Ref: J-1814, N-106/114]. Private, Militia, Union Company, 4th Battalion, 1780-1781 [Ref: N-86/105, M-230].
CHAPMAN, Thomas. Private in the militia who was draughted on August 30, 1781 to reinforce the American Army and to serve in the Maryland Continental Troops until December 10, 1781; honorably discharged on December 3, 1781 [Ref: D-387, I-10]. Private aboard the barge *Fearnought* under Capt. Levin Spedden; enlisted May 28, 1782; height not stated; dark complexion; born in Talbot County [Ref: D-611].
CHAPMAN, William. Private, Militia, Volunteer Company, 4th Battalion, 1780-1781 [Ref: N-86/105, M-229].
CHEAVES, Robert. Private, Militia, Hearts of Oak Company, 38th Battalion, 1780-1781 [Ref: N-86/105, M-234].
CHEESLY (CHEESLEY), James. Private, Militia, 2nd Volunteer Company, 4th Battalion, 1777-1778 [Ref: N-86/105, M-225]. Private, Militia, Volunteer Company, 4th Battalion, 1780-1781 [Ref: N-86/105, M-229]. Private (substitute), Maryland Line; honorably discharged on December 3, 1781 [Ref: I-11, D-407].
CHEESLY (CHEESLEY), Jonathan. Private, Militia, 2nd Volunteer Company, 4th Battalion, 1777-1778 [Ref: N-86/105, M-224]. Private, Militia, Volunteer Company, 4th Battalion, 1780-1781 [Ref: N-86/105, M-229]. Private in the militia who was draughted on August 30, 1781 to reinforce the American Army

and to serve in the Maryland Continental Troops until December 10, 1781 [Ref: D-387].

CHEESLY, Robert. Private, Militia, Volunteer Company, 4th Battalion, 1780-1781 [Ref: N-86/105, M-229]. Served in the Maryland Line; honorably discharged on December 3, 1781 [Ref: I-10, D-407].

CHEVOUS (CHEVERS), John. Private, Militia, Wye Company, 4th Battalion, 1777-1778 [Ref: N-86/105, M-222]. Took the Oath of Allegiance and Fidelity on or about March 1, 1778 [Ref: J-1814, N-106/114, which listed the name as "John Chevers"]. Private, Militia, Wye Company, 4th Battalion, 1780-1781 [Ref: N-86/105, M-228].

CHEZUM (CHEEZUM), Daniel. Took the Oath of Allegiance and Fidelity on or about March 1, 1778 [Ref: J-1814, N-106/114]. Private, Militia, Sword in Hand Company, 4th Battalion, 1780-1781 [Ref: N-86/105, M-231].

CHIPMAN, Hannah. See "William Horney," q.v.

CHIPMAN, Mary. See "John Horney," q.v.

CHIPPEY, Joshua. Private, 4th Independent Company of Maryland Regular Troops, Capt. James Hindman's Company, September, 1776 muster roll; enlisted January 28, 1776 [Ref: D-24].

CHRISTIAN (CRISTIAN), Daniel. Private, Militia, Hand & Hand Company, 4th Battalion, 1777-1778 [Ref: N-86/105, M-226]. Private, Militia, Hand in Hand Company, 4th Battalion, 1780-1781 [Ref: N-86/105, M-233].

CLAGGETT, Bishop. See "Samuel Chamberlaine," q.v.

CLARK, John. Private, Militia, Union Company, 4th Battalion, 1777-1778 [Ref: N-86/105, M-223]. Private, Militia, Union Company, 4th Battalion, 1780-1781 [Ref: N-86/105, M-230].

CLARK, Joshua. Private, Militia, Hand & Hand Company, 4th Battalion, 1777-1778 [Ref: N-86/105, M-225]. Took the Oath of Allegiance and Fidelity on or about March 1, 1778; name listed twice [Ref: J-1814, N-106/114]. Private, Militia, Hand in Hand Company, 4th Battalion, 1780-1781 [Ref: N-86/105, M-232].

CLARK, Parrott. Private, Militia, Hand in Hand Company, 4th Battalion, 1780-1781 [Ref: N-86/105, M-232].

CLARK, Richard. Private (substitute), Maryland Line; honorably discharged on December 3, 1781 [Ref: I-11].

CLARK, William. Private, Militia, Capt. Thomas Bullen's Company; no date was given; possibly late 1775 or early 1776 [Ref: Z-3].

CLARK, William. Second Lieutenant, Militia, 4th Battalion, April 9, 1778. First Lieutenant, Militia, Bullinbrook Company, December 3, 1779 through 1781 [Ref: N-99, M-231, M-63, E-24, F-28]. Took the Oath of Allegiance and Fidelity on or about March 1, 1778 [Ref: J-1814, N-106/114].

CLARK, William Jr. Private, Militia, Bullin Brook Company, 4th Battalion, 1777-1778 [Ref: N-86/105, M-224]. Private, Militia, Bullinbrook Company, 4th Battalion, 1780-1781 [Ref: N-86/105, M-231].

CLARKE, William. Took the Oath of Allegiance and Fidelity on or about March 1, 1778 [Ref: J-1814, N-106/114].

CLASH, James. Took the Oath of Allegiance and Fidelity on or after March 1, 1778 [Ref: J-1814, N-106/114].

CLASH, John. Took the Oath of Allegiance and Fidelity on or after March 1, 1778 [Ref: J-1814, N-106/114].

CLASH, Jonathan. Private, Militia, Third Haven Company, who was draughted on May 1, 1781 to serve until December 10, 1781 in the Maryland Continental Troops [Ref: D-371]. Took the Oath of Allegiance and Fidelity on or after March 1, 1778 [Ref: J-1814, N-106/114].

CLASH, Richard. Private, Maryland Line; honorably discharged in 1781 [Ref: D-407].

CLAYLAND, Harris. See "Francis Baker," q.v.

CLAYLAND, William. Private, Militia, Miles River Company, 38th Battalion, 1777-1778 [Ref: N-86/105, M-227]. Took the Oath of Allegiance and Fidelity on or about March 1, 1778 [Ref: J-1814, N-106/114].

CLAYTON, William. Captain, Militia, 4th Battalion, May 23, 1776 [Ref: M-63, A-438].

CLEMMONS, John. Private, Militia, Bullin Brook Company, 4th Battalion, 1777-1778 [Ref: N-86/105, M-224]. Private, Militia, Bullinbrook Company, 4th Battalion, 1780-1781 [Ref: N-86/105, M-231, which listed the name as "John Clemmonse"].

CLIFF (CLIFT), James. Private, Militia, Bullin Brook Company, 4th Battalion, 1777-1778 [Ref: N-86/105, M-224]. Took the Oath of Allegiance and Fidelity on or about March 1, 1778 [Ref: J-1814, N-106/114]. Private, 5th Maryland Line, enlisted May 14, 1778 and reported "died, time unknown" in May, 1779 [Ref: D-192].

CLOGG, Robert. Took the Oath of Allegiance and Fidelity on or about March 1, 1778 [Ref: J-1814, N-106/114].

CLOYD, Hugh. Took the Oath of Allegiance and Fidelity on or about March 1, 1778 [Ref: J-1814, N-106/114].

CLOYD, Thomas. Private, Militia, Bullin Brook Company, 4th Battalion, 1777-1778 [Ref: N-86/105, M-224].

COBURN, Henry. Private, Militia, Hearts of Oak Company, 38th Battalion, 1780-1781 [Ref: N-86/105, M-234].

COBURN, James. Private, 4th Independent Company of Maryland Regular Troops, Capt. James Hindman's Company, September, 1776 muster roll; enlisted January 31, 1776 [Ref: D-24].

COBURN, Jonathan. Private, Militia, Hearts of Oak Company, 38th Battalion, 1780-1781 [Ref: N-86/105, M-234]. Took the Oath of Allegiance and Fidelity on or after March 1, 1778 [Ref: J-1814, N-106/114, which listed the name as "Jonathan Colebourne"].

COBURN, Lambert (Lambeth). Private, Militia, Volunteer Company, 4th Battalion, 1777-1778 [Ref: N-86/105, M-223]. Took the Oath of Allegiance and Fidelity on or after March 1, 1778 [Ref: J-1814, N-106/114, which listed the name as "Lambeth Cobourne"]. Private, Militia, Volunteer Company, 4th Battalion, 1780-1781 [Ref: N-86/105, M-230].

COBURN (COLEBURN), Thomas. Private, Militia, Capt. Thomas Bullen's Company; no date was given; possibly late 1775 or early 1776 [Ref: Z-3]. Private, Militia, Third Haven Company, 4th Battalion, 1777-1778 [Ref: N-86/105, M-225, which listed the name as "Thomas Coleburn"]. Private, Militia, Third Haven Company, 4th Battalion, 1780-1781 [Ref: N-86/105, M-232].

COCHRAN (COKEHRAN), John. Took the Oath of Allegiance and Fidelity on or about March 1, 1778 [Ref: J-1814, N-106/114].

COCKAYNE, Carter. Ensign, Militia, 38th Battalion, April 9, 1778 [Ref: M-63, E-25]. Sergeant, Militia, Volunteer Company, 4th Battalion, 1780-1781 [Ref: N-92, M-229]. Took the Oath of Allegiance and Fidelity on or about March 1, 1778 [Ref: J-1814, N-106/114].

COCKAYNE, Francis. See "Francis Cocking," q.v.

COCKAYNE (COCKIN), Jonathan. Private, Militia, Volunteer Company, 4th Battalion, 1780-1781 [Ref: N-86/105, M-229]. Second Lieutenant, Militia, 4th Battalion, November 4, 1782 [Ref: M-63, I-298, which listed the name as "Jonathan Cockin"].

COCKAYNE, Samuel. Took the Oath of Allegiance and Fidelity on or about March 1, 1778 [Ref: J-1814, N-106/114].

COCKBURN, Jonathan. Private, Militia, Hearts of Oak Company, 38th Battalion, 1777-1778 [Ref: N-86/105, M-226].

COCKBURN, Solomon. Private, Militia, Hearts of Oak Company, 38th Battalion, 1777-1778 [Ref: N-86/105, M-226].

COCKEY, Elizabeth. See "Daniel Lambdin," q.v.

COCKEY, John. Private, Militia, Hearts of Oak Company, 38th Battalion, 1777-1778 [Ref: N-86/105, M-226]. Corporal, Militia, Hearts of Oak Company, 38th Battalion, 1780-1781 [Ref: N-104, M-234].

COCKIN, Jonathan. See "Jonathan Cockayne," q.v.

COCKING, Francis. Private, Militia, Capt. Thomas Bullen's Company; no date was given; possibly late 1775 or early 1776 [Ref: Z-3].

COCKRAIN, John. Private, Militia, Sword in Hand Company, 4th Battalion, 1777-1778 [Ref: N-86/105, M-224]. Private, Militia, Sword in Hand Company, 4th Battalion, 1780-1781 [Ref: N-86/105, M-231].

COCKRAL, John. Took the Oath of Allegiance and Fidelity on or about March 1, 1778 [Ref: J-1814, N-106/114].

COFFIN (COFFREE?), Samuel. Private, Militia, Union Company, 4th Battalion, 1780-1781 [Ref: N-86/105, M-230].

COFFREE, John Robert Samuel. Private, Militia, Union Company, who was draughted on May 1, 1781 to serve until December 10, 1781 in the Maryland Continental Troops [Ref: D-371].

COLBERT, John Sr. Private, Militia, Miles River Company, 38th Battalion, 1780-1781 [Ref: N-86/105, M-235].

COLE, Peter. Private, Militia, 2nd Volunteer Company, 4th Battalion, 1777-1778 [Ref: N-86/105, M-225]. Private, Militia, Volunteer Company, 4th Battalion, 1780-1781 [Ref: N-86/105, M-229]. Took the Oath of Allegiance and Fidelity on or about March 1, 1778 [Ref: J-1814, N-106/114].

COLE, Robert. Private, Militia, Wye Company, 4th Battalion, 1777-1778 [Ref: N-86/105, M-222]. Took the Oath of Allegiance and Fidelity on or about March 1, 1778 [Ref: J-1814, N-106/114].

COLEMAN, Charlotte. See "Thomas Barnett Sewell," q.v.

COLEMAN, Thomas. Private, Militia, 4th Battalion, Capt. Greenbury Goldsborough's Company, reviewed and passed July 27, 1776 [Ref: D-67].

COLESTON (COLISTON, COLSTON, COLESON), Henry. Ensign, Militia, 38th Battalion, April 9, 1778 [Ref: M-63, E-25]. Second Lieutenant, Militia, Hearts of Oak Company, 38th Battalion, March 12, 1779 through 1781 [Ref: N-94, N-104, M-234, M-64, F-28]. Took the Oath of Allegiance and Fidelity on or about March 1, 1778 [Ref: J-1814, N-106/114].

COLESTON (COLSTON), James. Private, Militia, Oxford Company, 38th Battalion, 1777-1778 [Ref: N-86/105, M-227]. Took the Oath of Allegiance and Fidelity on or about March 1, 1778 [Ref: J-1814, N-106/114]. Private, Militia, Oxford Company, 38th Battalion, 1780-1781 [Ref: N-86/105, M-235].

COLESTON (COLSTON), Jeremiah. Involved with the collection of salt in Talbot County which led to a dispute, armed confrontation, and a letter of explanation to Gen. Chamberlaine on December 30, 1776 [Ref: B-562, B-564, C-16]. He appears to have been from Caroline County, but took the Oath of Allegiance and Fidelity on or after March 1, 1778 in Talbot County [Ref: J-1814, N-106/114]. "Jeremiah Collson" was a private in the militia of Talbot County, Hearts of Oak Company, 38th Battalion, 1780-1781 [Ref: N-86/105, M-235]. See "William Milward," q.v.

COLESTON (COLISTON, COLSTON), John. Private, Militia, Oxford Company, 38th Battalion, 1777-1778 [Ref: N-86/105, M-228]. Took the Oath of Allegiance and Fidelity on or about March 1, 1778 [Ref: J-1814, N-106/114]. Private, Militia, Oxford Company, 38th Battalion, 1780-1781 [Ref: N-86/105, M-235].

COLESTON (COLISTON), Samuel. Private, Militia, Oxford Company, 38th Battalion, 1780-1781 [Ref: N-86/105, M-235].

COLESTON (COLSTON), William. Private, Militia, Oxford Company, 38th Battalion, 1777-1778 [Ref: N-86/105, M-227]. Took the Oath of Allegiance and Fidelity on or about March 1, 1778 [Ref: J-1814, N-106/114]. Private, Militia, Oxford Company, 38th Battalion, 1780-1781 [Ref: N-86/105, M-235].

COLLISON, Edward. Private, Militia, Bayside Company, 38th Battalion, 1780-1781 [Ref: N-86/105, M-233].
COLLISON, George. Private, Militia, Bayside Company, 38th Battalion, 1777-1778 [Ref: N-86/105, M-228]. Took the Oath of Allegiance and Fidelity on or about March 1, 1778 [Ref: J-1814, N-106/114, which listed the name as "George Collinson"]. Private, Militia, Bayside Company, 38th Battalion, 1780-1781 [Ref: N-86/105, M-233].
COLLISON, James. Private, Militia, Bayside Company, 38th Battalion, 1777-1778 [Ref: N-86/105, M-228]. Took the Oath of Allegiance and Fidelity on or after March 1, 1778 [Ref: J-1814, N-106/114]. Private, Militia, Bayside Company, 38th Battalion, 1780-1781 [Ref: N-86/105, M-233]. Draughted on May 1, 1781 to serve until December 10, 1781 in the Maryland Continental Troops [Ref: D-370].
COLVERT, John. Private, Militia, Miles River Company, 38th Battalion, 1777-1778 [Ref: N-86/105, M-227].
COLVERT, Thomas. Private, 4th Independent Company of Maryland Regular Troops, Capt. James Hindman's Company, September, 1776 muster roll; enlisted January 25, 1776 [Ref: D-24]. Took the Oath of Allegiance and Fidelity on or about March 1, 1778 [Ref: J-1814, N-106/114].
COMERFORD, Mary. See "Richard Johns," q.v.
COMERFORD (COMMERFORD), Thomas. Private, Militia, Hand & Hand Company, 4th Battalion, 1777-1778 [Ref: N-86/105, M-226]. Took the Oath of Allegiance and Fidelity on or about March 1, 1778 [Ref: J-1814, N-106/114]. Private, Militia, Hand in Hand Company, 4th Battalion, 1780-1781 [Ref: N-86/105, M-232].
CONDON (CONDAN), James. Private, Militia, 2nd Volunteer Company, 4th Battalion, 1777-1778 [Ref: N-86/105, M-224]. Private, Militia, Volunteer Company, 4th Battalion, 1780-1781 [Ref: N-86/105, M-229].
CONDON, Lambert (Lamboth). Private, Militia, Miles River Company, 38th Battalion, 1777-1778 [Ref: N-86/105, M-227]. Took the Oath of Allegiance and Fidelity on or about March 1, 1778 [Ref: J-1814, N-106/114]. Private, Militia, Miles River Company, 38th Battalion, 1780-1781 [Ref: N-86/105, M-235].
CONDON, William. Took the Oath of Allegiance and Fidelity on or about March 1, 1778 [Ref: J-1814, N-106/114]. Private (substitute), 5th Maryland Line; enlisted May 10, 1777; discharged in May, 1780 by Col. Forrest and subsequently discharged on December 3, 1781 by the Council of Maryland [Ref: I-11, D-407, D-191].
CONNER, William. Private, Militia, Bullin Brook Company, 4th Battalion, 1777-1778 [Ref: N-86/105, M-224].
CONNERLY, Henry. See "Henry Connolly," q.v.
CONNERLY, John. Took the Oath of Allegiance and Fidelity on or after March 1, 1778 [Ref: J-1814, N-106/114].

CONNERLY (CONNERLEY), Lawrence. Private, 4th Independent Company of Maryland Regular Troops, Capt. James Hindman's Company, September, 1776 muster roll; enlisted January 25, 1776 [Ref: D-24].

CONNERLY, Thomas. Private, 4th Independent Company of Maryland Regular Troops, Capt. James Hindman's Company, September, 1776 muster roll; enlisted January 25, 1776 [Ref: D-25].

CONNOLLY, Elizabeth. See "John Stevens," q.v.

CONNOLLY (CONNERLY), Henry. Private, Militia, United Company, 38th Battalion, 1777-1778 [Ref: N-86/105, M-227, which listed the name as "Henry Connerly"]. Took the Oath of Allegiance and Fidelity on or about March 1, 1778 [Ref: J-1814, N-106/114, which listed the name as "Henry Connerly"]. See "Henry Connolly," q.v. Private, Militia, United Company, 38th Battalion, 1780-1781 [Ref: N-86/105, M-233, which listed the name as "Henry Connolly"]. One "Henry Connolly" was born in St. Peter's Parish, Talbot County, on February 23, 1734, a son of William and Rachel Connolly [Ref: V-90].

CONNOLLY, John. Private, Militia, Third Haven Company, 4th Battalion, 1780-1781 [Ref: N-86/105, M-232].

CONNOLLY, John. Second Lieutenant, Militia, Third Haven Company, 4th Battalion, April 9, 1778 [Ref: N-91, M-64, E-24].

CONNOLLY, Rachel. See "Henry Connolly," q.v.

CONNOLLY, William. See "Henry Connolly," q.v.

COOK, Elizabeth. See "George Cook," q.v.

COOK, George. Private, Militia, Union Company, 4th Battalion, 1780-1781 [Ref: N-86/105, M-229]. One George Cook, son of James and Elizabeth, was born in St. Peter's Parish, Talbot County, on November 23, 1748 [Ref: V-91].

COOK, George. Private, Militia, Oxford Company, 38th Battalion, 1777-1778 [Ref: N-86/105, M-228]. Private, Militia, Oxford Company, 38th Battalion, 1780-1781 [Ref: N-86/105, M-235].

COOK, James. See "George Cook," q.v.

COOK, John. Private, Militia, Bayside Company, 38th Battalion, 1780-1781 [Ref: N-86/105, M-233]. Waterman on the barge *Intrepid* in 1781 [Ref: D-610].

COOMBES, Edward. Private, Militia, Capt. Thomas Bullen's Company; no date was given; possibly late 1775 or early 1776 [Ref: Z-3].

COOPER, Benjamin. Took the Oath of Allegiance and Fidelity on or after March 1, 1778 [Ref: J-1814, N-106/114].

COOPER, Charles. Private, 4th Independent Company of Maryland Regular Troops, Capt. James Hindman's Company, September, 1776 muster roll; enlisted January 25, 1776 [Ref: D-24].

COOPER, Christopher. Private, Militia, Sword in Hand Company, 4th Battalion, 1777-1778 [Ref: N-86/105, M-224]. Private, Militia, Sword in Hand Company, 4th Battalion, 1780-1781 [Ref: N-86/105, M-231].

COOPER, Haddaway. Private, Militia, Bayside Company, 38th Battalion, 1777-1778 [Ref: N-86/105, M-228]. Took the Oath of Allegiance and Fidelity on or after March 1, 1778 [Ref: J-1814, N-106/114]. Private, Militia, Bayside Company, 38th Battalion, 1780-1781 [Ref: N-86/105, M-233].

COOPER, John. Private, Militia, Capt. Thomas Bullen's Company; no date was given; possibly late 1775 or early 1776 [Ref: Z-3].

COOPER, John. Private, Militia, Broad Creek Company, 38th Battalion, 1777-1778 [Ref: N-86/105, M-226]. Private, Militia, Broad Creek Company, 38th Battalion, 1780-1781 [Ref: N-86/105, M-234]. Private in the militia who was draughted on August 30, 1781 to reinforce the American Army and to serve in the Maryland Continental Troops until December 10, 1781 [Ref: D-387].

COOPER, John. Private, Militia, Third Haven Company, 4th Battalion, 1777-1778 [Ref: N-86/105, M-225]. Private, Militia, Third Haven Company, 4th Battalion, 1780-1781 [Ref: N-86/105, M-232].

COOPER, John. Took the Oath of Allegiance and Fidelity on or after March 1, 1778 [Ref: J-1814, N-106/114].

COOPER, Nathaniel. Captain, Militia, Hand in Hand Company, 4th Battalion, May 13, 1776 through November 4, 1782; succeeded [Ref: N-91, N-101, M-232, M-64, E-24, F-298]. Took the Oath of Allegiance and Fidelity on or about March 1, 1778 [Ref: J-1814, N-106/114].

COOPER, Nathaniel Jr. Private, Militia, Hand & Hand Company, 4th Battalion, 1777-1778 [Ref: N-86/105, M-226].

COOPER, Richard. Private, Militia, Broad Creek Company, 38th Battalion, 1777-1778 [Ref: N-86/105, M-226]. Took the Oath of Allegiance and Fidelity on or after March 1, 1778 [Ref: J-1814, N-106/114]. Private, Militia, Broad Creek Company, 38th Battalion, 1780-1781 [Ref: N-86/105, M-234].

COOPER, Thomas. Private, Militia, Broad Creek Company, 38th Battalion, 1780-1781 [Ref: N-86/105, M-234].

COOPER, Thomas. Private, Militia, Union Company, 4th Battalion, 1780-1781 [Ref: N-86/105, M-230].

COOPER, Thomas. Private, Militia, Bayside Company, 38th Battalion, 1780-1781 [Ref: N-86/105, M-233]. Draughted on May 1, 1781 to serve until December 10, 1781 in the Maryland Continental Troops [Ref: D-370].

COOPER, William. Private, Militia, Bayside Company, 38th Battalion, 1777-1778 [Ref: N-86/105, M-228].

COOPER, William Jr. Took the Oath of Allegiance and Fidelity on or after March 1, 1778 [Ref: J-1814, N-106/114].

CORK (CAULK?), Daniel. Waterman on the barge *Intrepid* in 1781 [Ref: D-610].

CORK (CAULK?), John. First Lieutenant, Militia, Broad Creek Company, 38th Battalion, April 9, 1778 through 1781 [Ref: N-94, N-103, M-234, M-64, E-25].

CORK (CAULK?), Michael. Private, Militia, Oxford Company, 38th Battalion, 1777-1778 [Ref: N-86/105, M-227].

CORKREL (CORKRILL), John. Private, Militia, Wye Company, 4th Battalion, 1777-1778 [Ref: N-86/105, M-222]. Private, Militia, Wye Company, 4th Battalion, 1780-1781 [Ref: N-86/105, M-228].

CORNER, Adam. Took the Oath of Allegiance and Fidelity on or about March 1, 1778 [Ref: J-1814, N-106/114].

CORNER, Noah. Private, Militia, Oxford Company, 38th Battalion, 1777-1778 [Ref: N-86/105, M-227]. Took the Oath of Allegiance and Fidelity on or after March 1, 1778 [Ref: J-1814, N-106/114]. Private, Militia, Oxford Company, 38th Battalion, 1780-1781 [Ref: N-105, M-235, which spelled the name "Noah Carner"].

CORNER, Solomon Jr. Private, Militia, Third Haven Company, 4th Battalion, 1777-1778 [Ref: N-86/105, M-225].

CORNER, William. Took the Oath of Allegiance and Fidelity on or about March 1, 1778 [Ref: J-1814, N-106/114].

CORNEY, James. Private, Militia, Bullin Brook Company, 4th Battalion, 1777-1778 [Ref: N-86/105, M-224].

CORNISH, Solomon. Private, Militia, Capt. Thomas Bullen's Company; no date was given; possibly late 1775 or early 1776 [Ref: Z-3].

CORNON, Thomas. Private, Militia, 2nd Volunteer Company, 4th Battalion, 1777-1778 [Ref: N-86/105, M-225].

COSLEY (COSLY), John. Private, Militia, Union Company, 4th Battalion, 1777-1778 [Ref: N-86/105, M-223]. Private, Militia, Union Company, 4th Battalion, 1780-1781 [Ref: N-86/105, M-230]. See "John Exley," q.v.

COTNER, John. Private, Militia, Wye Company, 4th Battalion, 1780-1781 [Ref: N-86/105, M-229].

COTNER, Thomas. Private, Militia, Wye Company, 4th Battalion, 1780-1781 [Ref: N-86/105, M-229].

COVEY (COVY), Henry. Private, Militia, Hand & Hand Company, 4th Battalion, 1777-1778 [Ref: N-86/105, M-225]. Private, Militia, Volunteer Company, 4th Battalion, 1780-1781 [Ref: N-86/105, M-229]. Took the Oath of Allegiance and Fidelity on or about March 1, 1778; name listed twice [Ref: J-1814, N-106/114].

COVEY, Richard. Private, Militia, Bayside Company, 38th Battalion, 1780-1781 [Ref: N-86/105, M-233].

COWARD, John. Took the Oath of Allegiance and Fidelity on or about March 1, 1778 [Ref: J-1814, N-106/114]. Rendered patriotic service by supplying bacon for the use of the Army in April, 1778 and also by hauling provisions [Ref: P-162, P-163].

COWARD, Richard. Private, Militia, Oxford Company, 38th Battalion, 1780-1781 [Ref: N-86/105, M-235]. Took the Oath of Allegiance and Fidelity on or about March 1, 1778 [Ref: J-1814, N-106/114].

COWARD, Thomas. First Lieutenant, Militia, 4th Battalion, May 16, 1776 [Ref: M-65, A-428].

COWARD, Thomas. Private, Militia, Oxford Company, 38th Battalion, 1780-1781 [Ref: N-86/105, M-235].
COWARD, William. Private, Militia, Oxford Company, 38th Battalion, 1777-1778 [Ref: N-86/105, M-228]. Took the Oath of Allegiance and Fidelity on or about March 1, 1778 [Ref: J-1814, N-106/114].
COWLEY, John. Took the Oath of Allegiance and Fidelity on or about March 1, 1778 [Ref: J-1814, N-106/114].
COX, Edward. Private, Militia, Union Company, 4th Battalion, 1780-1781 [Ref: N-86/105, M-230].
COX, George. Private, Militia, Broad Creek Company, 38th Battalion, 1777-1778 [Ref: N-86/105, M-227]. Private, Militia, Hearts of Oak Company, 38th Battalion, 1780-1781 [Ref: N-86/105, M-234].
COX, Isaac Jr. Private, Militia, Third Haven Company, 4th Battalion, 1780-1781 [Ref: N-86/105, M-232]. Private in the militia who was draughted on August 30, 1781 to reinforce the American Army and to serve in the Maryland Continental Troops until December 10, 1781 [Ref: D-387].
COX, John. Private, Militia, Capt. Thomas Bullen's Company; no date was given; possibly late 1775 or early 1776 [Ref: Z-3].
COX, Joseph. Private, Militia, Third Haven Company, 4th Battalion, 1777-1778 [Ref: N-86/105, M-225]. Joseph Cox, son of Joseph and Mary Cox, was born in St. Peter's Parish, Talbot County, on February 15, 1729 [Ref: V-67].
COX, Nathaniel. Private, Militia, Capt. Thomas Bullen's Company; no date was given; possibly late 1775 or early 1776 [Ref: Z-3].
COX, Mary. See "Joseph Cox," q.v.
COX, Nicholas. Private, Militia, Union Company, 4th Battalion, 1780-1781 [Ref: N-86/105, M-229]. Took the Oath of Allegiance and Fidelity on or about March 1, 1778 [Ref: J-1814, N-106/114].
COX, Powell. Took the Oath of Allegiance and Fidelity on or about March 1, 1778 [Ref: J-1814, N-106/114].
COX, William. Took the Oath of Allegiance and Fidelity on or after March 1, 1778 [Ref: J-1814, N-106/114].
COXLEY, John. See "John Exley," q.v.
CRADDOCK, Isaac. Took the Oath of Allegiance and Fidelity on or about March 1, 1778 [Ref: J-1814, N-106/114].
CRAIG, James. Private, Militia, Miles River Company, 38th Battalion, 1777-1778 [Ref: N-86/105, M-227]. Took the Oath of Allegiance and Fidelity on or about March 1, 1778 [Ref: J-1814, N-106/114].
CRAY, Alexander. Private, Militia, Oxford Company, 38th Battalion, 1777-1778 [Ref: N-86/105, M-228]. Took the Oath of Allegiance and Fidelity on or about March 1, 1778; name listed twice [Ref: J-1814, N-106/114]. Private, Militia, Oxford Company, 38th Battalion, 1780-1781 [Ref: N-86/105, M-235]. Waterman on the barge *Intrepid* in 1781 [Ref: D-610].

CRAY, James. Private, Militia, Oxford Company, 38th Battalion, 1777-1778 [Ref: N-86/105, M-228]. Took the Oath of Allegiance and Fidelity on or about March 1, 1778 [Ref: J-1814, N-106/114]. Private, Militia, Oxford Company, 38th Battalion, 1780-1781 [Ref: N-86/105, M-235].

CRISALL, John. Received an invoice from Peregrine Tilghman, Purchasing Agent, regarding the flour aboard the vessel *Nancy* on May 12, 1780 [Ref: P-290].

CRISP, Benjamin. Private, 4th Independent Company of Maryland Regular Troops, Capt. James Hindman's Company, September, 1776 muster roll; enlisted January 30, 1776 [Ref: D-24].

CRISP, John. Private, Militia, Union Company, 4th Battalion, 1780-1781 [Ref: N-86/105, M-230].

CRONEEN, Daniel (of Caroline County). Took the Oath of Allegiance and Fidelity on or about March 1, 1778 [Ref: J-1814, N-106/114].

CRONEY, Daniel. Private, Militia, Hand & Hand Company, 4th Battalion, 1777-1778 [Ref: N-86/105, M-225].

CRONEY, James. Private, Militia, Wye Company, 4th Battalion, 1777-1778 [Ref: N-86/105, M-222].

CROOKSHANKS (CRUIKSHANKS), Charles. Private, Militia, Oxford Company, 38th Battalion, 1777-1778 [Ref: N-86/105, M-228]. Took the Oath of Allegiance and Fidelity on or after March 1, 1778 [Ref: J-1814, N-106/114].

CROSS, Bristow. Private, Maryland Line; honorably discharged on December 3, 1781 [Ref: I-10].

CROSS, Robert. Private, Militia, Miles River Company, 38th Battalion, 1780-1781 [Ref: N-86/105, M-235]. There was a Robert Cross who was a fifer in the 5th Maryland Line (enlisted March 19, 1777), was a private on January 1, 1778, and then a fifer again on August 20, 1778 [Ref: D-191].

CROUCH, James. Private, Militia, Union Company, 4th Battalion, 1780-1781 [Ref: N-86/105, M-229]. Private aboard the barge *Fearnought* under Capt. Levin Spedden; enlisted June 5, 1782; 5'5" tall; dark complexion; born in Talbot County [Ref: D-612].

CROWDER, John. Private, Militia, 4th Battalion, Capt. Greenbury Goldsborough's Company, reviewed and passed July 27, 1776 [Ref: D-67]. Private, Militia, Sword in Hand Company, 4th Battalion, 1777-1778 [Ref: N-86/105, M-224]. Took the Oath of Allegiance and Fidelity on or about March 1, 1778 [Ref: J-1814, N-106/114]. Private, Militia, Sword in Hand Company, 4th Battalion, 1780-1781 [Ref: N-86/105, M-231, which listed the name as "John Crouder"]. Private in the militia who was draughted on August 30, 1781 to reinforce the American Army and to serve in the Maryland Continental Troops until December 10, 1781 [Ref: D-387].

CRUMP, John. Private, Militia, 2nd Volunteer Company, 4th Battalion, 1777-1778 [Ref: N-86/105, M-224]. Took the Oath of Allegiance and Fidelity on or about March 1, 1778 [Ref: J-1814, N-106/114].

CRYER, John. Private, Militia, Bayside Company, 38th Battalion, 1777-1778 [Ref: N-86/105, M-228]. Private, Militia, Bayside Company, 38th Battalion, 1780-1781 [Ref: N-86/105, M-233]. Took the Oath of Allegiance and Fidelity on or about March 1, 1778 [Ref: J-1814, N-106/114].
CUMMINGS (CUMMINS), James. Corporal, Militia, Bayside Company, 38th Battalion, 1780-1781 [Ref: N-102, M-233]. Took the Oath of Allegiance and Fidelity on or after March 1, 1778 [Ref: J-1814, N-106/114].
CUMMINGS (CUMMINS), John. Private, Militia, Bayside Company, 38th Battalion, 1777-1778 [Ref: N-86/105, M-228]. Private, Militia, Bayside Company, 38th Battalion, 1780-1781 [Ref: N-86/105, M-233].
CUMMINGS (CUMMINS), Nathan. Private (subtitute), Maryland Line; honorably discharged on December 3, 1781 [Ref: I-11].
CUMMINGS (CUMMINS), Nicholas. Private, Militia, Bayside Company, 38th Battalion, 1777-1778 [Ref: N-86/105, M-228]. Took the Oath of Allegiance and Fidelity on or after March 1, 1778 [Ref: J-1814, N-106/114]. Private, Militia, Bayside Company, 38th Battalion, 1780-1781 [Ref: N-86/105, M-233].
CUMMINGS (CUMMINS), Solomon. Private, Militia, Bayside Company, 38th Battalion, 1780-1781 [Ref: N-86/105, M-233].
CUMMINGS, Thomas. Private, Militia, Bayside Company, 38th Battalion, 1777-1778 [Ref: N-86/105, M-228]. Took the Oath of Allegiance and Fidelity on or after March 1, 1778 [Ref: J-1814, N-106/114].
CUMMINS, Thomas Jr. Private, Bayside Company, 38th Battalion, 1780-1781 [Ref:
CUMMINS, William. Private, Militia, Volunteer Company, 4th Battalion, 1777-1778 [Ref: N-86/105, M-223]. Private, Militia, Volunteer Company, 4th Battalion, 1780-1781 [Ref: N-86/105, M-230].
CUMMINS, William. Private, Militia, Bayside Company, 38th Battalion, 1777-1778 [Ref: N-86/105, M-228]. Private, Militia, Bayside Company, 38th Battalion, 1780-1781 [Ref: N-86/105, M-233].
CUMMINS, William. Took the Oath of Allegiance and Fidelity on or after March 1, 1778 [Ref: J-1814, N-106/114].
CURRIER, Samuel. See "Joseph Dawson," q.v.
CUTHCART (CUTCART), John. Private, Militia, Capt. Thomas Bullen's Company; no date was given; possibly late 1775 or early 1776 [Ref: Z-3].
CUTHCART, Thomas. Private, Militia, Bullin Brook Company, 4th Battalion, 1777-1778 [Ref: N-86/105, M-224]. Took the Oath of Allegiance and Fidelity on or about March 1, 1778 [Ref: J-1814, N-106/114].
DAFFIN, Charles. Private, Militia, United Company, 38th Battalion, 1777-1778 [Ref: N-86/105, M-227].
DARDAN, Richard. Private, Militia, Volunteer Company, 4th Battalion, 1777-1778 [Ref: N-86/105, M-223].
DARDEN (DARDIN), Joseph. Took the Oath of Allegiance and Fidelity on or after March 1, 1778 [Ref: J-1814, N-106/114]. Private (substitute), Militia,

Volunteer Company, 4th Battalion, 1780-1781 [Ref: N-86/105, M-230]. Rendered patriotic service by supplying bacon for the use of the Army in April, 1778 [Ref: P-161].

DARDEN, Stephen. Private (substitute), Militia, Union Company, 4th Battalion, 1780-1781 [Ref: N-86/105, M-229].

DAREN, Henry. Private, Militia, Volunteer Company, 4th Battalion, 1780-1781 [Ref: N-86/105, M-230].

DAUGHERTY, John. See "John Dohorty," q.v.

DAVIS, Henry. Private, Militia, 4th Battalion, Capt. Greenbury Goldsborough's Company, reviewed and passed July 27, 1776 [Ref: D-68]. Private, Militia, 2nd Volunteer Company, 4th Battalion, 1777-1778 [Ref: N-86/105, M-225]. Private, Militia, Volunteer Company, 4th Battalion, 1780-1781 [Ref: N-86/105, M-229].

DAVIS, Joseph. Private, Militia, Third Haven Company, 4th Battalion, 1777-1778 [Ref: N-86/105, M-225]. Private, Militia, Third Haven Company, 4th Battalion, 1780-1781 [Ref: N-86/105, M-232].

DAVIS, Robert. Private, Militia, Miles River Company, 38th Battalion, 1777-1778 [Ref: N-86/105, M-227]. Private, Militia, Miles River Company, 38th Battalion, 1780-1781 [Ref: N-86/105, M-235].

DAVIS, Thomas. Private, 4th Independent Company of Maryland Regular Troops, Capt. James Hindman's Company, September, 1776 muster roll; enlisted January 27, 1776 [Ref: D-24].

DAVIS, William. Private, Militia, United Company, 38th Battalion, 1777-1778 [Ref: N-86/105, M-227]. Private, Militia, United Company, 38th Battalion, 1780-1781 [Ref: N-86/105, M-234].

DAWSON, Deborah. See "Joseph Dawson," q.v.

DAWSON, Elizabeth. See "John Gibson" and "Woolman Gibson" and "Thomas Auld," q.v.

DAWSON, George. Captain, Militia, 38th Battalion, April 9, 1778 through November 4, 1782; succeeded [Ref: M-68, E-24, I-498]. Appointed a Justice of the Peace on July 22, 1778 [Ref: E-163].

DAWSON, George Impey (Impy). Captain, Militia, Bayside Company, 38th Battalion, 1778-1781 [Ref: N-95, N-102. M-233]. Took the Oath of Allegiance and Fidelity on or about March 1, 1778 [Ref: J-1814, N-106/114].

DAWSON, Hugh. Private, Militia, Broad Creek Company, 38th Battalion, 1777-1778 [Ref: N-86/105, M-226]. Private, Militia, Broad Creek Company, 38th Battalion, 1780-1781 [Ref: N-86/105, M-234].

DAWSON, Impey. Took the Oath of Allegiance and Fidelity on or about March 1, 1778 [Ref: J-1814, N-106/114].

DAWSON, James. Private, Militia, Union Company, 4th Battalion, 1780-1781 [Ref: N-86/105, M-229].

DAWSON, James. Private, Militia, Sword in Hand Company, 4th Battalion, 1777-1778 [Ref: N-86/105, M-224]. Private, Militia, Sword in Hand Company, 4th Battalion, 1780-1781 [Ref: N-86/105, M-231].
DAWSON, John. Private, Militia, Hearts of Oak Company, 38th Battalion, 1777-1778 [Ref: N-86/105, M-226]. Private, Militia, Hearts of Oak Company, 38th Battalion, 1780-1781; name listed twice [Ref: N-86/105, M-234, M-235].
DAWSON, John. Private, Militia, Sword in Hand Company, 4th Battalion, 1777-1778 [Ref: N-86/105, M-224]. Private, Militia, Sword in Hand Company, 4th Battalion, 1780-1781 [Ref: N-86/105, M-231].
DAWSON, John. Private, Militia, Broad Creek Company, 38th Battalion, 1780-1781 [Ref: N-86/105, M-234].
DAWSON, John. Took the Oath of Allegiance and Fidelity on or about March 1, 1778 [Ref: J-1814, N-106/114].
DAWSON, John Impey. Second Lieutenant, Militia, 38th Battalion, May 23, 1776 [Ref: M-68, A-438].
DAWSON, Joseph. Private, Militia, Broad Creek Company, 38th Battalion, 1777-1778 [Ref: N-86/105, M-226]. Private, Militia, United Company, 38th Battalion, 1780-1781 [Ref: N-86/105, M-233]. Waterman on the barge *Intrepid* in 1781 [Ref: D-610]. Placed on the pension rolls as a private in the Maryland Line on June 30, 1818, aged 62, with an annual allowance of $96 effective April 30, 1818; reported dead, but no date was given [Ref: X-41/514]. His pension application (S34733) states he applied on April 13, 1818 at Easton, Talbot County, Maryland, declaring that he had enlisted there on February 15, 1777, and served under Capt. James Henry of the 5th Maryland Line until the latter's resignation in 1778; then he served under Capt. George Hambleton until the latter was taken prisoner at the defeat of General Gates. He then served under Capt. Perry Benson, now General Benson, until the Battle of Eutaw Springs in which he was wounded, taken prisoner, and the held until the end of the war. On March 31, 1818, Perry Benson made affidavit as to the service of Joseph Dawson. On March 23, 1820, Joseph Dawson, age 60, resident of Easton, repeated his declaration of service and loyalty, and he stated he had no property. His total annual income was $176 as follows: salary as bailiff in Easton, $80; clerk in market, $40; sexton in church, $16; and, Maryland pension as a wounded soldier, $40. He further stated that he was afflicted with rheumatism. As for his family: wife Deborah was aged about 40; Mary, aged between 6 and 7; and; Leah, aged between 3 and 4. In 1837 Samuel Currier stated that Joseph's children were then living in Baltimore [Ref: W-917, Y-785, U-32:4 (1944), pp. 107-108]. This appears to be the same person as Joseph Harrington Dawson (1758-1822) who was a private in the 5th Maryland Line, enlisted February 15, 1777, and served under Captains James Henry and Perry Benson. He married Mary Haddaway circa 1785 and their son William Dawson was born on August 23, 1805, married Sophia Kemp on November 18, 1828, and died on October 11, 1861 at Mayo, Maryland. Joseph died on October 3,

1822 and his wife Mary died on January 3, 1831 at Mayo in Anne Arundel County, Maryland. They are buried in the Dawson Cemetery [Ref: Maryland Society, Sons of the American Revolution, Membership Application No. 3026 (National No. 132985) approved on May 22, 1989, for Compatriot Robert Preston Taylor of Friendship, Maryland; also, *DAR Patriot Index*, Vol. I, p. 181]. Additional research may be necessary before drawing conclusions.

DAWSON, Leah. See "Joseph Dawson," q.v.

DAWSON, Mary. See "Joseph Dawson," q.v.

DAWSON, Nicholas. Private, Militia, Bayside Company, 38th Battalion, 1777-1778 [Ref: N-86/105, M-228]. Took the Oath of Allegiance and Fidelity on or about March 1, 1778 [Ref: J-1814, N-106/114]. Private, Militia, Bayside Company, 38th Battalion, 1780-1781 [Ref: N-86/105, M-233].

DAWSON, Perry (Certificate from Queen Anne's County). Took the Oath of Allegiance and Fidelity on or about March 1, 1778 [Ref: J-1814, N-106/114].

DAWSON, Ralph. Private, Militia, Broad Creek Company, 38th Battalion, 1777-1778 [Ref: N-86/105, M-226]. Took the Oath of Allegiance and Fidelity on or about March 1, 1778 [Ref: J-1814, N-106/114]. Private, Militia, Broad Creek Company, 38th Battalion, 1780-1781 [Ref: N-86/105, M-234]. Ralph Dawson appears on "a list of men blown up in the barges" in 1782 [Ref: D-615].

DAWSON, Richard. Private, Militia, Bayside Company, 38th Battalion, 1777-1778 [Ref: N-86/105, M-228].

DAWSON, Robert. Corporal, Militia, Broad Creek Company, 38th Battalion, 1780-1781 [Ref: N-103, M-234]. Took the Oath of Allegiance and Fidelity on or about March 1, 1778 [Ref: J-1814, N-106/114].

DAWSON, Robert Jr. Corporal, Militia, Broad Creek Company, 38th Battalion, 1780-1781 [Ref: N-103, M-234].

DAWSON, Sarah. See "Oakley Haddaway," q.v.

DAWSON, Thomas. Private, Militia, Union Company, 4th Battalion, 1777-1778 [Ref: N-86/105, M-223]. Took the Oath of Allegiance and Fidelity on or about March 1, 1778 [Ref: J-1814, N-106/114].

DAWSON, Thomas. Militia officer (rank not stated) by August 14, 1777 when the Maryland Council appointed him to take charge of the magazine in Talbot County and "ordered that said magazine be hereafter guarded by a sergeant and four men til further order." [Ref: M-68, C-334]. Assistant Purchasing Agent, 1778 [Ref: P-162].

DAWSON, William. Private, Militia, Broad Creek Company, 38th Battalion, 1777-1778 [Ref: N-86/105, M-226]. Private, Militia, Broad Creek Company, 38th Battalion, 1780-1781 [Ref: N-86/105, M-234].

DAWSON, William. Took the Oath of Allegiance and Fidelity on or about March 1, 1778 [Ref: J-1814, N-106/114, which listed the name as "William Dawson, Shff."]. Appointed a Justice of the Peace on November 20, 1779 and January 17, 1782, at which time he was also app;ointed a Judge of the Orphans Court [Ref: I-46, and F-22, which listed the name as "William Dowson"]. Rendered patriotic service by supplying wheat for the use of the Army in February, 1780 [Ref: P-269]. See "Joseph Dawson," q.v.

DEE, Elijer. Private, Militia, Hand & Hand Company, 4th Battalion, 1777-1778 [Ref: N-86/105, M-225]. Private, 5th Maryland Line, enlisted May 11, 1778 and still in service in November, 1780 [Ref: D-199, which listed the name as "Elijah Dee (or Dean)"].

DELAHAY, Henry. Private, Militia, Third Haven Company, 4th Battalion, 1777-1778 [Ref: N-86/105, M-225]. Private, Militia, Third Haven Company, 4th Battalion, 1780-1781 [Ref: N-86/105, M-232]. Took the Oath of Allegiance and Fidelity on or after March 1, 1778 [Ref: J-1814, N-106/114].

DELAHAY (DELEHAY), Henry. Private, Militia, Capt. Thomas Bullen's Company; no date was given; possibly late 1775 or early 1776 [Ref: Z-3]. Private, Militia, Oxford Company, 38th Battalion, 1780-1781 [Ref: N-86/105, M-235]. Private, Oxford Company, draughted on May 1, 1781 to serve until December 10, 1781 in the Maryland Continental Troops [Ref: D-371, which listed the name as "Jr."].

DELAHAY, James. Second Lieutenant, Militia, Oxford Company, 38th Battalion, 1778-1781 [Ref: N-93, N-105, M-235]. Took the Oath of Allegiance and Fidelity on or after March 1, 1778 [Ref: J-1814, N-106/114].

DELAHAY (DELEHAY), James Jr. Private, Militia, Capt. Thomas Bullen's Company; no date was given; possibly late 1775 or early 1776 [Ref: Z-3].

DELAHAY (DELEHAY), John Mc. Private, Militia, Capt. Thomas Bullen's Company; no date was given; possibly late 1775 or early 1776 [Ref: Z-3].

DELAHAY, Mark. Private, Militia, Bullin Brook Company, 4th Battalion, 1777-1778 [Ref: N-86/105, M-224]. Took the Oath of Allegiance and Fidelity on or after March 1, 1778 [Ref: J-1814, N-106/114]. Private, Militia, Bullinbrook Company, 4th Battalion, 1780-1781 [Ref: N-86/105, M-231].

DELAHAY (DELIHAY, DELEHAY), Thomas. Sergeant, Militia, Capt. Thomas Bullen's Company; no date was given; possibly late 1775 or early 1776 [Ref: Z-3]. Second Lieutenant, Militia, 38th Battalion, May 16, 1776 [Ref: M-69, A-428]. Thomas might be the "Capt. Delahay" referred to in a letter from Robert Lloyd Nichols to the Maryland Council on May 29, 1776 [Ref: A-451, A-452]. He was paid by the Maryland Council of Safety for services rendered on July 26, 1776, £3 15s. [Ref: B-118]. Since there was more then one man with this name, additional research will be necessary before drawing conclusions.

DELAHAY, Thomas. Private, Militia, Third Haven Company, 4th Battalion, 1777-1778 [Ref: N-86/105, M-225]. Private, Militia, Third Haven Company, 4th Battalion, 1780-1781 [Ref: N-86/105, M-232].

DELAHAY, Thomas Jr. Took the Oath of Allegiance and Fidelity on or about March 1, 1778 [Ref: J-1814, N-106/114].

DELAHAY (DELEHAY), William. Private, Militia, Capt. Thomas Bullen's Company; no date was given; possibly late 1775 or early 1776 [Ref: Z-3].

Private, Militia, Third Haven Company, 4th Battalion, 1780-1781 [Ref: N-86/105, M-232].
DENNY, Benjamin. Private, Militia, Hearts of Oak Company, 38th Battalion, 1777-1778 [Ref: N-86/105, M-226]. Private, Militia, Hearts of Oak Company, 38th Battalion, 1780-1781 [Ref: N-86/105, M-235].
DENNY, James Earle. He was paid £6 10s. by the Maryland Council of Safety on October 12, 1776, "for collecting & ascertaining the number of souls in Talbot County." [Ref: B-337]. Private, Militia, Hearts of Oak Company, 38th Battalion, 1777-1778 [Ref: N-86/105, M-226, which listed the name as "James Erl Denny"]. Took the Oath of Allegiance and Fidelity on or about March 1, 1778 [Ref: J-1814, N-106/114, which listed the name as "James Earle Denny"]. Rendered patriotic service by supplying bacon for the use of the Army in June, 1778 [Ref: P-174, which listed the name as "James C. Denny"]. Private, Militia, Hearts of Oak Company, 38th Battalion, 1780-1781 [Ref: N-86/105, M-235, which listed the name as "James E. Denny"]. See "Henry Banning," q.v.
DENNY, Joseph. Private, Militia, Broad Creek Company, 38th Battalion, 1777-1778 [Ref: N-86/105, M-226].
DENNY, Joseph. Private, Militia, Union Company, 4th Battalion, 1780-1781 [Ref: N-86/105, M-230].
DENNY, Joseph. Private, Militia, Hearts of Oak Company, 38th Battalion, 1780-1781 [Ref: N-86/105, M-235].
DENNY, Joseph. Took the Oath of Allegiance and Fidelity on or about March 1, 1778 [Ref: J-1814, N-106/114].
DENNY, Peter (1757-   ). Born in St. Peter's Parish, Talbot County, on December 19, 1757, a son of Peter Denny [Ref: K-55]. Private, Militia, Union Company, 4th Battalion, 1777-1778 [Ref: N-86/105, M-223]. Private, 1st Maryland Line, enlisted May 20, 1778 and reportedly "deserted" on August 30, 1778 [Ref: D-101]. Private, Militia, Union Company, 4th Battalion, 1780-1781 [Ref: N-86/105, M-230]. There was also a Peter Denny who was born in Maryland on October 21, 1740, married Esther Downes, was an ensign in the revolution, and died on September 7, 1804 [Ref: Y-818]. Additional research may be necessary before drawing conclusions.
DENNY, Richard. Private, Militia, Hearts of Oak Company, 38th Battalion, 1780-1781 [Ref: N-86/105, M-235]. Took the Oath of Allegiance and Fidelity on or about March 1, 1778 [Ref: J-1814, N-106/114].
DEVEREUX, James. Private, 4th Independent Company of Maryland Regular Troops, Capt. James Hindman's Company, September, 1776 muster roll; enlisted January 29, 1776 [Ref: D-24].
DICKINSON, Anne. See "James Dickinson," q.v.
DICKINSON, Charles. See "John Dickinson," q.v.
DICKINSON, Henry (1760-   ). Born in St. Peter's Parish, Talbot County, on March 15, 1760, a son of John and Ann Dickinson [Ref: K-55]. Private, Militia, Union Company, 4th Battalion, 1780-1781 [Ref: N-86/105, M-230].

DICKINSON, James (1745-   ). Born in St. Peter's Parish, Talbot County, on September 25, 1745, son of Wiliam and Anne Dickinson [Ref: V-91]. Private, Militia, Bullin Brook Company, 4th Battalion, 1777-1778 [Ref: N-86/105, M-224]. Took the Oath of Allegiance and Fidelity on or after March 1, 1778 [Ref: J-1814, N-106/114].

DICKINSON, James Jr. Private (substitute), Militia, Bullinbrook Company, 4th Battalion, 1780-1781 [Ref: N-86/105, M-231].

DICKINSON, John. Private, Militia, Union Company, 4th Battalion, 1777-1778 [Ref: N-86/105, M-223]. Private, Militia, Union Company, 4th Battalion, 1780-1781 [Ref: N-86/105, M-230]. One John Dickinson married Ann Trippe in St. Peter's Parish, Talbot County, on March 30, 1758. Their sons were Charles (born February 23, 1759), Henry (born March 15, 1760), and Philip (born January 24, 1762). [Ref: K-55]. Another John Dickinson married Sarah Lloyd, daughter of James Lloyd. Also, "John Dickinson (of Dorset County)" took the Oath of Allegiance and Fidelity on or about March 1, 1778 in Talbot County [Ref: J-1814, N-106/114]. Additional research will be necessary before drawing conclusions. See "Henry Dickinson" and "James Lloyd," q.v.

DICKINSON, Philip. See "John Dickinson," q.v.

DICKINSON, Samuel. Private, Militia, Volunteer Company, 4th Battalion, 1777-1778 [Ref: N-86/105, M-223]. Private, Militia, Volunteer Company, 4th Battalion, 1780-1781 [Ref: N-86/105, M-230]. Rendered patriotic service by supplying pork for the use of the Army in May, 1778 [Ref: P-164].

DICKINSON, William. Lieutenant, Militia, Capt. Thomas Bullen's Company; no date was given; possibly late 1775 or early 1776 [Ref: Z-3]. See "James Dickinson," q.v.

DIXON, John. Private, Militia, Capt. Thomas Bullen's Company; no date was given; possibly late 1775 or early 1776 [Ref: Z-3].

DIXON, John Jr. Private, Militia, Volunteer Company, 4th Battalion, 1780-1781 [Ref: N-86/105, M-229].

DIXON, Robert. Private, Militia, 2nd Volunteer Company, 4th Battalion, 1777-1778 [Ref: N-86/105, M-224]. Private, Militia, Volunteer Company, 4th Battalion, 1780-1781 [Ref: N-86/105, M-229].

DIXON, William. Private, Militia, 2nd Volunteer Company, 4th Battalion, 1777-1778 [Ref: N-86/105, M-225]. Took the Oath of Allegiance and Fidelity on or after March 1, 1778 [Ref: J-1814, N-106/114]. Private, Militia, Volunteer Company, 4th Battalion, 1780-1781 [Ref: N-86/105, M-229].

DOBSON, Isaac. Private, Militia, Volunteer Company, 4th Battalion, 1780-1781 [Ref: N-86/105, M-229]. Took the Oath of Allegiance and Fidelity on or about March 1, 1778 [Ref: J-1814, N-106/114].

DOBSON, John. Private, 4th Independent Company of Maryland Regular Troops, Capt. James Hindman's Company, September, 1776 muster roll; enlisted January 31, 1776; reportedly died before September, 1776 muster [Ref: D-25].

DOBSON, John. Private, Militia, Volunteer Company, 4th Battalion, 1780-1781 [Ref: N-86/105, M-229].
DODSON, Robert. Private, Militia, United Company, 38th Battalion, 1780-1781 [Ref: N-86/105, M-233].
DODSON, Thomas. Sergeant, Militia, United Company, 38th Battalion, 1780-1781 [Ref: N-102, M-233].
DOHORTY (DORHORTY, DAUGHERTY), John. Captain, Militia, 4th Battalion, May 13, 1776 [Ref: M-67, A-429]. Captain, Volunteer Company, 4th Battalion, 1780 to at least November 4, 1782 [Ref: N-87, N-96, M-229, and I-298, which listed the name as "John Dorhorty"].
DOMOKOY, Jonathan. Private, Militia, Oxford Company, 38th Battalion, 1777-1778 [Ref: N-86/105, M-227].
DORET(?), Henry. Private, Militia, Bayside Company, 38th Battalion, 1777-1778 [Ref: N-86/105, M-228].
DORGAN, James. See "John Dorgin," q.v.
DORGAN (DORGIN), John (1760-1839). Private, Militia, 4th Battalion, Capt. Greenbury Goldsborough's Company, reviewed and passed July 27, 1776 [Ref: D-68]. Placed on the pension rolls on March 5, 1833, aged 74, as a private in the Maryland Continental service; annual allowance of $26.66 effective March 4, 1831 [Ref: X-51/514]. In his pension application (S8352) on November 20, 1832 he stated he was born in Queen Anne's County, Maryland on September 25, 1760 and moved with his parents (not named) to St. Michael's in Talbot County when quite young. He was a private in the Maryland Boat Service and enlisted in the Flying Camp under Capt. Greenbury Goldsborough. William Richardson was the colonel; later joined with his company in the Army under General Washington, en route to New York, at the Battle of Brunswick. Later stationed at Staten Island and on to White Plains. At the end he returned to St. Marshalls Falls *[sic]* in Talbot County, Maryland. He also served under Capt. Course [Coursey] on the galley *Chester*. John Dorgin died on September 27, 1839 and his son James Dorgan *[sic]* then lived in Talbot County [Ref: W-1002, and J-1814, which contained a pension abstract]. See "Nathan Porter," q.v.
DORHORTY, John. Captain, Militia, 4th Battalion, April 9, 1778 [Ref: M-70, E-24].
DORNAHOY (DOMAHOY?), John. Took the Oath of Allegiance and Fidelity on or about March 1, 1778 [Ref: J-1814, N-106/114].
DORSET (DORSETT), Henry. Private, Militia, Bayside Company, 38th Battalion, 1777-1778 [Ref: N-86/105, M-228]. Private, Militia, Bayside Company, 38th Battalion, 1780-1781 [Ref: N-86/105, M-233].
DOWNES, Esther. See "Peter Denny," q.v.
DOWNES, John. See "John Stevens," q.v.
DOWNS, Elbert. Private, Militia, Union Company, 4th Battalion, 1777-1778 [Ref: N-86/105, M-223].

DOWRY, James. Second Lieutenant, Militia, Broad Creek Company, 38th Battalion, April 9, 1778 [Ref: M-71, E-25].
DOWSON, William. See "William Dawson," q.v.
DRAPER, Edward. Private, Militia, Union Company, 4th Battalion, 1780-1781 [Ref: N-86/105, M-230].
DRUMMOND, Stephen. Private, Militia, Bullinbrook Company, 4th Battalion, 1780-1781 [Ref: N-86/105, M-231].
DUDLEY, Elizabeth. See "George Dudley," q.v.
DUDLEY, George (1733-   ). Born in St. Peter's Parish, Talbot County, on September 26, 1733, son of James and Elizabeth Dudley [Ref: V-70]. Private, Militia, Hand & Hand Company, 4th Battalion, 1777-1778 [Ref: N-86/105, M-226]. Private, Militia, Hand in Hand Company, 4th Battalion, 1780-1781 [Ref: N-86/105, M-233].
DUDLEY, James. Private, Militia, Hand in Hand Company, 4th Battalion, 1780-1781 [Ref: N-86/105, M-232]. See "George Dudley," q.v.
DUDLEY, Mary. See "Thomas Dudley," q.v.
DUDLEY, Richard (c1750-1801). Private, Militia, Hand & Hand Company, 4th Battalion, 1777-1778 [Ref: N-86/105, M-226]. Private, Militia, Hand in Hand Company, 4th Battalion, 1780-1781 [Ref: N-86/105, M-233]. Richard Dudley was born in Maryland circa 1750, married Mary Manship, served as a private in the revolution, and died in October, 1801 [Ref: Y-884].
DUDLEY, Samuel. Private, Militia, Hand in Hand Company, 4th Battalion, 1780-1781 [Ref: N-86/105, M-232]. See "Thomas Dudley," q.v.
DUDLEY, Thomas (1737-   ). Born in St. Peter's Parish, Talbot County, on August 18, 1737, son of Samuel and Mary Dudley [Ref: V-79]. Private, Militia, Hand & Hand Company, 4th Battalion, 1777-1778 [Ref: N-86/105, M-226]. Private, Militia, Hand in Hand Company, 4th Battalion, 1780-1781 [Ref: N-86/105, M-232].
DUDLEY, William. Private, Militia, Hand in Hand Company, 4th Battalion, 1780-1781 [Ref: N-86/105, M-233].
DULING, Delahay. Private, 4th Independent Company of Maryland Regular Troops, Capt. James Hindman's Company, September, 1776 muster roll; enlisted January 26, 1776 [Ref: D-24].
DULING (DULEN), Edward. Private, Militia, Capt. Thomas Bullen's Company; no date was given; possibly late 1775 or early 1776 [Ref: Z-3].
DULING (DULIN, DEWLING), Elijah. Private, Militia, Sword in Hand Company, 4th Battalion, 1777-1778 [Ref: N-86/105, M-224]. Took the Oath of Allegiance and Fidelity on or after March 1, 1778 [Ref: J-1814, N-106/114]. Private, Militia, Sword in Hand Company, 4th Battalion, 1780-1781 [Ref: N-86/105, M-231].
DULING (DULIN), Holiday. Private, Militia, Miles River Company, 38th Battalion, 1777-1778 [Ref: N-86/105, M-227].

DULING (DEWLING), James. Private, Militia, 2nd Volunteer Company, 4th Battalion, 1777-1778 [Ref: N-86/105, M-225]. Private, Militia, Volunteer Company, 4th Battalion, 1780-1781 [Ref: N-86/105, M-229].
DULING (DULIN, DEWLING), John. Private, Militia, Sword in Hand Company, 4th Battalion, 1777-1778 [Ref: N-86/105, M-224]. Took the Oath of Allegiance and Fidelity on or after March 1, 1778 [Ref: J-1814, N-106/114]. Private, Militia, Sword in Hand Company, 4th Battalion, 1780-1781 [Ref: N-86/105, M-231]. Draughted on May 1, 1781 to serve until December 10, 1781 in the Maryland Continental Troops [Ref: D-370].
DULING (DULIN), Joseph. Took the Oath of Allegiance and Fidelity on or after March 1, 1778 [Ref: J-1814, N-106/114].
DULING, Nathan. Private, 4th Independent Company of Maryland Regular Troops, Capt. James Hindman's Company, September, 1776 muster roll; enlisted January 25, 1776 [Ref: D-24]. Private, Militia, Bullinbrook Company, 4th Battalion, 1780-1781 [Ref: N-86/105, M-231].
DULING (DEWLING), William. Private, Militia, Sword in Hand Company, 4th Battalion, 1777-1778 [Ref: N-86/105, M-224]. Private, Militia, Sword in Hand Company, 4th Battalion, 1780-1781 [Ref: N-86/105, M-231].
DUNCAN, John. Private, Militia, Volunteer Company, 4th Battalion, 1777-1778 [Ref: N-86/105, M-223]. Took the Oath of Allegiance and Fidelity on or after March 1, 1778 [Ref: J-1814, N-106/114]. Private, Militia, Third Haven Company, 4th Battalion, 1780-1781 [Ref: N-86/105, M-232].
DUNN, Patrick. Private, Militia, 2nd Volunteer Company, 4th Battalion, 1777-1778 [Ref: N-86/105, M-224].
DURDAN, Joseph. Private, Militia, Volunteer Company, 4th Battalion, 1777-1778 [Ref: N-86/105, M-223].
DURDAN, Stevin. Private, Militia, Union Company, 4th Battalion, 1777-1778 [Ref: N-86/105, M-223].
DURGAN, John. Private, Militia, United Company, 38th Battalion, 1780-1781 [Ref: N-86/105, M-233].
DWIGGINS, Lydia. See "Robert Dwiggins," q.v.
DWIGGINS, Robert. Second Lieutenant, Militia, Wye Company, 4th Battalion, June 17, 1777 [Ref: M-72]. Robert Dwiggins was born circa 1740-1745, married Lydia ----, was a second lieutenant in th revolution, and died before May, 1789 [Ref: Y-907].
DWIGGINS, Robert. Private, Militia, Wye Company, 4th Battalion, 1780-1781 [Ref: N-86/105, M-229].
EARLE, James. See "Peregrine Tilghman," q.v.
EASLEY, Richard. Private, Militia, Oxford Company, 38th Battalion, 1777-1778 [Ref: N-86/105, M-227]. Draughted on May 1, 1781 to serve until December 10, 1781 in the Maryland Continental Troops [Ref: D-371].

EASON, John. Private, Militia, Capt. Thomas Bullen's Company; no date was given; possibly late 1775 or early 1776 [Ref: Z-3]. Took the Oath of Allegiance and Fidelity on or about March 1, 1778 [Ref: J-1814, N-106/114].

EASON, Samuel. Private, Militia, Bullin Brook Company, 4th Battalion, 1777-1778 [Ref: N-86/105, M-224]. Private, Militia, Bullinbrook Company, 4th Battalion, 1780-1781 [Ref: N-86/105, M-231]. Took the Oath of Allegiance and Fidelity on or about March 1, 1778 [Ref: J-1814, N-106/114].

EATON, Edward. Private, Militia, Hearts of Oak Company, 38th Battalion, 1777-1778 [Ref: N-86/105, M-226]. Took the Oath of Allegiance and Fidelity on or about March 1, 1778 [Ref: J-1814, N-106/114]. Private, Militia, Hearts of Oak Company, 38th Battalion, 1780-1781 [Ref: N-86/105, M-235].

EATON, John. Private, Militia, Hearts of Oak Company, 38th Battalion, 1777-1778 [Ref: N-86/105, M-226]. Took the Oath of Allegiance and Fidelity on or about March 1, 1778 [Ref: J-1814, N-106/114]. Private, Militia, Hearts of Oak Company, 38th Battalion, 1780-1781 [Ref: N-86/105, M-235].

EATON, Richard. Private, Militia, Hearts of Oak Company, 38th Battalion, 1777-1778 [Ref: N-86/105, M-226]. Took the Oath of Allegiance and Fidelity on or about March 1, 1778 [Ref: J-1814, N-106/114]. Private, Militia, Hearts of Oak Company, 38th Battalion, 1780-1781 [Ref: N-86/105, M-235]. Gunner on the barge *Intrepid* in 1781 [Ref: D-610]. Private aboard the barge *Fearnought* under Capt. Levin Spedden; enlisted May 29, 1782; 6' tall; dark complexion; born in Talbot County [Ref: D-611]. There was also a Richard Eaton who was a private in the 5th Maryland Line, enlisted December 10, 1776 and discharged on December 10, 1779 (time expired). [Ref: D-203]. Additional research may be necessary before drawing conclusions.

ECCLESTON, Jarvis (Jervis). Took the Oath of Allegiance and Fidelity on or about March 1, 1778 [Ref: J-1814, N-106/114]. Private, 5th Maryland Line, enlisted June 16, 1779 and still in service in October, 1780 [Ref: D-203].

EDGAR, Adam. Private, Militia, Bayside Company, 38th Battalion, 1777-1778 [Ref: N-86/105, M-228]. Took the Oath of Allegiance and Fidelity on or after March 1, 1778 [Ref: J-1814, N-106/114].

EDGAR, Joseph. Private, Militia, Bayside Company, 38th Battalion, 1777-1778 [Ref: N-86/105, M-228]. Took the Oath of Allegiance and Fidelity on or after March 1, 1778 [Ref: J-1814, N-106/114]. Private, Militia, Bayside Company, 38th Battalion, 1780-1781 [Ref: N-86/105, M-233].

EDMONDSON, Ann. See "Christopher Birckhead" and "Pollard Edmondson," q.v.

EDMONDSON, Harriott and Horatio. See "Pollard Edmondson," q.v.

EDMONDSON, James and John. See "Pollard Edmondson," q.v.

EDMONDSON, Lucretia. See "Pollard Edmondson," q.v.

EDMONDSON, Peter. Private, Militia, Union Company, 4th Battalion, 1777-1778 [Ref: N-86/105, M-223]. Private, Militia, Union Company, 4th Battalion, 1780-1781 [Ref: N-86/105, M-230].

EDMONDSON, Pollard (c1718-1794). Son of John Edmondson and Margaret Pollard, he married first to Mary Dickinson in 1738 and second to Rachel Birckhead (widow of Philip McManus and daughter of Christopher Birckhead) in 1765. His children were: James (died circa 1774); Pollard; Horatio (died 1810); John; Lucretia (1766-1826); Ann; Mary; Harriott; and, Sarah. Pollard was a soldier in the colonial troop of horse in 1748. He served in the Maryland Lower House, 1751-1776, 1785, and attended the Maryland Convention in 1776 [Ref: O-28, R-72, R-74, R-302]. Took the Oath of Allegiance and Fidelity on or about March 1, 1778 [Ref: J-1814, N-106/114]. See "Christopher Birckhead" and "Edward Harris," q.v.

EDMONDSON, Pollard (of Pollard). Third Lieutenant, 4th Independent Company of Regulars in January, 1776; resigned in March, 1776 [Ref: R-302].

EDMONDSON, Samuel. Quartermaster, 5th Maryland Line, December 10, 1776; resigned October 14, 1777 [Ref: D-203]. Took the Oath of Allegiance and Fidelity on or about March 1, 1778 [Ref: J-1814, N-106/114].

EDMONDSON, Samuel Jr. Private, Militia, Union Company, 4th Battalion, 1777-1778 [Ref: N-86/105, M-223].

EDMONDSON, Sarah. See "Pollard Edmondson" and "Edward Harris" and "Thomas Ray," q.v.

EDMONDSON, William. Private, Militia, Wye Company, 4th Battalion, 1777-1778 [Ref: N-86/105, M-222]. Private, Militia, Wye Company, 4th Battalion, 1780-1781 [Ref: N-86/105, M-228].

EDMONDSON, William Clayton. Took the Oath of Allegiance and Fidelity on or about March 1, 1778 [Ref: J-1814, N-106/114].

EDWARDS, John. Private, Militia, Third Haven Company, 4th Battalion, 1777-1778 [Ref: N-86/105, M-225]. Took the Oath of Allegiance and Fidelity on or about March 1, 1778; name listed twice [Ref: J-1814, N-106/114]. Private, Militia, Third Haven Company, 4th Battalion, 1780-1781 [Ref: N-86/105, M-232].

ELBERT, Catharine Rebecca. See "John L. Elbert," q.v.

ELBERT, John L. (1760-1835). Apothecary and Surgeon's Mate, General Hospital, Maryland Continental Line. "The name of John L. Elbert, as returned in the Miscellaneous Roll on the Officers' Book as an apothecary in the General Hospital, the Army Books in the 3rd Auditor's Office, show that he received commutation pay as an apothecary of the General Hospital. Bounty Land Warrant No. 2593 for 300 acres issued September 22, 1781 to John L. Elbert as Surgeon's Mate, he being at the time legally entitled to 450 acres as an apothecary, a warrant has therefore been granted for 150 acres to make up the deficiency of the original grant. See No. 2157, new series, Dup. Warrant Book, W. Gordon, Clerk. August 16, 1836. Easton, Talbot County, Maryland, July 8, 1836: Dr. Tristram Thomas and Solomon Bassett [Barrett], a Revolutionary soldier, state they were acquainted with the late Dr. John L. Elbert, who was a surgeon in the Revolutionary Army and that John L. Elbert, now of Talbot

County and William G. Elbert, late of Queen Anne's County, were the sons of the late Dr. John L. Elbert, a surgeon in the Maryland Line, Continental Army. Papers also show the baptism of daughter Catharine Rebecca Elbert. (No other family data)." [Ref: U-30:2 (1942), pp. 55-56]. John also received bounty land warrants #2157-150 and #645-300-22 in September, 1791. His son John L. Elbert made inquiry on July 8, 1834 at which time the surviving children were listed as John L. Elbert, John Nicholson Elbert, William Gibson Elbert, and Rebecca (Catharine Rebecca) Elbert [Ref: W-1095]. John L. Elbert was born in Maryland on April 12, 1760, married Elizabeth Sudler, served as a surgeon's mate in the revolution, and died on July 10, 1835 [Ref: Y-939]. See "John Gibson," q.v.

ELBERT, John Nicholson. See "John L. Elbert," q.v.

ELBERT, Joshua. Took the Oath of Allegiance and Fidelity on or about March 1, 1778 [Ref: J-1814, N-106/114]. Private, Militia, Wye Company, 4th Battalion, 1780-1781 [Ref: N-86/105, M-229].

ELBERT, Rebecca. See "John L. Elbert," q.v.

ELBERT, William Gibson. See "John L. Elbert," q.v.

ELDRAKE, James. Private, Militia, Capt. Thomas Bullen's Company; no date was given; possibly late 1775 or early 1776 [Ref: Z-3].

ELDRAKE, James Jr. Private, Militia, Capt. Thomas Bullen's Company; no date was given; possibly late 1775 or early 1776 [Ref: Z-3].

ELDRICK, John. Private, Militia, Volunteer Company, 4th Battalion, 1777-1778 [Ref: N-86/105, M-223]. Took the Oath of Allegiance and Fidelity on or after March 1, 1778 [Ref: J-1814, N-106/114]. Private, Militia, Volunteer Company, 4th Battalion, 1780-1781 [Ref: N-86/105, M-230].

ELLIOTT, Edward. Took the Oath of Allegiance and Fidelity on or about March 1, 1778 [Ref: J-1814, N-106/114].

ELLIOTT, Henry. Private, Militia, Bayside Company, 38th Battalion, 1780-1781 [Ref: N-86/105, M-233].

ELLIS, Robert. Private, 4th Independent Company of Maryland Regular Troops, Capt. James Hindman's Company, September, 1776 muster roll; enlisted January 23, 1776 [Ref: D-24].

ELSBY, Thomas. Private, Militia, Bullin Brook Company, 4th Battalion, 1777-1778 [Ref: N-86/105, M-224].

EMERSON, Mary. See "Robert Goldsborough IV," q.v.

EMIHALL, John. Private, Militia, Oxford Company, 38th Battalion, 1777-1778 [Ref: N-86/105, M-227].

EMORY, John. Private, 4th Independent Company of Maryland Regular Troops, Capt. James Hindman's Company, September, 1776 muster roll; enlisted January 26, 1776 [Ref: D-23].

EMPSON, John. Private, Militia, 4th Battalion, Capt. Greenbury Goldsborough's Company, reviewed and passed July 27, 1776 [Ref: D-68].

ESGATE, Thomas. Took the Oath of Allegiance and Fidelity on or about March 1, 1778 [Ref: J-1814, N-106/114].
EUBANK (EUBANKS), Adam. Private, Militia, 2nd Volunteer Company, 4th Battalion, 1777-1778 [Ref: N-86/105, M-225].
EUBANK (EUBANKS), Edward. Private, Militia, Volunteer Company, 4th Battalion, 1780-1781 [Ref: N-86/105, M-229].
EUBANK, James. Took the Oath of Allegiance and Fidelity on or about March 1, 1778 [Ref: J-1814, N-106/114]. Private, Militia, Hearts of Oak Company, 38th Battalion, 1780-1781 [Ref: N-86/105, M-235].
EUBANK, John. Took the Oath of Allegiance and Fidelity on or about March 1, 1778 [Ref: J-1814, N-106/114].
EUBANK (EWBANKS), Jonathan. See "Richard Eubank," q.v.
EUBANK (EWBANKS), Richard. Took the Oath of Allegiance and Fidelity on or about March 1, 1778 [Ref: J-1814, N-106/114]. Private aboard the barge *Fearnought* under Capt. Levin Spedden; enlisted June 11, 1782; 5'10" tall; fair complexion; born in Talbot County [Ref: D-612]. "Richd. Ewbanks" and "Jona. Ewbanks" were privates in the 5th Maryland Line; Richard enlisted May 9, 1778 and Jonathan enlisted May 13, 1778; both reportedly "deserted" on July 2, 1778 [Ref: D-203]. Additional research may be necessary before drawing conclusions.
EUBANK (EUBANKS, EWBANKS), Thomas. Took the Oath of Allegiance and Fidelity on or about March 1, 1778 [Ref: J-1814, N-106/114]. Private, Militia, Volunteer Company, 4th Battalion, 1780-1781 [Ref: N-86/105, M-229]. Private aboard the barge *Fearnought* under Capt. Levin Spedden; enlisted May 28, 1782; 6' tall; fair complexion; born in Talbot County [Ref: D-611].
EVANS, Elizabeth. See "Turbutt Wright," q.v.
EVANS, Peregrine. Private, 4th Independent Company of Maryland Regular Troops, Capt. James Hindman's Company, September, 1776 muster roll; enlisted February 19, 1776 [Ref: D-24].
EXLEY (COXLEY, COSLEY?), John. Sergeant, Militia, Capt. Thomas Bullen's Company; no date was given; possibly late 1775 or early 1776 [Ref: Z-3; name difficult to read; looks like Exley or Coxley; could be Cosley].
FAIRBANKS (FAIRBANK), Daniel. Private, Militia, Broad Creek Company, 38th Battalion, 1777-1778 [Ref: N-86/105, M-227]. Took the Oath of Allegiance and Fidelity on or after March 1, 1778 [Ref: J-1814, N-106/114]. Private, Militia, Broad Creek Company, 38th Battalion, 1780-1781 [Ref: N-86/105, M-234].
FAIRBANKS (FAIRBANK), David. Took the Oath of Allegiance and Fidelity on or about March 1, 1778 [Ref: J-1814, N-106/114]. Sergeant, Militia, Broad Creek Company, 38th Battalion, 1780-1781 [Ref: N-103, M-234].
FAIRBANKS (FAIRBANK), James. Private, Militia, 4th Battalion, Capt. Greenbury Goldsborough's Company, reviewed and passed July 27, 1776 [Ref: D-68]. Private, Militia, Broad Creek Company, 38th Battalion, 1777-1778 [Ref:

N-86/105, M-226]. Private, Militia, Broad Creek Company, 38th Battalion, 1780-1781 [Ref: N-86/105, M-234]. See "John Bartlett," q.v.

FAIRBANKS, James. Private, Militia, Hand & Hand Company, 4th Battalion, 1777-1778 [Ref: N-86/105, M-225]. One James Fairbanks married Elizabeth Troth, served as a private in the revolution, and died after March 18, 1813 [Ref: Y-981].

FAIRBANKS, Peter. Private, Militia, Broad Creek Company, 38th Battalion, 1780-1781; name listed twice [Ref: N-86/105, M-234].

FAIRBANKS, Sarah. See "John Bartlett," q.v.

FAIRBANKS, Thomas. Private, Militia, Broad Creek Company, 38th Battalion, 1780-1781 [Ref: N-86/105, M-234].

FAIRBROTHERS, James. Private, Militia, Bullinbrook Company, 4th Battalion, 1780-1781 [Ref: N-86/105, M-231].

FAIRFIELD, John. Private, Militia, Hand & Hand Company, 4th Battalion, 1777-1778 [Ref: N-86/105, M-225].

FALLEN (FALLING, FOLLIN), Acquilla (Aquilla). Private, Militia, Wye Company, 4th Battalion, 1777-1778 [Ref: N-86/105, M-223, which listed the name as "Aquilla Follin"]. Took the Oath of Allegiance and Fidelity on or about March 1, 1778 [Ref: J-1814, N-106/114]. Private, Militia, Wye Company, 4th Battalion, 1780-1781 [Ref: N-86/105, M-229].

FANTHAM, John. Took the Oath of Allegiance and Fidelity on or about March 1, 1778 [Ref: J-1814, N-106/114].

FAREWELL, Nicholas. Private, 4th Independent Company of Maryland Regular Troops, Capt. James Hindman's Company, September, 1776 muster roll; enlisted January 26(?), 1776 [Ref: D-24].

FARGUSON, James. Private, Militia, 4th Battalion, Capt. Greenbury Goldsborough's Company, reviewed and passed July 27, 1776 [Ref: D-68].

FARIS, John. Private aboard the barge *Fearnought* under Capt. Levin Spedden; enlisted June 29, 1782 [Ref: D-612, which listed the name as "John Faris (Fanis?)"].

FARIS, Thomas. See "Thomas Pharis," q.v.

FARQUSON, James. Private, Militia, Miles River Company, 38th Battalion, 1780-1781 [Ref: N-86/105, M-235].

FARQUSON, William. Private, Militia, Miles River Company, 38th Battalion, 1780-1781 [Ref: N-86/105, M-235]. Private, Militia, Miles River Company, 38th Battalion, 1780-1781 [Ref: N-86/105, M-235, which listed the name as "William Ferguson(?)].

FARQUSTON, Robert. Ensign, Militia, Miles River Company, 38th Battalion, 1780-1781 [Ref: M-235].

FARRINGTON, Abraham. Private, Militia, Third Haven Company, 4th Battalion, 1780-1781 [Ref: N-86/105, M-232].

FARROW, Samuel. Private, Militia, Bullinbrook Company, 4th Battalion, 1780-1781 [Ref: N-86/105, M-231].

FARROWFIELD, John. Took the Oath of Allegiance and Fidelity on or about March 1, 1778 [Ref: J-1814, N-106/114].

FAULKNER, Dorias. See "Isaac Faulkner, Jr.," q.v.

FAULKNER, Greenbury. Private, Militia, Volunteer Company, 4th Battalion, 1780-1781 [Ref: N-86/105, M-229].

FAULKNER (FALKNER), Hinson (Hynson). Private, Militia, 2nd Volunteer Company, 4th Battalion, 1777-1778 [Ref: N-86/105, M-225]. Took the Oath of Allegiance and Fidelity on or about March 1, 1778 [Ref: J-1814, N-106/114]. Private (substitute), Militia, Volunteer Company, 4th Battalion, 1780-1781 [Ref: N-86/105, M-229]. Private in the militia who was draughted on August 30, 1781 to reinforce the American Army and to serve in the Maryland Continental Troops until December 10, 1781 [Ref: D-387].

FAULKNER (FALKNER), Isaac. Private, Militia, 2nd Volunteer Company, 4th Battalion, 1777-1778 [Ref: N-86/105, M-225]. Took the Oath of Allegiance and Fidelity on or about March 1, 1778 [Ref: J-1814, N-106/114]. Private, Militia, Volunteer Company, 4th Battalion, 1780-1781 [Ref: N-86/105, M-229]. Private (draught), Maryland Line; honorably discharged on February 4, 1782 [Ref: I-67].

FAULKNER, Isaac Jr. Private, Militia, Volunteer Company, 4th Battalion, 1780-1781 [Ref: N-86/105, M-229]. Private in the militia who was draughted on August 30, 1781 to reinforce the American Army and to serve in the Maryland Continental Troops until December 10, 1781 [Ref: D-387]. "Isaac Falkner, son of Isaac and Dorias" was born in St. Peter's Parish, Talbot County, on July 16, 1734 [Ref: V-71].

FAULKNER (FALKNER), Jacob. Private, Militia, Hand & Hand Company, 4th Battalion, 1777-1778 [Ref: N-86/105, M-225].

FAULKNER, Jacob Jr. Private, Militia, Hand & Hand Company, 4th Battalion, 1777-1778 [Ref: N-86/105, M-225].

FAULKNER, James. Private, Militia, Volunteer Company, 4th Battalion, 1780-1781 [Ref: N-86/105, M-229].

FAULKNER, Joshua. Took the Oath of Allegiance and Fidelity on or about March 1, 1778 [Ref: J-1814, N-106/114]. Private, Militia, Volunteer Company, 4th Battalion, 1780-1781 [Ref: N-86/105, M-229].

FAULKNER, Levi (Levy). Private, Militia, 2nd Volunteer Company, 4th Battalion, 1777-1778 [Ref: N-86/105, M-225]. Took the Oath of Allegiance and Fidelity on or about March 1, 1778 [Ref: J-1814, N-106/114]. Private, Militia, Volunteer Company, 4th Battalion, 1780-1781 [Ref: N-86/105, M-229]. Private in the militia who was draughted on August 30, 1781 to reinforce the American Army and to serve in the Maryland Continental Troops until December 10, 1781 [Ref: D-387].

FAULKNER, Thomas. Took the Oath of Allegiance and Fidelity on or about March 1, 1778 [Ref: J-1814, N-106/114].

FAUNTLEROY (FOUNTLEROY, FONTLERAY), John. First Lieutenant, Militia, 4th Battalion, 1778 [Ref: N-88, M-76, E-24]. Appointed a Justice of the Peace on November 20, 1779 [Ref: F-22].
FAUNTLEROY, John. Private, Militia, Wye Company, 4th Battalion, 1780-1781 [Ref: M-228].
FEARN (FEARNS), John. Private, Militia, Sword in Hand Company, 4th Battalion, 1777-1778 [Ref: N-86/105, M-224]. Private, Militia, Sword in Hand Company, 4th Battalion, 1780-1781 [Ref: N-86/105, M-231].
FERGUSON, Mary. See "Joseph Leonard," q.v.
FERGUSON, Robert. Private, 4th Independent Company of Maryland Regular Troops, Capt. James Hindman's Company, September, 1776 muster roll; enlisted February 19, 1776 [Ref: D-24].
FERRIL, Phil. Private, Militia, Union Company, 4th Battalion, 1777-1778 [Ref: N-86/105, M-223].
FERRY, John. Private, Militia, Wye Company, 4th Battalion, 1777-1778 [Ref: N-86/105, M-222].
FITZGERALD (FITZGERRALD), Thomas. Private, Militia, 2nd Volunteer Company, 4th Battalion, 1777-1778 [Ref: N-86/105, M-225]. Took the Oath of Allegiance and Fidelity on or about March 1, 1778 [Ref: J-1814, N-106/114].
FITZHUGH, Daniel Dulany. See "William Maynadier," q.v.
FITZJIFFERAS, Aaron. Private, Militia, Sword in Hand Company, 4th Battalion, 1780-1781 [Ref: M-231].
FITZPATRICK, David. Private, Militia, 4th Battalion, Capt. Greenbury Goldsborough's Company, reviewed and passed July 27, 1776 [Ref: D-68].
FITZPATRICK, William. Private, Militia, 4th Battalion, Capt. Greenbury Goldsborough's Company, reviewed and passed July 27, 1776 [Ref: D-68].
FLEMING (FLEMMING), David. Private, Militia, Union Company, 4th Battalion, 1777-1778 [Ref: N-86/105, M-223]. Took the Oath of Allegiance and Fidelity on or about March 1, 1778 [Ref: J-1814, N-106/114].
FLEMING (FLEMMING), James. Private, Militia, Union Company, 4th Battalion, 1780-1781 [Ref: N-86/105, M-230]. Private aboard the barge *Fearnought* under Capt. Levin Spedden; enlisted May 28, 1782; 5'11" tall; fair complexion; born in Talbot County [Ref: D-611].
FLEMING, John. Private, 4th Independent Company of Maryland Regular Troops, Capt. James Hindman's Company, September, 1776 muster roll; enlisted January 25(?), 1776 [Ref: D-24]. Private, Militia, Bullin Brook Company, 4th Battalion, 1777-1778 [Ref: N-86/105, M-224]. Private, Militia, Bullinbrook Company, 4th Battalion, 1780-1781 [Ref: N-86/105, M-231].
FLEMING, John. Private, Militia, Volunteer Company, 4th Battalion, 1780-1781 [Ref: N-86/105, M-229].

FLEMING, John. Private, Militia, Union Company, 4th Battalion, 1777-1778 [Ref: N-86/105, M-223]. Sergeant, Militia, Union Company, 4th Battalion, 1780-1781 [Ref: N-97, M-229].

FLEMING, Thomas. Private, Militia, Bullin Brook Company, 4th Battalion, 1777-1778 [Ref: N-86/105, M-224]. Private, Militia, Bullinbrook Company, 4th Battalion, 1780-1781 [Ref: N-86/105, M-231].

FLEMMING, John. Took the Oath of Allegiance and Fidelity on or about March 1, 1778; name listed twice [Ref: J-1814, N-106/114].

FLEMMING, Rachel. See "Thomas Buckley," q.v.

FLOYD, Jonathan (1744-   ). Born in St. Peter's Parish, Talbot County, on November 19, 1744, a son of Joseph and Mary Floyd [Ref: V-81]. Private, Militia, 4th Battalion, Capt. Greenbury Goldsborough's Company, reviewed and passed July 27, 1776 [Ref: D-67]. Private, Militia, Sword in Hand Company, 4th Battalion, 1777-1778 [Ref: N-86/105, M-224]. Took the Oath of Allegiance and Fidelity on or about March 1, 1778 [Ref: J-1814, N-106/114]. Private, Militia, Sword in Hand Company, 4th Battalion, 1780-1781 [Ref: N-86/105, M-231].

FLOYD, Joseph. Private, Militia, Capt. Thomas Bullen's Company; no date was given; possibly late 1775 or early 1776 [Ref: Z-3]. See "Jonathan Floyd," q.v.

FLOYD, Mary. See "Jonathan Floyd," q.v.

FLOYD, Robert. Private, Militia, Volunteer Company, 4th Battalion, 1780-1781 [Ref: N-86/105, M-229].

FLYNN, James. Private, Militia, Capt. Thomas Bullen's Company; no date was given; possibly late 1775 or early 1776 [Ref: Z-3].

FOCUM, Charles. Took the Oath of Allegiance and Fidelity on or about March 1, 1778 [Ref: J-1814, N-106/114].

FOLLIN, Aquilla. See "Acquilla Fallin," q.v.

FOREMAN, Henrietta Maria. See "Peregrine Tilghman," q.v.

FOREMAN, Perry. Private, 5th Maryland Line, enlisted February 3, 1777 and "left out" in April, 1778 [Ref: D-205].

FOREMAN, Samuel. Private, Militia, Wye Company, 4th Battalion, 1780-1781 [Ref: N-86/105, M-228].

FORESAIN, George. Private, Militia, 2nd Volunteer Company, 4th Battalion, 1777-1778 [Ref: N-86/105, M-224]. Private, Militia, Volunteer Company, 4th Battalion, 1780-1781 [Ref: N-86/105, M-229].

FORESAIN (FORESON), James. Private, Militia, 2nd Volunteer Company, 4th Battalion, 1777-1778 [Ref: N-86/105, M-224]. Took the Oath of Allegiance and Fidelity on or about March 1, 1778; name listed twice - once as "James Foreson" and once as "James Forson" [Ref: J-1814, N-106/114].

FOSTER, Elizabeth. See "Rigby Foster" and "William Foster," q.v.

FOSTER, James. Private, Militia, Volunteer Company, 4th Battalion, 1780-1781 [Ref: N-86/105, M-229].

FOSTER, Joseph. Private, Militia, Bullin Brook Company, 4th Battalion, 1777-1778 [Ref: N-86/105, M-224].
FOSTER, Joseph. Private, Militia, Volunteer Company, 4th Battalion, 1777-1778 [Ref: N-86/105, M-223].
FOSTER, Mark. Private, Militia, 2nd Volunteer Company, 4th Battalion, 1777-1778 [Ref: N-86/105, M-225]. Private, 5th Maryland Line, enlisted May 15, 1778 and still in service in November, 1780 [Ref: D-205].
FOSTER, Nathan. Private, Militia, 2nd Volunteer Company, 4th Battalion, 1777-1778 [Ref: N-86/105, M-225]. Took the Oath of Allegiance and Fidelity on or about March 1, 1778 [Ref: J-1814, N-106/114]. Private, Militia, Volunteer Company, 4th Battalion, 1780-1781 [Ref: N-86/105, M-229]. Draughted on May 1, 1781 to serve until December 10, 1781 in the Maryland Continental Troops; honorably discharged on December 3, 1781 [Ref: D-371, I-10]. One Nathaniel Foster ws a private in the 5th Maryland Line who enlisted on May 30, 1778 and was still in service in January, 1780 [Ref: D-205]. Additional research may be necessary before drawing conclusions.
FOSTER, Peter. Private, Militia, Volunteer Company, 4th Battalion, 1777-1778 [Ref: N-86/105, M-224].
FOSTER, Rigby (1744-   ). Born in St. Peter's Parish, Talbot County, on September 22, 1744, a son of Rigby and Elizabeth Foster [Ref: V-88]. Private, 5th Maryland Line, enlisted May 30, 1777 and still in service in November, 1780 [Ref: D-204]. Private, Militia, Hand in Hand Company, 4th Battalion, 1781 [Ref: M-232, N-86/105]. Took the Oath of Allegiance and Fidelity on or about March 1, 1778 [Ref: J-1814, N-106/114]. See "William Foster," q.v.
FOSTER, Stephen. Private, 5th Maryland Line, enlisted June 2, 1778 and served with Gen. Pulaski [Ref: D-205].
FOSTER, William (1737-   ). Born in St. Peter's Parish, Talbot County, on May 12, 1737, a son of Rigby and Elizabeth Foster [Ref: V-88]. Private, Militia, Bullin Brook Company, 4th Battalion, 1777-1778 [Ref: N-86/105, M-224]. Took the Oath of Allegiance and Fidelity on or after March 1, 1778 [Ref: J-1814, N-106/114]. Private, Militia, Bullinbrook Company, 4th Battalion, 1780-1781 [Ref: N-86/105, M-231].
FOUNTAIN, Massey. Took the Oath of Allegiance and Fidelity on or about March 1, 1778 [Ref: J-1814, N-106/114].
FOUNTAIN, Samuel. Private, Militia, Wye Company, 4th Battalion, 1780-1781 [Ref: N-86/105, M-228].
FOUNTAIN, Samuel Jr. Recommended to be commissioned an ensign on June 12, 1777 [Ref: P-110].
FOWLER, Robert. Private, Militia, 2nd Volunteer Company, 4th Battalion, 1777-1778 [Ref: N-86/105, M-224].
FRAMPTON, Elizabeth. See "Richard Frampton," q.v.

FRAMPTON, John. Private, Militia, Hand & Hand Company, 4th Battalion, 1777-1778; name listed twice [Ref: N-86/105, M-225, M-226]. Private, Militia, Hand in Hand Company, 4th Battalion, 1780-1781 [Ref: N-86/105, M-232].

FRAMPTON, Joseph. Private, Militia, Hand & Hand Company, 4th Battalion, 1777-1778 [Ref: N-86/105, M-226]. Took the Oath of Allegiance and Fidelity on or about March 1, 1778; name listed twice [Ref: J-1814, N-106/114]. Private, Militia, Hand in Hand Company, 4th Battalion, 1780-1781 [Ref: N-86/105, M-232].

FRAMPTON, Richard. Private, Militia, Hand & Hand Company, 4th Battalion, 1777-1778 [Ref: N-86/105, M-226]. Took the Oath of Allegiance and Fidelity on or about March 1, 1778 [Ref: J-1814, N-106/114]. Private, Militia, Hand in Hand Company, 4th Battalion, 1780-1781 [Ref: N-86/105, M-232]. One Richard Frampton, son of Elizabeth Frampton, was born in St. Peter's Parish, Talbot County, on June 3, 1727 [Ref: V-67].

FRAMPTON, Robert. Private, Militia, Hand & Hand Company, 4th Battalion, 1777-1778 [Ref: N-86/105, M-226]. Took the Oath of Allegiance and Fidelity on or about March 1, 1778 [Ref: J-1814, N-106/114]. Private, Militia, Hand in Hand Company, 4th Battalion, 1780-1781 [Ref: N-86/105, M-232]. Draughted on May 1, 1781 to serve until December 10, 1781 in the Maryland Continental Troops [Ref: D-371].

FRAMPTON, Thomas. Private, Militia, Hand & Hand Company, 4th Battalion, 1777-1778 [Ref: N-86/105, M-226]. Took the Oath of Allegiance and Fidelity on or about March 1, 1778 [Ref: J-1814, N-106/114]. Private, Militia, Hand in Hand Company, 4th Battalion, 1780-1781 [Ref: N-86/105, M-232].

FRAMPTON, William. Private, Militia, Hand & Hand Company, 4th Battalion, 1777-1778 [Ref: N-86/105, M-225]. Private, Militia, Hand in Hand Company, 4th Battalion, 1780-1781 [Ref: N-86/105, M-232].

FRANCIS, Ann. See "James Tilghman" and "Tench Tilghman" and "Lloyd Tilghman," q.v.

FRANCIS, Tench. See "Tench Tilghman," q.v.

FRANTIM, John. Private, Militia, Bullin Brook Company, 4th Battalion, 1777-1778 [Ref: N-86/105, M-224].

FRANTOM, Joseph. Private, Militia, Bullin Brook Company, 4th Battalion, 1777-1778 [Ref: N-86/105, M-224]. Rendered patriotic service by supplying bacon for the use of the Army in April, 1778 and also by hauling provisions [Ref: P-163].

FRAY, Phil. Private, Militia, Capt. Thomas Bullen's Company; no date was given; possibly late 1775 or early 1776 [Ref: Z-3].

FRAY, William. Private, Militia, Capt. Thomas Bullen's Company; no date was given; possibly late 1775 or early 1776 [Ref: Z-3].

FRAZIER, Levin. Corporal, 4th Independent Company of Maryland Regular Troops, September, 1776 muster roll; enlisted as a private on February 11, 1776 [Ref: D-23].

FRAZIER, William. Third Lieutenant, 4th Independent Company of Maryland Regular Troops, September, 1776 muster roll; commissioned March 7, 1776 [Ref: D-23]. First Lieutenant, 5th Maryland Line, December 10, 1776 [Ref: D-204].

FRISBY, Elizabeth. See "James Lloyd," q.v.

FRISBY, Peregrine. See "James Lloyd," q.v.

FRISBY, Susanna. See "Peregrine Tilghman," q.v.

FROTH, George. Took the Oath of Allegiance and Fidelity sometime between May and September, 1780 [Ref: L-111].

GALLAHAN (GALLAGHANE), James. Private, Militia, Wye Company, 4th Battalion, 1777-1778 [Ref: N-86/105, M-223]. Private, Militia, Wye Company, 4th Battalion, 1780-1781 [Ref: N-86/105, M-229].

GANNON, Thomas. Private, Militia, Wye Company, 4th Battalion, 1777-1778 [Ref: N-86/105, M-222].

GARDIN, Robert. Private, Militia, Hand & Hand Company, 4th Battalion, 1777-1778 [Ref: N-86/105, M-225].

GARDINER (GARDNER), Charles. Captain, Militia, Miles River Company, 38th Battalion, April 12, 1780 through 1781 [Ref: N-105, M-235, M-77, F-139]. Took the Oath of Allegiance and Fidelity on or about March 1, 1778 [Ref: J-1814, N-106/114]. Appointed a Justice of the Peace and a Judge of the Orphans Court on January 17, 1782 [Ref: I-46, which listed the name as "Charles Gardner"].

GARDINER (GARDENER), Charles. Private, Militia, Miles River Company, 38th Battalion, 1777-1778 [Ref: N-86/105, M-227].

GARDNER, John. Private, Militia, Wye Company, 4th Battalion, 1780-1781 [Ref: N-86/105, M-229].

GAREY, George. Private, Militia, 4th Battalion, Capt. Greenbury Goldsborough's Company, reviewed and passed July 27, 1776 [Ref: D-68]. Corporal, 5th Maryland Line, enlisted February 4, 1777; sergeant, July 1, 1779; discharged February 4, 1780 [Ref: D-208].

GAREY, Henry. Took the Oath of Allegiance and Fidelity on or about March 1, 1778 [Ref: J-1814, N-106/114].

GAREY (GARY), Jonathan. Private, Militia, Wye Company, 4th Battalion, 1777-1778 [Ref: N-86/105, M-222].

GAREY (GARY), William. Private, Militia, Hand & Hand Company, 4th Battalion, 1777-1778 [Ref: N-86/105, M-226]. Took the Oath of Allegiance and Fidelity on or about March 1, 1778 [Ref: J-1814, N-106/114]. Private, Militia, Hand in Hand Company, 4th Battalion, 1780-1781 [Ref: N-86/105, M-233].

GARKEE, William. Private, Militia, Capt. Thomas Bullen's Company; no date was given; possibly late 1775 or early 1776 [Ref: Z-3].

GARLAND, Jeremiah. Ensign, Militia, 4th Battalion, April 9, 1778. Second Lieutenant, Militia, Wye Company, 4th Battalion, 1780-1781 [Ref: N-88, N-96,

M-228, M-77, E-24, P-175]. Took the Oath of Allegiance and Fidelity on or about March 1, 1778 [Ref: J-1814, N-106/114].

GARLAND, Traverse (Travis). Private, Militia, Hand & Hand Company, 4th Battalion, 1777-1778 [Ref: N-86/105, M-225]. Sergeant, Militia, Volunteer Company, 4th Battalion, 1780-1781 [Ref: N-86/105, M-229]. Took the Oath of Allegiance and Fidelity on or about March 1, 1778 [Ref: J-1814, N-106/114].

GARLAND, William. Ensign, Militia, commissioned and drafted on July 31, 1778 [Ref: M-77, E-172].

GARRON (GARREN), Jacob. Private, Militia, Wye Company, 4th Battalion, 1777-1778 [Ref: N-86/105, M-222]. Private, Militia, Wye Company, 4th Battalion, 1780-1781 [Ref: N-86/105, M-229].

GARROTT, John. Private, 4th Independent Company of Maryland Regular Troops, Capt. James Hindman's Company, September, 1776 muster roll; enlisted February 10, 1776 [Ref: D-25].

GASKEN (GASHEN?), Greenwood. Private, Militia, Capt. Thomas Bullen's Company; no date was given; possibly late 1775 or early 1776 [Ref: Z-3].

GATES, General. See "Joseph Dawson," q.v.

GATES, Henry. Private, 4th Independent Company of Maryland Regular Troops, Capt. James Hindman's Company, September, 1776 muster roll; enlisted January 25(?), 1776 [Ref: D-24].

GAUSE, James. Private, Militia, Union Company, 4th Battalion, 1777-1778 [Ref: N-86/105, M-223]. Took the Oath of Allegiance and Fidelity on or about March 1, 1778 [Ref: J-1814, N-106/114].

GELON, James. See "James Gilon," q.v.

GEORGE, Richard. Private, Militia, Wye Company, 4th Battalion, 1777-1778 [Ref: N-86/105, M-222]. Took the Oath of Allegiance and Fidelity on or about March 1, 1778 [Ref: J-1814, N-106/114]. Private, Militia, Wye Company, 4th Battalion, 1780-1781 [Ref: N-86/105, M-228].

GERMAN, William. Private, Militia, Wye Company, 4th Battalion, 1777-1778 [Ref: N-86/105, M-223]. Private, Militia, Wye Company, 4th Battalion, 1780-1781 [Ref: N-86/105, M-229].

GIBSON, Anna. See "John Gibson," q.v.

GIBSON, Elizabeth. See "John Gibson" and "Woolman Gibson, of John," q.v.

GIBSON, Jacob. Captain, Militia, Wye Company, 4th Battalion, May 13, 1776 [Ref: M-78].

GIBSON, Jacob. Private, Militia, Union Company, 4th Battalion, 1777-1778 [Ref: N-86/105, M-223]. Private, Militia, Wye Company, 4th Battalion, 1780-1781 [Ref: N-86/105, M-228].

GIBSON, Jacob Jr. Took the Oath of Allegiance and Fidelity on or about March 1, 1778 [Ref: J-1814, N-106/114]. Private, Militia, Union Company, 4th Battalion, 1780-1781 [Ref: N-86/105, M-230].

GIBSON, James. Ensign, Militia, 4th Battalion, May 16, 1776 [Ref: M-78, A-429].

GIBSON, John (c1730-1790). Son of Woolman Gibson and Elizabeth Dawson, he married Elizabeth ---- by 1766 and their children were: Woolman Jr.; John III (died in 1819); Elizabeth (married first to John Thomas and second to ---- Stewart); Mary (married Richard Tilghman); and, Anna (married first to Dr. John Elbert and second to Dr. William E. Seth). John Gibson was appointed Court Justice in 1774 and 1778, Committee of Observation in 1775, Justice of the Orphans Court in 1777, Justice of the Peace in 1778, Commissary for Horses in 1778, and Judge of the Court of Appeals for Tax Assessment in 1786 [Ref: R-74, R-76, R-78, R-80, R-82, R-86, R-349, R-350, C-274, E-163]. Since his son was John Gibson 3rd, John was probably the "John Gibson, Jr." who took the Oath of Allegiance and Fidelity on or about March 1, 1778 [Ref: J-1814, N-106/114]. See "Woolman Gibson (of John)," q.v.

GIBSON, John Jr. Private, Militia, Miles River Company, 38th Battalion, 1777-1778 [Ref: N-86/105, M-227].

GIBSON, John 3rd. Private, Militia, Wye Company, 4th Battalion, 1777-1778 [Ref: N-86/105, M-222, which listed the name without the "3rd"]. Private, Militia, Wye Company, 4th Battalion, 1780-1781 [Ref: N-86/105, M-228]. See "John Gibson," q.v.

GIBSON, Jonathan. Private, Militia, 4th Battalion, Capt. Greenbury Goldsborough's Company, reviewed and passed July 27, 1776 [Ref: D-67]. Ensign, Militia, May 23, 1776 [Ref: A-438]. Took the Oath of Allegiance and Fidelity on or about March 1, 1778 [Ref: J-1814, N-106/114]. Paid £9 for services rendered on March 11, 1779, by Col. Christopher Birkhead [Ref: E-319]. See "Woolman Gibson" and "Jonathan Hopkins," q.v.

GIBSON, Maria. See "Richard Tilghman, Jr.," q.v.

GIBSON, Mary. See "Woolman Gibson" and "Richard Tilghman, Jr.," q.v.

GIBSON, Rachel. See "Jonathan Hopkins," q.v.

GIBSON, William. See "Jonathan Hopkins," q.v.

GIBSON, Woolman. Son of Woolman Gibson and Elizabeth Dawson, he married Rachel Hopkins (widow) and they had these children: John, Jonathan (died in 1783); Woolman (captain, 1776; died in 1781); Jacob; and, Mary (married Samuel Seney). Woolman served in the Maryland Lower House, 1758-1766, was a lieutenant in the colonial militia in 1748, and a captain by 1759. Took the Oath of Allegiance and Fidelity on or about March 1, 1778 [Ref: J-1814, N-106/114]. Appointed a Justice of the Peace on January 17, 1782 [Ref: I-46]. He died in 1786 [Ref: R-351]. See "John Gibson" and "Jonathan Hopkins," q.v.

GIBSON, Woolman. Private, Militia, Hand & Hand Company, 4th Battalion, 1777-1778 [Ref: N-86/105, M-225]. Second Lieutenant, Militia, Miles River Company, 38th Battalion, April 9, 1778 [Ref: N-92, M-78, E-25]. One Woolman Gibson was appointed "Auctioner" for Talbot County by the Maryland Council on March 2, 1781 [Ref: G-334].

GIBSON, Woolman Jr. Took the Oath of Allegiance and Fidelity on or about March 1, 1778 [Ref: J-1814, N-106/114]. Private, Militia, Miles River

Company, 38th Battalion, 1777-1778 [Ref: N-86/105, M-227, which listed the name without the "Jr."]. Corporal, Militia, Miles River Company, 38th Battalion, 1780-1781 [Ref: N-105, M-235]. See "John Gibson," q.v.

GIBSON, Woolman 3rd. Private, Militia, Wye Company, 4th Battalion, 1777-1778 [Ref: N-86/105, M-222, which listed the name as "Woolman Gibson 3rd"]. First Lieutenant, Militia, Wye Company, 4th Battalion, June 17, 1777 [Ref: M-78, which listed the name as "Woolman Gibson IV"]. Captain, Militia, Wye Company, 4th Battalion, April 9, 1778 to 1781 [Ref: N-88, N-96, M-228, M-78, E-24]. Took the Oath of Allegiance and Fidelity on or about March 1, 1778 [Ref: J-1814, N-106/114]. Appointed a Justice of the Peace on December 4, 1779 [Ref: F-31, which listed the name as "Woolman Gibson 3d"]. A son of Woolman and Rachel Gibson, Capt. Woolman Gibson died in 1781 [Ref: R-351].

GIBSON, Woolman (of John). First Lieutenant, Militia, 4th Battalion, Capt. Greenbury Goldsborough's Company, July 1, 1776 [Ref: D-67, M-78, A-539]. A son of John and Elizabeth Gibson, Woolman married Frances Reynolds by 1778 and apparently died without issue. He served in the Maryland Lower House between 1782 and 1792, was a Court Justice from 1779 to at least 1794, and died circa 1798 [Ref: R-352, R-87, R-88].

GIDDIS, William. Private, Militia, Volunteer Company, 4th Battalion, 1777-1778 [Ref: N-86/105, M-223]. Took the Oath of Allegiance and Fidelity on or about March 1, 1778 [Ref: J-1814, N-106/114].

GILES, John. Private, Militia, Capt. Thomas Bullen's Company; no date was given; possibly late 1775 or early 1776 [Ref: Z-3].

GILES, Samuel. Private, 4th Independent Company of Maryland Regular Troops, Capt. James Hindman's Company, September, 1776 muster roll; enlisted January 28, 1776 [Ref: D-24].

GILHUST, Robert. Private, Militia, Wye Company, 4th Battalion, 1777-1778 [Ref: N-86/105, M-222].

GILL, Ase. Private, Militia, Hand in Hand Company, 4th Battalion, 1780-1781 [Ref: N-86/105, M-232].

GILL, Moses. Private, Militia, Hand in Hand Company, 4th Battalion, 1780-1781 [Ref: N-86/105, M-232].

GILON (GELON), James. Private, Militia, 2nd Volunteer Company, 4th Battalion, 1777-1778 [Ref: N-86/105, M-225]. Sergeant, Militia, Volunteer Company, 4th Battalion, 1780-1781 [Ref: N-86/105, M-229, which listed the name as "James Gilon (Gelson)"]. Took the Oath of Allegiance and Fidelity on or about March 1, 1778 [Ref: J-1814, N-106/114, which listed the name as "James Gelon"].

GILON (GELON, GELAND), John. Private, Militia, 2nd Volunteer Company, 4th Battalion, 1777-1778 [Ref: N-86/105, M-224]. Took the Oath of Allegiance and Fidelity on or about March 1, 1778 [Ref: J-1814, N-106/114, which listed the name as "John Geland"]. Private, 5th Maryland Line, enlissted June 6, 1778 [Ref: D-209, which listed the name as "John Gelon"].

GILON (GELON), John Jr. Private, Militia, 2nd Volunteer Company, 4th Battalion, 1777-1778 [Ref: N-86/105, M-225].
GILPIN, Isaac. Private, Militia, Union Company, 4th Battalion, 1780-1781 [Ref: N-86/105, M-229]. Took the Oath of Allegiance and Fidelity on or after March 1, 1778 [Ref: J-1814, N-106/114].
GLEVE, George. Private, Militia, United Company, 38th Battalion, 1777-1778 [Ref: N-86/105, M-227].
GOLDER, Archibald (Clerk). Served on a Committee of Inquiry on April 14, 1780 with regards to the accounting of provisions by Peregrine Tilghman, Purchasing Agent [Ref: P-283].
GOLDSBOROUGH, Ann (Anna). See "Howes Goldsborough" and "John Goldsborough," q.v.
GOLDSBOROUGH, Caroline. See "John Goldsborough, Jr.," q.v.
GOLDSBOROUGH, Charles. See "Howes Goldsborough" and "John Goldsborough" and "Robert Goldsborough IV," q.v.
GOLDSBOROUGH, Elizabeth. See "Howes Goldsborough" and "John Goldsboorugh" and "Robert Goldsborough IV," q.v.
GOLDSBOROUGH, Greenberry (Greenbury). Private, Militia, Union Company, 4th Battalion, 1777-1778 [Ref: N-86/105, M-223]. Private, Militia, Oxford Company, 38th Battalion, 1780-1781 [Ref: N-86/105, M-235, which listed the name as "Greenbury Goldsbury"]. Draughted on May 1, 1781 to serve until December 10, 1781 in the Maryland Continental Troops [Ref: D-371].
GOLDSBOROUGH, Greenbury (1742-1829). Son of John Goldsborough and Anne Turbutt (daughter of Foster Turbutt), he was born on April 23, 1742, married (wife's name not known), and died on February 19, 1829 [Ref: R-359, Y-1181]. Appointed by the Maryland Council of Safety on January 27, 1776, to collect gold and silver coin in Talbot County to comply with the Resolve of Congress [Ref: A-132]. Captain, Militia, Sword in Hand Company, 4th Battalion, May 13, 1776 to June 17, 1777; resigned [Ref: B-244, D-67, M-79]. Took the Oath of Allegiance and Fidelity on or about March 1, 1778 [Ref: J-1814, N-106/114]. See "John Goldsborough," q.v.
GOLDSBOROUGH, Henry. See "Howes Goldsborough" and "James Tilghman, Jr.," q.v.
GOLDSBOROUGH, Howes (1747-1797). Son of Robert Goldsborough (c1704-1777) and Mary Anne Turbutt (widow of John Robins and daughter of Foster Turbutt), he was born on September 4, 1717, married his second cousin Rebecca Goldsborough, daughter of Robert Goldsborough (1733-1788), on November 16, 1773, and had these children: Sarah (born 1774); Robert (1776-1777); Mary Ann (1778-c1812); Charles (1779-1824); Robert Yerbury (1782-c1805); Henry Turbutt (1783-1785); William Henry (1785-1842); Ann (1787-1855); Howes (born 1789, became a physician); Rebecca (1790-1792); Elizabeth (died in infancy in 1791); and, Henry (1792-1832). Howes served in the Maryland Lower House between 1777 and 1785, was a Court Justice from

1777 to at least 1782, Justice of the Orphans Court from 1777 to at least 1783, Justice of the Peace in 1778 and 1779, Commissioner of the Tax from 1777 to at least 1792, and Associate Justice, Second District, 1795. Howes died on January 30, 1797 [Ref: R-78, R-80, R-90, R-358, E-163, F-22, Y-1181].

GOLDSBOROUGH, John (1711-1778). Son of Robert Goldsborough and Elizabeth Greenberry, he was born on October 12, 1711 and married first to Anne Turbutt in 1733 and second to Mary Skinner (widow of John Lookerman and daughter of Richard Skinner) by 1774. His children were: Robert (died 1770); John (Register of Wills in Dorchester County, 1777-1803); Greenbury (captain in 1776); Charles; William (lieutenant in 1776, major in 1794); Robert (became a physician); Elizabeth; Anne; Henrietta Maria; Mary; and, Anna Maria. John served in the Maryland Lower House from 1742 to 1764, was a Justice of the Court of Oyer and Terminer and Gaol Delivery, 1768-1771, and attended the Maryland Convention on July 3, 1776 for the purpose of forming a new government. He was selected one of the judges of election for Talbot County on November 8, 1776 and was appointed a Justice of the Orphans Court on June 4, 1777. On January 9, 1778 the Maryland Council issued a Special Commission of Oyer & Terminer & Goal Delivery for the Eastern Shore according to the late Act of Assembly and directed in Talbot County" to John Goldsborough and four others to be Judges of the Special Court. John died on June 18, 1778 [Ref: C-463, C-538, O-35, O-55, R-359, C-274, Y-1181]. See "Greenbury Goldsborough" and "James Tilghman, Jr.," q.v.

GOLDSBOROUGH, John Jr. (1740-1803). Son of John Goldsborough (1711-1778) and Anne Turbutt, he was born on March 26, 1740, married Caroline Goldsborough, and died on November 18, 1803 [Ref: Y-1181]. Took the Oath of Allegiance and Fidelity on or about March 1, 1778 [Ref: J-1814, N-106/114], which noted "Certificate from Dorset County"]. Register of Wills in Dorchester County from 1777 to 1803, among other county offices [Ref: R-359].

GOLDSBOROUGH, Mary. See "Howes Goldsborough" and "John Goldsborough," q.v.

GOLDSBOROUGH, Nicholas (1759-   ). Born on February 23, 1759, son of Nicholas Goldsborough (1726-1777), he married Sarah Harrison (born August 28, 1757) on May 6, 1788 in St. Peter's Parish, Talbot County [Ref: K-57]. Private, Militia, Oxford Company, 38th Battalion, 1777-1778 [Ref: N-86/105, M-227]. Private, Militia, Oxford Company, 38th Battalion, 1780-1781 [Ref: N-86/105, M-235]. Took the Oath of Allegiance and Fidelity on or about March 1, 1778 [Ref: J-1814, N-106/114]. See "Tench Tilghman" and "John Singleton," q.v.

GOLDSBOROUGH, Rebecca. See "Howes Goldsborough," q.v.

GOLDSBOROUGH, Robert. See "Howes Goldsborough" and "John Goldsborough" and "Robert Goldsborough IV" and "William Goldsborough," q.v.

GOLDSBOROUGH, Robert IV (1740-1798). Son of Robert Goldsborough (c1704-1777) and Sarah Nichols, he married Mary Emerson in 1768 and had these children: Robert (died in infancy); Robert Henry (died young); Robert Henry (1779-1836); Elizabeth (who married Charles Goldsborough, Governor of Maryland in 1819); and, another daughter (name unknown). Robert served in the Maryland Lower House, 1774-1779, was a Judge of the General Court, 1784-1798, and a member of the Constitution Ratification Committee in 1788 [Ref: R-80, R-363]. Lieutenant, Militia, January 3, 1776 to June 10, 1777; resigned [Ref: M-79]. There was also a Robert Goldsborough (1733-1788) who married Sarah Yerbury and rendered patriotic service during the revolution [Ref: Y-1181]. Additional research may be necessary before drawing conclusions.

GOLDSBOROUGH, Sarah. See "Howes Goldsborough" and "John Singleton," q.v.

GOLDSBOROUGH, William (1750-1801). Son of Robert Goldsborough (c1704-1777) and Mary Anne Turbutt (widow of John Robins and daughter of Foster Turbutt), William apparently never married. He served in the Maryland Lower House, 1777-1779, and was a Court Justice, 1779-1785, Justice of the Orphans Court, 1779-1784, and Commissioner of the Tax (appointed 1786). [Ref: R-80, R-366, F-22, I-46]. On February 7, 1776, James Lloyd Chamberlain wrote to the Maryland Council of Safety: "I am requested to enclose you the commission [first lieutenant] granted to Mr. William Goldsborough, who to gratify his parents, has declined the acceptance thereof." [Ref: A-140, A-159]. However, he may have been the William Goldsborough who was commissioned a captain in the militia, 4th Battalion, on April 9, 1778 [Ref: N-88, M-79, E-24]. Took the Oath of Allegiance and Fidelity on or about March 1, 1778 [Ref: J-1814, N-106/114].

GOLDSBOROUGH, William (1759-1794). Private, Militia, 4th Battalion, Capt. Greenbury Goldsborough's Company, reviewed and passed July 27, 1776 [Ref: D-67]. Second Lieutenant, Militia, Sword in Hand Company, 4th Battalion, April 9, 1778 through 1781 [Ref: N-86, N-99, M-230, M-79, E-24, which listed the name as "Jr."]. Took the Oath of Allegiance and Fidelity on or about March 1, 1778 [Ref: J-1814, N-106/114]. He was nicknamed "Hessian Billy" because he killed three Hessian soldiers who simultaneously attacked him. He never married; subsequently joined the Society of the Cincinnati [Ref: R-359]. See "John Goldsborough," q.v.

GOODY (GOODAY, GOODDEY), William. Private, Militia, Third Haven Company, 4th Battalion, 1777-1778 [Ref: N-86/105, M-225]. Took the Oath of Allegiance and Fidelity on or about March 1, 1778 [Ref: J-1814, N-106/114]. Private, Militia, Third Haven Company, 4th Battalion, 1780-1781 [Ref: N-86/105, M-232].

GORDON, Alexander. Private, Militia, Hearts of Oak Company, 38th Battalion, 1777-1778 [Ref: N-86/105, M-226]. Took the Oath of Allegiance and Fidelity on or about March 1, 1778 [Ref: J-1814, N-106/114]. On August 3, 1778

Alexander Gordon gave a deposition in Talbot County that he was employed by [Blair] McClannengan on the [privateer] sloop *Dolphin* when the sloop *Polly* was robbed by armed men with bayonets at the mouth of the Pocomoke... [Ref: O-111].

GORDON, John. Took the Oath of Allegiance and Fidelity on or about March 1, 1778 [Ref: J-1814, N-106/114].

GORDON, Richard. Private, Militia, Broad Creek Company, 38th Battalion, 1777-1778 [Ref: N-86/105, M-226].

GORDON, Thomas. Private, Militia, Volunteer Company, 4th Battalion, 1780-1781 [Ref: N-86/105, M-230].

GORDON, Thomas. Captain, Militia, 4th Battalion, May 13, 1776. Recommended to be promoted to Second Major, June 17, 1777 [Ref: M-79]. Took the Oath of Allegiance and Fidelity on or about March 1, 1778 [Ref: J-1814, N-106/114].

GORDON, W. See "John L. Elbert," q.v.

GORE, John. Private, Militia, Sword in Hand Company, 4th Battalion, 1777-1778 [Ref: N-86/105, M-224]. Took the Oath of Allegiance and Fidelity on or about March 1, 1778 [Ref: J-1814, N-106/114]. Private, Militia, Sword in Hand Company, 4th Battalion, 1780-1781 [Ref: N-86/105, M-231].

GORE, Samuel. Private, Militia, 2nd Volunteer Company, 4th Battalion, 1777-1778 [Ref: N-86/105, M-225]. Took the Oath of Allegiance and Fidelity on or about March 1, 1778; name listed twice [Ref: J-1814, N-106/114]. Private, Militia, Volunteer Company, 4th Battalion, 1780-1781 [Ref: N-86/105, M-229].

GORE, Walter (Walker?). Private, Militia, 2nd Volunteer Company, 4th Battalion, 1777-1778 [Ref: N-86/105, M-225]. Private, Militia, Volunteer Company, 4th Battalion, 1780-1781 [Ref: N-86/105, M-229, which listed the name as "Walker Gore"].

GORE, William. Private, Militia, Volunteer Company, 4th Battalion, 1777-1778 [Ref: N-86/105, M-223]. Private, Militia, Volunteer Company, 4th Battalion, 1780-1781 [Ref: N-86/105, M-230].

GOSSAGE, Charles. Private, Militia, United Company, 38th Battalion, 1777-1778 [Ref: N-86/105, M-227]. Took the Oath of Allegiance and Fidelity on or after March 1, 1778 [Ref: J-1814, N-106/114]. Private, Militia, United Company, 38th Battalion, 1780-1781 [Ref: N-86/105, M-233].

GOSSAGE, Daniel. Private, Militia, United Company, 38th Battalion, 1777-1778 [Ref: N-86/105, M-227]. Private, Militia, United Company, 38th Battalion, 1780-1781 [Ref: N-86/105, M-233].

GOSSAGE, John. Took the Oath of Allegiance and Fidelity on or about March 1, 1778 [Ref: J-1814, N-106/114]..

GOSSAGE, Robert. Private, Militia, United Company, 38th Battalion, 1777-1778 [Ref: N-86/105, M-227]. Took the Oath of Allegiance and Fidelity on or about March 1, 1778 [Ref: J-1814, N-106/114, which listed the name as "Robert

Gausage"]. Sergeant, Militia, United Company, 38th Battalion, 1780-1781 [Ref: N-102, M-233].

GRACE, Abell or Abel (1743-   ). Born in St. Peter's Parish, Talbot County, on March 9, 1743, a son of William and Mary Grace [Ref: V-89]. Private, Militia, Capt. Thomas Bullen's Company; no date was given; possibly late 1775 or early 1776 [Ref: Z-3]. Private, Militia, 2nd Volunteer Company, 4th Battalion, 1777-1778 [Ref: N-86/105, M-224]. Took the Oath of Allegiance and Fidelity on or about March 1, 1778 [Ref: J-1814, N-106/114]. Ensign, Militia, April 9, 1778. First Lieutenant, Militia, Volunteer Company, 4th Battalion, from 1780 through at least November 4, 1782 [Ref: N-87, N-96, M-229, M-79, E-24, I-498].

GRACE, James. Private, Militia, United Company, 38th Battalion, 1777-1778 [Ref: N-86/105, M-227]. Took the Oath of Allegiance and Fidelity on or about March 1, 1778 [Ref: J-1814, N-106/114]. Private, Militia, United Company, 38th Battalion, 1780-1781 [Ref: N-86/105, M-234].

GRACE, John. Private, Militia, United Company, 38th Battalion, 1777-1778 [Ref: N-86/105, M-227]. Private, Militia, United Company, 38th Battalion, 1780-1781 [Ref: N-86/105, M-233].

GRACE, Mary. See "William Grace" and "Abell Grace," q.v.

GRACE, Nathan (Nathaniel). Took the Oath of Allegiance and Fidelity on or about March 1, 1778 [Ref: J-1814, N-106/114, which listed the name as "Nathan Grace"]. Private, Militia, 8th Class, United Company, 38th Battalion, 1780-1781 [Ref: N-86/105, M-234].

GRACE, Nathaniel. Private, Militia, United Company, 38th Battalion, 1777-1778 [Ref: N-86/105, M-227]. Took the Oath of Allegiance and Fidelity on or about March 1, 1778 [Ref: J-1814, N-106/114]. Private, Militia, 7th Class, United Company, 38th Battalion, 1780-1781 [Ref: N-86/105, M-233]. One "Nathl. Grace" appears on "a list of men blown up in the barges" in 1782 [Ref: D-615].

GRACE, William (1742-   ). Born in St. Peter's Parish, Talbot County, on June 14, 1742, a son of William and Mary Grace [Ref: V-89]. Private, Militia, Broad Creek Company, 38th Battalion, 1777-1778 [Ref: N-86/105, M-226]. Took the Oath of Allegiance and Fidelity on or about March 1, 1778 [Ref: J-1814, N-106/114]. Private, Militia, Broad Creek Company, 38th Battalion, 1780-1781 [Ref: N-86/105, M-234]. See "Abell Grace," q.v.

GRAHAM, Joseph. Sergeant, Militia, United Company, 38th Battalion, 1780-1781 [Ref: N-102, M-233]. Took the Oath of Allegiance and Fidelity on or about March 1, 1778 [Ref: J-1814, N-106/114].

GRAINGER, Richard. Private, Militia, Hand in Hand Company, 4th Battalion, 1780-1781 [Ref: N-86/105, M-232].

GRASON, Richard. First Lieutenant, Militia, Miles River Neck Company, January 3, 1776, and subsequently listed in the 20th battalion of militia in Queen Anne's County [Ref: M-80].

GRAY, Rubin. Private, Militia, Volunteer Company, 4th Battalion, 1780-1781 [Ref: N-86/105, M-229].

GREEN, Andrew. Private, Militia, Sword in Hand Company, 4th Battalion, 1777-1778 [Ref: N-86/105, M-224]. Took the Oath of Allegiance and Fidelity on or about March 1, 1778 [Ref: J-1814, N-106/114]. Private, Militia, Sword in Hand Company, 4th Battalion, 1780-1781 [Ref: N-86/105, M-231].

GREEN, John. Private, Militia, 4th Battalion, Capt. Greenbury Goldsborough's Company, reviewed and passed July 27, 1776 [Ref: D-68].

GREENBERRY, Elizabeth. See "John Goldsborough," q.v.

GREENHAWK, John. Private, Militia, Volunteer Company, 4th Battalion, 1780-1781 [Ref: N-86/105, M-229].

GREENHAWK, Richard. Private, Militia, 2nd Volunteer Company, 4th Battalion, 1777-1778 [Ref: N-86/105, M-225]. Took the Oath of Allegiance and Fidelity on or about March 1, 1778 [Ref: J-1814, N-106/114].

GREENHAWK, Thomas. Took the Oath of Allegiance and Fidelity on or about March 1, 1778 [Ref: J-1814, N-106/114].

GREGORY, James. Private, Militia, Sword in Hand Company, 4th Battalion, 1777-1778 [Ref: N-86/105, M-224]. Took the Oath of Allegiance and Fidelity on or about March 1, 1778; name listed twice [Ref: J-1814, N-106/114].

GREGORY, James Sr. Private, Militia, Sword in Hand Company, 4th Battalion, 1780-1781 [Ref: N-86/105, M-231]. Took the Oath of Allegiance and Fidelity on or after March 1, 1778 [Ref: J-1814, N-106/114, which listed the name without the "Sr."].

GREGORY, John. Private, Militia, Sword in Hand Company, 4th Battalion, 1780-1781 [Ref: N-86/105, M-231]. Took the Oath of Allegiance and Fidelity on or about March 1, 1778; name listed twice [Ref: J-1814, N-106/114].

GREGORY, William. Private, Militia, Sword in Hand Company, 4th Battalion, 1777-1778 [Ref: N-86/105, M-224]. Took the Oath of Allegiance and Fidelity on or about March 1, 1778 [Ref: J-1814, N-106/114]. Private, Militia, Sword in Hand Company, 4th Battalion, 1780-1781 [Ref: N-86/105, M-231].

GRIFFIN, Edward. Private, Militia, Capt. Thomas Bullen's Company; no date was given; possibly late 1775 or early 1776 [Ref: Z-3]. Private, Militia, Wye Company, 4th Battalion, 1777-1778 [Ref: N-86/105, M-222].

GRIFFIN, Francis. Took the Oath of Allegiance and Fidelity on or about March 1, 1778 [Ref: J-1814, N-106/114].

GRIFFIN, Robert. Private, Militia, Hand in Hand Company, 4th Battalion, 1780-1781 [Ref: N-86/105, M-232].

GRIFFIN, Robert. Private, Militia, Wye Company, 4th Battalion, 1777-1778 [Ref: N-86/105, M-222]. Private, Militia, Wye Company, 4th Battalion, 1780-1781 [Ref: N-86/105, M-229].

GRIFFIN, Robert. Took the Oath of Allegiance and Fidelity on or about March 1, 1778 [Ref: J-1814, N-106/114].

GRIFFITH, Edward. Took the Oath of Allegiance and Fidelity on or about March 1, 1778 [Ref: J-1814, N-106/114].

GROVES, Thomas. Private, Militia, Broad Creek Company, 38th Battalion, 1777-1778 [Ref: N-86/105, M-227]. Private, Militia, United Company, 38th Battalion, 1780-1781 [Ref: N-86/105, M-233].
GUEST, Job. Private, Militia, Capt. Thomas Bullen's Company; no date was given; possibly late 1775 or early 1776 [Ref: Z-3].
GULLY, Ball. Took the Oath of Allegiance and Fidelity on or after March 1, 1778 [Ref: J-1814, N-106/114].
GULLY, Bartholomew. Private, Militia, Third Haven Company, 4th Battalion, 1777-1778 [Ref: N-86/105, M-225].
GULLY, Charles. Private, Militia, Union Company, 4th Battalion, 1780-1781 [Ref: N-86/105, M-230].
GULLY, Charles. Private, Militia, Third Haven Company, 4th Battalion, 1777-1778 [Ref: N-86/105, M-225]. Private, Militia, Third Haven Company, 4th Battalion, 1780-1781 [Ref: N-86/105, M-232].
HADDAMAN, ----. Captain, Militia, 38th Battalion, May 23, 1776 [Ref: M-81, A-438].
HADDAWAY, Daniel. Private, Militia, United Company, 38th Battalion, 1777-1778 [Ref: N-86/105, M-227]. Private, Militia, United Company, 38th Battalion, 1780-1781 [Ref: N-86/105, M-233].
HADDAWAY, George. Took the Oath of Allegiance and Fidelity on or after March 1, 1778 [Ref: J-1814, N-106/114].
HADDAWAY, James. Private, Militia, Broad Creek Company, 38th Battalion, 1777-1778 [Ref: N-86/105, M-226]. Private, Militia, Broad Creek Company, 38th Battalion, 1780-1781 [Ref: N-86/105, M-234].
HADDAWAY, John. Private, Militia, Bayside Company, 38th Battalion, 1777-1778 [Ref: N-86/105, M-228]. Ensign, Militia, Bayside Company, 38th Battalion, April 9, 1778 to June 15, 1780; resigned [Ref: N-95, M-81, E-25].
HADDAWAY, John. Private, Militia, Bayside Company, 38th Battalion, 1777-1778 [Ref: N-86/105, M-228].
HADDAWAY, John. Private, Militia, Broad Creek Company, 38th Battalion, 1777-1778 [Ref: N-86/105, M-227]. Private, Militia, Broad Creek Company, 38th Battalion, 1780-1781 [Ref: N-86/105, M-234].
HADDAWAY, John. Took the Oath of Allegiance and Fidelity on or about March 1, 1778; name listed twice [Ref: J-1814, N-106/114].
HADDAWAY, Lucretia. See "Oakley Haddaway," q.v.
HADDAWAY, Mary. See "Joseph Dawson," q.v.
HADDAWAY, Oakley (c1752-1792). Private, Militia, 4th Battalion, Capt. Greenbury Goldsborough's Company, reviewed and passed July 27, 1776 [Ref: D-68]. Took the Oath of Allegiance and Fidelity on or about March 1, 1778 [Ref: J-1814, N-106/114]. Private, Militia, Bayside Company, 38th Battalion, 1780-1781 [Ref: N-86/105, M-233]. Lieutenant on the barge *Intrepid* on June 14, 1781 [Ref: D-609]. Lieutenant on the barge *Terrible* from July 10, 1782 to August 2, 1782 [Ref: D-610]. Oakley Haddaway was born in Maryland circa

1752, married first to Sarah Dawson and second to Lucretia Haddaway, was a first lieutenant in the revolution, and died on June 10, 1792 [Ref: Y-1260].

HADDAWAY, Peter. Private, Militia, Broad Creek Company, 8th Class, 38th Battalion, 1777-1778 [Ref: N-86/105, M-227].

HADDAWAY, Peter. Private, Militia, Broad Creek Company, 7th Class, 38th Battalion, 1777-1778 [Ref: N-86/105, M-227].

HADDAWAY, Peter. Private, Militia, Broad Creek Company, 38th Battalion, 1780-1781 [Ref: N-86/105, M-234].

HADDAWAY, Robert. First Lieutenant, Militia, Bayside Company, 38th Battalion, April 9, 1778 through 1781 [Ref: N-95, N-102, M-233, M-81, E-24]. Took the Oath of Allegiance and Fidelity on or about March 1, 1778 [Ref: J-1814, N-106/114].

HADDAWAY, Robert. Private, Militia, Broad Creek Company, 38th Battalion, 1777-1778 [Ref: N-86/105, M-226]. Took the Oath of Allegiance and Fidelity on or after March 1, 1778 [Ref: J-1814, N-106/114].

HADDAWAY, Rolen. Private, Militia, Broad Creek Company, 38th Battalion, 1777-1778 [Ref: N-86/105, M-226].

HADDAWAY, Sarah. See "Edward Auld," q.v.

HADDAWAY, Thomas. Private, Militia, Bayside Company, 38th Battalion, 1777-1778 [Ref: N-86/105, M-228].

HADDAWAY, Thomas Lambden. Private, Militia, 4th Battalion, Capt. Greenbury Goldsborough's Company, reviewed and passed July 27, 1776 [Ref: D-68]. Private, Militia, Bayside Company, 38th Battalion, 1777-1778 [Ref: N-86/105, M-228]. Private, Militia, Bayside Company, 38th Battalion, 1780-1781 [Ref: N-86/105, M-233].

HADDAWAY, Thomas Lurty. Private, Militia, Bayside Company, 38th Battalion, 1780-1781 [Ref: N-102, M-233].

HADDAWAY, William. Private, Militia, Bayside Company, 38th Battalion, 1777-1778 [Ref: N-86/105, M-228]. Private, Militia, Bayside Company, 38th Battalion, 1780-1781 [Ref: N-86/105, M-233].

HADDAWAY, William. Private, Militia, Broad Creek Company, 38th Battalion, 1777-1778 [Ref: N-86/105, M-226]. Private, Militia, Broad Creek Company, 38th Battalion, 1780-1781 [Ref: N-86/105, M-234].

HADDAWAY, William. Private in the militia who was draughted on August 30, 1781 to reinforce the American Army and to serve in the Maryland Continental Troops until December 10, 1781 [Ref: D-387].

HADDAWAY, William Jr. Took the Oath of Allegiance and Fidelity on or after March 1, 1778 [Ref: J-1814, N-106/114].

HADDAWAY, William Webb (1711-c1786). Took the Oath of Allegiance and Fidelity on or about March 1, 1778 [Ref: J-1814, N-106/114]. He married Frances Harrison, and died before October 16, 1786 [Ref: Y-1260, and S-I:26, which called him "colonel"]. See "Edward Auld," q.v.

HADDAWAY, William Webb Jr. (1736-1810). Captain, Militia, 38th Battalion, May 13, 1776 [Ref: M-81]. On November 25, 1777 the Maryland Council ordered the Treasurer of the Eastern Shore to "pay to William Webb Haddaway £2050 for erecting salt works in Talbot County." [Ref: C-425]. Took the Oath of Allegiance and Fidelity on or about March 1, 1778 [Ref: J-1814, N-106/114]. William was a Lieutenant Colonel, Militia, 38th Battalion, April 9, 1778, and was probably the "Col. Haddaway of Talbot County engaged to man our boats with a number of volunteers in order to assist in clearing the bay of the enemy..." as recorded in the proceedings of the Council of Maryland on September 9 and 23, 1780 [Ref: F-284, G-118, M-81, E-24]. The Treasurer of Maryland paid Col. William Webb Haddaway £5 6s. 11p. for services rendered on October 14, 1780 [Ref: F-327]. He married Sarah Lambdin and died on November 11, 1810 [Ref: Y-1260].

HALL, George. Private, Militia, Wye Company, 4th Battalion, 1777-1778 [Ref: N-86/105, M-222]. Took the Oath of Allegiance and Fidelity on or about March 1, 1778 [Ref: J-1814, N-106/114]. Private, Militia, Wye Company, 4th Battalion, 1780-1781 [Ref: N-86/105, M-228].

HALL, John. Private, Militia, Wye Company, 4th Battalion, 1780-1781 [Ref: N-86/105, M-229].

HALL, John. Private, Militia, Bayside Company, 38th Battalion, 1777-1778 [Ref: N-86/105, M-228]. Sergeant, Militia, Bayside Company, 38th Battalion, 1780-1781 [Ref: N-102, M-233].

HALL, John. Paid £6 10s. by the Maryland Council of Safety on October 12, 1776, "for collecting & ascertaining the number of souls in Talbot County." [Ref: B-337]. Took the Oath of Allegiance and Fidelity on or about March 1, 1778 [Ref: J-1814, N-106/114].

HALL, Robert. Ensign, Militia, 4th Battalion, May 23, 1776. Second Lieutenant, Militia, April 9, 1778. First Lieutenant, Militia, Wye Company, 4th Battalion, 1780-1781 [Ref: M-82, A-438, E-24, N-88, N-96, M-228]. Took the Oath of Allegiance and Fidelity on or about March 1, 1778 [Ref: J-1814, N-106/114]. Appointed as Inspector of Tobacco at Emerson's Landing on August 30, 1780 [Ref: F-271].

HALL, Thomas. Sergeant, 4th Independent Company of Maryland Regular Troops, September, 1776 muster roll; enlisted January 20, 1776 [Ref: D-23].

HAMBLETON, George. See "Joseph Dawson," q.v.

HAMBLETON (HAMILTON), John. Second Lieutenant, Militia, United Company, 38th Battalion, April 9, 1778 through 1781 [Ref: N-93, N-102, M-233, M-82, E-25]. Took the Oath of Allegiance and Fidelity on or about March 1, 1778 [Ref: J-1814, N-106/114].

HAMBLETON, John 3rd. Private, Militia, United Company, 38th Battalion, 1777-1778 [Ref: N-86/105, M-227].

HAMBLETON, Mary. See "Hugh Sherwood, of Huntington," q.v.

HAMBLETON, Philemon (Philimon). Private, Militia, United Company, 38th Battalion, 1777-1778 [Ref: N-86/105, M-227]. Took the Oath of Allegiance and Fidelity on or about March 1, 1778 [Ref: J-1814, N-106/114]. Private, Militia, United Company, 38th Battalion, 1780-1781 [Ref: N-86/105, M-233].

HAMBLETON, William. Captain, Militia, Broad Creek Company, 38th Battalion, May 13, 1776 through 1781 [Ref: N-94, N-103 M-234, M-82, M-83]. Took the Oath of Allegiance and Fidelity on or about March 1, 1778 [Ref: J-1814, N-106/114].

HAMBLETON, William. Private, Militia, United Company, 38th Battalion, 1777-1778; name listed twice [Ref: N-86/105, M-227]. One William Hambleton was appointed a Justice of the Peace on November 21, 1778 [Ref: E-250].

HAMBLETON, William Jr. Took the Oath of Allegiance and Fidelity on or about March 1, 1778 [Ref: J-1814, N-106/114].

HAMILTON, Elizabeth. See "James Hindman," q.v.

HAMILTON, William 3rd. Private, Militia, 2nd Volunteer Company, 4th Battalion, 1777-1778 [Ref: N-86/105, M-225]. Private, Militia, Volunteer Company, 4th Battalion, 1780-1781 [Ref: N-86/105, M-229].

HANCOCK, John. Took the Oath of Allegiance and Fidelity on or about March 1, 1778 [Ref: J-1814, N-106/114]. Rendered patriotic service by hiring a cart and team for the use of the Army in June, 1778 [Ref: P-175].

HANCOCK (HANDCOCK), John. Private, Militia, Volunteer Company, 4th Battalion, 1777-1778 [Ref: N-86/105, M-223]. Private, Militia, Volunteer Company, 4th Battalion, 1780-1781 [Ref: N-86/105, M-230].

HANDY, Jacob. Private, Militia, Union Company, 4th Battalion, 1777-1778 [Ref: N-86/105, M-223].

HARDCASTLE, James. Private, Militia, Hand in Hand Company, 4th Battalion, 1780-1781 [Ref: N-86/105, M-232].

HARDCASTLE, John. Ensign, Militia, Hand in Hand Company, 4th Battalion, April 9, 1778 through 1781 [Ref: N-91, N-101, M-232, M-84, E-24]. Took the Oath of Allegiance and Fidelity on or about March 1, 1778 [Ref: J-1814, N-106/114].

HARDCASTLE, Peter. Sergeant, 4th Independent Company of Maryland Regular Troops, September, 1776 muster roll; enlisted January 26, 1776 [Ref: D-23].

HARDCASTLE, William. Private, Militia, Wye Company, 4th Battalion, 1780-1781 [Ref: N-86/105, M-229].

HARDIKIN (HARDICKIN), Matthew. Private, 4th Independent Company of Maryland Regular Troops, Capt. James Hindman's Company, September, 1776 muster roll; enlisted January 23, 1776 [Ref: D-25]. Took the Oath of Allegiance and Fidelity on or about March 1, 1778 [Ref: J-1814, N-106/114]. Sergeant, Militia, Bullinbrook Company, 4th Battalion, 1780-1781 [Ref: N-99, M-231].

HARDING (HARDIN), James. Private, Militia, Bullin Brook Company, 4th Battalion, 1777-1778 [Ref: N-86/105, M-224]. Took the Oath of Allegiance and Fidelity on or about March 1, 1778 [Ref: J-1814, N-106/114]. Private,

Militia, Bullinbrook Company, 4th Battalion, 1780-1781 [Ref: N-86/105, M-231, which listed the name as "James Harding"].

HARDING, John. Private, Militia, Capt. Thomas Bullen's Company; no date was given; possibly late 1775 or early 1776 [Ref: Z-3].

HARDING (HARDIN), Joseph Jr. (1750-   ). Born in St. Peter's Parish, Talbot County, on May 18, 1750, son of Joseph Harding [Ref: V-91]. Private, Militia, Capt. Thomas Bullen's Company; no date was given; possibly late 1775 or early 1776 [Ref: Z-3, which listed the name as "Joseph Harding" without the "Jr."]. Private, Militia, Bullin Brook Company, 4th Battalion, 1777-1778 [Ref: N-86/105, M-224]. Took the Oath of Allegiance and Fidelity on or about March 1, 1778 [Ref: J-1814, N-106/114].

HARDING (HARDIN), Joseph Sr. Took the Oath of Allegiance and Fidelity on or about March 1, 1778 [Ref: J-1814, N-106/114]. Rendered patriotic service by supplying bacon and hauling provisions for the use of the Army in April, 1778 [Ref: P-163].

HARDING, Robert. Private, Militia, Capt. Thomas Bullen's Company; no date was given; possibly late 1775 or early 1776 [Ref: Z-3].

HARMAN, Henry. Took the Oath of Allegiance and Fidelity on or about March 1, 1778 [Ref: J-1814, N-106/114].

HARMON, John. Took the Oath of Allegiance and Fidelity on or after March 1, 1778 [Ref: J-1814, N-106/114].

HARNEY, Thomas. See "Thomas Horney," q.v.

HARPER, Thomas. Private, Militia, Union Company, 4th Battalion, 1777-1778 [Ref: N-86/105, M-223].

HARRINGTON, Anthony (1762-c1836). Private, Maryland Line. Pension application S31108 was filed in 1832 in Madison County, Kentucky, stating he was born in Talbot County, Maryland in 1762 and enlisted there in 1778. No family information was given. He died in Kentucky before October 3, 1836 [Ref: W-1527, Y-1318].

HARRINGTON, David. Took the Oath of Allegiance and Fidelity on or about March 1, 1778 [Ref: J-1814, N-106/114].

HARRINGTON, David Jr. Took the Oath of Allegiance and Fidelity on or about March 1, 1778 [Ref: J-1814, N-106/114].

HARRINGTON, James. Private, Militia, Bullinbrook Company, 4th Battalion, 1780-1781 [Ref: N-86/105, M-231]. Took the Oath of Allegiance and Fidelity on or about March 1, 1778; name listed twice [Ref: J-1814, N-106/114].

HARRINGTON, Joseph. Took the Oath of Allegiance and Fidelity on or about March 1, 1778 [Ref: J-1814, N-106/114].

HARRINGTON, Nathan. Private, 4th Independent Company of Maryland Regular Troops, Capt. James Hindman's Company, September, 1776 muster roll; enlisted January 28, 1776 [Ref: D-24].

HARRINGTON, Richard. Private, Militia, Miles River Company, 38th Battalion, 1777-1778 [Ref: N-86/105, M-227]. Took the Oath of Allegiance and Fidelity on or about March 1, 1778 [Ref: J-1814, N-106/114]. Ensign, Militia, 38th Battalion, April 12, 1780 [Ref: M-84, F-140]. First Lieutenant, Militia, Miles River Company, 38th Battalion, from 1781 to at least November 4, 1782 [Ref: N-105, M-235, M-84, I-298].

HARRINGTON, William. Private, Militia, Wye Company, 4th Battalion, 1777-1778 [Ref: N-86/105, M-222]. Took the Oath of Allegiance and Fidelity on or about March 1, 1778 [Ref: J-1814, N-106/114]. Private, Militia, Bullinbrook Company, 4th Battalion, 1780-1781 [Ref: N-86/105, M-231]. See "William Herrington," q.v.

HARRIS, Edward (c1757-c1837). Served from Talbot County in the Maryland Lower House, 1783-1784, but spent most of his life in Queen Anne's County. "No land was found listed in his name in Talbot County in 1783, but he married the daughter of a Talbot County legislator, and it was probably through her dower that he was elected a delegate from Talbot County." His wife was Sarah Edmondson, a daughter of Pollard Edmondson [Ref: R-412, R-88].

HARRIS (HARRISS), Henry (1735-   ). Born in St. Peter's Parish, Talbot County, on May 1, 1735, son of Henry and Mary Harris [Ref: V-79]. Private, Militia, Capt. Thomas Bullen's Company; no date was given; possibly late 1775 or early 1776 [Ref: Z-3]. Private, Militia, Bullin Brook Company, 4th Battalion, 1777-1778 [Ref: N-86/105, M-224]. Took the Oath of Allegiance and Fidelity on or after March 1, 1778 [Ref: J-1814, N-106/114]. Private, Militia, Bullinbrook Company, 4th Battalion, 1780-1781 [Ref: N-86/105, M-231].

HARRIS (HARRISS), James. Private, Militia, Bayside Company, 38th Battalion, 1780-1781 [Ref: N-86/105, M-233].

HARRIS (HARRISS), John. Private, Militia, Volunteer Company, 4th Battalion, 1780-1781 [Ref: N-86/105, M-230]. Took the Oath of Allegiance and Fidelity on or about March 1, 1778 [Ref: J-1814, N-106/114].

HARRIS (HARRISS), Jonathan. Private, Militia, Hearts of Oak Company, 38th Battalion, 1777-1778 [Ref: N-86/105, M-226]. Private, Militia, Hearts of Oak Company, 38th Battalion, 1780-1781 [Ref: N-86/105, M-235].

HARRIS, Mary. See "Henry Harris," q.v.

HARRIS (HARRISS, HERRISS), Noah. Took the Oath of Allegiance and Fidelity on or about March 1, 1778 [Ref: J-1814, N-106/114]. Private, Militia, Bayside Company, 38th Battalion, 1780-1781 [Ref: N-86/105, M-233].

HARRIS (HARRISS), Risdon (Risden). Private, Militia, Bayside Company, 38th Battalion, 1777-1778 [Ref: N-86/105, M-228]. Took the Oath of Allegiance and Fidelity on or about March 1, 1778 [Ref: J-1814, N-106/114]. Private, Militia, Bayside Company, 38th Battalion, 1780-1781 [Ref: N-86/105, M-233].

HARRIS (HARRISS), Solomon. Private, 4th Independent Company of Maryland Regular Troops, Capt. James Hindman's Company, September, 1776 muster roll; enlisted February 5, 1776 [Ref: D-24]. Private, Militia, 4th Battalion, Capt. Greenbury Goldsborough's Company, reviewed and passed July 27, 1776 [Ref: D-68]. Private, Militia, Wye Company, 4th Battalion, 1777-1778 [Ref: N-

86/105, M-222]. Took the Oath of Allegiance and Fidelity on or about March 1, 1778 [Ref: J-1814, N-106/114]. Private, Militia, Bullinbrook Company, 4th Battalion, 1780-1781 [Ref: N-86/105, M-231].

HARRIS (HARRISS), William. Private, Militia, Bullin Brook Company, 4th Battalion, 1777-1778 [Ref: N-86/105, M-224]. Private, Militia, Bullinbrook Company, 4th Battalion, 1780-1781 [Ref: N-86/105, M-231].

HARRIS (HARRISS), William. Private, Militia, Hand & Hand Company, 4th Battalion, 1777-1778 [Ref: N-86/105, M-226]. Took the Oath of Allegiance and Fidelity on or after March 1, 1778 [Ref: J-1814, N-106/114].

HARRISON, Ann. See "Christopher Birckhead," q.v.

HARRISON, Benjamin. Private, Militia, Broad Creek Company, 38th Battalion, 1780-1781 [Ref: N-86/105, M-234]. Took the Oath of Allegiance and Fidelity on or after March 1, 1778 [Ref: J-1814, N-106/114].

HARRISON, Edward. Private, Militia, Capt. Thomas Bullen's Company; no date was given; possibly late 1775 or early 1776 [Ref: Z-3]. Private, Militia, Bayside Company, 38th Battalion, 1780-1781 [Ref: N-86/105, M-233].

HARRISON, Frances. See "Hugh Auld" and William Webb Haddaway," q.v.

HARRISON, Issable. See "John Harrison" and "William Harrison," q.v.

HARRISON, James. Took the Oath of Allegiance and Fidelity on or about March 1, 1778 [Ref: J-1814, N-106/114].

HARRISON, John. Private, Militia, Bayside Company, 38th Battalion, 1777-1778 [Ref: N-86/105, M-228]. Private, Militia, 5th Class, Bayside Company, 38th Battalion, 1780-1781 [Ref: N-86/105, M-233].

HARRISON, John. Private, Militia, 8th Class, Bayside Company, 38th Battalion, 1780-1781 [Ref: N-86/105, M-233].

HARRISON, John. Private, Militia, Oxford Company, 38th Battalion, 1777-1778 [Ref: N-86/105, M-227].

HARRISON, John. Took the Oath of Allegiance and Fidelity on or about March 1, 1778 [Ref: J-1814, N-106/114]. One John Harrison, son of William and Issable Harrison, was born in St. Peter's Parish, Talbot County, on October 6, 1741 [Ref: V-81].

HARRISON, John Jr. (Oxford Neck). Took the Oath of Allegiance and Fidelity on or after March 1, 1778 [Ref: J-1814, N-106/114]. Private, Militia, Oxford Company, 38th Battalion, 1780-1781 [Ref: N-86/105, M-235]. Draughted on May 1, 1781 to serve until December 10, 1781 in the Maryland Continental Troops [Ref: D-371].

HARRISON, Jonathan Jr. Private, Militia, United Company, 38th Battalion, 1777-1778 [Ref: N-86/105, M-227]. Private, Militia, United Company, 38th Battalion, 1780-1781 [Ref: N-86/105, M-233].

HARRISON, Joseph. Second Lieutenant, Militia, 38th Battalion, May 16, 1776 [Ref: M-85, A-428].

HARRISON, Joseph. Private, Militia, Broad Creek Company, 38th Battalion, 1777-1778 [Ref: N-86/105, M-227]. Took the Oath of Allegiance and Fidelity on or after March 1, 1778 [Ref: J-1814, N-106/114]. Private, Militia, Broad Creek Company, 38th Battalion, 1780-1781 [Ref: N-86/105, M-234].

HARRISON, Joseph Jr. Took the Oath of Allegiance and Fidelity on or after March 1, 1778 [Ref: J-1814, N-106/114].

HARRISON, Joseph 3rd. Private, Militia, United Company, 38th Battalion, 1780-1781 [Ref: N-86/105, M-233].

HARRISON, Joseph (of Thomas). Private, Militia, United Company, 38th Battalion, 1780-1781 [Ref: N-86/105, M-233].

HARRISON, Nathaniel. Private, Militia, United Company, 38th Battalion, 1780-1781 [Ref: N-86/105, M-233].

HARRISON, Robert. First Lieutenant, Militia, 38th Battalion, May 16, 1776 [Ref: M-85, A-428].

HARRISON, Robert. Private, Militia, Bayside Company, 38th Battalion, 1780-1781 [Ref: N-86/105, M-233].

HARRISON, Robert. Private, Militia, United Company, 38th Battalion, 1780-1781 [Ref: N-86/105, M-233].

HARRISON, Robert. Private, Militia, Broad Creek Company, 38th Battalion, 1777-1778 [Ref: N-86/105, M-226]. Private, Militia, Broad Creek Company, 38th Battalion, 1780-1781 [Ref: N-86/105, M-234]. One Robert Harrison appears on "a list of men blown up in the barges" in 1782 [Ref: D-615].

HARRISON, Robert. Took the Oath of Allegiance and Fidelity on or after March 1, 1778 [Ref: J-1814, N-106/114].

HARRISON, Sarah. See "Nicholas Goldsborough," q.v.

HARRISON, Solomon. Private, Militia, Bayside Company, 38th Battalion, 1777-1778 [Ref: N-86/105, M-228]. Corporal, Militia, Bayside Company, 38th Battalion, 1780-1781 [Ref: N-102, M-233].

HARRISON, Stephen. Private, Militia, 4th Battalion, Capt. Greenbury Goldsborough's Company, reviewed and passed July 27, 1776 [Ref: D-68].

HARRISON, Thomas. Ensign, Militia, 38th Battalion, May 16, 1776. Ensign, Militia, United Company, 38th Battalion, April 9, 1778 through 1781 [Ref: N-93, N-102, M-233, M-85, A-428, E-25]. Took the Oath of Allegiance and Fidelity on or after March 1, 1778 [Ref: J-1814, N-106/114]. On January 9, 1778 the Maryland Council issued a Special Commission of Oyer & Terminer & Goal Delivery for the Eastern Shore according to the late Act of Assembly and directed in Talbot County" to Thomas Harrison and four others to be Judges of the Special Court [Ref: C-463, C-538].

HARRISON, Thomas Jr. Private, Militia, United Company, 38th Battalion, 1777-1778 [Ref: N-86/105, M-227, which listed the name without the "Jr."]. Sergeant, Militia, United Company, 38th Battalion, 1780-1781 [Ref: N-102, M-233].

HARRISON, William. Private, Militia, United Company, 38th Battalion, 1777-1778 [Ref: N-86/105, M-227]. Private, Militia, United Company, 38th Battalion, 1780-1781 [Ref: N-86/105, M-233].

HARRISON, William. Private, Militia, Broad Creek Company, 38th Battalion, 1777-1778 [Ref: N-86/105, M-226]. Private, Militia, Broad Creek Company, 38th Battalion, 1780-1781 [Ref: N-86/105, M-234].
HARRISON, William ("of James T. P."). Private in the militia who was draughted on August 30, 1781 to reinforce the American Army and to serve in the Maryland Continental Troops until December 10, 1781 [Ref: D-387].
HARRISON, William Jr. Private, Militia, United Company, 38th Battalion, 1777-1778 [Ref: N-86/105, M-227]. Private, Militia, United Company, 38th Battalion, 1780-1781 [Ref: N-86/105, M-233]. William Harrison, son of William and Issable Harrison, was born in St. Peter's Parish, Talbot County, on August 31, 1743 [Ref: V-81]. See "John Harrison," q.v.
HARRISON, William Sr. Private, Militia, United Company, 38th Battalion, 1780-1781 [Ref: N-86/105, M-233].
HART (HEART), Christopher. Private, Militia, Wye Company, 4th Battalion, 1777-1778 [Ref: N-86/105, M-222]. Took the Oath of Allegiance and Fidelity on or about March 1, 1778 [Ref: J-1814, N-106/114]. Private, Militia, Wye Company, 4th Battalion, 1780-1781 [Ref: N-86/105, M-229].
HART, Mary. See "William Benny," q.v.
HART (HEART), William. Private, Militia, Miles River Company, 38th Battalion, 1777-1778 [Ref: N-86/105, M-227]. Took the Oath of Allegiance and Fidelity on or about March 1, 1778 [Ref: J-1814, N-106/114]. Private, Militia, Miles River Company, 38th Battalion, 1780-1781 [Ref: N-86/105, M-235].
HARWOOD, Henry Hall. See "Edward Lloyd," q.v.
HARWOOD, Nathaniel. Private, 5th Maryland Line, enlisted April 22, 1778; transferred to Invalids Corps on June 10, 1778 [Ref: D-213].
HARWOOD, Peter. Private, Militia, Volunteer Company, 4th Battalion, 1780-1781 [Ref: N-86/105, M-229].
HARWOOD, Richard. Private, Militia, Union Company, 4th Battalion, 1777-1778 [Ref: N-86/105, M-223]. Took the Oath of Allegiance and Fidelity on or about March 1, 1778 [Ref: J-1814, N-106/114]. Paid 12s. 8p. for services rendered on March 11, 1779, by Col. Christopher Birkhead [Ref: E-319]. Private (substitute), Militia, Union Company, 4th Battalion, 1780-1781 [Ref: N-86/105, M-230].
HARWOOD, Risdon (Rizden). Took the Oath of Allegiance and Fidelity on or about March 1, 1778 [Ref: J-1814, N-106/114]. Private, Militia, Union Company, 4th Battalion, 1777-1778 [Ref: N-86/105, M-223].
HARWOOD, Robert. Private, Militia, 2nd Volunteer Company, 4th Battalion, 1777-1778 [Ref: N-86/105, M-225]. Took the Oath of Allegiance and Fidelity on or about March 1, 1778 [Ref: J-1814, N-106/114].
HARWOOD, Robert 3rd. Took the Oath of Allegiance and Fidelity on or about March 1, 1778 [Ref: J-1814, N-106/114].
HARWOOD, Samuel. Private, Militia, Union Company, 4th Battalion, 1777-1778 [Ref: N-86/105, M-223].

HARWOOD, Sharp. Private, Militia, Union Company, 4th Battalion, 1780-1781 [Ref: N-86/105, M-230].

HARWOOD, Thomas. Private, Militia, 2nd Volunteer Company, 4th Battalion, 1777-1778 [Ref: N-86/105, M-225]. Private, Militia, Volunteer Company, 4th Battalion, 1780-1781 [Ref: N-86/105, M-229].

HASELDINE (HAZLEDINE), Francis. Private, 4th Independent Company of Maryland Regular Troops, Capt. James Hindman's Company, September, 1776 muster roll; enlisted January 25, 1776 [Ref: D-24].

HASELDINE (HAZELDINE), James. Private, Militia, Miles River Company, 38th Battalion, 1777-1778 [Ref: N-86/105, M-227]. Took the Oath of Allegiance and Fidelity on or about March 1, 1778 [Ref: J-1814, N-106/114]. Private, Militia, Volunteer Company, 4th Battalion, 1780-1781 [Ref: N-86/105, M-229].

HASELDINE (HAZELDINE), Richard. Took the Oath of Allegiance and Fidelity on or about March 1, 1778 [Ref: J-1814, N-106/114]. Private, Militia, Volunteer Company, 4th Battalion, 1780-1781 [Ref: N-86/105, M-229].

HASELDINE, William. Private, Militia, Miles River Company, 38th Battalion, 1777-1778 [Ref: N-86/105, M-227].

HAWKINS, James. Private, Militia, Wye Company, 4th Battalion, 1777-1778 [Ref: N-86/105, M-222].

HAYS, Richard. Private, Militia, Third Haven Company, 4th Battalion, 1777-1778 [Ref: N-86/105, M-225]. Took the Oath of Allegiance and Fidelity on or about March 1, 1778 [Ref: J-1814, N-106/114].

HAYWARD, George. See "William Hayward," q.v.

HAYWARD, Henrietta. See "William Hayward," q.v.

HAYWARD, Sarah. See "William Hayward," q.v.

HAYWARD, Thomas. See "William Hayward," q.v.

HAYWARD, William (c1735-1791). He married Margaret Robins on November 29, 1760 in St. Peter's Parish, Talbot County, and their children were: Henrietta Maria (born October 19, 1761 and died October 23, 1761); Sarah (born August 15, 1763 and died October 8, 1764); George Robins (born September 16, 1767 and died December 11, 1811); and, Thomas [Ref: K-55, K-57]. William initially resided in Somerset County where he was Acting Clerk of Indictments, 1750-1752, served in the Maryland Lower House, 1762-1763, and was a Court Justice, 1763. By 1767 he had moved to Talbot County where he held these offices: Justice, Provincial Court, 1771-1776; Rent Roll Keeper, 1772-1773; Judge, Admiralty Court, 1776; and, Third Council of Safety, 1776. [Ref: R-427]. Took the Oath of Allegiance and Fidelity on or after March 1, 1778 [Ref: J-1814, N-106/114]. This William Hayward was the uncle, not the father, of William Hayward, Jr. (c1758-1834). [Ref: R-208]. See "James Lloyd Chamberlaine," q.v.

HEFFERNON (HEFFERSON?), Robert. Private, 4th Independent Company of Maryland Regular Troops, Capt. James Hindman's Company, September, 1776 muster roll; enlisted January 30, 1776 [Ref: D-25]. Private, Militia, Hand & Hand Company, 4th Battalion, 1777-1778 [Ref: N-86/105, M-226]. Private in the militia who was draughted on August 30, 1781 to reinforce the American Army and to serve in the Maryland Continental Troops until December 10, 1781 [Ref: D-387].

HELMSLEY, William, Esq. (Certificate from Queen Anne's County). Took the Oath of Allegiance and Fidelity on or about March 1, 1778 [Ref: J-1814, N-106/114].

HELSBY, Elizabeth. See "John Helsby," q.v.

HELSBY, John (1727-). Born in St. Peter's Parish, Talbot County, on January 6, 1727, son of Thomas and Elizabeth Helsby [Ref: V-67]. Took the Oath of Allegiance and Fidelity on or about March 1, 1778 [Ref: J-1814, N-106/114]. John Helsby again took the Oath of Allegiance and Fidelity sometime between May and September, 1780 [Ref: L-112].

HELSBY, John Jr. Private, Militia, Capt. Thomas Bullen's Company; no date was given; possibly late 1775 or early 1776 [Ref: Z-3]. Took the Oath of Allegiance and Fidelity on or after March 1, 1778 [Ref: J-1814, N-106/114, which listed the name as "Jr."].

HELSBY, Thomas. Private, Militia, Bullinbrook Company, 4th Battalion, 1780-1781 [Ref: N-86/105, M-231]. See "John Helsby," q.v.

HELSBY, Thomas Jr. Private, Militia, Capt. Thomas Bullen's Company; no date was given; possibly late 1775 or early 1776 [Ref: Z-3].

HELSBY, Thomas (of William). Private, Militia, Bullinbrook Company, 4th Battalion, 1780-1781 [Ref: N-86/105, M-231]. Thomas Hilsby (of William) was draughted on August 30, 1781 to reinforce the American Army and to serve in the Maryland Continental Troops until December 10, 1781 [Ref: D-387].

HELSBY, William Jr. Private, Militia, Volunteer Company, 4th Battalion, 1780-1781 [Ref: N-86/105, M-230].

HELSBY, William Long. Private, Militia, Third Haven Company, 4th Battalion, 1777-1778 [Ref: N-86/105, M-225]. Took the Oath of Allegiance and Fidelity on or after March 1, 1778 [Ref: J-1814, N-106/114]. Private, Militia, Third Haven Company, 4th Battalion, 1780-1781 [Ref: N-86/105, M-232, which listed the name as "William Lang Helsbey"].

HEMSLEY, Maria Lloyd. See "Peregrine Tilghman," q.v.

HEMSLEY, Thomas. See "James Tilghman, Jr.," q.v.

HEMSLEY, William (1736/7-1812). Rendered patriotic service by supplying wheat for the use of the Army in January and April, 1780 [Ref: P-266, P-282, R-825].

HENDRICK, James. Private, Militia, Volunteer Company, 4th Battalion, 1780-1781 [Ref: N-86/105, M-229].

HENNON, Hall. Private, Militia, United Company, 38th Battalion, 1777-1778 [Ref: N-86/105, M-227].

HENRIX, Edward. Private, Militia, Sword in Hand Company, 4th Battalion, 1777-1778 [Ref: N-86/105, M-224]. Private, Militia, Sword in Hand Company, 4th Battalion, 1780-1781 [Ref: N-86/105, M-231]. Took the Oath of Allegiance and Fidelity on or about March 1, 1778; name listed twice [Ref: J-1814, N-106/114].

HENRY, James. See "Joseph Dawson," q.v.

HERON, James. Took the Oath of Allegiance and Fidelity on or about March 1, 1780 [Ref: J-1814, N-106/114].

HERON, John. Private, Militia, Union Company, 4th Battalion, 1777-1778 [Ref: N-86/105, M-223]. Took the Oath of Allegiance and Fidelity on or about March 1, 1778 [Ref: J-1814, N-106/114]. Private, Militia, Union Company, 4th Battalion, 1780-1781 [Ref: N-86/105, M-230].

HERON, Peter. Took the Oath of Allegiance and Fidelity on or about March 1, 1778 [Ref: J-1814, N-106/114].

HERRINGTON, William. Private, Militia, Capt. Thomas Bullen's Company; no date was given; possibly late 1775 or early 1776 [Ref: Z-3]. See "William Harrington," q.v.

HEWEY (HEWIE), John. Private, Militia, 4th Battalion, Capt. Greenbury Goldsborough's Company, reviewed and passed July 27, 1776 [Ref: D-68]. Private, Militia, Miles River Company, 38th Battalion, 1777-1778 [Ref: N-86/105, M-227]. Took the Oath of Allegiance and Fidelity on or about March 1, 1778 [Ref: J-1814, N-106/114, which listed the name as "John Hewie"]. Private, Militia, Miles River Company, 38th Battalion, 1780-1781 [Ref: N-86/105, M-235].

HEWEY, Jonathan. Private, Militia, 2nd Volunteer Company, 4th Battalion, 1777-1778 [Ref: N-86/105, M-225]. Took the Oath of Allegiance and Fidelity on or about March 1, 1778 [Ref: J-1814, N-106/114].

HEWEY (HEWIE), Robert. Took the Oath of Allegiance and Fidelity on or about March 1, 1778 [Ref: J-1814, N-106/114, which listed the name as "Robert Hewie"].

HEWEY, Thomas. Private, Militia, Miles River Company, 38th Battalion, 1780-1781 [Ref: N-86/105, M-235].

HEWEY (HEWIE), Woolman. Private, Militia, Miles River Company, 38th Battalion, 1777-1778 [Ref: N-86/105, M-227]. Took the Oath of Allegiance and Fidelity on or about March 1, 1778 [Ref: J-1814, N-106/114, which listed the name as "Woolman Hewie"]. Sergeant, Militia, Miles River Company, 38th Battalion, 1780-1781 [Ref: N-105, M-235].

HEWS, James. See "James Hughs," q.v.

HICKSON, Richard. Private, Militia, Capt. Thomas Bullen's Company; no date was given; possibly late 1775 or early 1776 [Ref: Z-3]. Private, Militia, Volunteer Company, 4th Battalion, 1777-1778 [Ref: N-86/105, M-223]. Private, Militia, Volunteer Company, 4th Battalion, 1780-1781 [Ref: N-86/105,

M-230]. Rendered patriotic service by supplying bacon for the use of the Army in April, 1778 [Ref: P-161].

HICKSON, Woolman. Private, Militia, Volunteer Company, 4th Battalion, 1780-1781 [Ref: N-86/105, M-230].

HIGBY, John. Private, Militia, Oxford Company, 38th Battalion, 1777-1778 [Ref: N-86/105, M-228]. Took the Oath of Allegiance and Fidelity on or after March 1, 1778 [Ref: J-1814, N-106/114].

HIGGINS, Daniel. Private, 4th Independent Company of Maryland Regular Troops, Capt. James Hindman's Company, September, 1776 muster roll; enlisted January 29, 1776 [Ref: D-24].

HIGGINS, Henry. Private, 4th Independent Company of Maryland Regular Troops, Capt. James Hindman's Company; enlisted January 26, 1776; honorably discharged July 28, 1776 [Ref: D-24]. Private, Militia, Bullin Brook Company, 4th Battalion, 1777-1778 [Ref: N-86/105, M-224]. Took the Oath of Allegiance and Fidelity on or after March 1, 1778 [Ref: J-1814, N-106/114]. Private, Militia, Third Haven Company, 4th Battalion, 1780-1781 [Ref: N-86/105, M-232].

HIGGINS, James. Private, Militia, Third Haven Company, 4th Battalion, 1777-1778 [Ref: N-86/105, M-225]. Took the Oath of Allegiance and Fidelity on or about March 1, 1778 [Ref: J-1814, N-106/114].

HIGGINS, James Saywell. Took the Oath of Allegiance and Fidelity on or about March 1, 1778 [Ref: J-1814, N-106/114].

HIGGINS, John. Private, Militia, Bullin Brook Company, 4th Battalion, 1777-1778 [Ref: N-86/105, M-224]. Took the Oath of Allegiance and Fidelity on or after March 1, 1778 [Ref: J-1814, N-106/114]. Private, Militia, Bullinbrook Company, 4th Battalion, 1780-1781 [Ref: N-86/105, M-231].

HIGGINS, John. Took the Oath of Allegiance and Fidelity on or about March 1, 1778 [Ref: J-1814, N-106/114]. Rendered patriotic service by supplying bacon for the use of the Army in June, 1778 [Ref: P-175].

HIGGINS, John Jr. Private, Militia, Capt. Thomas Bullen's Company; no date was given; possibly late 1775 or early 1776 [Ref: Z-3]. Private, Militia, Bullinbrook Company, 4th Battalion, 1780-1781 [Ref: N-86/105, M-231].

HIGGINS, Thomas. Private, Militia, Bullin Brook Company, 4th Battalion, 1777-1778 [Ref: N-86/105, M-224]. Took the Oath of Allegiance and Fidelity on or about March 1, 1778; name listed twice [Ref: J-1814, N-106/114]. Private, Militia, Bullinbrook Company, 4th Battalion, 1780-1781 [Ref: N-86/105, M-231].

HIGGINS, William. Private, Militia, Bullin Brook Company, 4th Battalion, 1777-1778 [Ref: N-86/105, M-224]. Took the Oath of Allegiance and Fidelity on or after March 1, 1778 [Ref: J-1814, N-106/114]. Corporal, Militia, Broad Creek Company, 38th Battalion, 1780-1781 [Ref: N-103, M-234]. Draughted on August 30, 1781 to reinforce the American Army and to serve in the Maryland Continental Troops until December 10, 1781 [Ref: D-387].

HILL, Thomas. Private, Militia, 4th Battalion, Capt. Greenbury Goldsborough's Company, reviewed and passed July 27, 1776 [Ref: D-68].

HINDMAN, Edward. Second Lieutenant, 4th Independent Company of Maryland Regular Troops, September, 1776 muster roll; commissioned January 5, 1776 or February 14, 1776, both dates were given [Ref: D-23, A-159]. Took the Oath of Allegiance and Fidelity on or about March 1, 1778 [Ref: J-1814, N-106/114]. Appointed a Justice of the Peace on July 22, 1778 [Ref: E-163].

HINDMAN, Jacob. See "James Hindman" and "William Hindman," q.v.

HINDMAN, James (1741-1830). Son of Jacob Hindman and Mary Trippe, he married first to Marian Anderson by 1774 and second to Elizabeth Hamilton in 1797, but apparently died without issue. James served in several capacities: Maryland Lower House, 1780-1784; Executive Council, 1777-1779, 1786-1789; Treasurer of the Eastern Shore, 1777-1778; Committee of Observation (elected 1775); Collector of Cloathing, 1777-1778; and, Deputy Assistant Commissary General of Purchases, 1779-1780. He later lived in Queen Anne's County by 1788 and in Baltimore City by 1809 [Ref: R-443, C-426, F-22, F-215]. Captain, 4th Independent Company of Maryland Regular Troops at Oxford; commissioned January 5, 1776. Lieutenant Colonel, 5th Maryland Line, December, 1776. Colonel before April 4, 1777 (date of resignation). Contractor for Horses by August 22, 1780 when he wrote to the governor regarding the purchase of flour and horses [Ref: B-118, D-23, P-311, R-443, R-84, R-86, R-87, R-88, R-89, F-256, D-212].

HINDMAN, John (1754-1827). On June 6, 1776, "the Council of Safety agree with Dr. John Hindman of Talbot County to pay him at the rate of £100 per annum for providing medicine for and attending Captain James Hindman's Independent Company of Regular Troops." [Ref: A-467]. Took the Oath of Allegiance and Fidelity on or about March 1, 1778 [Ref: J-1814, N-106/114]. Surgeon, 5th Maryland Line, from December 10, 1776 to January 13, 1778 (date of resignation). [Ref: D-212]. John Hindman was born in Maryland on January 24, 1754, married Mary Ann Latcha, and died in 1827 [Ref: Y-1431].

HINDMAN, William (1743-1822). Son of Jacob Hindman and Mary Trippe, he never married, but devoted his life to public service: Maryland Convention, 1775; Senate, 1776-1793; United States Congress, 1794-1801; United States Senate, 1801; Treasurer, Eastern Shore, 1775-1777; Clerk, Eastern Shore Branch of the Maryland Council of Safety, 1775; Justice of the Peace, 1778; Executive Council, 1789-1791; Secretary, Committee of Observation, 1775; Judge of the Orphans Court, 1778; Board of Visitors, Washington College, 1782; and, Delegate to the Continental Congress, 1784-1786 [Ref: A-3, R-76, R-78, R-80, R-82, R-84, R-86, R-87, R-88, R-89, R-90, R-445, O-1, O-4, E-250]. He may be the William Hindman who was recommended to be first lieutenant in Union Company, 4th Militia Battalion, on June 17, 1777 [Ref: M-87]. He also rendered patriotic service by supplying wheat for the use of the Army in February, 1780 [Ref: P-269].

HOBBS, John. Private, Militia, Hand in Hand Company, 4th Battalion, 1780-1781 [Ref: N-86/105, M-232].
HOBBS, John. Private, Militia, Volunteer Company, 4th Battalion, 1780-1781 [Ref: N-86/105, M-229].
HOBBS, John. Took the Oath of Allegiance and Fidelity on or about March 1, 1778 [Ref: J-1814, N-106/114].
HOBBS, Joseph. Private, Militia, 2nd Volunteer Company, 4th Battalion, 1777-1778 [Ref: N-86/105, M-225, which listed the name as "Joseph Hobs"]. Took the Oath of Allegiance and Fidelity on or about March 1, 1778 [Ref: J-1814, N-106/114]. Private, Militia, Volunteer Company, 4th Battalion, 1780-1781 [Ref: N-86/105, M-229].
HOLLADAY (HOLLIDAY), James. Private, Militia, Union Company, 4th Battalion, 1777-1778 [Ref: N-86/105, M-223]. Private, Militia, Union Company, 4th Battalion, 1780-1781 [Ref: N-86/105, M-229].
HOLLAND, Arthor. Private, Militia, Bullin Brook Company, 4th Battalion, 1777-1778 [Ref: N-86/105, M-224].
HOLLAND, James. Took the Oath of Allegiance and Fidelity on or about March 1, 1778 [Ref: J-1814, N-106/114].
HOLLAND, John. Private, Militia, 4th Battalion, Capt. Greenbury Goldsborough's Company, reviewed and passed July 27, 1776 [Ref: D-67].
HOLLAND, William. Private, Militia, Miles River Company, 38th Battalion, 1777-1778 [Ref: N-86/105, M-227]. Private, Militia, Miles River Company, 38th Battalion, 1780-1781 [Ref: N-86/105, M-235].
HOLLAND, Zachariah. Took the Oath of Allegiance and Fidelity on or about March 1, 1778 [Ref: J-1814, N-106/114].
HOLLYDAY, Anna Maria. See "Samuel Chamberlaine," q.v.
HOLLYDAY, Henrietta. See "Samuel Chamberlaine," q.v.
HOLLYDAY, Henry. Rendered patriotic service by supplying wheat for the use of the Army in February, 1780, and three horses in July, 1780 [Ref: P-267, G-34]. On July 28, 1780, James Hindman, Contractor for Horses in Talbot County, advised Governor Lee and the Maryland Council, in part, that he "received of Mr. Henry Hollyday, a non-juror of this county, three horses, and expect in a few days to receive five or six more from other non-jurors..." [Ref: G-34]. See "Samuel Chamberlaine," q.v.
HOLMES, Francis (1744-   ). Born in St. Peter's Parish, Talbot County, on January 24, 1744, a son of Ralph and Frances Holmes [Ref: V-81]. Private, Militia, Oxford Company, 38th Battalion, 1777-1778 [Ref: N-86/105, M-227]. Private, Militia, Oxford Company, 38th Battalion, 1780-1781 [Ref: N-86/105, M-235].
HOLMES, John Jr. Private, Militia, Volunteer Company, 4th Battalion, 1780-1781 [Ref: N-86/105, M-230].
HOLMES, Paul. Private, Militia, Capt. Thomas Bullen's Company; no date was given; possibly late 1775 or early 1776 [Ref: Z-3].

HOLMES, Ralph. Private, Militia, Capt. Thomas Bullen's Company; no date was given; possibly late 1775 or early 1776 [Ref: Z-3]. See "Francis Holmes" and "Solomon Holmes," q.v.

HOLMES, Ralph Jr. Private, Militia, Capt. Thomas Bullen's Company; no date was given; possibly late 1775 or early 1776 [Ref: Z-3].

HOLMES, Solomon. Took the Oath of Allegiance and Fidelity on or after March 1, 1778 [Ref: J-1814, N-106/114]. One Solomon Holmes, son of Ralph and Frances Holmes, was born in St. Peter's Parish, Talbot County, on March 9, 1734 [Ref: V-81]. See "Solomon Holmes, Sr.," q.v.

HOLMES, Solomon Jr. Private, Militia, Third Haven Company, 4th Battalion, 1777-1778 [Ref: N-86/105, M-225]. Waterman on the barge *Intrepid* in 1781 [Ref: D-610, which listed the name without the "Jr."].

HOLMES, Solomon Sr. Private, Militia, Third Haven Company, 4th Battalion, 1777-1778 [Ref: N-86/105, M-225, which listed the name without the "Sr."]. Private, Militia, Third Haven Company, 4th Battalion, 1780-1781 [Ref: N-86/105, M-232].

HOLMES, Thomas Jr. Private, Militia, Third Haven Company, 4th Battalion, 1780-1781 [Ref: N-86/105, M-232].

HOLT, Elizabeth. See "John Holt," q.v.

HOLT, James. Private, Militia, Capt. Thomas Bullen's Company; no date was given; possibly late 1775 or early 1776 [Ref: Z-3]. Private, Militia, Volunteer Company, 4th Battalion, 1780-1781 [Ref: N-86/105, M-230]. Waterman on the barge *Intrepid* in 1781 [Ref: D-610].

HOLT, John. Private in the militia who was draughted on August 30, 1781 to reinforce the American Army and to serve in the Maryland Continental Troops until December 10, 1781; honorably discharged on December 3, 1781 [Ref: D-387, I-10]. One John Holt, son of John and Elizabeth, was born in St. Peter's Parish, Talbot County, on April 6, 1728 [Ref: V-86].

HOOK, James. First Lieutenant, Militia, Volunteer Company, 4th Battalion, April 9, 1778 [Ref: N-87, M-88, E-24]. Took the Oath of Allegiance and Fidelity on or about March 1, 1778 [Ref: J-1814, N-106/114].

HOPKINS, Benjamin. Private, Militia, Hearts of Oak Company, 38th Battalion, 1777-1778 [Ref: N-86/105, M-226].

HOPKINS, Daniel. Private, Militia, United Company, 38th Battalion, 1780-1781 [Ref: N-86/105, M-233].

HOPKINS, Dennis. Private, Militia, Oxford Company, 38th Battalion, 1777-1778 [Ref: N-86/105, M-227]. Private, Militia, Oxford Company, 38th Battalion, 1780-1781 [Ref: N-86/105, M-235]. "Dennis Hopkins, Meeting House" took the Oath of Allegiance and Fidelity on or about March 1, 1778 [Ref: J-1814, N-106/114].

HOPKINS, Denny. Private, Militia, Hearts of Oak Company, 38th Battalion, 1777-1778 [Ref: N-86/105, M-226]. Private, Militia, Hearts of Oak Company, 38th Battalion, 1780-1781 [Ref: N-86/105, M-235].

HOPKINS, Francis. Private, Militia, Hand in Hand Company, 4th Battalion, 1780-1781 [Ref: N-86/105, M-232].
HOPKINS, Francis Jr. Private, Militia, Hearts of Oak Company, 38th Battalion, 1780-1781 [Ref: N-86/105, M-234].
HOPKINS, Hugh. Corporal, Militia, United Company, 38th Battalion, 1780-1781 [Ref: N-102, M-233].
HOPKINS, James (1757-   ). Born in St. Peter's Parish, Talbot County, on September 11, 1757, a son of Peter and Sarah Hopkins, and married Lucany [Lurany?] Cook in June, 1796 [Ref: K-55. K-57]. Private, Militia, Oxford Company, 38th Battalion, 1777-1778 [Ref: N-86/105, M-227]. Private, Militia, Oxford Company, 38th Battalion, 1780-1781 [Ref: N-86/105, M-235].
HOPKINS, James. Private, Militia, Volunteer Company, 4th Battalion, 1777-1778 [Ref: N-86/105, M-223]. Private, Militia, Hearts of Oak Company, 38th Battalion, 1780-1781 [Ref: N-86/105, M-235].
HOPKINS, James. Private, Militia, Third Haven Company, 4th Battalion, 1777-1778 [Ref: N-86/105, M-225]. Private, Militia, Bullinbrook Company, 4th Battalion, 1780-1781 [Ref: N-86/105, M-231].
HOPKINS, James (Bay S. Neck). Took the Oath of Allegiance and Fidelity on or after March 1, 1778 [Ref: J-1814, N-106/114].
HOPKINS, James Jr. Took the Oath of Allegiance and Fidelity on or after March 1, 1778 [Ref: J-1814, N-106/114].
HOPKINS, John. Private, 4th Independent Company of Maryland Regular Troops, Capt. James Hindman's Company, September, 1776 muster roll; enlisted February 2, 1776 [Ref: D-24]. Private, Militia, Oxford Company, 38th Battalion, 1777-1778 [Ref: N-86/105, M-228].
HOPKINS, John. Private, Militia, Union Company, 4th Battalion, 1777-1778 [Ref: N-86/105, M-223].
HOPKINS, John Johnnings. Took the Oath of Allegiance and Fidelity on or about March 1, 1778 [Ref: J-1814, N-106/114]. "J. J. Hopkins" was a private in the militia, United Company, 38th Battalion, 1777-1778 [Ref: N-86/105, M-227].
HOPKINS, John Jr. Private, Militia, United Company, 38th Battalion, 1780-1781 [Ref: N-86/105, M-234].
HOPKINS, John 3rd. Private, Militia, Hearts of Oak Company, 38th Battalion, 1777-1778 [Ref: N-86/105, M-226]. Private, Militia, Hearts of Oak Company, 38th Battalion, 1780-1781 [Ref: N-86/105, M-234].
HOPKINS, Jonathan. Private, Militia, Miles River Company, 38th Battalion, 1780 [Ref: N-86/105, M-235]. Took the Oath of Allegiance and Fidelity on or about March 1, 1778 [Ref: J-1814, N-106/114]. On Novmember 15, 1780, Rachel Gibson, wife of Woolman Gibson, petitioned the Governor and Congress asking for the discharge of her son Jonathan Hopkins, her son by a former marriage, who was "deficient in his intellect" and having "straggled away last winter was induced to enlist" on the galley *Chester*. She stated he was unfit for service and was exposed to the "mockery and insult of the sailors and to the

hazard of being corrupted by their example and of learning the bad words." Her petition was written by Rev. John Gordon, Rector of St. Michael's Parish, and endorsed by him, Jonathan Gibson, Joseph Bruff, John Broome, Richard Parrott, and William Gibson [Ref: F-367].

HOPKINS, Joseph. Private, Militia, United Company, 38th Battalion, 1777-1778 [Ref: N-86/105, M-227].

HOPKINS, Joseph. Private, Militia, Hearts of Oak Company, 38th Battalion, 1777-1778 [Ref: N-86/105, M-226]. Private, Militia, Hearts of Oak Company, 38th Battalion, 1780-1781 [Ref: N-86/105, M-235].

HOPKINS, Joseph. Took the Oath of Allegiance and Fidelity on or about March 1, 1778 [Ref: J-1814, N-106/114].

HOPKINS, Joseph (of Benjamin). Private in the militia who was draughted on August 30, 1781 to reinforce the American Army and to serve in the Maryland Continental Troops until December 10, 1781 [Ref: D-387].

HOPKINS, Joshua. Private, Militia, Hearts of Oak Company, 38th Battalion, 1777-1778 [Ref: N-86/105, M-226]. Private, Militia, Hearts of Oak Company, 38th Battalion, 1780-1781 [Ref: N-86/105, M-235, which listed the name as "Hashua Hopkins"].

HOPKINS, Lambert. Private, Militia, Union Company, 4th Battalion, 1780-1781 [Ref: N-86/105, M-230].

HOPKINS, Lucy. See "John Bruff," q.v.

HOPKINS, Moses. Private, Militia, Oxford Company, 38th Battalion, 1777-1778 [Ref: N-86/105, M-227]. Took the Oath of Allegiance and Fidelity on or after March 1, 1778 [Ref: J-1814, N-106/114]. Private, Militia, Oxford Company, 38th Battalion, 1780-1781 [Ref: N-86/105, M-235].

HOPKINS, Nathaniel. Private, Militia, Sword in Hand Company, 4th Battalion, 1777-1778 [Ref: N-86/105, M-224]. Took the Oath of Allegiance and Fidelity on or about March 1, 1778 [Ref: J-1814, N-106/114]. Private, Militia, Sword in Hand Company, 4th Battalion, 1780-1781 [Ref: N-86/105, M-231].

HOPKINS, Peter (1759-   ). Born in St. Peter's Parish, Talbot County, on September 8, 1759, a son of Peter and Sarah Hopkins [Ref: K-55]. Private, Militia, Oxford Company, 38th Battalion, 1777-1778 [Ref: N-86/105, M-227]. See "James Hopkins," q.v.

HOPKINS, Rachel. See "Woolman Gibson" and "Jonathan Hopkins," q.v.

HOPKINS, Richard. Private, Militia, Bullinbrook Company, 4th Battalion, 1780-1781 [Ref: N-86/105, M-231]. Took the Oath of Allegiance and Fidelity on or about March 1, 1778 [Ref: J-1814, N-106/114].

HOPKINS, Richard Jr. Private, Militia, Hearts of Oak Company, who was draughted on May 1, 1781 to serve until December 10, 1781 in the Maryland Continental Troops [Ref: D-370].

HOPKINS, Robert. Private in the militia who was draughted on August 30, 1781 to reinforce the American Army and to serve in the Maryland Continental Troops until December 10, 1781 [Ref: D-387].

HOPKINS, Robert. Private, Militia, Miles River Company, 38th Battalion, 1777-1778 [Ref: N-86/105, M-227]. Took the Oath of Allegiance and Fidelity on or about March 1, 1778 [Ref: J-1814, N-106/114]. Private, Militia, Miles River Company, 38th Battalion, 1780-1781 [Ref: N-86/105, M-235].

HOPKINS, Sarah. See "James Hopkins" and "Peter Hopkins," q.v.

HOPKINS, Thomas. Captain, Militia, United Company, 38th Battalion, April 9, 1778 through 1781 [Ref: N-93, N-102, M-233, M-89, E-25]. Took the Oath of Allegiance and Fidelity on or about March 1, 1778 [Ref: J-1814, N-106/114]. Paid for his recruiting services in Talbot County by the Collector of the Tax on January 13, 1780 [Ref: F-57].

HOPKINS, Thomas. Private, Militia, Third Haven Company, 4th Battalion, 1780-1781 [Ref: N-86/105, M-232].

HOPKINS, William. Private, Militia, United Company, 38th Battalion, 1777-1778 [Ref: N-86/105, M-227]. Took the Oath of Allegiance and Fidelity on or about March 1, 1778 [Ref: J-1814, N-106/114]. Private, Militia, United Company, 38th Battalion, 1780-1781 [Ref: N-86/105, M-233].

HORNEY, James. Private, Militia, Bullinbrook Company, 4th Battalion, 1780-1781 [Ref: N-86/105, M-231]. Took the Oath of Allegiance and Fidelity on or about March 1, 1778 [Ref: J-1814, N-106/114].

HORNEY, John (1749-1821). Private, Militia, Bayside Company, 38th Battalion, 1777-1778 [Ref: N-86/105, M-228, which listed the name as "Jr."]. Private, 5th Maryland Line, enlisted on June 6, 1778 and discharged on March 20, 1779 [Ref: D-213]. Private, Militia, Bayside Company, 38th Battalion, 1780-1781 [Ref: N-86/105, M-233, which listed the name as "Jr."]. John Horney was born in Maryland on March 1, 1749, married Mary Chipman, was a private in the revolution, and died in North Carolina on July 22, 1821 [Ref: Y-1485].

HORNEY, Philemon. Waterman on the barge *Intrepid* in 1781 [Ref: D-610].

HORNEY, Philip (1758-1821). Took the Oath of Allegiance and Fidelity on or about March 1, 1778 [Ref: J-1814, N-106/114]. Philip Horney was born in Maryland in 1758, married first to Sarah Manlove and second to Nancy Ann Carter, rendered patriotic service during the revolution, and died in North Carolina in 1821 [Ref: Y-1485].

HORNEY, Solomon. Private, Militia, 4th Battalion, Capt. Greenbury Goldsborough's Company, reviewed and passed July 27, 1776 [Ref: D-68]. Private, Militia, Bayside Company, 38th Battalion, 1777-1778 [Ref: N-86/105, M-228]. Private, Militia, Bayside Company, 38th Battalion, 1780-1781 [Ref: N-86/105, M-233].

HORNEY, Thomas. Private, Militia, Bayside Company, 38th Battalion, 1777-1778 [Ref: N-86/105, M-228]. Private, 5th Maryland Line, enlisted on June 6, 1778 and discharged on March 20, 1779 [Ref: D-213]. Private, Militia, Bayside Company, 38th Battalion, 1780-1781 [Ref: N-86/105, M-233, which listed the name as "Thomas Harney"].

HORNEY, William. Private, Militia, 2nd Volunteer Company, 4th Battalion, 1777-1778 [Ref: N-86/105, M-225]. Private, 5th Maryland Line, enlisted May 12, 1778 and still in service in November, 1780 [Ref: D-213]. In November, 1810, the Treasurer of Maryland was directed to pay annually to William Horney, of Talbot County, an old revolutionary soldier, a sum of money, quarterly payments, equal to half pay of a soldier during the war aforesaid, as a further remuneration to said William Horney for the services rendered his country, and as a relief from the indigence and misery which attend his decrepitude and old age. [Ref: T-356]. There was also a William Horney who was born in Maryland circa 1750-1751, married Hannah Chipman, served as a private in the revolution, and died in Ohio in 1829 [Ref: Y-1485]. Additional research will be necessary before drawing conclusions.

HUDSON, John. See "Walter Hudson," q.v.

HUDSON, Mary Anne. See "Walter Hudson," q.v.

HUDSON, Thomas. Private, Militia, Capt. Thomas Bullen's Company; no date was given; possibly late 1775 or early 1776 [Ref: Z-3].

HUDSON, Walter (1743-   ). Born in St. Peter's Parish, Talbot County, on July 27, 1743, a son of John and Mary Anne Hudson [Ref: V-81]. Took the Oath of Allegiance and Fidelity on or about March 1, 1778 [Ref: J-1814, N-106/114].

HUGGINS, Benjamin. Private, Militia, Hand & Hand Company, 4th Battalion, 1777-1778 [Ref: N-86/105, M-226].

HUGHES, Andrew. Private, 4th Independent Company of Maryland Regular Troops, Capt. James Hindman's Company, September, 1776 muster roll; enlisted January 20, 1776 [Ref: D-24].

HUGHES (HEWS), Christian. Private, Militia, Sword in Hand Company, 4th Battalion, 1777-1778 [Ref: N-86/105, M-224]. Private, Militia, Sword in Hand Company, 4th Battalion, 1780-1781 [Ref: N-86/105, M-231].

HUGHES (HUGHS), Christopher. Private, Militia, Sword in Hand Company, 4th Battalion, 1780-1781 [Ref: N-86/105, M-231].

HUGHES (HEWES), James. Private, Militia, United Company, 38th Battalion, 1777-1778 [Ref: N-86/105, M-227]. Took the Oath of Allegiance and Fidelity on or about March 1, 1778 [Ref: J-1814, N-106/114, which listed the name as "James Hewes"]. Private, Militia, United Company, 38th Battalion, 1780-1781 [Ref: N-86/105, M-233].

HUGHES (HUGHS), John. Private, 4th Independent Company of Maryland Regular Troops, Capt. James Hindman's Company; enlisted January 25, 1776; reported missing on August 27, 1776 at the Battle of Long Island [Ref: D-24]. Private, Militia, Bayside Company, 38th Battalion, 1780-1781 [Ref: N-86/105, M-233]. See "James Lloyd Chamberlaine," q.v.

HULL, Daniel. Took the Oath of Allegiance and Fidelity on or about March 1, 1778 [Ref: J-1814, N-106/114].

HULL, John. Private, Militia, Bullin Brook Company, 4th Battalion, 1777-1778 [Ref: N-86/105, M-224]. Private, Militia, Bullinbrook Company, 4th Battalion, 1780-1781 [Ref: N-86/105, M-231].
HULL, John. Private, Militia, 2nd Volunteer Company, 4th Battalion, 1777-1778 [Ref: N-86/105, M-225]. Took the Oath of Allegiance and Fidelity on or about March 1, 1778 [Ref: J-1814, N-106/114].
HULL, Nathaniel. Private, Militia, Bullin Brook Company, 4th Battalion, 1777-1778 [Ref: N-86/105, M-224]. Took the Oath of Allegiance and Fidelity on or about March 1, 1778 [Ref: J-1814, N-106/114]. Private, Militia, Bullinbrook Company, 4th Battalion, 1780-1781 [Ref: N-86/105, M-231].
HUMBEY, John. Private, 4th Independent Company of Maryland Regular Troops, Capt. James Hindman's Company, September, 1776 muster roll; enlisted February 8, 1776 [Ref: D-24].
HUMES, William. Private, Militia, 2nd Volunteer Company, 4th Battalion, 1777-1778 [Ref: N-86/105, M-224].
HUNT, George. Private, Militia, Sword in Hand Company, 4th Battalion, 1777-1778 [Ref: N-86/105, M-224]. Took the Oath of Allegiance and Fidelity on or about March 1, 1778; name listed twice [Ref: J-1814, N-106/114]. Private, Militia, Sword in Hand Company, 4th Battalion, 1780-1781 [Ref: N-86/105, M-231].
HUNT, James. Private, Militia, Broad Creek Company, 38th Battalion, 1777-1778 [Ref: N-86/105, M-226]. Took the Oath of Allegiance and Fidelity on or after March 1, 1778 [Ref: J-1814, N-106/114].
HUNT, John. Private, Militia, Volunteer Company, 4th Battalion, 1780-1781 [Ref: N-86/105, M-229].
HUNT, John. Sergeant, Militia, Broad Creek Company, 38th Battalion, 1780-1781 [Ref: N-103, M-234].
HUNT, Joseph. Private, Militia, Broad Creek Company, 38th Battalion, 1780-1781 [Ref: N-86/105, M-234].
HUNT, Margaret. See "William Jones, Jr.," q.v.
HUNT, Peter. Private, Militia, Broad Creek Company, 38th Battalion, 1777-1778 [Ref: N-86/105, M-226]. Took the Oath of Allegiance and Fidelity on or about March 1, 1778; name listed twice [Ref: J-1814, N-106/114].
HUNT, Samuel. Private, Militia, Broad Creek Company, 38th Battalion, 1777-1778 [Ref: N-86/105, M-226]. Private, Militia, Broad Creek Company, 38th Battalion, 1780-1781 [Ref: N-86/105, M-234].
HUNTER, James. Private, Militia, Capt. Thomas Bullen's Company; no date was given; possibly late 1775 or early 1776 [Ref: Z-3]. Private (substitute), Maryland Line; honorably discharged on December 3, 1781 [Ref: I-11].
HURLEY, John. Private, Militia, Bullin Brook Company, 4th Battalion, 1777-1778 [Ref: N-86/105, M-224].
HURRY, Thomas. Private, Militia, Volunteer Company, 4th Battalion, 1780-1781 [Ref: N-86/105, M-229].

HUSSAY, Woolman. Private, Militia, Volunteer Company, 4th Battalion, 1780-1781 [Ref: N-86/105, M-229].
HUTCHINGS, James. Private, Militia, Hand & Hand Company, 4th Battalion, 1777-1778 [Ref: N-86/105, M-226].
HUTCHINGS, Samuel. Private, Militia, Hand & Hand Company, 4th Battalion, 1777-1778 [Ref: N-86/105, M-225].
HUTCHINSON, John. Private, Militia, Capt. Thomas Bullen's Company; no date was given; possibly late 1775 or early 1776 [Ref: Z-3].
IMPY, Michael. Private, 5th Maryland Line, enlisted June 4, 1778 and discharged March 19, 1779 [Ref: D-219].
IRVINE, Alexander. Took the Oath of Allegiance and Fidelity on or about March 1, 1778 [Ref: J-1814, N-106/114].
IRVINE, Charles Edward. Took the Oath of Allegiance and Fidelity on or about March 1, 1778 [Ref: J-1814, N-106/114].
JACKSON, Edward. Private, Militia, Volunteer Company, 4th Battalion, 1780-1781 [Ref: N-86/105, M-229].
JACKSON, Isaac. Took the Oath of Allegiance and Fidelity on or after March 1, 1778 [Ref: J-1814, N-106/114].
JACKSON, Jacob. Gunner on the barge *Fearnought* under Capt. Levin Spedden in 1782 [Ref: D-613].
JACKSON, James. Private, Militia, 2nd Volunteer Company, 4th Battalion, 1777-1778 [Ref: N-86/105, M-224]. Took the Oath of Allegiance and Fidelity on or about March 1, 1778 [Ref: J-1814, N-106/114].
JACKSON, John. Private, Militia, Union Company, 4th Battalion, 1777-1778 [Ref: N-86/105, M-223]. Private, Militia, Union Company, 4th Battalion, 1780-1781 [Ref: N-86/105, M-230]. Rendered patriotic service by hauling provisions for the use of the Army in June, 1778 [Ref: P-176].
JACKSON, Joseph. Private, 4th Independent Company of Maryland Regular Troops, Capt. James Hindman's Company, September, 1776 muster roll; enlisted January 28, 1776 [Ref: D-24].
JACKSON, Thomas. Private, Militia, Hand & Hand Company, 4th Battalion, 1777-1778 [Ref: N-86/105, M-226]. Took the Oath of Allegiance and Fidelity on or about March 1, 1778 [Ref: J-1814, N-106/114].
JACKSON, William. Private, Militia, Wye Company, 4th Battalion, 1780-1781 [Ref: N-86/105, M-229]. Took the Oath of Allegiance and Fidelity on or about March 1, 1778 [Ref: J-1814, N-106/114].
JACOBS, John. Took the Oath of Allegiance and Fidelity on or about March 1, 1778 [Ref: J-1814, N-106/114].
JACOBS, John Jr. Private aboard the barge *Fearnought* under Capt. Levin Spedden; enlisted May 28, 1782; 5'6" tall; dark complexion; born in Talbot County [Ref: D-611].
JACOBS, Levin. Private, Militia, Union Company, 4th Battalion, 1780-1781 [Ref: N-86/105, M-230]. Waterman on the barge *Intrepid* in 1781 [Ref: D-610].

JADVIN, Robert. Private, Militia, Hand in Hand Company, 4th Battalion, 1780-1781 [Ref: N-86/105, M-232].
JADVIN, Thomas. Private, Militia, Hand in Hand Company, 4th Battalion, 1780-1781 [Ref: N-86/105, M-232].
JAMES, Alexander. Private, Militia, Oxford Company, 38th Battalion, 1777-1778 [Ref: N-86/105, M-228]. Took the Oath of Allegiance and Fidelity on or after March 1, 1778 [Ref: J-1814, N-106/114]. Private, Militia, Oxford Company, 38th Battalion, 1780-1781 [Ref: N-86/105, M-235].
JAMES, Joseph. Private, Militia, Capt. Thomas Bullen's Company; no date was given; possibly late 1775 or early 1776 [Ref: Z-3].
JAMES, Obediah. Private, Militia, Capt. Thomas Bullen's Company; no date was given; possibly late 1775 or early 1776 [Ref: Z-3].
JAMES, Robert. Private, Militia, Capt. Thomas Bullen's Company; no date was given; possibly late 1775 or early 1776 [Ref: Z-3].
JAMES, Solomon. Ensign, Militia, 4th Battalion, May 16, 1776 [Ref: M-92, A-428].
JEFFERS, Jacob. Private, 4th Independent Company of Maryland Regular Troops, Capt. James Hindman's Company, September, 1776 muster roll; enlisted January 28, 1776 [Ref: D-24].
JEFFERS, Peter. Private, 4th Independent Company of Maryland Regular Troops, Capt. James Hindman's Company, September, 1776 muster roll; enlisted January 27, 1776 [Ref: D-24].
JEFFERS, Reuben. Private, 4th Independent Company of Maryland Regular Troops, Capt. James Hindman's Company, September, 1776 muster roll; enlisted January 28, 1776 [Ref: D-24].
JEFFERSON, George. Private, Militia, Broad Creek Company, 38th Battalion, 1780-1781 [Ref: N-86/105, M-234].
JEFFERSON, James. Private, Militia, United Company, 38th Battalion, 1777-1778 [Ref: N-86/105, M-227]. Private, Militia, Broad Creek Company, 38th Battalion, 1780-1781 [Ref: N-86/105, M-234].
JEFFERSON, Thomas. Private, Militia, Broad Creek Company, 38th Battalion, 1777-1778 [Ref: N-86/105, M-226, which listed the name as "Thomas Jepherson"]. Private, Militia, Broad Creek Company, 38th Battalion, 1780-1781; name listed twice [Ref: N-86/105, M-234].
JEFFERSON (JEFFERNON?), Robert. Private, Militia, Hand & Hand Company, 4th Battalion, 1777-1778 [Ref: N-86/105, M-226].
JENKENSON, John. Private, Militia, Wye Company, 4th Battalion, 1777-1778 [Ref: N-86/105, M-223].
JENKINS, George. Private, Militia, Capt. Thomas Bullen's Company; no date was given; possibly late 1775 or early 1776 [Ref: Z-3]. Private, Militia, Volunteer Company, 4th Battalion, 1777-1778 [Ref: N-86/105, M-223]. Took the Oath of Allegiance and Fidelity on or about March 1, 1778 [Ref: J-1814, N-

106/114]. Private, Militia, Volunteer Company, 4th Battalion, 1780-1781 [Ref: N-86/105, M-230].
JENKINS, John. Private, Militia, Union Company, 4th Battalion, 1780-1781 [Ref: N-86/105, M-230].
JENKINS, Joseph. Private (substitute), 5th Maryland Line, enlisted March 16, 1777; honorably discharged on March 16, 1780 or December 3, 1781, both dates were given [Ref: I-11, D-218]. There may have been two men with this name. Additional research will be necessary before drawing conclusions.
JENKINS, Matthew. Private, Militia, Capt. Thomas Bullen's Company; no date was given; possibly late 1775 or early 1776 [Ref: Z-3].
JENKINS, Matthew Lewis. Took the Oath of Allegiance and Fidelity on or after March 1, 1778 [Ref: J-1814, N-106/114].
JENKINS, Samuel. Private, Militia, Capt. Thomas Bullen's Company; no date was given; possibly late 1775 or early 1776 [Ref: Z-3]. Private, Militia, Third Haven Company, 4th Battalion, 1777-1778 [Ref: N-86/105, M-225]. Private, 5th Maryland Line, enlisted on February 18, 1777 and transferred out on October 1, 1779, "not heard of since." [Ref: D-218]. Private, Militia, Third Haven Company, 4th Battalion, 1780-1781 [Ref: N-86/105, M-232]. Draughted on May 1, 1781 to serve until December 10, 1781 in the Maryland Continental Troops [Ref: D-371]. There may be more then one man with this name. Additional research will be necessary before drawing conclusions.
JENKINS, Thomas. Second Lieutenant, Militia, [72nd?] Volunteer Company, April 9, 1778 [Ref: M-92, E-24]. Took the Oath of Allegiance and Fidelity on or about March 1, 1778 [Ref: J-1814, N-106/114].
JENKINS, Thomas Jr. Took the Oath of Allegiance and Fidelity on or about March 1, 1778 [Ref: J-1814, N-106/114].
JENKINS, Walter. Ensign, Militia, Bullinbrook Company, 4th Battalion, December 3, 1779 through 1781 [Ref: N-99, M-231, M-92, F-28]. Took the Oath of Allegiance and Fidelity on or about March 1, 1778; name listed twice [Ref: J-1814, N-106/114].
JENKINS, William. Private, 4th Independent Company of Maryland Regular Troops, Capt. James Hindman's Company, September, 1776 muster roll; enlisted January 22, 1776 [Ref: D-24].
JOB, Thomas. Took the Oath of Allegiance and Fidelity on or about March 1, 1778 [Ref: J-1814, N-106/114].
JOHNS, Benjamin (1746-1791). Son of Benjamin Johns and Rachel Harris, of Calvert County (Quakers), he was a cabinetmaker and apparently moved to Talbot County with his brother Richard by 1771 [Ref: R-490]. Private, Militia, Sword in Hand Company, 4th Battalion, 1780-1781 [Ref: N-86/105, M-231]. See "Richard Johns," q.v.
JOHNS, Elizabeth. See "James Tilghman," q.v.
JOHNS, Margaret. See "Richard Johns," q.v.

JOHNS, Richard (1748-1796). Son of Benjamin Johns and Rachel Harris, of Calvert County (Quakers), he apparently removed to Talbot County with his brother Benjamin by 1771. He allied himself with the Anglicans of that county and married first to Mary Comerford by 1773 and second to Margaret ----. His only child Benjamin Franklin Johns (1778-1797) left Maryland for Kentucky a few months before his death [Ref: R-490]. Richard served in the Maryland Lower House, 1779-1780, as a Court Justice between 1777 and 1795, Justice of the Orphans Court, 1779-1789 [Ref: R-82, R-490, E-250, I-46]. First Lieutenant, Militia, Hand in Hand Company, 4th Battalion, April 9, 1778. Captain, November 4, 1782 [Ref: N-91, N-101, M-232, M-92, E-24, I-298]. Took the Oath of Allegiance and Fidelity on or about March 1, 1778 [Ref: J-1814, N-106/114]. Appointed a Justice of the Peace on July 22, 1778 [Ref: E-163].

JOHNSON, Henry. Private, Militia, Sword in Hand Company, 4th Battalion, 1777-1778 [Ref: N-86/105, M-224]. Took the Oath of Allegiance and Fidelity on or about March 1, 1778 [Ref: J-1814, N-106/114].

JOHNSON, Henry Jr. Private, Militia, Sword in Hand Company, 4th Battalion, 1780-1781 [Ref: N-86/105, M-231].

JOHNSON, John. Private, Militia, Capt. Thomas Bullen's Company; no date was given; possibly late 1775 or early 1776 [Ref: Z-3]. Private, Militia, Volunteer Company, 4th Battalion, 1777-1778 [Ref: N-86/105, M-223]. Took the Oath of Allegiance and Fidelity on or about March 1, 1778 [Ref: J-1814, N-106/114]. Private, Militia, Volunteer Company, 4th Battalion, 1780-1781 [Ref: N-86/105, M-230].

JOHNSON, John Jr. Private, Militia, Bullin Brook Company, 4th Battalion, 1777-1778 [Ref: N-86/105, M-224].

JOHNSON, Randel. Private, Militia, Capt. Thomas Bullen's Company; no date was given; possibly late 1775 or early 1776 [Ref: Z-3].

JOHNSON, Randolph. First Lieutenant, Militia, 4th Battalion, April 9, 1778. Captain, Militia, Bullinbrook Company, 4th Battalion, December 3, 1779 through 1781 [Ref: N-99, M-231, M-93, E-24, F-28]. Took the Oath of Allegiance and Fidelity on or about March 1, 1778 [Ref: J-1814, N-106/114].

JOHNSON, Thomas. Private, Militia, Capt. Thomas Bullen's Company; no date was given; possibly late 1775 or early 1776 [Ref: Z-3]. Took the Oath of Allegiance and Fidelity on or about March 1, 1778 [Ref: J-1814, N-106/114].

JOHNSON, Thomas. Took the Oath of Allegiance and Fidelity on or about March 1, 1778 [Ref: J-1814, N-106/114].

JONES, Benjamin. See "William Jones, Jr.," q.v.

JONES, Christian. See "John Jones," q.v.

JONES, David (1743-   ). Born in St. Peter's Parish, Talbot County, on November 19, 1743, a son of John and Mary Jones [Ref: V-80]. Private, Militia, Bullin Brook Company, 4th Battalion, 1777-1778 [Ref: N-86/105, M-224]. Took the Oath of Allegiance and Fidelity on or about March 1, 1778 [Ref: J-1814, N-

106/114]. Private, Militia, Bullinbrook Company, 4th Battalion, 1780-1781 [Ref: N-86/105, M-231].

JONES, Edward. Private, Militia, 4th Battalion, Capt. Greenbury Goldsborough's Company, reviewed and passed July 27, 1776 [Ref: D-68].

JONES, Eliza Ann. See "William Jones, Jr.," q.v.

JONES, Elizabeth. See "Richard Jones" and "Solomon Jones" and "Thomas Jones," q.v.

JONES, Evin (Evan). Private, Militia, Bullin Brook Company, 4th Battalion, 1777-1778 [Ref: N-86/105, M-224]. Took the Oath of Allegiance and Fidelity on or about March 1, 1778 [Ref: J-1814, N-106/114]. Private, Militia, Bullinbrook Company, 4th Battalion, 1780-1781 [Ref: N-86/105, M-231].

JONES, James. Private, 4th Independent Company of Maryland Regular Troops, Capt. James Hindman's Company, September, 1776 muster roll; enlisted January 22, 1776 [Ref: D-24].

JONES, James. Private, Militia, Bayside Company, 38th Battalion, 1777-1778 [Ref: N-86/105, M-228]. Private, Militia, Bayside Company, 38th Battalion, 1780-1781 [Ref: N-86/105, M-233].

JONES, James. Private, Militia, Broad Creek Company, 38th Battalion, 1777-1778 [Ref: N-86/105, M-226]. Private, Militia, Broad Creek Company, 38th Battalion, 1780-1781 [Ref: N-86/105, M-234].

JONES, James. Private, Militia, Wye Company, 4th Battalion, 1780-1781 [Ref: N-86/105, M-228].

JONES, James. Sergeant, Militia, Bullinbrook Company, 4th Battalion, 1780-1781 [Ref: M-231].

JONES, James. Took the Oath of Allegiance and Fidelity on or after March 1, 1778 [Ref: J-1814, N-106/114].

JONES, James (of John). Took the Oath of Allegiance and Fidelity on or after March 1, 1778 [Ref: J-1814, N-106/114].

JONES, James Sr. Took the Oath of Allegiance and Fidelity on or about March 1, 1778 [Ref: J-1814, N-106/114].

JONES, John. Private, Militia, Capt. Thomas Bullen's Company; no date was given; possibly late 1775 or early 1776 [Ref: Z-3]. Private, Militia, Bayside Company, 38th Battalion, 1777-1778 [Ref: N-86/105, M-228]. Took the Oath of Allegiance and Fidelity on or about March 1, 1778 [Ref: J-1814, N-106/114]. Private, Militia, Bayside Company, 38th Battalion, 1780-1781 [Ref: N-86/105, M-233]. One John Jones, son of John and Mary Jones, was born in St. Peter's Parish, Talbot County, on February 21, 1730. Another John Jones, son of John and Christian Jones, was born on April 28, 1732. And another John Jones, son of John Jones of Bullenbrook and Rachel his wife, was born on April 13, 1743 [Ref: V-68, V-83, V-88]. Since there were several men with this name, additional research will be necessary before drawing conclusions. See "Richard Jones" and "Solomon Jones" and "Thomas Jones" and "David Jones," q.v.

JONES, John. Private, Militia, Wye Company, 4th Battalion, 1777-1778 [Ref: N-86/105, M-222]. Took the Oath of Allegiance and Fidelity on or about March 1, 1778 [Ref: J-1814, N-106/114].
JONES, John. Private, Militia, Union Company, 4th Battalion, 1777-1778 [Ref: N-86/105, M-223]. Took the Oath of Allegiance and Fidelity on or about March 1, 1778 [Ref: J-1814, N-106/114].
JONES, John (Tanner). Private, Militia, Capt. Thomas Bullen's Company; no date was given; possibly late 1775 or early 1776 [Ref: Z-3].
JONES, Joseph. Private, Militia, Third Haven Company, 4th Battalion, 1777-1778 [Ref: N-86/105, M-225]. Took the Oath of Allegiance and Fidelity on or about March 1, 1778 [Ref: J-1814, N-106/114].
JONES, Levi. See "William Jones, Jr.," q.v.
JONES, Margaret. See "William Jones, Jr.," q.v.
JONES, Mary. See "John Jones" and "David Jones," q.v.
JONES, Matilda. See "William Jones, Jr.," q.v.
JONES, Pierce. Private, Militia, Volunteer Company, 4th Battalion, 1780-1781 [Ref: N-86/105, M-230].
JONES, Rachel. See "John Jones," q.v.
JONES, Richard. Private, Militia, Sword in Hand Company, 4th Battalion, 1777-1778 [Ref: N-86/105, M-224]. Took the Oath of Allegiance and Fidelity on or about March 1, 1778 [Ref: J-1814, N-106/114]. Private, Militia, Sword in Hand Company, 4th Battalion, 1780-1781 [Ref: N-86/105, M-231]. One Richard Jones, a son of John and Elizabeth Jones, was born in St. Peter's Parish, Talbot County, on November 6, 1734 [Ref: V-88].
JONES, Robert. Private, Militia, Broad Creek Company, 38th Battalion, 1777-1778 [Ref: N-86/105, M-226]. Took the Oath of Allegiance and Fidelity on or after March 1, 1778 [Ref: J-1814, N-106/114].
JONES, Robert Jr. Private, Militia, Broad Creek Company, 38th Battalion, 1780-1781 [Ref: N-86/105, M-234].
JONES, Rubin. Private, Militia, Broad Creek Company, 38th Battalion, 1780-1781 [Ref: N-86/105, M-234].
JONES, Solomon. Paid £6 10s. by the Maryland Council of Safety on October 12, 1776, "for collecting & ascertaining the number of souls in Talbot County." [Ref: B-337]. Private, Militia, Bullin Brook Company, 4th Battalion, 1777-1778 [Ref: N-86/105, M-224]. Private, Militia, Third Haven Company, 4th Battalion, 1780-1781 [Ref: N-86/105, M-232]. One Solomon Jones was born in St. Peter's Parish, Talbot County, on May 29, 1741, a son of John and Elizabeth Jones [Ref: V-88].
JONES, Solomon Jr. Took the Oath of Allegiance and Fidelity on or after March 1, 1778 [Ref: J-1814, N-106/114].
JONES, Thomas. Private, Militia, Hearts of Oak Company, 38th Battalion, 1780-1781 [Ref: N-86/105, M-234].

JONES, Thomas. Private, Militia, Third Haven Company, 4th Battalion, 1780-1781 [Ref: N-86/105, M-232].

JONES, Thomas. Private who enlisted on March 20, 1781 to serve 3 years in the Maryland Continental Troops [Ref: D-371].

JONES, Thomas. Took the Oath of Allegiance and Fidelity on or about March 1, 1778 [Ref: J-1814, N-106/114]. One Thomas Jones was born in St. Peter's Parish, Talbot County, on January 21, 1743, a son of John and Elizabeth Jones [Ref: V-88].

JONES, William. Private, Militia, Broad Creek Company, 38th Battalion, 1777-1778 [Ref: N-86/105, M-227]. Private, Militia, Broad Creek Company, 38th Battalion, 1780-1781 [Ref: N-86/105, M-234].

JONES, William Jr. Private, Militia, Broad Creek Company, 38th Battalion, 1777-1778 [Ref: N-86/105, M-226, which listed the name without the "Jr."]. Private, Militia, Broad Creek Company, 38th Battalion, 1780-1781 [Ref: N-86/105, M-234]. Draughted on May 1, 1781 to serve until December 10, 1781 in the Maryland Continental Troops [Ref: D-370]. William Jones married Margaret Hunt in Talbot County in January, 1791, and died in November, 1822. Margaret Jones, widow, applied for a pension (W4248) in Baltimore City on September 20, 1842, age 75, stating that William lived in Talbot County at the time of his enlistment in the Maryland Line. Their children were Matilda, Eliza Ann, Benjamin, Levi and William, and they had 20 grandchildren (not named) in 1842 [Ref: W-1884].

JORDAN, Absolom. Private, Militia, Capt. Thomas Bullen's Company; no date was given; possibly late 1775 or early 1776 [Ref: Z-3].

JORDAN, Thomas. Private, Militia, Union Company, 4th Battalion, 1777-1778 [Ref: N-86/105, M-223]. Took the Oath of Allegiance and Fidelity on or about March 1, 1778 [Ref: J-1814, N-106/114].

JUDAN, Nathaniel. Private, Militia, Capt. Thomas Bullen's Company; no date was given; possibly late 1775 or early 1776 [Ref: Z-3].

JUMP, Jacob. Took the Oath of Allegiance and Fidelity on or about March 1, 1778 [Ref: J-1814, N-106/114].

KEARSE, James. Private in the militia who was draughted on August 30, 1781 to reinforce the American Army and to serve in the Maryland Continental Troops until December 10, 1781 [Ref: D-387].

KEES (KEER?), Thomas. Private, Militia, Oxford Company, 38th Battalion, 1777-1778 [Ref: N-86/105, M-228]. Private, Militia, Hearts of Oak Company, 38th Battalion, 1780-1781 [Ref: N-86/105, M-234].

KEETS, John. Took the Oath of Allegiance and Fidelity on or after March 1, 1778 [Ref: J-1814, N-106/114].

KEITHLY (KEETHLY, KEATHLY), Jacob. Private, Militia, Broad Creek Company, 38th Battalion, 1777-1778 [Ref: N-86/105, M-227]. Private, Militia, Miles River Company, 38th Battalion, 1780-1781 [Ref: N-86/105, M-235].

KEITHLY (KEATHLY), James. Private, Militia, Hearts of Oak Company, 38th Battalion, 1777-1778 [Ref: N-86/105, M-226]. Private, Militia, Hearts of Oak Company, 38th Battalion, 1780-1781 [Ref: N-86/105, M-234].

KELLY, Roger. Private, Militia, 4th Battalion, Capt. Greenbury Goldsborough's Company, reviewed and passed July 27, 1776 [Ref: D-67]. Private, Militia, Third Haven Company, 4th Battalion, 1780-1781 [Ref: N-86/105, M-232].

KELSOE, Ellen or Eleanor. See "Henry Lowe," q.v.

KEMP, Benjamin. Sergeant, Militia, Third Haven Company, 4th Battalion, 1780-1781 [Ref: M-232]. Took the Oath of Allegiance and Fidelity on or after March 1, 1778 [Ref: J-1814, N-106/114].

KEMP, Benjamin. Private, Militia, Bayside Company, 38th Battalion, 1777-1778 [Ref: N-86/105, M-228]. Took the Oath of Allegiance and Fidelity on or about March 1, 1778 [Ref: J-1814, N-106/114].

KEMP, Benjamin Jr. Private, Militia, Bayside Company, 38th Battalion, 1780-1781 [Ref: N-86/105, M-233].

KEMP, Elizabeth. See "James Ball," q.v.

KEMP, Henry. Took the Oath of Allegiance and Fidelity on or about March 1, 1778 [Ref: J-1814, N-106/114].

KEMP, James Jr. Private, Militia, Hand & Hand Company, 4th Battalion, 1777-1778 [Ref: N-86/105, M-226]. Private, Militia, Hand in Hand Company, 4th Battalion, 1780-1781 [Ref: N-86/105, M-232].

KEMP, John. Private, Militia, Hand & Hand Company, 4th Battalion, 1777-1778 [Ref: N-86/105, M-226]. Private, Militia, Hand in Hand Company, 4th Battalion, 1780-1781 [Ref: N-86/105, M-232].

KEMP, Joseph. Private, Militia, Bayside Company, 38th Battalion, 1777-1778; name listed twice [Ref: N-86/105, M-228]. Private, Militia, Bayside Company, 38th Battalion, 1780-1781 [Ref: N-86/105, M-233].

KEMP, Joseph. Private, Militia, Third Haven Company, 4th Battalion, 1777-1778 [Ref: N-86/105, M-225]. Private, Militia, Third Haven Company, 4th Battalion, 1780-1781 [Ref: N-86/105, M-232].

KEMP, Joseph Jr. Took the Oath of Allegiance and Fidelity on or after March 1, 1778 [Ref: J-1814, N-106/114].

KEMP, Joseph (of John). Took the Oath of Allegiance and Fidelity on or after March 1, 1778 [Ref: J-1814, N-106/114].

KEMP, Quinton. Private, Militia, Third Haven Company, 4th Battalion, 1777-1778 [Ref: N-86/105, M-225].

KEMP, Robert. Private, Militia, Third Haven Company, who was draughted on May 1, 1781 to serve until December 10, 1781 in the Maryland Continental Troops [Ref: D-371].

KEMP, Sophia. See "Joseph Dawson," q.v.

KEMP, Thomas. Private, Militia, Hearts of Oak Company, 38th Battalion, 1777-1778 [Ref: N-86/105, M-226]. Took the Oath of Allegiance and Fidelity on or

about March 1, 1778 [Ref: J-1814, N-106/114]. Private, Militia, Hearts of Oak Company, 38th Battalion, 1780-1781 [Ref: N-86/105, M-235].
KEMP, William. Private, Militia, Wye Company, 4th Battalion, 1780-1781 [Ref: N-86/105, M-229].
KENDALL, Thomas. Private, Militia, Hand in Hand Company, 4th Battalion, 1780-1781 [Ref: N-86/105, M-232].
KENDRICK (KINDRICK), James. Private, Militia, 2nd Volunteer Company, 4th Battalion, 1777-1778 [Ref: N-86/105, M-224]. Draughted on May 1, 1781 to serve until December 10, 1781 in the Maryland Continental Troops [Ref: D-371].
KENNARD, Joshua (Certificate from Queen Anne's County). Took the Oath of Allegiance and Fidelity on or about March 1, 1778 [Ref: J-1814, N-106/114].
KENNEDY, James. Private, Militia, 2nd Volunteer Company, 4th Battalion, 1777-1778 [Ref: N-86/105, M-225, which listed the name as "James Kennday"]. Took the Oath of Allegiance and Fidelity on or about March 1, 1778 [Ref: J-1814, N-106/114]. Private (substitute), Militia, Volunteer Company, 4th Battalion, 1780-1781 [Ref: N-86/105, M-229].
KENNEY, William. Private, 4th Independent Company of Maryland Regular Troops, Capt. James Hindman's Company, September, 1776 muster roll; enlisted January 26(?), 1776 [Ref: D-24].
KENT, John. Private, Militia, Capt. Thomas Bullen's Company; no date was given; possibly late 1775 or early 1776 [Ref: Z-3].
KERR, David. Private, Militia, Oxford Company, 38th Battalion, 1777-1778 [Ref: N-86/105, M-228].
KERSEY, Brian. Private, 3rd Maryland Line, 1777 [Ref: D-129].
KERSEY, John. Private, Militia, Capt. Thomas Bullen's Company; no date was given; possibly late 1775 or early 1776 [Ref: Z-3]. Sergeant, Militia, Bayside Company, 38th Battalion, 1780-1781 [Ref: N-102, M-233]. Took the Oath of Allegiance and Fidelity on or after March 1, 1778 [Ref: J-1814, N-106/114]. See "Henry Banning," q.v.
KERSEY (KERSY), John. Private, Militia, Union Company, 4th Battalion, 1777-1778 [Ref: N-86/105, M-223]. Private, Militia, Union Company, 4th Battalion, 1780-1781 [Ref: N-86/105, M-230].
KERSEY, Peter. Took the Oath of Allegiance and Fidelity on or about March 1, 1778 [Ref: J-1814, N-106/114].
KEY, Francis Scott. See "Edward Lloyd," q.v.
KEYS, Thomas. Private, Militia, Miles River Company, 38th Battalion, 1777-1778 [Ref: N-86/105, M-227]. Took the Oath of Allegiance and Fidelity on or about March 1, 1778 [Ref: J-1814, N-106/114].
KIEGHLEY, James. Took the Oath of Allegiance and Fidelity on or about March 1, 1778 [Ref: J-1814, N-106/114].
KING, Thomas. Private, Militia, Union Company, 4th Battalion, 1777-1778 [Ref: N-86/105, M-223]. Private, Militia, Union Company, 4th Battalion, 1780-1781

[Ref: N-86/105, M-230]. Took the Oath of Allegiance and Fidelity on or about March 1, 1778 [Ref: J-1814, N-106/114].
KINNARD, Ebenezer. Private, Militia, Wye Company, 4th Battalion, 1777-1778 [Ref: N-86/105, M-222]. Took the Oath of Allegiance and Fidelity on or about March 1, 1778 [Ref: J-1814, N-106/114]. Private, Militia, Volunteer Company, 4th Battalion, 1780-1781 [Ref: N-86/105, M-229].
KINNARD, James. Private, Militia, Wye Company, 4th Battalion, 1780-1781 [Ref: N-86/105, M-229]. Draughted on May 1, 1781 to serve until December 10, 1781 in the Maryland Continental Troops [Ref: D-371].
KINNARD, Joshua. Private, Militia, Wye Company, 4th Battalion, 1777-1778 [Ref: N-86/105, M-222]. Private (substitute), Militia, Wye Company, 4th Battalion, 1780-1781 [Ref: N-86/105, M-229].
KINNARD, Richard. Private, Militia, Wye Company, 4th Battalion, 1780-1781 [Ref: N-86/105, M-228].
KINNEMONT (KENNEMENT, KINNIMONT), Hopkins. Private, Militia, Miles River Company, 38th Battalion, 1777-1778 [Ref: N-86/105, M-227]. Took the Oath of Allegiance and Fidelity on or about March 1, 1778 [Ref: J-1814, N-106/114].
KINNEMONT, John. Private, Militia, United Company, 38th Battalion, 1780-1781 [Ref: N-86/105, M-233].
KINNEMONT, Philip. Private, Militia, Volunteer Company, 4th Battalion, 1780-1781 [Ref: N-86/105, M-229].
KINNEMONT (KINNERNET?), Solomon. Private, Militia, Miles River Company, 2nd Class, 38th Battalion, 1777-1778 [Ref: N-86/105, M-227].
KINNEMONT (KINNIMONT), Solomon. Private, Militia, Miles River Company, 4th Class, 38th Battalion, 1777-1778 [Ref: N-86/105, M-227].
KINNEMONT (KININMONT), Solomon. Took the Oath of Allegiance and Fidelity on or about March 1, 1778 [Ref: J-1814, N-106/114].
KIRBY (KERBY), Aaron (c1755/1760-1826). Private, Militia, 2nd Volunteer Company, 4th Battalion, 1777-1778 [Ref: N-86/105, M-225]. Private, Militia, Volunteer Company, 4th Battalion, 1780-1781 [Ref: N-86/105, M-229]. Abner Kirby was born circa 1755-1760, married Rebecca ----, served as a private in the revolution, and died before December 5, 1826 in Maryland [Ref: Y-1694].
KIRBY (KERBY), Abner. Private, Militia, Hand & Hand Company, 4th Battalion, 1777-1778 [Ref: N-86/105, M-226]. Private, Militia, Hand in Hand Company, 4th Battalion, 1780-1781 [Ref: N-86/105, M-232].
KIRBY (KERBY), Anthony. Private, Militia, Hearts of Oak Company, 38th Battalion, 1777-1778 [Ref: N-86/105, M-226]. Took the Oath of Allegiance and Fidelity on or about March 1, 1778 [Ref: J-1814, N-106/114]. Private, Militia, Hearts of Oak Company, 38th Battalion, 1780-1781 [Ref: N-86/105, M-234]. Draughted on May 1, 1781 to serve until December 10, 1781 in the Maryland Continental Troops [Ref: D-370].

KIRBY, Benjamin. Private, Militia, Hand & Hand Company, 4th Battalion, 1777-1778 [Ref: N-86/105, M-225]. Took the Oath of Allegiance and Fidelity on or after March 1, 1778 [Ref: J-1814, N-106/114].

KIRBY (KERBY), Benjamin. Private, Militia, Sword in Hand Company, 4th Battalion, 1777-1778 [Ref: N-86/105, M-224]. Private, Militia, Sword in Hand Company, 4th Battalion, 1780-1781 [Ref: N-86/105, M-231]. Took the Oath of Allegiance and Fidelity on or about March 1, 1778 [Ref: J-1814, N-106/114].

KIRBY (KERBY), Benjamin. Private, Militia, Hearts of Oak Company, 38th Battalion, 1780-1781 [Ref: N-86/105, M-235]. Took the Oath of Allegiance and Fidelity on or about March 1, 1778 [Ref: J-1814, N-106/114].

KIRBY, Bill. See "David Kirby," q.v.

KIRBY (KERBY), Cloudsberry (Cloudsbury). Private, Militia, Sword in Hand Company, 4th Battalion, 1777-1778 [Ref: N-86/105, M-224]. Private, Militia, Sword in Hand Company, 4th Battalion, 1780-1781 [Ref: N-86/105, M-231]. Took the Oath of Allegiance and Fidelity on or about March 1, 1778 [Ref: J-1814, N-106/114].

KIRBY (KERBY), Cloudsbury. Private, Militia, Hearts of Oak Company, 38th Battalion, 1780-1781 [Ref: N-86/105, M-234]. Took the Oath of Allegiance and Fidelity on or after March 1, 1778 [Ref: J-1814, N-106/114].

KIRBY (KERBY), Daniel. Private, Militia, 2nd Volunteer Company, 4th Battalion, 1777-1778 [Ref: N-86/105, M-225]. Private, Militia, Volunteer Company, 4th Battalion, 1780-1781 [Ref: N-86/105, M-229].

KIRBY (KERBY), David. Private, Militia, 2nd Volunteer Company, 4th Battalion, 1777-1778 [Ref: N-86/105, M-225]. Took the Oath of Allegiance and Fidelity on or after March 1, 1778 [Ref: J-1814, N-106/114]. Private, Militia, Hand in Hand Company, 4th Battalion, 1780-1781 [Ref: N-86/105, M-232].

KIRBY, David (of Bill). Private, Militia, Volunteer Company, 4th Battalion, 1780-1781 [Ref: N-86/105, M-229].

KIRBY (KERBY), Emory. Private, Militia, Hearts of Oak Company, 38th Battalion, 1777-1778 [Ref: N-86/105, M-226]. Private, Militia, Union Company, 4th Battalion, 1780-1781 [Ref: N-86/105, M-230].

KIRBY, Hinson (Hynson). Took the Oath of Allegiance and Fidelity on or about March 1, 1778; name listed twice [Ref: J-1814, N-106/114].

KIRBY (KERBY), John. Private, Militia, 2nd Volunteer Company, 4th Battalion, 1777-1778 [Ref: N-86/105, M-224]. Private, Militia, Volunteer Company, 4th Battalion, 1780-1781 [Ref: N-86/105, M-229].

KIRBY (KERBY), John. Private, Militia, United Company, 38th Battalion, 1780-1781 [Ref: N-86/105, M-233]. Private in the militia who was draughted on August 30, 1781 to reinforce the American Army and to serve in the Maryland Continental Troops until December 10, 1781 [Ref: D-387].

KIRBY, John. Seaman whose name appears on "a list of men blown up in the barges" in 1782 [Ref: D-615].

KIRBY, John. Took the Oath of Allegiance and Fidelity on or after March 1, 1778 [Ref: J-1814, N-106/114].
KIRBY (KERBY), John Jr. Private, Militia, Sword in Hand Company, 4th Battalion, 1777-1778 [Ref: N-86/105, M-224]. Private, Militia, Sword in Hand Company, 4th Battalion, 1780-1781 [Ref: N-86/105, M-231].
KIRBY (KERBY), Lambert. Private, Militia, Sword in Hand Company, 4th Battalion, 1777-1778 [Ref: N-86/105, M-224]. Private, Militia, Volunteer Company, 4th Battalion, 1780-1781 [Ref: N-86/105, M-229]. Took the Oath of Allegiance and Fidelity on or about March 1, 1778 [Ref: J-1814, N-106/114].
KIRBY (KERBY), Lambert Jr. Took the Oath of Allegiance and Fidelity on or about March 1, 1778 [Ref: J-1814, N-106/114]. Private, Militia, Sword in Hand Company, 4th Battalion, 1780-1781 [Ref: N-86/105, M-231].
KIRBY, Michael. Took the Oath of Allegiance and Fidelity on or about March 1, 1778; name listed twice [Ref: J-1814, N-106/114].
KIRBY (KERBY), Michael Jr. Private, Militia, Sword in Hand Company, 4th Battalion, 1777-1778 [Ref: N-86/105, M-224]. Private, Militia, Sword in Hand Company, 4th Battalion, 1780-1781 [Ref: N-86/105, M-231].
KIRBY (KERBY), Morris. Private, Militia, 2nd Volunteer Company, 4th Battalion, 1777-1778 [Ref: N-86/105, M-225]. Private, Militia, Volunteer Company, 4th Battalion, 1780-1781 [Ref: N-86/105, M-229].
KIRBY (KERBY), Moses. Private, Militia, Hand & Hand Company, 4th Battalion, 1777-1778 [Ref: N-86/105, M-225]. Private, Militia, Hand in Hand Company, 4th Battalion, 1780-1781 [Ref: N-86/105, M-232].
KIRBY (KERBY), Nathan. Private, Militia, Sword in Hand Company, 4th Battalion, 1777-1778 [Ref: N-86/105, M-224]. Took the Oath of Allegiance and Fidelity on or about March 1, 1778; name listed twice [Ref: J-1814, N-106/114]. Private, Militia, Sword in Hand Company, 4th Battalion, 1780-1781 [Ref: N-86/105, M-231]. One "Nathaniel Kerby" was a private in the 5th Maryland Line who enlisted on June 6, 1778 and was in service until February, 1779, "not heard of." [Ref: D-221]. Additional research may be necessary before drawing conclusions.
KIRBY (KERBY), Parrott (Parot). Private, Militia, 2nd Volunteer Company, 4th Battalion, 1777-1778 [Ref: N-86/105, M-225]. Took the Oath of Allegiance and Fidelity on or about March 1, 1778 [Ref: J-1814, N-106/114].
KIRBY, Rebecca. See "Abner Kirby," q.v.
KIRBY, Richard. Private, Militia, Volunteer Company, 4th Battalion, 1780-1781 [Ref: N-86/105, M-229].
KIRBY (KERBY), Richard. Private, Militia, Hand in Hand Company, 4th Battalion, 1780-1781 [Ref: N-86/105, M-232].
KIRBY (KERBY), Robert Jr. Private, Militia, Hand & Hand Company, 4th Battalion, 1777-1778 [Ref: N-86/105, M-225].

KIRBY (KERBY), Samuel. Private, Militia, Hearts of Oak Company, 38th Battalion, 1780-1781 [Ref: N-86/105, M-234].

KIRBY, Thomas. Private, Militia, 2nd Volunteer Company, 4th Battalion, 1777-1778 [Ref: N-86/105, M-224].

KIRBY, William. Took the Oath of Allegiance and Fidelity on or after March 1, 1778 [Ref: J-1814, N-106/114].

KNAPP (NAPP), Thomas. Private, Militia, 4th Battalion, Capt. Greenbury Goldsborough's Company, reviewed and passed July 27, 1776 [Ref: D-67]. Private, Militia, Bullin Brook Company, 4th Battalion, 1777-1778 [Ref: N-86/105, M-224, which listed the name as "Thomas Napp"]. Private, Militia, Bullinbrook Company, 4th Battalion, 1780-1781 [Ref: N-86/105, M-231, which listed the name as "Thomas Napp"].

KNIGHT, Lucretia. See "Joseph Pippen," q.v.

KNIGHT, William. Private, Militia, 4th Battalion, Capt. Greenbury Goldsborough's Company, reviewed and passed July 27, 1776 [Ref: D-67].

KNOTTS, Nathan. Private, Militia, Miles River Company, 38th Battalion, 1780-1781 [Ref: N-86/105, M-235].

KNOWLES, John. Took the Oath of Allegiance and Fidelity on or after March 1, 1778 [Ref: J-1814, N-106/114].

KNOWLES, John. Private, Militia, Third Haven Company, 4th Battalion, 1780-1781 [Ref: N-86/105, M-232].

KNOWLES (NOWLS), John. Private, Militia, Bullin Brook Company, 4th Battalion, 1777-1778 [Ref: N-86/105, M-224, which listed the name as "John Nowls"]. Private, Militia, Bullinbrook Company, 4th Battalion, 1780-1781 [Ref: N-86/105, M-231].

KNOWLES (NOWELS), Joseph. Private, Militia, Capt. Thomas Bullen's Company; no date was given; possibly late 1775 or early 1776 [Ref: Z-3]. Private, Militia, 4th Battalion, Capt. Greenbury Goldsborough's Company, reviewed and passed July 27, 1776 [Ref: D-68, which listed the name as "Joseph Nowels"].

KNOWLY, William. Private, Militia, Sword in Hand Company, 4th Battalion, 1780-1781 [Ref: N-86/105, M-231].

LAMAX, William. See "William Lomax," q.v.

LAMBDIN, Ann. See "James Lowe" and "John Lowe" and "William Lowe," q.v.

LAMBDIN (LAMBDEN), Daniel. Private, Militia, Bayside Company, 38th Battalion, 1777-1778 [Ref: N-86/105, M-228]. Private, Militia, Bayside Company, 38th Battalion, 1780-1781; name listed twice [Ref: N-86/105, M-233]. One Daniel Lambden was a first lieutenant in the militia, 4th Battalion, on November 4, 1782 [Ref: M-96, I-298]. One Daniel Lambdin was born on May 16, 1759, married Mary Spry, served in the revolution, and died on September 7, 1809 [Ref: Y-1730]. Another Daniel Lambdin, son of William Lambdin, Jr., married first to Elizabeth Truitt and second to Elizabeth Cockey

[Ref: S-II:509]. Since there was also a soldier named "Daniel Lambdin, Jr.," q.v., additional research will be necessary before drawing conclusions.

LAMBDIN (LAMBDEN, LAMDIN), Daniel Jr. Private, Militia, Bayside Company, 38th Battalion, 1780-1781 [Ref: N-86/105, M-233]. Took the Oath of Allegiance and Fidelity on or after March 1, 1778 [Ref: J-1814, N-106/114]. Private, Militia, Hand in Hand Company, 4th Battalion, 1780-1781 [Ref: N-86/105, M-233, which listed the name as "Daniel Lambdon, Jr."]. See the other "Daniel Lambdin," q.v.

LAMBDIN (LAMBDEN), Robert (1728-1795). Born on February 8, 1728, a son of Daniel Lambdin and Judith Sands, Robert married first to Frances Lowe and second to Mary Leeds in 1790, served as an ensign in the revolution, and died on September 26, 1795 [Ref: S-II:509, Y-1730]. Ensign, Militia, Bayside Company, March 3, 1776 [Ref: M-96]. Took the Oath of Allegiance and Fidelity on or after March 1, 1778 [Ref: J-1814, N-106/114].

LAMBDIN (LAMBDEN, LAMDEN), Robert Jr. Private, Militia, Bayside Company, 38th Battalion, 1777-1778 [Ref: N-86/105, M-228]. Took the Oath of Allegiance and Fidelity on or after March 1, 1778 [Ref: J-1814, N-106/114]. Private, Militia, Bayside Company, 38th Battalion, 1780-1781 [Ref: N-86/105, M-233].

LAMBDIN, Sarah. See "William Webb Haddaway, Jr.," q.v.

LAMBDIN (LAMBDEN), William (1755-1823). Took the Oath of Allegiance and Fidelity on or after March 1, 1778 [Ref: J-1814, N-106/114]. Private, Militia, Bayside Company, 38th Battalion, 1780-1781 [Ref: N-86/105, M-233]. Private in the militia who was draughted on August 30, 1781 to reinforce the American Army and to serve in the Maryland Continental Troops until December 10, 1781 [Ref: D-387]. William Lambdin was born on July 24, 1755, married Dorcas Morsell, served as a private in the revolution, and died on June 25, 1823 [Ref: Y-1730].

LAMBDIN (LAMBDEN), William. Captain, Militia, 38th Battalion, November 4, 1782 [Ref: M-96, I-298].

LAMBDIN, William Jr. See "Wrightson Lambdin" and "Daniel Lambdin," q.v.

LAMBDIN (LAMBDEN), Wrightson. Son of William Lambdin, Jr. and his second wife Catherine Wrightson, he was on the militia list in Talbot County in 1777 and died in 1812 [Ref: S-II:509]. Private, Militia, Bayside Company, 38th Battalion, 1777-1778 [Ref: N-86/105, M-228]. Private, Militia, Bayside Company, 38th Battalion, 1780-1781 [Ref: N-86/105, M-233].

LANDMAN, Daniel. Private, Militia, Volunteer Company, 4th Battalion, 1777-1778 [Ref: N-86/105, M-223]. Private, Militia, Volunteer Company, 4th Battalion, 1780-1781 [Ref: N-86/105, M-230].

LANE, James. Private, Militia, Wye Company, 4th Battalion, 1777-1778; name listed twice [Ref: N-86/105, M-222]. Private, Militia, Wye Company, 4th Battalion, 1780-1781 [Ref: N-86/105, M-228].

LANE, Timothy. See "Timothy Lane Price," q.v.

LANE, William. Private, Militia, Wye Company, 4th Battalion, 1777-1778 [Ref: N-86/105, M-222]. Private, Militia, Wye Company, 4th Battalion, 1780-1781 [Ref: N-86/105, M-228]. Private in the militia who was draughted on August 30, 1781 to reinforce the American Army and to serve in the Maryland Continental Troops until December 10, 1781 [Ref: D-387].

LANGSTON (SANGSTON?), Isaac. Took the Oath of Allegiance and Fidelity sometime between May and September, 1780 [Ref: L-115].

LANGSTON (SANGSTON?), James. Took the Oath of Allegiance and Fidelity sometime between May and September, 1780 [Ref: L-115].

LARIMORE, Alexander. Private, Militia, Broad Creek Company, 1st Class, 38th Battalion, 1777-1778 [Ref: N-86/105, M-226].

LARIMORE, Alexander. Private, Militia, Broad Creek Company, 2nd Class, 38th Battalion, 1777-1778 [Ref: N-86/105, M-226].

LARIMORE (LARYMORE), Alexander Jr. Private, Militia, Broad Creek Company, 38th Battalion, 1780-1781 [Ref: N-86/105, M-234].

LARIMORE, James. Private, Militia, Broad Creek Company, 38th Battalion, 1777-1778 [Ref: N-86/105, M-226]. Private, Militia, Broad Creek Company, 38th Battalion, 1780-1781 [Ref: N-86/105, M-234].

LARIMORE, John. Private, Militia, Broad Creek Company, 38th Battalion, 1780-1781 [Ref: N-86/105, M-234].

LARIMORE, John. Private, Militia, Bayside Company, 38th Battalion, 1780-1781 [Ref: N-86/105, M-233]. Private, Militia, Bayside Company, 38th Battalion, 1777-1778 [Ref: N-86/105, M-228].

LARIMORE (LARYMORE), John. Took the Oath of Allegiance and Fidelity on or after March 1, 1778 [Ref: J-1814, N-106/114].

LARIMORE, Jonathan. Private, Militia, Broad Creek Company, 38th Battalion, 1780-1781 [Ref: N-86/105, M-234]. Private, Militia, Broad Creek Company, 38th Battalion, 1777-1778 [Ref: N-86/105, M-227].

LARIMORE (LARYMORE), Joseph. Private, Militia, Broad Creek Company, 38th Battalion, 1777-1778 [Ref: N-86/105, M-227]. Took the Oath of Allegiance and Fidelity on or after March 1, 1778 [Ref: J-1814, N-106/114].

LARIMORE (LARYMORE), Richard. Private, Militia, Broad Creek Company, 38th Battalion, 1780-1781 [Ref: N-86/105, M-234].

LARIMORE, Robert. Private, Militia, Broad Creek Company, 38th Battalion, 1780-1781 [Ref: N-86/105, M-234]. Private, Militia, Broad Creek Company, 38th Battalion, 1777-1778 [Ref: N-86/105, M-226].

LARIMORE (LARRIMORE, LARYMORE), Thomas. Private, Militia, Sword in Hand Company, 4th Battalion, 1777-1778 [Ref: N-86/105, M-224]. Took the Oath of Allegiance and Fidelity on or about March 1, 1778 [Ref: J-1814, N-106/114]. Private, Militia, Sword in Hand Company, 4th Battalion, 1780-1781 [Ref: N-86/105, M-231].

LARUDEN, Thomas. Waterman on the barge *Intrepid* in 1781 [Ref: D-610].

LARY (LAREY), Dennis. Took the Oath of Allegiance and Fidelity on or about March 1, 1778 [Ref: J-1814, N-106/114].
LARY, Denny. Private, Militia, Union Company, 4th Battalion, 1777-1778 [Ref: N-86/105, M-223].
LARY, Jonathan. Private, Militia, Volunteer Company, 4th Battalion, 1780-1781 [Ref: N-86/105, M-229].
LATCHA, Mary Ann. See "John Hindman," q.v.
LATHMAN, John Jr. Private, Militia, Capt. Thomas Bullen's Company; no date was given; possibly late 1775 or early 1776 [Ref: Z-3].
LATTERMAN (LATHERMAN, LOTTERMAN), Conrad Lewis. Took the Oath of Allegiance and Fidelity on or about March 1, 1778 [Ref: J-1814, N-106/114, which listed the name as "Conrad Lewis Latherman"]. Private, Militia, Miles River Company, 38th Battalion, 1777-1778 [Ref: N-86/105, M-227, which listed the name as "Lewis Latterman"]. Private, Militia, Miles River Company, 38th Battalion, 1780-1781 [Ref: N-86/105, M-235, which listed the name as "Dr. C. Lewis Lotterman"].
LAVIL, William. See "William Lovel," q.v.
LEADENHAM (LADANHAM), Edward (1742-1831). Private, Militia, Broad Creek Company, 38th Battalion, 1777-1778 [Ref: N-86/105, M-226]. Private, Militia, Broad Creek Company, 38th Battalion, 1780-1781 [Ref: N-86/105, M-234]. Edward Leadenham was born in Maryland in 1742, married Nancy ----, served in the revolution, and died on August 21, 1821 [Ref: Y-1763].
LEADENHAM (LEDDENHAM), John. Private, Militia, Broad Creek Company, 38th Battalion, 1780-1781 [Ref: N-86/105, M-234]. Took the Oath of Allegiance and Fidelity on or after March 1, 1778 [Ref: J-1814, N-106/114].
LEADENHAM, Nancy. See "Edward Leadenham," q.v.
LEADENHAM (LEDDENHAM), Nathaniel. Private, Militia, Broad Creek Company, 38th Battalion, 1777-1778 [Ref: N-86/105, M-227]. Private, 5th Maryland Line, enlisted June 6, 1778 and reportedly "deserted" in February, 1779 [Ref: D-223, which listed the name as "Nathl. Ledenham"]. Private, Militia, Broad Creek Company, 38th Battalion, 1780-1781 [Ref: N-86/105, M-234].
LECOMPTE, Anthony (c1726-c1790). Took the Oath of Allegiance and Fidelity on or about March 1, 1778 [Ref: J-1814, N-106/114, which listed the name as "Anthny Lecompt"]. Anthony Lecompte was born in Maryland circa 1726, married Mary Sewell, rendered patriotic service during the revolution, and died circa 1790 [Ref: Y-1759].
LEE, Charles. Private, Militia, Bullin Brook Company, 4th Battalion, 1777-1778 [Ref: N-86/105, M-224].
LEE, Jeremiah. Private, Militia, Hand & Hand Company, 4th Battalion, 1777-1778 [Ref: N-86/105, M-225]. Took the Oath of Allegiance and Fidelity on or about March 1, 1778 [Ref: J-1814, N-106/114]. Private, 5th Maryland Line, enlisted

May 19, 1778; first muster in July, 1779; present on October, 1780; "died some short time after this says Capt. Benson." [Ref: D-223, D-224].

LEE, John. Corporal, Militia, Bullinbrook Company, 4th Battalion, 1780-1781 [Ref: M-231]. Took the Oath of Allegiance and Fidelity on or about March 1, 1778 [Ref: J-1814, N-106/114].

LEE, John Jr. Private, Militia, Bullin Brook Company, 4th Battalion, 1777-1778 [Ref: N-86/105, M-224]. Took the Oath of Allegiance and Fidelity on or about March 1, 1778 [Ref: J-1814, N-106/114].

LEE, Mary. See "Richard Linthicum," q.v.

LEE, Oliver. Private, Militia, Bullinbrook Company, 4th Battalion, 1780-1781 [Ref: N-86/105, M-231].

LEE, Temperance. See "Joseph Pippen," q.v.

LEE, William. Private aboard the barge *Fearnought* under Capt. Levin Spedden; enlisted May 29, 1782; 6'2" tall; fair complexion; born in Talbot County [Ref: D-611].

LEE, William. Took the Oath of Allegiance and Fidelity on or about March 1, 1778 [Ref: J-1814, N-106/114].

LEEDS, Lucretia. See "John Bozman," q.v.

LEEDS, Mary. See "Robert Lambdin," q.v.

LEGG, Anna. See "Thomas Legg," q.v.

LEGG, Edward. See "Greenwood Legg," q.v.

LEGG (LEG), Greenwood (1747-   ). Born in St. Peter's Parish, Talbot County, on October 4, 1747 about 10 o'clock in the morning, son of Edward and Mary Legg [Ref: K-55, V-91]. Private, Militia, Union Company, 4th Battalion, 1777-1778 [Ref: N-86/105, M-223]. Private, Militia, Hand in Hand Company, 4th Battalion, 1780-1781 [Ref: N-86/105, M-233].

LEGG, Mary. See "Greenwood Legg," q.v.

LEGG, Rebecca. See "Thomas Legg," q.v.

LEGG, Samuel (c1730-c1790). Private, Maryland troops; married Mary Clayland [Ref: Y-1777].

LEGG, Thomas (c1752-1803). Born circa 1752 in Maryland, rendered patriotic service during the revolution, married first to Anna ---- and second to Rebecca ----, and died before May, 1803 in Pennsylvania [Ref: Y-1777].

LEMDERGIN, William. Took the Oath of Allegiance and Fidelity on or about March 1, 1778 [Ref: J-1814, N-106/114].

LEONARD, James. Private, Militia, Hearts of Oak Company, 38th Battalion, 1777-1778 [Ref: N-86/105, M-226]. Took the Oath of Allegiance and Fidelity on or about March 1, 1778 [Ref: J-1814, N-106/114].

LEONARD, James Hopkins. Private, Militia, Hearts of Oak Company, 38th Battalion, 1777-1778 [Ref: N-86/105, M-226, which listed the name as "James Hopkin Leonard"]. Private, Militia, Hearts of Oak Company, 38th Battalion, 1780-1781 [Ref: N-86/105, M-235, which mistakenly listed the name as "James K. Leonard" rather than "James H. Leonard"].

LEONARD, John. Private, Militia, Hearts of Oak Company, 38th Battalion, 1777-1778 [Ref: N-86/105, M-226]. Took the Oath of Allegiance and Fidelity on or about March 1, 1778 [Ref: J-1814, N-106/114]. Private, Militia, Hearts of Oak Company, 38th Battalion, 1780-1781 [Ref: N-86/105, M-234].
LEONARD, John Jr. Took the Oath of Allegiance and Fidelity on or about March 1, 1778 [Ref: J-1814, N-106/114].
LEONARD, John Cook. Corporal, Militia, Hearts of Oak Company, 38th Battalion, 1780-1781 [Ref: N-104, M-234].
LEONARD, Jonathan. Private, Militia, Hearts of Oak Company, 38th Battalion, 1777-1778 [Ref: N-86/105, M-226]. Private, Militia, Hearts of Oak Company, 38th Battalion, 1780-1781 [Ref: N-86/105, M-234].
LEONARD, Jonathan. Private, Militia, United Company, 38th Battalion, 1777-1778 [Ref: N-86/105, M-227]. Private, Militia, United Company, 38th Battalion, 1780-1781 [Ref: N-86/105, M-233].
LEONARD, Jonathan. Took the Oath of Allegiance and Fidelity on or after March 1, 1778 [Ref: J-1814, N-106/114].
LEONARD, Joseph. Private, Militia, Hearts of Oak Company, 38th Battalion, 1780-1781 [Ref: N-86/105, M-235]. Draughted on May 1, 1781 to serve until December 10, 1781 in the Maryland Continental Troops [Ref: D-370]. One Joseph Leonard married Mary Ferguson in Talbot County by license dated February 8, 1821. He died in 1834 about a mile from Trappe in Talbot County. Mary Leonard, widow, applied for a pension (R6293) at Easton on December 21, 1857, but it was rejected [Ref: W-2058].
LEONARD, Thomas. Private, Militia, Hearts of Oak Company, 38th Battalion, 1780-1781 [Ref: N-86/105, M-234]. Took the Oath of Allegiance and Fidelity on or about March 1, 1778 [Ref: J-1814, N-106/114].
LEONARD, Thomas Jr. Private, Militia, Hearts of Oak Company, 38th Battalion, 1777-1778 [Ref: N-86/105, M-226].
LEONARD, William. Private, Militia, Hearts of Oak Company, 38th Battalion, 1780-1781 [Ref: N-86/105, M-234]. Private, Militia, Hearts of Oak Company, 38th Battalion, 1777-1778 [Ref: N-86/105, M-226].
LEVERTON, John Foster. Private, 4th Independent Company of Maryland Regular Troops, Capt. James Hindman's Company, September, 1776 muster roll; enlisted January 28, 1776 [Ref: D-24].
LEVICK, Solomon. Private, Militia, Wye Company, 4th Battalion, 1777-1778 [Ref: N-86/105, M-222]. Took the Oath of Allegiance and Fidelity on or about March 1, 1778 [Ref: J-1814, N-106/114].
LEWIS, Isaac. Private, Militia, 4th Battalion, Capt. Greenbury Goldsborough's Company, reviewed and passed July 27, 1776 [Ref: D-67].
LIDDLE, John. Private, Militia, 2nd Volunteer Company, 4th Battalion, 1777-1778 [Ref: N-86/105, M-224].

LILES, Thomas. Private, 4th Independent Company of Maryland Regular Troops, Capt. James Hindman's Company, September, 1776 muster roll; enlisted February 2, 1776 [Ref: D-25].
LINTHICUM, Richard (1752-c1817). Took the Oath of Allegiance and Fidelity on or about March 1, 1778 [Ref: J-1814, N-106/114, which listed the name as "Richard Linthricum"]. Drummer, Militia, Broad Creek Company, 38th Battalion, 1780-1781 [Ref: N-103, M-234]. Richard Linthicum was born on April 12, 1752, served as a drummer in the revolution, married Mary Lee, and died after August 24, 1817 [Ref: Y-1810].
LITTLETON, John. Private, Militia, Third Haven Company, 4th Battalion, 1777-1778 [Ref: N-86/105, M-225, which listed the name as "John Liddleton"]. Private, Militia, Third Haven Company, 4th Battalion, 1780-1781 [Ref: N-86/105, M-232]. Took the Oath of Allegiance and Fidelity on or after March 1, 1778 [Ref: J-1814, N-106/114].
LLOYD, Anne. See "Matthew Tilghman" and "Edward Lloyd," q.v.
LLOYD, Deborah. See "Peregrine Lloyd" and "James Lloyd," q.v.
LLOYD, Edward (1744-1796). Son of Edward Lloyd and Anne Rousby, he married Elizabeth Tayloe on November 12, 1767 and their children were: Edward (1770-1834, married Sally Scott Murray and became Governor of Maryland in 1809); Anne (married Richard Tasker Lowndes); Rebecca (married Joseph Hopper Nicholson); Elizabeth (married Henry Hall Harwood); Eleanor (married Charles Lowndes); Maria (married Richard William West); and, Mary (married Francis Scott Key). Col. Edward Lloyd served in the Maryland Lower House, 1771-1776, attended the Maryland Conventions in 1775 and 1776, and was a colonel by January, 1778. He also served in the Senate, 1781-1793, and on the Executive Council, 1777-1779. He was a member of the First Council of Safety in 1775. He was also elected a Delegate to the Continental Congress in 1779 (did not serve, but was elected again in 1783). He was appointed by the Maryland Council of Safety on January 27, 1776, to collect gold and silver coin in Talbot County to comply with the Resolve of Congress. He was still active in military affairs as late as November, 1780. He also attended the Constitution Ratification Convention in 1788. Throughout most of his life he was afflicted with the gout which oftentimes hampered him in the performance of his duties; nevertheless, he maintained a high social position. One of his interests was thoroughbred horse racing and he was steward of the Annapolis Jockey Club before the Revolution. He was instrumental in reviving the sport after the war [Ref: A-3, O-1, O-4, O-28, R-537, R-538, R-70, R-71, R-72, R-76, R-84, R-89, R-90, R-91, F-356].
LLOYD, Eleanor. See "Edward Lloyd," q.v.
LLOYD, Henrietta. See "James Lloyd Chamberlaine" and "Samuel Chamberlaine," q.v.
LLOYD, James. Captain, Militia, 4th Battalion, May 16, 1776 [Ref: M-98, A-428]. Took the Oath of Allegiance and Fidelity on or about March 1, 1778 [Ref: J-

1814, N-106/114, which listed the name as "James Loyd"]. On March 23, 1781, James Lloyd wrote to the Council of the Eastern Shore of Maryland stating, in part, that he had "made application some time ago to the Governor and Council for a command in the Select Militia the result of which I have not yet been made acquainted with ... I served the Campaign of 1777 as volunteer Aide de Camp to General Greene to which at that time was annexed the rank of major. I need not adduce any arguments, I presume to prove that I am ... eligible to an appointment on this service ... by your putting it in my power to be serviceable to my country." [Ref: H-143]. James Lloyd, son of James, was born on March 16, 1716/7 and lived at Parsons Landing in Talbot County, He was a Justice of Talbot County, 1751-1769. and was commissioned a captain of a company of the 4th Battalion on May 16, 1776. He married Elizabeth Frisby, daughter of Peregrine Frisby of Cecil County, and their children were: Thomas; Sarah (married John Dickinson); Deborah (married Edward Martin); and, Robert Grundy (married Mary Ruth). [Ref: S-II:177].

LLOYD, James. Private, Militia, Third Haven Company, 4th Battalion, 1780-1781 [Ref: N-86/105, M-232].

LLOYD, Joseph. Corporal, 5th Maryland Line, enlisted September 22, 1777 and still in service in January, 1780 [Ref: D-223].

LLOYD, Margaret. See "Richard Tilghman, Jr.," q.v.

LLOYD, Maria. See "Edward Lloyd," q.v.

LLOYD, Mary. See "Edward Lloyd," q.v.

LLOYD, Rebecca. See "Edward Lloyd," q.v.

LLOYD, Robert. Private, Militia, Third Haven Company, 4th Battalion, 1780-1781 [Ref: N-86/105, M-232]. See "James Lloyd," q.v.

LLOYD, Sarah. See "James Lloyd," q.v.

LLOYD, Thomas. See "James Lloyd," q.v.

LOMAX, William. Private, Militia, Third Haven Company, 4th Battalion, 1777-1778 [Ref: N-86/105, M-225, which listed the name as "William Lamax"]. Took the Oath of Allegiance and Fidelity on or about March 1, 1778 [Ref: J-1814, N-106/114].

LOOKERMAN, John. See "John Goldsborough," q.v.

LOTTERMAN, Doctor. See "Conrad Lewis Latterman," q.v.

LOVE, James. Private, Militia, Union Company, 4th Battalion, 1780-1781 [Ref: N-86/105, M-229]. Private, Militia, United Company, 38th Battalion, 1777-1778 [Ref: N-86/105, M-227].

LOVE, John. Private, Militia, Union Company, 4th Battalion, 1780-1781 [Ref: N-86/105, M-230].

LOVE, John. Private, Militia, Volunteer Company, 4th Battalion, 1780-1781 [Ref: N-86/105, M-230]. Private, Militia, Volunteer Company, 4th Battalion, 1777-1778 [Ref: N-86/105, M-223].

LOVE, Thomas. Private, Militia, Union Company, 4th Battalion, 1780-1781 [Ref: N-86/105, M-230]. Private, Militia, Union Company, 4th Battalion, 1777-1778

[Ref: N-86/105, M-223]. Took the Oath of Allegiance and Fidelity on or about March 1, 1778 [Ref: J-1814, N-106/114].

LOVE, Thomas Jr. Took the Oath of Allegiance and Fidelity on or about March 1, 1778 [Ref: J-1814, N-106/114].

LOVE, William. Private, Militia, Hand & Hand Company, 4th Battalion, 1777-1778 [Ref: N-86/105, M-225]. Private, Militia, Hand in Hand Company, 4th Battalion, 1780-1781 [Ref: N-86/105, M-232]. Took the Oath of Allegiance and Fidelity on or about March 1, 1778 [Ref: J-1814, N-106/114].

LOVEDAY, Nicholas. Private, Militia, Union Company, 4th Battalion, 1777-1778 [Ref: N-86/105, M-223]. Private, Militia, Sword in Hand Company, 4th Battalion, 1780-1781 [Ref: N-86/105, M-231]. Second Lieutenant, Militia, November 4, 1782 [Ref: M-98, I-298].

LOVEDAY, Thomas. Private, Militia, Hand in Hand Company, 4th Battalion, 1780-1781 [Ref: N-86/105, M-232]. Private, Militia, Hand & Hand Company, 4th Battalion, 1777-1778 [Ref: N-86/105, M-226]. Took the Oath of Allegiance and Fidelity on or about March 1, 1778 [Ref: J-1814, N-106/114].

LOVEDAY, William. Private, Militia, Sword in Hand Company, 4th Battalion, 1780-1781 [Ref: N-86/105, M-231]. Private, Militia, Union Company, 4th Battalion, 1777-1778 [Ref: N-86/105, M-223]. Took the Oath of Allegiance and Fidelity on or about March 1, 1778 [Ref: J-1814, N-106/114].

LOVEL (LAVIL, LEVILL?), William. Private, Militia, Union Company, 4th Battalion, 1777-1778 [Ref: N-86/105, M-223, which listed the name as "William Levill(?)"]. Took the Oath of Allegiance and Fidelity on or about March 1, 1778 [Ref: J-1814, N-106/114]. Private (substitute), Militia, Union Company, 4th Battalion, 1780-1781 [Ref: N-86/105, M-230, which listed the name as "William Lavil"].

LOWE, Ann. See "James Lowe," q.v.

LOWE, Catherine. See "James Lowe," q.v.

LOWE, Elizabeth. See "James Lowe," q.v.

LOWE, Ellen or Eleanor. See "Henry Lowe," q.v.

LOWE, Frances. See "Robert Lambdin," q.v.

LOWE, Henry. Private, Militia, Capt. Thomas Bullen's Company; no date was given; possibly late 1775 or early 1776 [Ref: Z-3]. Private, Militia, 2nd Volunteer Company, 4th Battalion, 1777-1778 [Ref: N-86/105, M-225]. Took the Oath of Allegiance and Fidelity on or about March 1, 1778 [Ref: J-1814, N-106/114]. Rendered patriotic service by supplying bacon for the use of the Army in May, 1778 [Ref: P-168]. Henry Lowe applied for a pension in Washington County, Virginia on August 19, 1818, aged 66, stating he had enlisted in Talbot County, Maryland. On January 17, 1821 he lived with his wife (not named) who was aged 50 and daughters (not named) who were aged 17 and 10. He married second to Ellen or Eleanor Kelsoe on July 21, 1836 in Washington County, Virginia. Eleanor Lowe, widow, applied for a pension (W8259) on June 28, 1853, 34 to 40 *[sic]*, stating Henry had died on May 21,

1845. She also applied for bounty land (#8454-160-55) on April 6, 1855, aged 40 [Ref: W-2130].

LOWE, James (1730-1802). Son of John Lowe and Elizabeth Auld, James married Ann Lambdin in 1758 and their children were: John (1759-1806); Elizabeth (born 1760); William (1761-1782); Thomas (1762-1763); Catherine (1764-1831); Ann (1768-1828); James (1770-c1812); Sarah (1771-c1823); Wrightson Lambdin (1773-1848); and, Mary Ann (1776-1835). Ann Lowe died on October 16, 1778 and James Lowe died in 1802 [Ref: S-I:20, S-II:506]. Ensign, Militia, 38th Battalion, May 23, 1776 [Ref: M-98, A-438]. Took the Oath of Allegiance and Fidelity on or after March 1, 1778 [Ref: J-1814, N-106/114].

LOWE, John (1759-1806). Born on January 8, 1759, eldest son of James Lowe and Ann Lambdin, he married Ruth Sears and died on June 18, 1806 [Ref: S-II:506]. Private, Militia, Bayside Company, 38th Battalion, 1777-1778 [Ref: N-86/105, M-228]. Sergeant, Militia, Bayside Company, 38th Battalion, 1780-1781 [Ref: N-102, M-233]. Took the Oath of Allegiance and Fidelity on or after March 1, 1778 [Ref: J-1814, N-106/114]. First Lieutenant, Militia, November 4, 1782 [Ref: M-98, I-298]. See "James Lambdin," q.v.

LOWE, Mary Ann. See "James Lowe," q.v.

LOWE, Nicholas. Private, Militia, Capt. Thomas Bullen's Company; no date was given; possibly late 1775 or early 1776 [Ref: Z-3].

LOWE, Sarah. See "James Lowe," q.v.

LOWE, Thomas. See "James Lowe," q.v.

LOWE (LOW), William (1761-1782). Born in Talbot County on April 22, 1761, second son of James Lowe and Ann Lambdin [Ref: S-II:506]. Private, Militia, Bayside Company, 38th Battalion, 1777-1778 [Ref: N-86/104, M-233]. Served aboard the barge *Fearnought* under Capt. Levin Spedden; enlisted May 30, 1782; 5'7" tall; fair complexion [Ref: D-611]. William Lowe was a lieutenant whose name appears on "a list of men blown up in the barges" in 1782 [Ref: D-615].

LOWE, Wrightson. See "James Lowe," q.v.

LOWNDES, Charles. See "Edward Lloyd," q.v.

LOWNDES, Richard Tasker. See "Edward Lloyd," q.v.

LOWRY (LOWERY), James. Took the Oath of Allegiance and Fidelity on or about March 1, 1778 [Ref: J-1814, N-106/114]. Second Lieutenant, Militia, Broad Creek Company, 38th Battalion, 1780-1781 [Ref: M-234, N-103, N-94, which spelled the name "Dowry"].

LOWRY, James Jr. Private, Militia, Broad Creek Company, 38th Battalion, 1777-1778 [Ref: N-86/105, M-226].

LOWRY, John. Private, Militia, Broad Creek Company, 38th Battalion, 1780-1781 [Ref: N-86/105, M-234]. Private, Militia, Broad Creek Company, 38th Battalion, 1777-1778 [Ref: N-86/105, M-226].

LOWRY (LOWREY), Joseph. Private, Militia, Broad Creek Company, 38th Battalion, 1780-1781 [Ref: N-86/105, M-234]. Private, Militia, Broad Creek

Company, 38th Battalion, 1777-1778 [Ref: N-86/105, M-227]. Took the Oath of Allegiance and Fidelity on or about March 1, 1778 [Ref: J-1814, N-106/114].

LOWRY (LOWREY), Robert. Took the Oath of Allegiance and Fidelity on or about March 1, 1778 [Ref: J-1814, N-106/114]. Private, Militia, Broad Creek Company, 38th Battalion, 1780-1781 [Ref: N-86/105, M-234]. Private, Militia, Broad Creek Company, 38th Battalion, 1777-1778 [Ref: N-86/105, M-227].

LOWTHER (LOUTHER, LOWDER), Robert. Private, Militia, Sword in Hand Company, 4th Battalion, 1777-1778 [Ref: N-86/105, M-224]. Took the Oath of Allegiance and Fidelity on or about March 1, 1778 [Ref: J-1814, N-106/114, which listed the name as "Robert Lowder"]. Private, Militia, Sword in Hand Company, 4th Battalion, 1780-1781 [Ref: N-86/105, M-231, which listed the name as "Robert Louther"].

LUCAS (LUCUS), David. Private, Militia, 2nd Volunteer Company, 4th Battalion, 1777 [Ref: N-86/105, M-225]. Recommened to be Second Lieutenant, June 17, 1777 [Ref: M-98]. Private, Militia, Volunteer Company, 4th Battalion, 1780-1781 [Ref: N-86/105, M-229].

LUCAS, Morgan. Private, Militia, Volunteer Company, 4th Battalion, 1780-1781 [Ref: N-86/105, M-229]. Took the Oath of Allegiance and Fidelity on or about March 1, 1778; name listed twice [Ref: J-1814, N-106/114].

LUCAS, Samuel. See "Joseph Benson," q.v.

LUMLEY, Thomas. Private, 4th Independent Company of Maryland Regular Troops, Capt. James Hindman's Company, September, 1776 muster roll; enlisted January 28, 1776 [Ref: D-24].

LUNDERGAN, William. Private, Militia, Miles River Company, 38th Battalion, 1777-1778 [Ref: N-86/105, M-227].

LUNDERKIN (LUNDERGIN), Richard. Private, Militia, 4th Battalion, Capt. Greenbury Goldsborough's Company, reviewed and passed July 27, 1776 [Ref: D-68].

MAARCY, William. Took the Oath of Allegiance and Fidelity on or about March 1, 1778 [Ref: J-1814, N-106/114].

MACESON, John. Private, Militia, Capt. Thomas Bullen's Company; no date was given; possibly late 1775 or early 1776 [Ref: Z-3].

MACKEY (MACKIE), Philip. Private, Militia, Bullin Brook Company, 4th Battalion, 1777-1778 [Ref: N-86/105, M-224]. Took the Oath of Allegiance and Fidelity on or after March 1, 1778 [Ref: J-1814, N-106/114, which listed the name as "Philip Mackie"]. Private, Militia, Bullinbrook Company, 4th Battalion, 1780-1781 [Ref: N-86/105, M-231]. One Philip Mackey, son of William and Sarah Mackey, was born in St. Peter's Parish, Talbot County, on June 6, 1731 [Ref: V-90].

MACKEY, Sarah. See "Philip Mackey," q.v.

MACKEY, William. Private, Militia, Bullinbrook Company, 4th Battalion, 1780-1781 [Ref: N-86/105, M-231]. Private, Militia, Bullin Brook Company, 4th Battalion, 1777-1778 [Ref: N-86/105, M-224]. See "Philip Mackey," q.v.

MACKIMMY, John. Private, Militia, Hand & Hand Company, 4th Battalion, 1777-1778 [Ref: N-86/105, M-226].

MACOTTER, Hez. Private, Militia, Capt. Thomas Bullen's Company; no date was given; possibly late 1775 or early 1776 [Ref: Z-3].

MADDING, Nathan. Private, 4th Independent Company of Maryland Regular Troops, Capt. James Hindman's Company, September, 1776 muster roll; enlisted February 2(?), 1776 [Ref: D-24]. Private, 5th Maryland Line, enlisted December 10, 1776 and discharged March 8, 1780 [Ref: D-226, which listed the name as "Nathan Maddin"].

MADDING, Sampson. Private, 5th Maryland Line, enlisted May 20, 1778 and discharged March 1, 1779 [Ref: D-227].

MADRID, William. Private, Militia, Volunteer Company, 4th Battalion, 1780-1781 [Ref: N-86/105, M-230]. Private, Militia, Volunteer Company, 4th Battalion, 1777-1778 [Ref: N-86/105, M-223].

MAGGS (MAGS), John. Private, Militia, 2nd Volunteer Company, 4th Battalion, 1777-1778 [Ref: N-86/105, M-225]. Private, Militia, Union Company, 4th Battalion, 1780-1781 [Ref: N-86/105, M-230].

MAINES, James. Took the Oath of Allegiance and Fidelity on or about March 1, 1778 [Ref: J-1814, N-106/114].

MAKEWAY, Ephraim. See "Ephraim McQuay," q.v.

MANLOVE, Sarah. See "Philip Horney," q.v.

MANNING, Nathaniel. See "John Stevens," q.v.

MANSFIELD, Levin. Private, Militia, Miles River Company, 38th Battalion, 1780-1781 [Ref: N-86/105, M-235].

MANSFIELD, Richard. Private, Militia, Broad Creek Company, 38th Battalion, 1780-1781 [Ref: N-86/105, M-234]. Private, Militia, Broad Creek Company, 38th Battalion, 1777-1778 [Ref: N-86/105, M-227].

MANSFIELD, Thomas. Private, Militia, Miles River Company, 38th Battalion, 1777-1778 [Ref: N-86/105, M-227]. Took the Oath of Allegiance and Fidelity on or about March 1, 1778 [Ref: J-1814, N-106/114, which listed the name as "Thomas Masfield"].

MANSHIP, Charles. Private, Militia, Hand & Hand Company, 4th Battalion, 1777-1778 [Ref: N-86/105, M-226]. Private, Militia, Hand in Hand Company, 4th Battalion, 1780-1781 [Ref: N-86/105, M-232]. Took the Oath of Allegiance and Fidelity on or about March 1, 1778 [Ref: J-1814, N-106/114].

MANSHIP, Henry. Private, Militia, Hand in Hand Company, 4th Battalion, 1780-1781 [Ref: N-86/105, M-233]. Private, Militia, Hand & Hand Company, 4th Battalion, 1777-1778 [Ref: N-86/105, M-226].

MANSHIP, Mary. See "Richard Dudley," q.v.

MAQUAY, Ephraim. See "Ephraim McQuay," q.v.

MARDRY (MARDARY), William. Private, Militia, 2nd Volunteer Company, who was draughted on May 1, 1781 to serve until December 10, 1781 in the Maryland Continental Troops [Ref: D-371]. Took the Oath of Allegiance and Fidelity on or after March 1, 1778 [Ref: J-1814, N-106/114].

MARKLAND, Charles. Private, Militia, Oxford Company, 38th Battalion, 1780-1781 [Ref: N-86/105, M-235]. One Charles Markland, son of Charles and Mary Markland, was born in St. Peter's Parish, Talbot County, on November 6, 1727 [Ref: V-85].

MARKLAND, Edward. Private, Militia, Oxford Company, 38th Battalion, 1777-1778 [Ref: N-86/105, M-227]. Took the Oath of Allegiance and Fidelity on or about March 1, 1778 [Ref: J-1814, N-106/114]. Private, Militia, Oxford Company, 38th Battalion, 1780-1781 [Ref: N-86/105, M-235]. Private in the militia who was draughted on August 30, 1781 to reinforce the American Army and to serve in the Maryland Continental Troops until December 10, 1781 [Ref: D-387].

MARKLAND, John. Ensign, Militia, Oxford Company, 38th Battalion, April 9, 1778 [Ref: N-93, M-106, E-25, which listed the name as "John Narkland"]. Appointed as a Judge of the Court of Appeals on May 27, 1778 [Ref: E-112]. Appointed as Inspector of Tobacco at Oxford on August 30, 1778 [Ref: F-271].

MARKLAND, Mary. See "Charles Markland," q.v.

MARSH, Edward. Private, Militia, Capt. Thomas Bullen's Company; no date was given; possibly late 1775 or early 1776 [Ref: Z-3].

MARSHALL (MARSHAL), Arthur (Arther). Took the Oath of Allegiance and Fidelity on or about March 1, 1778 [Ref: J-1814, N-106/114]. Private, Militia, Hearts of Oak Company, 38th Battalion, 1777-1778 [Ref: N-86/105, M-226]. Private, Militia, Hearts of Oak Company, 38th Battalion, 1780-1781 [Ref: N-86/105, M-234].

MARSHALL, Elijah. Private, Militia, United Company, 38th Battalion, 1777-1778 [Ref: N-86/105, M-227, which listed the name as "Lijah Marshall"]. Private, Militia, United Company, 38th Battalion, 1780-1781 [Ref: N-86/105, M-233].

MARSHALL, James. Private, Militia, Hearts of Oak Company, 38th Battalion, 1780-1781 [Ref: N-86/105, M-234]. Private, Militia, Hearts of Oak Company, 38th Battalion, 1777-1778 [Ref: N-86/105, M-226]. Took the Oath of Allegiance and Fidelity on or about March 1, 1778 [Ref: J-1814, N-106/114].

MARSHALL (MARSHAL), John. Private, Militia, Hearts of Oak Company, 38th Battalion, 1777-1778 [Ref: N-86/105, M-226].

MARSHALL, Joseph. Private, Militia, Hearts of Oak Company, 38th Battalion, 1780-1781 [Ref: N-86/105, M-234]. Private, Militia, Hearts of Oak Company, 38th Battalion, 1777-1778 [Ref: N-86/105, M-226]. Took the Oath of Allegiance and Fidelity on or about March 1, 1778 [Ref: J-1814, N-106/114].

MARSHALL, Meredith (Meredeth). Private, Militia, Hearts of Oak Company, 38th Battalion, 1777-1778 [Ref: N-86/105, M-226]. Private, Militia, Hearts of Oak Company, 38th Battalion, 1780-1781 [Ref: N-86/105, M-235, which listed the

name as "Marydeth Marshall"]. Took the Oath of Allegiance and Fidelity on or about March 1, 1778 [Ref: J-1814, N-106/114].
MARSHALL, Richard. Took the Oath of Allegiance and Fidelity on or about March 1, 1778 [Ref: J-1814, N-106/114].
MARSHALL, Solomon. Private, Militia, Capt. Thomas Bullen's Company; no date was given; possibly late 1775 or early 1776 [Ref: Z-3].
MARSHALL, William. Private, Militia, Hearts of Oak Company, 38th Battalion, 1780-1781 [Ref: N-86/105, M-234].
MARSHALL, William. Private, Militia, Third Haven Company, 4th Battalion, 1777-1778 [Ref: N-86/105, M-225]. Private, Militia, Third Haven Company, 4th Battalion, 1780-1781 [Ref: N-86/105, M-232].
MARSHALL, William ("at J. Ll. Chamberlaine's"). Took the Oath of Allegiance and Fidelity on or after March 1, 1778 [Ref: J-1814, N-106/114].
MARSHALL, William Jr. Took the Oath of Allegiance and Fidelity on or after March 1, 1778 [Ref: J-1814, N-106/114]. Private, Militia, Hearts of Oak Company, 38th Battalion, 1780-1781 [Ref: N-86/105, M-234].
MARTIN, Edward. See "James Lloyd," q.v.
MARTIN, Ennalls (1758-   ). Born in St. Peter's Parish, Talbot County, on August 23, 1758, a son of Thomas Martin Jr. and wife Mary [Ref: K-55]. Surgeon's Mate, Hospital Department, Maryland Line. On January 17, 1833 the Treasurer of the Western Shore was directed to pay to Dr. Ennals Martin, of Talbot County, a surgeon's mate during the Revolutionary War, half yearly, half pay of surgeon's mate, for the services rendered by him during said war. [Ref: T-373]. Placed on the pension rolls on July 16, 1822 with an annual allowance of $480 effective March 4, 1831 [Ref: X-51/514].
MARTIN, Henry. Private, 4th Independent Company of Maryland Regular Troops, Capt. James Hindman's Company, September, 1776 muster roll; enlisted as a private on January 20, 1776 [Ref: D-24]. Private (substitute), Militia, Volunteer Company, 4th Battalion, 1780-1781 [Ref: N-86/105, M-230].
MARTIN, Henry. Private, Militia, Volunteer Company, 4th Battalion, 1777-1778 [Ref: N-86/105, M-223]. Took the Oath of Allegiance and Fidelity on or about March 1, 1778 [Ref: J-1814, N-106/114].
MARTIN, Henry. Private, Militia, Volunteer Company, 4th Battalion, 1777-1778 [Ref: N-86/105, M-223]. Took the Oath of Allegiance and Fidelity on or after March 1, 1778 [Ref: J-1814, N-106/114].
MARTIN, Henry Jr. Took the Oath of Allegiance and Fidelity on or about March 1, 1778 [Ref: J-1814, N-106/114]. Private (substitute), Militia, Volunteer Company, 4th Battalion, 1780-1781 [Ref: N-86/105, M-230].
MARTIN, John. Private, Militia, Miles River Company, 38th Battalion, 1780-1781 [Ref: N-86/105, M-235].
MARTIN, Joseph. See "John Stevens," q.v.
MARTIN, Mary. See "Richard Martin" and "Tristram Martin" and "Ennalls Martin" and "Thomas Martin 3rd," q.v.

MARTIN, Nicholas (c1749-1783). Son of Philip Martin and Phebe Bowdle, Nicholas apparently never married and served for a brief period in the Maryland Lower House in 1780. He was Senior Captain for Stephen Steward & Son, of West River, Anne Arundel County, shipbuilders, shipowners, and merchants; master of the sloop *Morris and Wallace* with letters of marque and reprisal dated October 19, 1777; commmander of the sloop *Porpus* with letters of marque and reprisal granted April 23, 1779; captain of the brig *Nesbitt* by March 8, 1781 to at least January, 1782; captain of the *Dauphin* which was captured on November 23, 1782 by a Guernsey privateer. Martin was imprisoned on the Isle of Jersey and apparently died by April 20, 1783 [Ref: R-84, R-578, R-579]. One Nicholas Martin was appointed a Justice of the Peace on November 21, 1778 [Ref: E-250].

MARTIN, Nicholas (1743-1808). Captain, Militia, 38th Battalion, May 16, 1776 [Ref: M-101, A-428]. He was a mariner, at least between 1770 and 1776, and served in the Maryland Assemblies of 1795, 1801 and 1802. There may be an identification problem with the other Capt. Nicholas Martin herein who was also a mariner [Ref: R-579]. One Nicholas Martin was appointed a Justice of the Peace on July 22, 1778 [Ref: E-163]. Capt. Nicholas Martin (1743-1808) married Hannah Oldham [Ref: Y-1909].

MARTIN, Nicholas. Private, Militia, Oxford Company, 38th Battalion, 1780-1781 [Ref: N-86/105, M-235].

MARTIN, Philip. Private, 3rd Maryland Line, enlisted August 4, 1777 [Ref: D-141]. Placed on the pension rolls (S34971) on January 4, 1819, age 72 (or age 68 in 1820; both ages were given), with an annual allowance of $96 effective May 22, 1818. He died on December 12, 1824; no family [Ref: X-41/514, W-2208]. See "Nicholas Martin," q.v.

MARTIN, Richard (1752-   ). Born in St. Peter's Parish, Talbot County, on June 21, 1752, son of Thomas and Mary Martin [Ref: K-55]. Private, Militia, Volunteer Company, 4th Battalion, 1777-1778 [Ref: N-86/105, M-223]. Took the Oath of Allegiance and Fidelity on or about March 1, 1778 [Ref: J-1814, N-106/114]. Private, Militia, Volunteer Company, 4th Battalion, 1780-1781 [Ref: N-86/105, M-230].

MARTIN, Robert. Private, Militia, Volunteer Company, 4th Battalion, 1780-1781 [Ref: N-86/105, M-230].

MARTIN, Solomon. Private, Militia, Volunteer Company, 4th Battalion, 1780-1781 [Ref: N-86/105, M-230]. Private, Militia, Volunteer Company, 4th Battalion, 1777-1778 [Ref: N-86/105, M-223]. Took the Oath of Allegiance and Fidelity on or after March 1, 1778 [Ref: J-1814, N-106/114].

MARTIN (MARTING), Thomas. Clerk in Capt. Thomas Bullen's Militia Company; no date was given; possibly late 1775 or early 1776 [Ref: Z-3]. Took the Oath of Allegiance and Fidelity on or about March 1, 1778 [Ref: J-1814, N-106/114]. See "Richard Martin" and "Tristram Martin," q.v.

MARTIN, Thomas Jr. Private, Militia, Volunteer Company, 4th Battalion, 1777-1778 [Ref: N-86/105, M-223]. Took the Oath of Allegiance and Fidelity on or about March 1, 1778 [Ref: J-1814, N-106/114]. Rendered patriotic service by supplying bacon for the use of the Army in May, 1778, and by supplying pork in June, 1778 [Ref: P-164, P-175]. Appointed a Justice of the Peace on July 22, 1778 [Ref: E-163]. Private (substitute), Militia, Volunteer Company, 4th Battalion, 1780-1781 [Ref: N-86/105, M-230]. See "Tristram Martin" and "Ennalls Martin" and "Thomas Martin 3rd," q.v.

MARTIN, Thomas 3rd (1749-). Born in St. Peter's Parish, Talbot County, on February 24, 1749, a son of Thomas Martin Jr. and his wife Mary [Ref: V-91]. Private, Militia, Volunteer Company, 4th Battalion, 1777-1778 [Ref: N-86/105, M-223].

MARTIN, Tristram (1753-). Born in St. Peter's Parish, Talbot County, on August 14, 1753, a son of Thomas Martin Jr. and wife Mary [Ref: K-55]. Took the Oath of Allegiance and Fidelity on or about March 1, 1778 [Ref: J-1814, N-106/114].

MARTIN, William. Took the Oath of Allegiance and Fidelity on or about March 1, 1778 [Ref: J-1814, N-106/114].

MARTIN, William Jr. Private, Militia, Capt. Thomas Bullen's Company; no date was given; possibly late 1775 or early 1776 [Ref: Z-3].

MARTIN, Zenas. Private, Militia, Capt. Thomas Bullen's Company; no date was given; possibly late 1775 or early 1776 [Ref: Z-3].

MARTINDALE, Perdue. Corporal, 4th Independent Company of Maryland Regular Troops, September, 1776 muster roll; enlisted January 28, 1776 [Ref: D-23].

MARTINDALE, William. Sergeant, 4th Independent Company of Maryland Regular Troops, September, 1776 muster roll; enlisted January 28, 1776 [Ref: D-23].

MASON, John. Private, Militia, Capt. Thomas Bullen's Company; no date was given; possibly late 1775 or early 1776 [Ref: Z-3]. Took the Oath of Allegiance and Fidelity on or about March 1, 1778 [Ref: J-1814, N-106/114].

MASON, William. Private, Militia, Broad Creek Company, 38th Battalion, 1780-1781 [Ref: N-86/105, M-234]. Private, Militia, Broad Creek Company, 38th Battalion, 1777-1778 [Ref: N-86/105, M-226]. Took the Oath of Allegiance and Fidelity on or after March 1, 1778 [Ref: J-1814, N-106/114].

MASTERSON, John. Private, 4th Independent Company of Maryland Regular Troops, Capt. James Hindman's Company, September, 1776 muster roll; enlisted January 28, 1776 [Ref: D-25].

MATHER, John. Private, Militia, Hearts of Oak Company, 38th Battalion, 1777-1778 [Ref: N-86/105, M-226]. Took the Oath of Allegiance and Fidelity on or about March 1, 1778 [Ref: J-1814, N-106/114].

MATTHEWS, Andrew. Private, Militia, Sword in Hand Company, 4th Battalion, 1777-1778 [Ref: N-86/105, M-224]. Took the Oath of Allegiance and Fidelity

on or about March 1, 1778 [Ref: J-1814, N-106/114]. Private, Militia, Sword in Hand Company, 4th Battalion, 1780-1781 [Ref: N-86/105, M-231].
MATTHEWS, Andrew. Private, Militia, Union Company, 4th Battalion, 1780-1781 [Ref: N-86/105, M-230].
MATTHEWS, David. Took the Oath of Allegiance and Fidelity on or about March 1, 1778 [Ref: J-1814, N-106/114].
MATTHEWS, James. Private, Militia, Hand in Hand Company, 4th Battalion, 1780-1781 [Ref: N-86/105, M-232].
MATTHEWS, Lewis. Took the Oath of Allegiance and Fidelity on or about March 1, 1778 [Ref: J-1814, N-106/114].
MATTHEWS, Thomas. Private, Militia, Sword in Hand Company, 4th Battalion, 1777-1778 [Ref: N-86/105, M-224]. Took the Oath of Allegiance and Fidelity on or after March 1, 1778 [Ref: J-1814, N-106/114].
MATTHEWS, William. Private, Militia, Hearts of Oak Company, 38th Battalion, 1777-1778 [Ref: N-86/105, M-226]. Took the Oath of Allegiance and Fidelity on or about March 1, 1778 [Ref: J-1814, N-106/114]. Drummer, Militia, Hearts of Oak Company, 38th Battalion, 1780-1781 [Ref: N-104, M-234].
MATTHEWS, William. Private, Militia, Sword in Hand Company, 4th Battalion, 1777-1778 [Ref: N-86/105, M-224]. Private, Militia, Sword in Hand Company, 4th Battalion, 1780-1781 [Ref: N-86/105, M-231]. Took the Oath of Allegiance and Fidelity on or after March 1, 1778 [Ref: J-1814, N-106/114].
MATTHEWS, William. Sergeant, Militia, Capt. Thomas Bullen's Company; no date was given; possibly late 1775 or early 1776 [Ref: Z-3]. Took the Oath of Allegiance and Fidelity on or about March 1, 1778 [Ref: J-1814, N-106/114].
MAY, Eliza. See "John Stevens," q.v.
MAYNADIER, Daniel. See "William Maynadier," q.v.
MAYNADIER, Elizabeth. See "William Maynadier," q.v.
MAYNADIER, Henry. See "William Maynadier," q.v.
MAYNADIER, Margaret. See "William Maynadier," q.v.
MAYNADIER, William (1747-1795). Eldest son of Rev. Daniel Maynadier and Mary Murray, of Dorchester County, he was born in St. Peter's Parish, Talbot County, on April 28, 1747, "being Tuesday, about 11 of the clock at night." [Ref: V-91]. William married his cousin Margaret Ennalls and their children were: William (married first to Sarah Scott Brown and second to Catherine Brown); Henry (never married); Daniel (never married); Margaret Murray (married Daniel Dulany Fitzhugh and died in 1840); and, Elizabeth. William was a Court Justice, 1777-1779, and served in the Maryland Lower House, 1781-1782 [Ref: R-86, R-585, R-586]. Captain, Militia, Third Haven Company, 4th Battalion, April 9, 1778 [Ref: N-91, M-101, E-24]. Took the Oath of Allegiance and Fidelity on or about March 1, 1778 [Ref: J-1814, N-106/114]. Appointed a Justice of the Peace on November 21, 1778 and November 20, 1779 [Ref: F-22, and E-250, which listed the name as "William Manadier"]. See "William Brinsfield," q.v.

MAYNADIER, William. Private, Militia, Third Haven Company, 4th Battalion, 1777-1778 [Ref: N-86/105, M-225].

MAYNARD, Foster (1742-1818). Private, Militia, Hearts of Oak Company, 38th Battalion, 1780-1781 [Ref: N-86/105, M-234]. Private, Militia, Hearts of Oak Company, 38th Battalion, 1777-1778 [Ref: N-86/105, M-226]. Took the Oath of Allegiance and Fidelity on or about March 1, 1778 [Ref: J-1814, N-106/114]. Foster Maynard was born in Maryland on June 17, 1742, married Margaret Aldern, served in the revolution, and died in December, 1818 [Ref: Y-1932].

McCALLUM (McCALLEM), Alexander. Private, Militia, Union Company, 4th Battalion, 1777-1778 [Ref: N-86/105, M-223]. Took the Oath of Allegiance and Fidelity on or about March 1, 1778 [Ref: J-1814, N-106/114]. Private (substitute), Militia, Union Company, 4th Battalion, 1780-1781 [Ref: N-86/105, M-230]. Rendered patriotic service by supplying bacon for the use of the Army in April, 1778 [Ref: P-162].

McCALLUM, William. Private (substitute), Militia, Union Company, 4th Battalion, 1780-1781 [Ref: M-229].

McCALLUM, William. Second Lieutenant, Militia, Union Company, 4th Battalion, April 9, 1778 [Ref: N-88, M-102, E-24]. Took the Oath of Allegiance and Fidelity on or about March 1, 1778 [Ref: J-1814, N-106/114].

McCANLY, Rachel. See "Thomas Barnett Sewell," q.v.

McCARTER, James. Private, Militia, Miles River Company, 38th Battalion, 1780-1781 [Ref: N-86/105, M-235]. Private, Militia, Miles River Company, 38th Battalion, 1777-1778 [Ref: N-86/105, M-227].

McCARTY, Charles. Private, Militia, Bayside Company, 38th Battalion, 1777-1778 [Ref: N-86/105, M-228].

McCLANNENGAN, Blair. See "Alexander Gordon," q.v.

McCLAYLAND, Alexander. Private, Militia, Capt. Thomas Bullen's Company; no date was given; possibly late 1775 or early 1776 [Ref: Z-3, which listed the name as "Alexr. Mackclayland"]. Private, Militia, Bullinbrook Company, 4th Battalion, 1780-1781 [Ref: N-86/105, M-231, which listed the name as "Elexr. McClayland"]. He may be the McClayland born on January 14, 1744 and listed in the St. Peter's Parish Register as "---- Macclayland, son of Alexander and wife." [Ref: V-88]. See "Findley McClayland," q.v.

McCLAYLAND, Findley (1740-). Born in St. Peter's Parish, Talbot County, on April 14, 1740, a son of Alexander and ---- Macclayland [Ref: V-88]. Private, Militia, Bullin Brook Company, 4th Battalion, 1777-1778 [Ref: N-86/105, M-224]. Took the Oath of Allegiance and Fidelity on or about March 1, 1778 [Ref: J-1814, N-106/114].

McCLAYLAND, John. Took the Oath of Allegiance and Fidelity on or after March 1, 1778 [Ref: J-1814, N-106/114].

McCLAYLAND, Thomas. Private, Militia, Third Haven Company, 4th Battalion, 1777-1778 [Ref: N-86/105, M-225]. Took the Oath of Allegiance and Fidelity on or after March 1, 1778 [Ref: J-1814, N-106/114].

McCOLLISTER, Roger. Private, Militia, 2nd Volunteer Company, 4th Battalion, 1777-1778 [Ref: N-86/105, M-225].

McCONIKIN, John. Private, Militia, Broad Creek Company, 38th Battalion, 1777-1778 [Ref: N-86/105, M-227].

McCORMACK, Dennis. Private (substitute), Militia, Wye Company, 4th Battalion, 1780-1781 [Ref: N-86/105, M-228].

McCULLOCH, John. Took the Oath of Allegiance and Fidelity on or about March 1, 1778 [Ref: J-1814, N-106/114].

McCULLOCK, Hugh. Private, Militia, Volunteer Company, 4th Battalion, 1780-1781 [Ref: N-86/105, M-229].

McCULLOCK, John. Private, Militia, Hand & Hand Company, 4th Battalion, 1777-1778 [Ref: N-86/105, M-226].

McDANIEL, Richard. Private, 4th Independent Company of Maryland Regular Troops, Capt. James Hindman's Company, September, 1776 muster roll; enlisted January 23, 1776 [Ref: D-24].

McDONALD, John. Private, Militia, Bayside Company, 38th Battalion, 1780-1781 [Ref: N-86/105, M-233].

McGINNY (McGINNEY, McGINEY), Daniel. Took the Oath of Allegiance and Fidelity on or after March 1, 1778 [Ref: J-1814, N-106/114]. Waterman on the barge *Intrepid* in 1781 [Ref: D-610].

McGINNY (McGUINA, McGUINIA), Daniel. Private, Militia, Third Haven Company, 4th Battalion, 1780-1781 [Ref: N-86/105, M-232].

McGINNY (McGINNEY), David. Private, Militia, Third Haven Company, 4th Battalion, 1777-1778 [Ref: N-86/105, M-225].

McGINNY (McGINNEY, McGUINA), James. Private, Militia, Third Haven Company, 4th Battalion, 1777-1778 [Ref: N-86/105, M-225]. Private, Militia, Miles River Company, 38th Battalion, 1780-1781 [Ref: N-86/105, M-235].

McGINNY (McGINNEY, MEGUINEY, McGUINA), John. Private, Militia, Capt. Thomas Bullen's Company; no date was given; possibly late 1775 or early 1776 [Ref: Z-3]. Private, Militia, Third Haven Company, 4th Battalion, 1777-1778 [Ref: N-86/105, M-225]. Took the Oath of Allegiance and Fidelity on or about March 1, 1778 [Ref: J-1814, N-106/114].

McGINNY (MEGUINEY), Michael. Private, Militia, Capt. Thomas Bullen's Company; no date was given; possibly late 1775 or early 1776 [Ref: Z-3].

McGINNY (McGUINA, McGAINA), Solomon. Private, Militia, Bullin Brook Company, 4th Battalion, 1777-1778 [Ref: N-86/105, M-224].

McGINNY (MEGUINEY), Thomas. Private, Militia, Capt. Thomas Bullen's Company; no date was given; possibly late 1775 or early 1776 [Ref: Z-3].

McGUIRE, Isaiah. Private, Militia, Bullin Brook Company, 4th Battalion, 1777-1778 [Ref: N-86/105, M-224]. Took the Oath of Allegiance and Fidelity on or after March 1, 1778 [Ref: J-1814, N-106/114].

McKEEL, Thomas. Sergeant, 1st Maryland Line, enlisted December 10, 1776. Ensign (no dated), but "never served." [Ref: D-13, D-136]. Placed on the pension rolls in Talbot County as a sergeant in the Maryland Line on February 13, 1819, aged 84, with an annual allowance of $96, but was dropped from the rolls under the Act of May 1, 1820 (reason not stated); pension had commenced on May 23, 1818 [Ref: X-41/514].

McKERNON, Daniel. Took the Oath of Allegiance and Fidelity on or about March 1, 1778 [Ref: J-1814, N-106/114].

McKINSEY, Alexander. Private, Militia, Oxford Company, 38th Battalion, 1777-1778 [Ref: N-86/105, M-228]. Took the Oath of Allegiance and Fidelity on or about March 1, 1778 [Ref: J-1814, N-106/114]. Private, Militia, Oxford Company, 38th Battalion, 1780-1781 [Ref: N-86/105, M-235].

McKINSEY, Alexander. Private, Militia, Volunteer Company, 4th Battalion, 1777-1778 [Ref: N-86/105, M-223].

McKNOULTY, John (Jr.). Corporal, Militia, Bayside Company, 38th Battalion, 1780-1781 [Ref: N-102, M-233].

McKNOULTY, Thomas. Private, Militia, Bayside Company, 38th Battalion, 1780-1781 [Ref: N-86/105, M-233].

McMAHAN, Elizabeh. See "James McMahan" and "John McMahan, Jr.," q.v.

McMAHAN (MACMAHAN), Grace. See "William Berridge," q.v.

McMAHAN (MACMAHAN), James (1757-   ). Born in St. Peter's Parish, Talbot County, on August 10, 1757, son of John and Elizabeth Macmahan [Ref: K-56]. Took the Oath of Allegiance and Fidelity on or after March 1, 1778 [Ref: J-1814, N-106/114]. See "Samuel McMahan," q.v.

McMAHAN (MACMAHAN), John. Private, Militia, Third Haven Company, 4th Battalion, 1777-1778 [Ref: N-86/105, M-225, which listed the name as "John Macmahan"]. Private, Militia, Third Haven Company, 4th Battalion, 1780-1781 [Ref: N-86/105, M-232]. See "James McMahan" and "John McMahan, Jr.," q.v.

McMAHAN (MACKMAYHAN), John. Private, Militia, Capt. Thomas Bullen's Company; no date was given; possibly late 1775 or early 1776 [Ref: Z-3, which listed the name as "John Mackmayhan"]. Private, Militia, Bullinbrook Company, 4th Battalion, 1780-1781 [Ref: N-86/105, M-231].

McMAHAN (MACKMAYHAWN), John Jr. Took the Oath of Allegiance and Fidelity on or after March 1, 1778 [Ref: J-1814, N-106/114]. "John Mackmayhawn, son of John and Elizabeth" was born in St. Peter's Parish, Talbot County, on September 20, 1739 [Ref: V-77].

McMAHAN, Richard. Took the Oath of Allegiance and Fidelity on or about March 1, 1778 [Ref: J-1814, N-106/114].

McMAHAN (MACKMAHAN), Samuel or Jams. Fifer, Militia, Bullinbrook Company, 4th Battalion, 1780-1781 [Ref: N-99, which listed the name as

"Samuel Mackmahan, fifer" and M-231, which listed the name as "Jams. Mackmahan, fifer"].

McMANUS, Philip. See "Pollard Edmondson," q.v.

McNAMARA, George. Private, 4th Independent Company of Maryland Regular Troops, Capt. James Hindman's Company; enlisted January 26, 1776; reportedly deserted August 3, 1776 [Ref: D-24].

McNEAL, Archibald. Took the Oath of Allegiance and Fidelity on or about March 1, 1778 [Ref: J-1814, N-106/114].

McNULTY, John. Private, Militia, Bayside Company, 38th Battalion, 1777-1778 [Ref: N-86/105, M-228].

McQUAY (MAQUAY, MAKEWAY), Ephraim. Private, Militia, 4th Battalion, Capt. Greenbury Goldsborough's Company, reviewed and passed July 27, 1776 [Ref: D-68, which listed the name as ""Ephraim Maquay"]. Private, Militia, Miles River Company, 38th Battalion, 1777-1778 [Ref: N-86/105, M-227, which listed the name as "Epheram McWay"]. Took the Oath of Allegiance and Fidelity on or about March 1, 1778 [Ref: J-1814, N-106/114, which listed the name as "Ephraim Makeway"].

McQUAY (MAKEWAY), Jeremiah. Took the Oath of Allegiance and Fidelity on or about March 1, 1778 [Ref: J-1814, N-106/114].

McQUAY, Jeremiah Jr. Private, Militia, Miles River Company, 38th Battalion, 1780-1781 [Ref: N-86/105, M-235].

McQUAY (McWAY), John. Private, Militia, Miles River Company, 38th Battalion, 1777-1778 [Ref: N-86/105, M-227]. Private, Militia, Miles River Company, 38th Battalion, 1780-1781 [Ref: N-86/105, M-235].

McQUAY, John. Private, Militia, Broad Creek Company, 38th Battalion, 1780-1781 [Ref: N-86/105, M-234].

McQUAY, Martin. Private, 5th Maryland Line, enlisted June 2, 1779 and still in service on January 1, 1780 [Ref: D-228].

McQUAY, Patrick. Private, Militia, Broad Creek Company, 38th Battalion, 1780-1781 [Ref: N-86/105, M-234]. Private, Militia, Broad Creek Company, 38th Battalion, 1777-1778 [Ref: N-86/105, M-227].

McQUAY (MAQUAY), Thomas. Private, Militia, 4th Battalion, Capt. Greenbury Goldsborough's Company, reviewed and passed July 27, 1776 [Ref: D-68]. Private, 5th Maryland Line, enlisted March 10, 1777 and discharged March 8, 1780 [Ref: D-226]. Private, Militia, Bayside Company, 38th Battalion, 1780-1781 [Ref: N-86/105, M-233].

McSWEENY, Jeremiah. Private, Militia, Miles River Company, 38th Battalion, 1780-1781 [Ref: N-86/105, M-235]. Took the Oath of Allegiance and Fidelity on or about March 1, 1778 [Ref: J-1814, N-106/114].

MEAD, James. Drummer, 4th Independent Company of Maryland Regular Troops, September, 1776 muster roll; enlisted March 16, 1776 [Ref: D-23].

MEAGHER, Peter. Private, Militia, 4th Battalion, Capt. Greenbury Goldsborough's Company, reviewed and passed July 27, 1776 [Ref: D-67].

MEARS, John. Private, Militia, Capt. Thomas Bullen's Company; no date was given; possibly late 1775 or early 1776 [Ref: Z-3]. Private, Militia, 4th Battalion, Capt. Greenbury Goldsborough's Company, reviewed and passed July 27, 1776 [Ref: D-67]. Took the Oath of Allegiance and Fidelity on or after March 1, 1778 [Ref: J-1814, N-106/114].

MEEDS (MEADS), Giles. Private, Militia, Union Company, 4th Battalion, 1777-1778 [Ref: N-86/105, M-223]. Took the Oath of Allegiance and Fidelity on or about March 1, 1778 [Ref: J-1814, N-106/114].

MEEDS, James. Private, Militia, Hand in Hand Company, 4th Battalion, 1780-1781 [Ref: N-86/105, M-232]. Took the Oath of Allegiance and Fidelity on or about March 1, 1778 [Ref: J-1814, N-106/114].

MEEDS, Thomas. Private, Militia, Hand in Hand Company, 4th Battalion, 1780-1781 [Ref: N-86/105, M-232]. Took the Oath of Allegiance and Fidelity on or about March 1, 1778 [Ref: J-1814, N-106/114].

MEHONY, Anthony. Took the Oath of Allegiance and Fidelity on or about March 1, 1778 [Ref: J-1814, N-106/114].

MELONY, William. Private, 4th Independent Company of Maryland Regular Troops, Capt. James Hindman's Company, September, 1776 muster roll; enlisted January 25, 1776 [Ref: D-25].

MERCHANT, James. Private, Militia, Union Company, 4th Battalion, 1777-1778 [Ref: N-86/105, M-223]. Private, Militia, Union Company, 4th Battalion, 1780-1781 [Ref: N-86/105, M-230]. Took the Oath of Allegiance and Fidelity on or about March 1, 1778 [Ref: J-1814, N-106/114].

MERCHANT, John. Private, Militia, Sword in Hand Company, 4th Battalion, 1777-1778 [Ref: N-86/105, M-224]. Took the Oath of Allegiance and Fidelity on or about March 1, 1778; name listed twice [Ref: J-1814, N-106/114]. Rendered patriotic service by supplying bacon for the use of the Army in May, 1778 [Ref: P-165].

MERCHANT, John Jr. Private, Militia, Sword in Hand Company, 4th Battalion, 1780-1781 [Ref: N-86/105, M-231].

MERCHANT, Joseph. Private, 4th Independent Company of Maryland Regular Troops, Capt. James Hindman's Company; enlisted January 28, 1776; reported missing on August 27, 1776 after the Battle of Long Island [Ref: D-24].

MERRICK, Aaron (Aron). Private, Militia, Volunteer Company, 4th Battalion, 1780-1781 [Ref: N-86/105, M-229]. Took the Oath of Allegiance and Fidelity on or about March 1, 1778 [Ref: J-1814, N-106/114].

MERRICK, Allen (Allin). Private, Militia, Third Haven Company, 4th Battalion, 1777-1778 [Ref: N-86/105, M-225].

MERRICK, Andrew. Private, Militia, Third Haven Company, 4th Battalion, 1777-1778 [Ref: N-86/105, M-225]. Took the Oath of Allegiance and Fidelity on or about March 1, 1778 [Ref: J-1814, N-106/114].

MERRICK, Daniel. Private, Militia, Union Company, 4th Battalion, 1780-1781 [Ref: N-86/105, M-230]. Took the Oath of Allegiance and Fidelity on or after

March 1, 1778 [Ref: J-1814, N-106/114]. One Daniel Merrick, son of Daniel and Mary, was born in St. Peter's Parish, Talbot County, on January 6, 1732 [Ref: V-70]. Another Daniel Merrick (1757-c1813) of Maryland also served in the revolution [Ref: Y-2005]. Additional research will be necessary before drawing conclusions.

MERRICK, James. Private, Militia, Capt. Thomas Bullen's Company; no date was given; possibly late 1775 or early 1776 [Ref: Z-3].

MERRICK, James Jr. Private, Militia, Capt. Thomas Bullen's Company; no date was given; possibly late 1775 or early 1776 [Ref: Z-3].

MERRICK, John. Private, Militia, Bullinbrook Company, 4th Battalion, 1780-1781 [Ref: N-86/105, M-231]. Private in the militia who was draughted on August 30, 1781 to reinforce the American Army and to serve in the Maryland Continental Troops until December 10, 1781; honorably discharged on December 3, 1781 [Ref: D-387, I-10].

MERRICK, John. Sergeant, Militia, Capt. Thomas Bullen's Company; no date was given; possibly late 1775 or early 1776 [Ref: Z-3].

MERRICK, John Jr. Private, Militia, Capt. Thomas Bullen's Company; no date was given; possibly late 1775 or early 1776 [Ref: Z-3].

MERRICK, Mary. See "Daniel Merrick," q.v.

MERRICK, Matthias (1747-   ). Born in St. Peter's Parish, Talbot County, on August 8, 1747, a "son of James Merrick Secundum and Mary his wife," he married Rebekah ---- and died after 1781 [Ref: V-90, Y-2006]. Private, Militia, Volunteer Company, 4th Battalion, 1780-1781 [Ref: N-86/105, M-230]. Private, Militia, Volunteer Company, 4th Battalion, 1777-1778 [Ref: N-86/105, M-223].

MERRICK, Rebekah. See "Matthias Merrick," q.v.

MERRICK, William. Private, Militia, Capt. Thomas Bullen's Company; no date was given; possibly late 1775 or early 1776 [Ref: Z-3].

MERRICK, William Levitt. Private aboard the barge *Fearnought* under Capt. Levin Spedden; enlisted on May 27, 1782; 5'5" tall; dark complexion; born in Talbot County [Ref: D-611]. He applied for a pension (S8892) in Dorchester County on August 6, 1832, age 73, stating he was born in Talbot County on October 20, 1759 and lived there at the time of his enlistment [Ref: W-2331].

MIDDLETON, William. Private, Militia, Wye Company, 4th Battalion, 1777-1778 [Ref: N-86/105, M-222].

MIERS, James. Private, Militia, Volunteer Company, 4th Battalion, 1777-1778 [Ref: N-86/105, M-223].

MILLER, Abner. Private, Militia, Wye Company, 4th Battalion, 1777-1778 [Ref: N-86/105, M-222]. Took the Oath of Allegiance and Fidelity on or about March 1, 1778 [Ref: J-1814, N-106/114].

MILLER, Charles. Private, Militia, Wye Company, 4th Battalion, 1777-1778 [Ref: N-86/105, M-222]. Took the Oath of Allegiance and Fidelity on or about March 1, 1778 [Ref: J-1814, N-106/114].

MILLER, Jeffery (Jeffrey). Private, Militia, Bullinbrook Company, 4th Battalion, 1780-1781 [Ref: N-86/105, M-231]. Private, Militia, Bullin Brook Company, 4th Battalion, 1777-1778 [Ref: N-86/105, M-224]. Took the Oath of Allegiance and Fidelity on or about March 1, 1778 [Ref: J-1814, N-106/114].

MILLER, John. Sergeant, 4th Independent Company of Maryland Regular Troops, September, 1776 muster roll; enlisted as a corporal on January 22, 1776 [Ref: D-23].

MILLINGTON, Alemby (Alimby, Alundy). Private, Militia, Wye Company, 4th Battalion, 1777-1778 [Ref: N-86/105, M-222]. Private, Militia, Wye Company, 4th Battalion, 1780-1781 [Ref: N-96, M-228]. In the proceedings of the Council of Maryland on September 10, 1781 is the following: "It appearing to this Board that Allemby Millington is an inhabitant of Talbot County and that he has stood his draught in that county and that the said Millington was draughted as an inhabitant of Caroline County to serve till the 10th of December next [in the Maryland Line] the said Allemby Millington is hereby discharged from the said draught in Caroline County." [Ref: G-618]. Earlier, on September 4, 1781. Christopher Birckhead, Talbot County Lieutenant, stated that Allemby Millington "has been for these several years past an enrolled militia man in this county. I have also a certificate from his captain that he attends constantly at the muster field and does his duty as a good soldier. He has also been classed and stood all the draughts in the county." It was recorded that he was "Discharged from the Draught in Caroline County 19th Sept. 1781, by Governor & Council." [Ref: H-476].

MILLINGTON, Isaac. Private, Militia, Hand in Hand Company, 4th Battalion, 1780-1781 [Ref: N-86/105, M-232]. Private, Militia, Hand & Hand Company, 4th Battalion, 1777-1778 [Ref: N-86/105, M-225]. Took the Oath of Allegiance and Fidelity on or about March 1, 1778 [Ref: J-1814, N-106/114].

MILLINGTON, John. Private, 4th Independent Company of Maryland Regular Troops, Capt. James Hindman's Company; enlisted February 15, 1776 [Ref: D-24]. On August 17, 1776, the Maryland Council of Safety ordered that "John Millington, of Capt. Hindman's Company, permitted to go to his home in Talbot County for the recovery of his health." [Ref: B-215].

MILLINGTON, Nicholson. Private, Militia, Wye Company, 4th Battalion, 1777-1778 [Ref: N-86/105, M-222].

MILLINGTON, Richard. Private, Militia, 5th Class, Hand & Hand Company, 4th Battalion, 1777-1778 [Ref: N-86/105, M-226]. Private, Militia, Hand in Hand Company, 4th Battalion, 1780-1781 [Ref: N-86/105, M-233].

MILLINGTON, Richard. Private, Militia, 8th Class, Hand & Hand Company, 4th Battalion, 1777-1778 [Ref: N-86/105, M-226]. Private, Militia, Hand in Hand Company, 4th Battalion, 1780-1781 [Ref: N-86/105, M-232].

MILLINGTON, Richard. Took the Oath of Allegiance and Fidelity on or about March 1, 1778 [Ref: J-1814, N-106/114].

MILLINGTON, William. Private, Militia, Hand & Hand Company, 4th Battalion, 1777-1778 [Ref: N-86/105, M-225].

MILLIS, Edward. Private, Militia, Wye Company, 4th Battalion, 1777-1778 [Ref: N-86/105, M-222]. Took the Oath of Allegiance and Fidelity on or about March 1, 1778 [Ref: J-1814, N-106/114].

MILLIS, James. Private, Militia, Union Company, 4th Battalion, 1777-1778 [Ref: N-86/105, M-223].

MILLS, John. Private, Militia, 4th Battalion, Capt. Greenbury Goldsborough's Company, reviewed and passed July 27, 1776 [Ref: D-67].

MILTON, Martha. See "John Bartlett," q.v.

MILWARD (MELWARD, MILLWARD), William. Deposed on December 30, 1776 regarding a dispute over the use and sale of salt, explaining that "he and his wife went to live at Plain Dealing in the spring of 1774 and his wife was employed to take charge of the house as housekeeper, at that time there was a quantity of salt in a house the key of which was delivered into his wife's care ... in January 1775 he did receive 514 bushels of salt for Mr. James Lloyd Chamberlaine and put it into the house above mentioned at Plain Dealing and that between October and Christmas of the same year he the deponent did measure and sell all the salt ... at 3 shillings per bushel ... and James Lloyd Chamberlaine did caution the deponent not to mix the new received salt which was his, with the old salt that was before in the house, as that did not belong to him, but to Tommy Chamberlain, a minor..." An armed confrontation also took place with a band of men led by Jeremiah Colston [Ref: B-562, A-563]. Recommended to be Second Lieutenant, Militia, Union Company, 4th Battalion, June 17, 1777 [Ref: M-104]. Took the Oath of Allegiance and Fidelity on or about March 1, 1778 [Ref: J-1814, N-106/114]. First Lieutenant, Militia, Union Company, 4th Battalion, April 9, 1778 through 1781 [Ref: N-88, N-97, M-229, M-104, E-24].

MITCHELL, Jacob. Took the Oath of Allegiance and Fidelity on or after March 1, 1778 [Ref: J-1814, N-106/114].

MONEY, Mary. See "Thomas Sherwood," q.v.

MOODY, William. Private, Militia, Capt. Thomas Bullen's Company; no date was given; possibly late 1775 or early 1776 [Ref: Z-3].

MOORE, Charles. Private, 4th Independent Company of Maryland Regular Troops, Capt. James Hindman's Company; enlisted January 12, 1776; reportedly deserted August 3, 1776 [Ref: D-24].

MOORE, Christopher. Private, Militia, Capt. Thomas Bullen's Company; no date was given; possibly late 1775 or early 1776 [Ref: Z-3, which listed the name as "Christr. Moor"].

MOORE, George. Private, Militia, Union Company, 4th Battalion, 1780-1781 [Ref: N-86/105, M-230].

MOORE, Richard. Private, Militia, Bullinbrook Company, 4th Battalion, 1780-1781 [Ref: N-86/105, M-231].

MOORE, William. Took the Oath of Allegiance and Fidelity on or about March 1, 1778 [Ref: J-1814, N-106/114].

MORGAN, James. Sergeant, 4th Independent Company of Maryland Regular Troops, September, 1776 muster roll; enlisted January 20, 1776 [Ref: D-23].

MORGAN, John. Private in the militia who was draughted on August 30, 1781 to reinforce the American Army and to serve in the Maryland Continental Troops until December 10, 1781 [Ref: D-387].

MORGAN, Thomas. Took the Oath of Allegiance and Fidelity on or about March 1, 1778 [Ref: J-1814, N-106/114].

MORGAN, Thomas Jr. Private, Militia, Union Company, 4th Battalion, 1777-1778 [Ref: N-86/105, M-223]. Private, Militia, Union Company, 4th Battalion, 1780-1781 [Ref: N-86/105, M-230]. Private (substitute), Maryland Line; honorably discharged on December 3, 1781 [Ref: I-11, which listed the name without the "Jr."].

MORGAN, Thomas Spry. Took the Oath of Allegiance and Fidelity on or about March 1, 1778 [Ref: J-1814, N-106/114].

MORGAN, William. Private, Militia, Sword in Hand Company, 4th Battalion, 1780-1781 [Ref: N-86/105, M-231]. Private, Militia, Sword in Hand Company, 4th Battalion, 1777-1778 [Ref: N-86/105, M-224]. Took the Oath of Allegiance and Fidelity on or about March 1, 1778; name listed twice [Ref: J-1814, N-106/114].

MORLING, Francis. Took the Oath of Allegiance and Fidelity on or about March 1, 1778 [Ref: J-1814, N-106/114].

MORRIS (MORRISS), David. Private, Militia, Bayside Company, 38th Battalion, 1777-1778 [Ref: N-86/105, M-228]. Private, Militia, Bayside Company, 38th Battalion, 1780-1781 [Ref: N-86/105, M-233].

MORRIS (MORRISS), James. Private, Militia, Hand in Hand Company, 4th Battalion, 1780-1781 [Ref: N-86/105, M-232]. Private in the militia who was draughted on August 30, 1781 to reinforce the American Army and to serve in the Maryland Continental Troops until December 10, 1781 [Ref: D-387].

MORRIS (MORRISS), John. Private, Militia, Hand & Hand Company, 4th Battalion, 1777-1778 [Ref: N-86/105, M-225]. Private, Militia, Hand in Hand Company, 4th Battalion, 1780-1781 [Ref: N-86/105, M-232].

MORRIS, William. Private, Militia, Hearts of Oak Company, 38th Battalion, 1777-1778 [Ref: N-86/105, M-226].

MORSEL, James. Took the Oath of Allegiance and Fidelity on or after March 1, 1778 [Ref: J-1814, N-106/114].

MORSELL, Dorcas. See "William Lambdin," q.v.

MORTON, Thomas. Took the Oath of Allegiance and Fidelity on or about March 1, 1778 [Ref: J-1814, N-106/114].

MULLIKIN (MULLICAN), Eleanor. See "John Mullikin," q.v.

MULLIKIN, James. Private, Militia, Volunteer Company, 4th Battalion, 1780-1781 [Ref: N-86/105, M-230]. Private, Militia, Volunteer Company, 4th

Battalion, 1777-1778 [Ref: N-86/105, M-223]. Took the Oath of Allegiance and Fidelity on or about March 1, 1778; name listed twice [Ref: J-1814, N-106/114].

MULLIKIN, James Jr. Took the Oath of Allegiance and Fidelity on or after March 1, 1778 [Ref: J-1814, N-106/114]. Private, Militia, Volunteer Company, 4th Battalion, 1780-1781 [Ref: N-86/105, M-230].

MULLIKIN, Jesse. Private, Militia, Volunteer Company, 4th Battalion, 1780-1781 [Ref: N-86/105, M-230]. Private, Militia, Volunteer Company, 4th Battalion, 1777-1778 [Ref: N-86/105, M-223].

MULLIKIN, John (1738-   ). Born in St. Peter's Parish, Talbot County, on November 15, 1738, son of William and Eleanor Mullican [Ref: V-79]. Private, Militia, Third Haven Company, 4th Battalion, 1780-1781 [Ref: N-86/105, M-232]. Took the Oath of Allegiance and Fidelity on or after March 1, 1778 [Ref: J-1814, N-106/114].

MULLIKIN, Mary. See "Samuel Mullikin" and "William Mullikin," q.v.

MULLIKIN, Patrick. Private, Militia, Capt. Thomas Bullen's Company; no date was given; possibly late 1775 or early 1776 [Ref: Z-3]. Private, Militia, Oxford Company, 38th Battalion, 1780-1781 [Ref: N-86/105, M-235]. Took the Oath of Allegiance and Fidelity on or after March 1, 1778 [Ref: J-1814, N-106/114]. See "William Mullikin," q.v.

MULLIKIN, Ruth. See "Henry Bowdle, Jr.," q.v.

MULLIKIN, Samuel (1754-   ). Born in St. Peter's Parish, Talbot County, on September 20, 1754, son of William and Mary Mullikin [Ref: K-55]. Private, Militia, Volunteer Company, 4th Battalion, 1777-1778 [Ref: N-86/105, M-223]. Took the Oath of Allegiance and Fidelity on or after March 1, 1778 [Ref: J-1814, N-106/114]. Private, Militia, Volunteer Company, 4th Battalion, 1780-1781 [Ref: N-86/105, M-230].

MULLIKIN, Samuel. Sergeant, Militia, Capt. Thomas Bullen's Company; no date was given; possibly late 1775 or early 1776 [Ref: Z-3].

MULLIKIN, Samuel Jr. Private, Militia, Capt. Thomas Bullen's Company; no date was given; possibly late 1775 or early 1776 [Ref: Z-3]. Private, Militia, Union Company, 4th Battalion, 1777-1778 [Ref: N-86/105, M-223, which listed the name without the "Jr."].

MULLIKIN, William (1737-   ). Born in St. Peter's Parish, Talbot County, on August 14, 1737, son of Patrick and Mary Mullican [Ref: V-79]. Private, Militia, Volunteer Company, 4th Battalion, 1780-1781 [Ref: N-86/105, M-230]. Took the Oath of Allegiance and Fidelity on or after March 1, 1778 [Ref: J-1814, N-106/114]. See "Samuel Mullikin" and "John Mullikin," q.v.

MURDOCH, Josias. Private, 4th Independent Company of Maryland Regular Troops, Capt. James Hindman's Company; enlisted January 31, 1776; reportedly deserted before September, 1776 muster roll [Ref: D-25].

MURPHY, John. Private, 4th Independent Company of Maryland Regular Troops, Capt. James Hindman's Company, September, 1776 muster roll; enlisted

February 7, 1776 [Ref: D-25]. Private, Militia, Hearts of Oak Company, 38th Battalion, 1777-1778 [Ref: N-86/105, M-226]. Took the Oath of Allegiance and Fidelity on or about March 1, 1778 [Ref: J-1814, N-106/114, which listed the name as "John Murphey"]. Private, Militia, Hearts of Oak Company, 38th Battalion, 1780-1781 [Ref: N-86/105, M-235].

MURPHY, John Jr. Private, Militia, Sword in Hand Company, 4th Battalion, 1780-1781 [Ref: N-86/105, M-231].

MURRAY, Henry (Certificate from Dorset County). Took the Oath of Allegiance and Fidelity on or about March 1, 1778 [Ref: J-1814, N-106/114].

MURRAY, Sally Scott. See "Edward Lloyd," q.v.

NABB, Charles. Took the Oath of Allegiance and Fidelity on or about March 1, 1778 [Ref: J-1814, N-106/114]. Rendered patriotic service by supplying wheat for the use of the Army in March, 1780 [Ref: P-278].

NABB, Charles Jr. Private, Militia, Sword in Hand Company, 4th Battalion, 1777-1778 [Ref: N-86/105, M-224, which listed the name without the "Jr."]. Private, Militia, Sword in Hand Company, 4th Battalion, 1780-1781 [Ref: N-86/105, M-231].

NABB, James. See "John Stevens," q.v.

NABB, John. Private, Militia, Sword in Hand Company, 4th Battalion, 1777-1778 [Ref: N-86/105, M-224]. Private, Militia, Sword in Hand Company, 4th Battalion, 1780-1781 [Ref: N-86/105, M-231]. Rendered patriotic service by supplying wheat for the use of the Army in April and June, 1780 [Ref: P-287, P-298].

NAPP, Thomas. See "Thomas Knapp," q.v.

NARKLAND, John. See "John Markland," q.v.

NASH, John. Private, Militia, Sword in Hand Company, 4th Battalion, 1777-1778 [Ref: N-86/105, M-224].

NASH, Page. Took the Oath of Allegiance and Fidelity on or after March 1, 1778 [Ref: J-1814, N-106/114].

NASH, Thomas. Private, Militia, United Company, 38th Battalion, 1780-1781 [Ref: N-86/105, M-233]. Private, Militia, United Company, 38th Battalion, 1777-1778 [Ref: N-86/105, M-227]. Took the Oath of Allegiance and Fidelity on or about March 1, 1778 [Ref: J-1814, N-106/114].

NEAL, Francis. Private, Militia, Third Haven Company, 4th Battalion, 1777-1778 [Ref: N-86/105, M-225].

NEAL (NEALL), George. Private, Militia, Capt. Thomas Bullen's Company; no date was given; possibly late 1775 or early 1776 [Ref: Z-3].

NEAL, Joseph. Private, Militia, Union Company, 4th Battalion, 1777-1778 [Ref: N-86/105, M-223]. Private, Militia, Union Company, 4th Battalion, 1780-1781 [Ref: N-86/105, M-230]. Private in the militia who was draughted on August 30, 1781 to reinforce the American Army and to serve in the Maryland Continental Troops until December 10, 1781 [Ref: D-387].

NEAL, Robert. Private, Militia, Union Company, 4th Battalion, 1780-1781 [Ref: N-86/105, M-229]. Private, Militia, Union Company, 4th Battalion, 1777-1778 [Ref: N-86/105, M-223]. Took the Oath of Allegiance and Fidelity on or about March 1, 1778 [Ref: J-1814, N-106/114].

NEAL, Samuel. Private, Militia, Union Company, 4th Battalion, 1777-1778 [Ref: N-86/105, M-223].

NEEDLES, Edward. Private, Militia, Union Company, 4th Battalion, 1777-1778 [Ref: N-86/105, M-223]. Took the Oath of Allegiance and Fidelity on or about March 1, 1778 [Ref: J-1814, N-106/114, which listed the name as "Edward Neadles"]. Private, Militia, Union Company, 4th Battalion, 1780-1781 [Ref: N-86/105, M-230].

NEEDLES, John. Took the Oath of Allegiance and Fidelity on or about March 1, 1778 [Ref: J-1814, N-106/114, which listed the name as "John Neadles"]. Rendered patriotic service by supplying bacon for the use of the Army in May, 1778 [Ref: P-169]. Sheriff of Talbot County in 1779 [Ref: F-132].

NEEDLES, Tristram (Tristam). Private, Militia, Union Company, 4th Battalion, 1777-1778 [Ref: N-86/105, M-223]. Private, Militia, Union Company, 4th Battalion, 1780-1781 [Ref: N-86/105, M-230].

NEEDLES, William. Private, Militia, Union Company, 4th Battalion, 1780-1781 [Ref: N-86/105, M-229].

NEGRO BRISTOL (a free man). Private in the militia who was draughted on August 30, 1781 to reinforce the American Army and to serve in the Maryland Continental Troops until December 10, 1781 [Ref: D-387].

NEGRO SPINDILOW (a free man). Private in the militia who was draughted on August 30, 1781 to reinforce the American Army and to serve in the Maryland Continental Troops until December 10, 1781 [Ref: D-387].

NEIGHBOURS, James. Private, Militia, Union Company, 4th Battalion, 1780-1781 [Ref: N-86/105, M-230]. Private aboard the barge *Fearnought* under Capt. Levin Spedden; enlisted June 4, 1782; 5'5" tall; fair complexion; born in Talbot County [Ref: D-612].

NEIGHBOURS, Levi. Private aboard the barge *Fearnought* under Capt. Levin Spedden; enlisted May 28, 1782; 5'7" tall; fair complexion; born in Talbot County [Ref: D-611].

NEIGHBOURS, Samuel. Private, Militia, 2nd Volunteer Company, 4th Battalion, 1777-1778 [Ref: N-86/105, M-225]. Took the Oath of Allegiance and Fidelity on or about March 1, 1778 [Ref: J-1814, N-106/114].

NEIGHBOURS, Samuel Jr. Private, Militia, Union Company, 4th Battalion, 1777-1778 [Ref: N-86/105, M-223, which listed the name without the "Jr."]. Private, Militia, Union Company, 4th Battalion, 1780-1781 [Ref: N-86/105, M-229]. Took the Oath of Allegiance and Fidelity on or about March 1, 1778 [Ref: J-1814, N-106/114].

NEIGHBOURS, Thomas. Private, Militia, Capt. Thomas Bullen's Company; no date was given; possibly late 1775 or early 1776 [Ref: Z-3]. Took the Oath of Allegiance and Fidelity on or about March 1, 1778 [Ref: J-1814, N-106/114].

NEIGHBOURS, Thomas (of Samuel). Private in the militia who was draughted on August 30, 1781 to reinforce the American Army and to serve in the Maryland Continental Troops until December 10, 1781 [Ref: D-387, which spelled the name "Nilghbours"].

NESMITH, John. Took the Oath of Allegiance and Fidelity on or about March 1, 1778 [Ref: J-1814, N-106/114].

NEWCOMB (NEWCOME), Robert. Private, Militia, 4th Battalion, Capt. Greenbury Goldsborough's Company, reviewed and passed July 27, 1776 [Ref: D-67]. Private, Militia, Hearts of Oak Company, 38th Battalion, 1777-1778 [Ref: N-86/105, M-226]. Took the Oath of Allegiance and Fidelity on or about March 1, 1778 [Ref: J-1814, N-106/114, which listed the name as "Robert Newcome"]. Private, 5th Maryland Line, enlisted March 1, 1778 and reportedly "deserted" on August 1, 1778 [Ref: D-234].

NEWCOMB (NEWCOME), Robert Jr. Took the Oath of Allegiance and Fidelity on or about March 1, 1778 [Ref: J-1814, N-106/114].

NEWNAM (NUNAM), Abner. Private, Militia, Hand in Hand Company, 4th Battalion, 1780-1781 [Ref: N-86/105, M-232]. Private, Militia, Hand & Hand Company, 4th Battalion, 1777-1778 [Ref: N-86/105, M-226].

NEWNAM (NUNAM), Daniel. Private, Militia, Sword in Hand Company, 4th Battalion, 1777-1778 [Ref: N-86/105, M-224]. Private, Militia, Sword in Hand Company, 4th Battalion, 1780-1781 [Ref: N-86/105, M-231]. Took the Oath of Allegiance and Fidelity on or about March 1, 1778 [Ref: J-1814, N-106/114].

NEWNAM, Edward. Private, Militia, Capt. Thomas Bullen's Company; no date was given; possibly late 1775 or early 1776 [Ref: Z-3].

NEWNAM (NUNAM), John. Private, Militia, Volunteer Company, 4th Battalion, 1777-1778 [Ref: N-86/105, M-223]. Took the Oath of Allegiance and Fidelity on or after March 1, 1778 [Ref: J-1814, N-106/114]. Private, Militia, Volunteer Company, 4th Battalion, 1780-1781 [Ref: N-86/105, M-230, which listed the name as "John Nunam"].

NEWNAM, John. Took the Oath of Allegiance and Fidelity on or about March 1, 1778; name listed twice [Ref: J-1814, N-106/114].

NEWNAM, Joseph. Private, Militia, 4th Battalion, Capt. Greenbury Goldsborough's Company, reviewed and passed July 27, 1776 [Ref: D-67]. Took the Oath of Allegiance and Fidelity on or about March 1, 1778 [Ref: J-1814, N-106/114].

NEWNAM, Risdon. Private, Militia, 4th Battalion, Capt. Greenbury Goldsborough's Company, reviewed and passed July 27, 1776 [Ref: D-67].

NICHOLS (NICKELS), John. Private, Militia, Union Company, 4th Battalion, 1777-1778 [Ref: N-86/105, M-223].

NICHOLS (NICOLS), Robert Lloyd. Appointed Paymaster of the Eastern Shore Troops in May, 1776, by the Maryland Council [Ref: A-451, A-452, B-183]. Second Major, Militia, 4th Battalion, January 1, 1776. Recommended to be First Major, June 17, 1777. Lieutenant Colonel, Militia, 4th Battalion, April 9, 1778 [Ref: N-90, M-107, E-24]. Took the Oath of Allegiance and Fidelity on or about March 1, 1778 [Ref: J-1814, N-106/114, which listed the name as "Loyd Robert Nicols"]. Appointed a Justice of the Peace on November 20, 1779 and January 17, 1782 [Ref: F-22, which listed the name as "Robert Lloyd Nicolls" and I-46, which listed the name as "Robert Lloyd Nicholls"].

NICHOLS (NICHOLLS), Samuel. Private, Militia, Wye Company, 4th Battalion, 1777-1778 [Ref: N-86/105, M-222]. Took the Oath of Allegiance and Fidelity on or about March 1, 1778 [Ref: J-1814, N-106/114].

NICHOLS, Sarah. See "Robert Goldsborough," q.v.

NICHOLSON, Daniel. Private, Militia, Wye Company, 4th Battalion, 1777-1778 [Ref: N-86/105, M-222].

NICHOLSON, Henrietta. See "John Bracco," q.v.

NICHOLSON, Joseph Hopper. See "Edward Lloyd," q.v.

NICKS, Joseph. Took the Oath of Allegiance and Fidelity on or about March 1, 1778 [Ref: J-1814, N-106/114].

NICOLS, Henry. See "Samuel Chamberlaine," q.v.

NICOLS, John. Private, Militia, Third Haven Company, 4th Battalion, 1777-1778 [Ref: N-86/105, M-225]. Private, Militia, Third Haven Company, 4th Battalion, 1780-1781 [Ref: N-86/105, M-232]. Took the Oath of Allegiance and Fidelity on or after March 1, 1778 [Ref: J-1814, N-106/114].

NICOLS (NICOLLS), Samuel. Appointed a Justice of the Peace on November 21, 1778 [Ref: E-250].

NICOLS, William. Private, Militia, Bullinbrook Company, 4th Battalion, 1780-1781 [Ref: N-86/105, M-231]. One William Nicols married Henrietta Maria Chamberlaine in St. Peter's Parish, Talbot County, on May 21, 1760 [Ref: K-55].

NISBITT, John. Private, Militia, Capt. Thomas Bullen's Company; no date was given; possibly late 1775 or early 1776 [Ref: Z-3].

NIX, George. Private, Militia, Hand & Hand Company, 4th Battalion, 1777-1778 [Ref: N-86/105, M-225].

NOLEY, William. Private, Militia, Sword in Hand Company, 4th Battalion, 1777-1778 [Ref: N-86/105, M-224].

NORRIS, James. Private, Militia, Third Haven Company, 4th Battalion, 1777-1778 [Ref: N-86/105, M-225]. Took the Oath of Allegiance and Fidelity on or after March 1, 1778 [Ref: J-1814, N-106/114].

NORRIS, John. Second Lieutenant, Militia, Bayside Company, January 3, 1776 [Ref: M-107].

NORRIS, Lambert. Took the Oath of Allegiance and Fidelity on or after March 1, 1778 [Ref: J-1814, N-106/114].

NORRIS, Philip. Private, Militia, Volunteer Company, 4th Battalion, 1780-1781 [Ref: N-86/105, M-229]. Private, Militia, 2nd Volunteer Company, 4th Battalion, 1777-1778 [Ref: N-86/105, M-225]. Took the Oath of Allegiance and Fidelity on or about March 1, 1778 [Ref: J-1814, N-106/114].

NORTH, George. On May 12, 1778, the Maryland Council ordered that the Sheriff of Talbot County may $32 to George North, the bounty for enlisting two recruits [Ref: E-77].

NORTH, Jacob. Private, Militia, 4th Battalion, Capt. Greenbury Goldsborough's Company, reviewed and passed July 27, 1776 [Ref: D-68]. Corporal, 5th Maryland Line, enlisted June 28, 1777; sergeant, June, 1778; and still in service on January 1, 1780 [Ref: D-234]. Jacob North was born in Maryland, married Ruth ----, and died before October 26, 1795 [Ref: Y-2159].

NORTH, Ruth. See "Jacob North," q.v.

NORTON, Richard. Private, Militia, Volunteer Company, 4th Battalion, 1780-1781 [Ref: N-86/105, M-229]. Private, Militia, 2nd Volunteer Company, 4th Battalion, 1777-1778 [Ref: N-86/105, M-225]. Private, Militia, Wye Company, 4th Battalion, 1780-1781 [Ref: N-86/105, M-229].

NORWOOD, Edward. Private, Militia, Hearts of Oak Company, 38th Battalion, 1780-1781 [Ref: N-86/105, M-235].

NORWOOD, John. Private, Militia, Hearts of Oak Company, 38th Battalion, 1780-1781 [Ref: N-86/105, M-235]. Private, Militia, Hearts of Oak Company, 38th Battalion, 1777-1778 [Ref: N-86/105, M-226]. Took the Oath of Allegiance and Fidelity on or about March 1, 1778 [Ref: J-1814, N-106/114].

NORWOOD, Joseph. Private, Militia, United Company, 38th Battalion, 1780-1781 [Ref: N-86/105, M-233]. Private in the militia who was draughted on August 30, 1781 to reinforce the American Army and to serve in the Maryland Continental Troops until December 10, 1781 [Ref: D-387].

NORWOOD, Joseph. Private, Militia, Oxford Company, 38th Battalion, 1777-1778 [Ref: N-86/105, M-228]. Took the Oath of Allegiance and Fidelity on or after March 1, 1778 [Ref: J-1814, N-106/114]. Private, Militia, Oxford Company, 38th Battalion, 1780-1781 [Ref: N-86/105, M-235].

NORWOOD, William. Took the Oath of Allegiance and Fidelity on or about March 1, 1778 [Ref: J-1814, N-106/114].

NORWOOD, William Jr. Private, Militia, Hearts of Oak Company, 38th Battalion, 1780-1781 [Ref: N-86/105, M-234]. Private, Militia, Hearts of Oak Company, 38th Battalion, 1777-1778 [Ref: N-86/105, M-226].

NOWLES, Joseph. See "Joseph Knowles," q.v.

NUNAM, Abner. See "Abner Newnam," q.v.

NUTTLE (NUTTALL), John. Took the Oath of Allegiance and Fidelity on or about March 1, 1778 [Ref: J-1814, N-106/114]. Private, Militia, Miles River Company, 38th Battalion, 1777-1778 [Ref: N-86/105, M-227].

NUTTLE, John Jr. Private, Militia, Miles River Company, 38th Battalion, 1780-1781 [Ref: N-86/105, M-235].

NUTTLE (NUTTELL), Philip. Private, Militia, Miles River Company, 38th Battalion, 1777-1778 [Ref: N-86/105, M-227].
NUTTLE, Phill. Private, Militia, Wye Company, 4th Battalion, 1780-1781 [Ref: N-86/105, M-228].
NUTTLE, Solomon. Private, Militia, Miles River Company, 38th Battalion, 1780-1781 [Ref: N-86/105, M-235].
NUTWELL, Thomas. Took the Oath of Allegiance and Fidelity on or about March 1, 1778 [Ref: J-1814, N-106/114]. Private, Militia, Hand & Hand Company, 4th Battalion, 1777-1778 [Ref: N-86/105, M-226, which listed the name as "Thomas Nutrell"].
O'BRYAN, John. Private, 4th Independent Company of Maryland Regular Troops, Capt. James Hindman's Company, September, 1776 muster roll; enlisted January 23, 1776 [Ref: D-24].
OGLE, James. Private, Militia, Capt. Thomas Bullen's Company; no date was given; possibly late 1775 or early 1776 [Ref: Z-3].
OLD, Hugh. See "Hugh Auld," q.v.
OLDFIELD, Henry (1737-   ). Born in St. Peter's Parish, Talbot County, on October 23, 1737, son of Henry and Sarah Oldfield [Ref: V-79]. Private, Militia, 4th Battalion, Capt. Greenbury Goldsborough's Company, reviewed and passed July 27, 1776 [Ref: D-68].
OLDFIELD, Sarah. See "Henry Oldfield," q.v.
OLDHAM, Hannah. See "Nicholas Martin," q.v.
ORAM (OREM, ORIM), Andrew. Private, Militia, 4th Battalion, Capt. Greenbury Goldsborough's Company, reviewed and passed July 27, 1776 [Ref: D-68]. Private, Militia, Hearts of Oak Company, 38th Battalion, 1777-1778 [Ref: N-86/105, M-226]. Took the Oath of Allegiance and Fidelity on or about March 1, 1778 [Ref: J-1814, N-106/114]. Sergeant, Militia, Hearts of Oak Company, 38th Battalion, 1780-1781 [Ref: N-104, M-234].
ORAM (OREM), Edward. Private, Militia, Oxford Company, 38th Battalion, 1777-1778 [Ref: N-86/105, M-227]. Private, Militia, Oxford Company, 38th Battalion, 1780-1781 [Ref: N-86/105, M-235].
ORAM, Hugh. Private, Militia, Oxford Company, 38th Battalion, 1777-1778 [Ref: N-86/105, M-227]. Took the Oath of Allegiance and Fidelity on or about March 1, 1778 [Ref: J-1814, N-106/114].
ORAM (OREM), Nicholas. Took the Oath of Allegiance and Fidelity on or about March 1, 1778 [Ref: J-1814, N-106/114]. Private, Militia, Hearts of Oak Company, 38th Battalion, 1777-1778 [Ref: N-86/105, M-226]. Private, Militia, Hearts of Oak Company, 38th Battalion, 1780-1781; name listed twice and spelled "Oram" and "Orem" [Ref: N-86/105, M-234, M-235].
ORAM (OREM), Spedden. Private, Militia, Oxford Company, 38th Battalion, 1780-1781 [Ref: N-86/105, M-235]. Waterman on the barge *Intrepid* in 1781 [Ref: D-610]. On February 18, 1825 the Treasurer of Maryland was directed to

pay to Spedden Orem, of Talbot County, half pay of a private as further remuneration for his services during the Revolutionary War. [Ref: T-379].

ORAM (OREM, ORIM), William. Private, Militia, Hearts of Oak Company, 38th Battalion, 1777-1778 [Ref: N-86/105, M-226]. Took the Oath of Allegiance and Fidelity on or about March 1, 1778 [Ref: J-1814, N-106/114]. Private, Militia, Hearts of Oak Company, 38th Battalion, 1780-1781 [Ref: N-86/105, M-234].

ORRELL, James. Corporal, 4th Independent Company of Maryland Regular Troops, September, 1776 muster roll; enlisted January 26, 1776 [Ref: D-23].

OSMOND (OSMON, OSMANT), John. Took the Oath of Allegiance and Fidelity on or about March 1, 1778 [Ref: J-1814, N-106/114]. Private, Militia, Miles River Company, 38th Battalion, 1777-1778 [Ref: N-86/105, M-227]. Corporal, Militia, Miles River Company, 38th Battalion, 1780-1781 [Ref: N-105, M-235].

OSMOND (OZMONT, AUSMAN), Jonathan. Private, Militia, Hand & Hand Company, 4th Battalion, 1777-1778 [Ref: N-86/105, M-225, which listed the name as "Jonathan Ausman"]. Private, Militia, Hand in Hand Company, 4th Battalion, 1780-1781 [Ref: N-86/105, M-232]. Took the Oath of Allegiance and Fidelity on or about March 1, 1778 [Ref: J-1814, N-106/114].

OSMOND (OSMENT, OZMOND, AUSMAN), Thomas. Private, Militia, Hand & Hand Company, 4th Battalion, 1777-1778 [Ref: N-86/105, M-225, which listed the name as "Thomas Ausman"]. Took the Oath of Allegiance and Fidelity on or about March 1, 1778 [Ref: J-1814, N-106/114]. Private, Militia, Hand in Hand Company, 4th Battalion, 1780-1781 [Ref: N-86/105, M-232]. Draughted on May 1, 1781 to serve until December 10, 1781 in the Maryland Continental Troops [Ref: D-371].

OXENHAM, Peter. Private, Militia, Hand in Hand Company, 4th Battalion, 1780-1781 [Ref: N-86/105, M-232].

OXENHAM, Richard (c1750-1797). Private, Militia, Third Haven Company, 4th Battalion, 1780-1781 [Ref: N-86/105, M-232]. Private, Militia, Hand & Hand Company, 4th Battalion, 1777-1778 [Ref: N-86/105, M-225]. Richard Oxenham was born circa 1750, married Elizabeth Rathall (Rathell), and died before March 14, 1797 [Ref: Y-2204].

OZBUN (OZBON), William. Private, Militia, 4th Battalion, Capt. Greenbury Goldsborough's Company, reviewed and passed July 27, 1776; name listed twice [Ref: D-67, D-68].

PALMER, Isaac. Private, Militia, Wye Company, 4th Battalion, 1780-1781 [Ref: N-86/105, M-229]. Private, Militia, Wye Company, 4th Battalion, 1777-1778 [Ref: N-86/105, M-222, which listed the name as "Isaac Pamer"].

PAMPHILION (PAMPILION), Nicholas. Took the Oath of Allegiance and Fidelity on or about March 1, 1778 [Ref: J-1814, N-106/114]. Private, Militia, Third Haven Company, 4th Battalion, 1780-1781 [Ref: N-86/105, M-232].

PARK, John. Private, Militia, Wye Company, 4th Battalion, 1780-1781 [Ref: N-86/105, M-228].

PARKER, Thomas. Private, Militia, 2nd Volunteer Company, 4th Battalion, 1777-1778 [Ref: N-86/105, M-224].

PARKERSON, Edward. Private, Militia, Union Company, 4th Battalion, 1777-1778 [Ref: N-86/105, M-223]. Private, Militia, Hand in Hand Company, 4th Battalion, 1780-1781 [Ref: N-86/105, M-232].

PARKS, John. Took the Oath of Allegiance and Fidelity on or about March 1, 1778 [Ref: J-1814, N-106/114].

PARRISH (PARISH), William. Private, Militia, 2nd Volunteer Company, 4th Battalion, 1777-1778 [Ref: N-86/105, M-225]. Private, Militia, Volunteer Company, 4th Battalion, 1780-1781 [Ref: N-86/105, M-229].

PARROTT, Aaron. Private, Militia, Hand in Hand Company, 4th Battalion, 1780-1781 [Ref: N-86/105, M-232]. Private, Militia, Hand & Hand Company, 4th Battalion, 1777-1778 [Ref: N-86/105, M-225].

PARROTT, Abner. Private, Militia, Bullinbrook Company, 4th Battalion, 1780-1781 [Ref: N-86/105, M-231]. Private, Militia, Bullin Brook Company, 4th Battalion, 1777-1778 [Ref: N-86/105, M-224]. Took the Oath of Allegiance and Fidelity on or after March 1, 1778 [Ref: J-1814, N-106/114].

PARROTT, Ann. See "Peter Parrott," q.v.

PARROTT, George (1730-   ). Born in St. Peter's Parish, Talbot County, on April 20, 1730, son of Joseph and Mary Parrott [Ref: V-67].Took the Oath of Allegiance and Fidelity on or about March 1, 1778 [Ref: J-1814, N-106/114].

PARROTT, Henry. Private, Militia, Third Haven Company, 4th Battalion, 1780-1781 [Ref: N-86/105, M-232]. Private, Militia, Third Haven Company, 4th Battalion, 1777-1778 [Ref: N-86/105, M-225]. Took the Oath of Allegiance and Fidelity on or after March 1, 1778 [Ref: J-1814, N-106/114].

PARROTT (PARRATT), James. Private, Militia, Capt. Thomas Bullen's Company; no date was given; possibly late 1775 or early 1776 [Ref: Z-3].

PARROTT, James. Private, Militia, Bullin Brook Company, 4th Battalion, 1777-1778 [Ref: N-86/105, M-224]. Private, Militia, Bullinbrook Company, 4th Battalion, 1780-1781 [Ref: N-86/105, M-231].

PARROTT, James. Private, Militia, Hand & Hand Company, 4th Battalion, 1777-1778 [Ref: N-86/105, M-225]. Took the Oath of Allegiance and Fidelity on or after March 1, 1778 [Ref: J-1814, N-106/114].

PARROTT, James (1756-1845). Took the Oath of Allegiance and Fidelity on or about March 1, 1778 [Ref: J-1814, N-106/114, which listed the name as "James Parrott, farmer"]. This might be the James Parrott who was born in Maryland in 1756, married first to Katherine Smith and second to Matilda Tharp, rendered patriotic service during the revolution, and died in 1845 in Indiana [Ref: Y-2238]. Since there were several men with this name, additional research will be necessary before drawing conclusions.

PARROTT, James Jr. Private, Militia, Hand & Hand Company, 4th Battalion, 1777-1778 [Ref: N-86/105, M-225]. Private, Militia, Hand in Hand Company, 4th Battalion, 1780-1781 [Ref: N-86/105, M-232].

PARROTT, Jane. See "Henry Banning," q.v.

PARROTT, John. Private, Militia, Volunteer Company, 4th Battalion, 1777-1778 [Ref: N-86/105, M-223]. Took the Oath of Allegiance and Fidelity on or after March 1, 1778 [Ref: J-1814, N-106/114]. Private, Militia, Volunteer Company, 4th Battalion, 1780-1781 [Ref: N-86/105, M-230].

PARROTT, John. Private, Militia, Hand & Hand Company, 4th Battalion, 1777-1778 [Ref: N-86/105, M-226]. Private, Militia, Hand in Hand Company, 4th Battalion, 1780-1781 [Ref: N-86/105, M-233]. Took the Oath of Allegiance and Fidelity on or about March 1, 1778 [Ref: J-1814, N-106/114].

PARROTT, John. Private, Militia, 4th Battalion, Capt. Greenbury Goldsborough's Company, reviewed and passed July 27, 1776 [Ref: D-68]. Rendered patriotic service by supplying bacon for the use of the Army in May, 1778 [Ref: P-169].

PARROTT, John Jr. Private, Militia, Volunteer Company, 4th Battalion, 1780-1781 [Ref: N-86/105, M-230]. Private, Militia, Volunteer Company, 4th Battalion, 1777-1778 [Ref: N-86/105, M-223].

PARROTT, Joseph. Private, Militia, Union Company, 4th Battalion, 1777-1778 [Ref: N-86/105, M-223]. See "George Parrott," q.v.

PARROTT, Mary. See "George Parrott," q.v.

PARROTT, Perry. Private, Militia, Sword in Hand Company, 4th Battalion, 1780-1781 [Ref: N-86/105, M-231]. Private, Militia, Sword in Hand Company, 4th Battalion, 1777-1778 [Ref: N-86/105, M-224]. Took the Oath of Allegiance and Fidelity on or about March 1, 1778 [Ref: J-1814, N-106/114]. Rendered patriotic service by supplying bacon for the use of the Army and by hauling provisions in May, 1778, and by supplying wheat in March, 1780 [Ref: P-172, P-275].

PARROTT, Peter. Private, Militia, Hand in Hand Company, 4th Battalion, 1780-1781 [Ref: N-86/105, M-232]. Took the Oath of Allegiance and Fidelity on or about March 1, 1778 [Ref: J-1814, N-106/114]. "Peter Parratt, son of Peter Parratt and Ann his wife, was born May --, 1736." [Ref: V-88].

PARROTT, Richard. First Lieutenant, Militia, Miles River Company, 38th Battalion, April 9, 1778 [Ref: N-92, M-110, E-25]. Took the Oath of Allegiance and Fidelity on or about March 1, 1778 [Ref: J-1814, N-106/114]. Rendered patriotic service by transporting bacon for the use of the Army in June, 1778 [Ref: P-173]. See "Jonathan Hopkins," q.v.

PARROTT, Saila (Salah). Private, Militia, Hand & Hand Company, 4th Battalion, 1777-1778 [Ref: N-86/105, M-226]. Private, Militia, Hand in Hand Company, 4th Battalion, 1780-1781 [Ref: N-86/105, M-232]. Took the Oath of Allegiance and Fidelity on or about March 1, 1778 [Ref: J-1814, N-106/114].

PARROTT, Slyter. Private, Militia, Sword in Hand Company, 4th Battalion, 1780-1781 [Ref: N-86/105, M-231]. Took the Oath of Allegiance and Fidelity on or about March 1, 1778 [Ref: J-1814, N-106/114].

PARROTT, Thomas. Private, Militia, Hand in Hand Company, 4th Battalion, 1780-1781 [Ref: N-86/105, M-232]. Private, Militia, Hand & Hand Company, 4th Battalion, 1777-1778 [Ref: N-86/105, M-225].

PARSONNETT, David. Private, Militia, Wye Company, 4th Battalion, 1780-1781 [Ref: N-86/105, M-228]. Private, Militia, Wye Company, 4th Battalion, 1777-1778 [Ref: N-86/105, M-222].

PARSONS (PEARSONS), Benjamin. Private, Militia, Third Haven Company, 4th Battalion, 1780-1781 [Ref: N-86/105, M-232]. Private, Militia, Third Haven Company, 4th Battalion, 1777-1778 [Ref: N-86/105, M-225].

PARSONS, James. Private, Militia, Oxford Company, 38th Battalion, 1777-1778 [Ref: N-86/105, M-228].

PARSONS (PEARSONS), Joseph. Private, Militia, Union Company, 4th Battalion, 1777-1778 [Ref: N-86/105, M-223]. Private, Militia, Union Company, 4th Battalion, 1780-1781 [Ref: N-86/105, M-230].

PASTERFIELD, Philip. See "Daniel Auld, Jr.," q.v.

PATTERSON, James. Private, Militia, Oxford Company, 38th Battalion, 1777-1778 [Ref: N-86/105, M-227]. Took the Oath of Allegiance and Fidelity on or after March 1, 1778 [Ref: J-1814, N-106/114].

PATTERSON, John. Private, Militia, Bullinbrook Company, 4th Battalion, 1780-1781 [Ref: N-86/105, M-231]. Private, Militia, Bullin Brook Company, 4th Battalion, 1777-1778 [Ref: N-86/105, M-224]. Rendered patriotic service by supplying bacon for the use of the Army in June, 1778 [Ref: P-175].

PATTINSON, Vincent. Private, Militia, Capt. Thomas Bullen's Company; no date was given; possibly late 1775 or early 1776 [Ref: Z-3].

PATTISON, Edward. Private, Militia, Third Haven Company, 4th Battalion, 1780-1781 [Ref: N-86/105, M-232].

PEARSON, Levi. Private, Militia, 2nd Volunteer Company, 4th Battalion, 1777-1778 [Ref: N-86/105, M-225]. Sergeant, Militia, Volunteer Company, 4th Battalion, 1780-1781 [Ref: N-96, M-229].

PEARSON, Thomas. Private, Militia, 2nd Volunteer Company, 4th Battalion, 1777-1778 [Ref: N-86/105, M-225].

PEARSON, William. Private, Militia, Volunteer Company, 4th Battalion, 1780-1781 [Ref: N-86/105, M-229]. Private, Militia, 2nd Volunteer Company, 4th Battalion, 1777-1778 [Ref: N-86/105, M-225].

PECKERN, Robert. See "Robert Pickering," q.v.

PECOR, Leon. See "Thomas Barnett Sewell," q.v.

PENNYMORE, Phil. Private, Militia, Capt. Thomas Bullen's Company; no date was given; possibly late 1775 or early 1776 [Ref: Z-3].

PENNYMORE, William. Private, Militia, Capt. Thomas Bullen's Company; no date was given; possibly late 1775 or early 1776 [Ref: Z-3].

PERRY, Charles. Rendered patriotic service by supplying a horse for the use of the Army in August, 1780 [Ref: P-310].

PERRY, Dionisious (Dionisius). Took the Oath of Allegiance and Fidelity on or about March 1, 1778 [Ref: J-1814, N-106/114]. Took the Oath of Allegiance and Fidelity on or after March 1, 1778 [Ref: J-1814, N-106/114].

PERRY, William. Attended the Maryland Convention on July 3, 1776 for the purpose of forming a new government, and was selected one of the judges of elections for Talbot County on November 8, 1776 [Ref: O-35, O-55]. Quartermaster, Militia, 4th Battalion, August 13, 1776 [Ref: M-111, B-198]. Took the Oath of Allegiance and Fidelity on or about March 1, 1778 [Ref: J-1814, N-106/114]. Justice of the Peace and Judge of the Orphans Court, appointed on November 21, 1778 and November 20, 1779 [Ref: E-250, F-22].

PHARIS (PHARRIS), Thomas. Private, Militia, Volunteer Company, 4th Battalion, 1780-1781 [Ref: N-86/105, M-230]. Private, Militia, Volunteer Company, 4th Battalion, 1777-1778 [Ref: N-86/105, M-223].

PHILIPS, John. Private, Militia, Wye Company, 4th Battalion, 1780-1781 [Ref: N-86/105, M-228].

PHILIPS, Philemon. Private, Militia, Volunteer Company, 4th Battalion, 1777-1778 [Ref: N-86/105, M-223].

PICKERING, Charles. Private, Militia, Oxford Company, 38th Battalion, 1777-1778 [Ref: N-86/105, M-228]. Private, Militia, Oxford Company, 38th Battalion, 1780-1781 [Ref: N-86/105, M-235].

PICKERING, Charles. Private, Militia, 2nd Volunteer Company, 4th Battalion, 1777-1778 [Ref: N-86/105, M-225]. Took the Oath of Allegiance and Fidelity on or after March 1, 1778 [Ref: J-1814, N-106/114].

PICKERING, Charles Jr. Private, Militia, Oxford Company, 38th Battalion, 1780-1781 [Ref: N-86/105, M-235]. Took the Oath of Allegiance and Fidelity on or about March 1, 1778 [Ref: J-1814, N-106/114, which listed the name without the "Jr."].

PICKERING, George. Private, Militia, Hearts of Oak Company, 38th Battalion, 1777-1778 [Ref: N-86/105, M-226]. Took the Oath of Allegiance and Fidelity on or about March 1, 1778 [Ref: J-1814, N-106/114]. Private, Militia, Union Company, 4th Battalion, 1780-1781 [Ref: N-86/105, M-230].

PICKERING, Peter. Waterman on the barge *Intrepid* in 1781 [Ref: D-610].

PICKERING, Robert. Private, Militia, Wye Company, 4th Battalion, 1777-1778 [Ref: N-86/105, M-222, which listed the name as "Robert Peckern"]. Private, Militia, Wye Company, 4th Battalion, 1780-1781 [Ref: N-86/105, M-228]. Took the Oath of Allegiance and Fidelity on or about March 1, 1778 [Ref: J-1814, N-106/114].

PINKIND, John. Private, Militia, Volunteer Company, 4th Battalion, 1780-1781 [Ref: N-86/105, M-229].

PINKIND, Michael. Private, Militia, Volunteer Company, 4th Battalion, 1780-1781 [Ref: N-86/105, M-229]. Private, Militia, 2nd Volunteer Company, 4th Battalion, 1777-1778 [Ref: N-86/105, M-225, which listed the name as "Michael Pinkins"].

PINKINE, Vincent. Private, Militia, 2nd Volunteer Company, 4th Battalion, 1777-1778 [Ref: N-86/105, M-225].

PIPPEN, Joseph (1752-1833). He applied for a pension in Edgecombe County, North Carolina on August 29, 1832, aged 80, stating he was born in Talbot County, Maryland and "at age 11 was moved to Halifax County, North Carolina." He later enlisted in the North Carolina Line and held the rank of ensign. He died on April 10, 1833. See pension file W5546 awarded to Temperance Pippen, his widow, in 1853 in Edgecombe County, North Carolina. She died on June 7, 1854 [Ref: W-2707]. Joseph Pippen married first to Lucretia Knight and second to Mrs. Temperance Lee [Ref: Y-2320].

PITTS, William. Private, 4th Independent Company of Maryland Regular Troops, Capt. James Hindman's Company, September, 1776 muster roll; enlisted January 25, 1776 [Ref: D-24].

PLOWMAN, James. Took the Oath of Allegiance and Fidelity on or about March 1, 1778 [Ref: J-1814, N-106/114].

PLOWMAN, James Jr. Private, Militia, Hand in Hand Company, who was draughted on May 1, 1781 to serve until December 10, 1781 in the Maryland Continental Troops [Ref: D-371].

PLUMMER, George. Private, Militia, Wye Company, 4th Battalion, 1780-1781 [Ref: N-86/105, M-229]. Private, Militia, Wye Company, 4th Battalion, 1777-1778 [Ref: N-86/105, M-222]. Took the Oath of Allegiance and Fidelity on or after March 1, 1778 [Ref: J-1814, N-106/114].

PLUMMER, Gewil(?). Private, Militia, Wye Company, 4th Battalion, 1780-1781 [Ref: N-86/105, M-228].

PLUMMER, Hopkins Kinnimont (of James). Private, Militia, Wye Company, 4th Battalion, 1780-1781 [Ref: N-86/105, M-228].

PLUMMER, James. See "Hopkins Kinnimont Plummer," q.v.

PLUMMER, John. Private, Militia, Bayside Company, 38th Battalion, 1780-1781 [Ref: N-86/105, M-233]. Took the Oath of Allegiance and Fidelity on or after March 1, 1778 [Ref: J-1814, N-106/114].

PLUMMER, John Jr. Private, Militia, Bayside Company, 38th Battalion, 1780-1781 [Ref: N-86/105, M-233].

PLUMMER, Levi. Private, Militia, Wye Company, 4th Battalion, 1777-1778 [Ref: N-86/105, M-222]. Took the Oath of Allegiance and Fidelity on or about March 1, 1778 [Ref: J-1814, N-106/114].

PLUMMER, Phil. Private, Militia, Bayside Company, 38th Battalion, 1777-1778 [Ref: N-86/105, M-228].

PLUMMER, Solomon. Took the Oath of Allegiance and Fidelity on or about March 1, 1778 [Ref: J-1814, N-106/114]. Private, Militia, Wye Company, 4th Battalion, 1780-1781 [Ref: N-86/105, M-228]. Draughted on May 1, 1781 to serve until December 10, 1781 in the Maryland Continental Troops [Ref: D-371]. In June, 1781, he petitioned Gov. Thomas Sim Lee as follows: "Humbly Sheweth. That Your Excellencies Petitioner (under a late Act of Assembly) among the other militia of the county afsd. [Talbot] have been classed, and draughted as an able bodied man; Tho' very infirm for some years past occasioned by an imposthum in his breast that broak & left him in a decline (as he thinks) which has rendered him unable to work or do duty as a soldier in the field, and now prevents him from marching out with the draughts from the county afsd. agreeable to orders of the Lieutenant and thereby has incurred the penalty of said Act. Your petitioner being so unfortunately circumstanced, humbly requests the interposition of Your Excellency in his behalf; that would be pleased to stay all further prosecution against him for not complying with the terms of the said Act or grant him such relief as to Your Excellency shall deem mete." Attested by: Moses Butler (made his mark), Thomas Plummer, and John Plummer. [Ref: H-332].

PLUMMER, Thomas. Private, Militia, Wye Company, 4th Battalion, 1777-1778 [Ref: N-86/105, M-222]. Took the Oath of Allegiance and Fidelity on or after March 1, 1778 [Ref: J-1814, N-106/114].

PLUNKETT, James. Private, Militia, Capt. Thomas Bullen's Company; no date was given; possibly late 1775 or early 1776 [Ref: Z-3].

POLK, Anna. See "Richard Tilghman, Jr.," q.v.

POLLARD, Margaret. See "Pollard Edmondson," q.v.

PONEY, George. Private, Militia, Union Company, 4th Battalion, 1780-1781 [Ref: N-86/105, M-230]. Draughted on May 1, 1781 to serve until December 10, 1781 in the Maryland Continental Troops [Ref: D-371].

PORTER, Francis. Ensign, Militia, Bayside Company, 38th Battalion, June 15, 1780 [Ref: N-102, M-233, M-111, F-195]. Took the Oath of Allegiance and Fidelity on or after March 1, 1778 [Ref: J-1814, N-106/114].

PORTER, Hugh. Private, Militia, United Company, 38th Battalion, 1777-1778 [Ref: N-86/105, M-227]. Private, Militia, United Company, 38th Battalion, 1780-1781 [Ref: N-86/105, M-233, which listed the name as "Hughs Porter"].

PORTER, James. Took the Oath of Allegiance and Fidelity on or about March 1, 1778 [Ref: J-1814, N-106/114].

PORTER, John. Private, Militia, Bayside Company, 38th Battalion, 1780-1781 [Ref: N-86/105, M-233]. Private, Militia, Bayside Company, 38th Battalion, 1777-1778 [Ref: N-86/105, M-228]. Took the Oath of Allegiance and Fidelity on or about March 1, 1778; name listed twice [Ref: J-1814, N-106/114].

PORTER, John Jr. Private, Militia, 2nd Volunteer Company, 4th Battalion, 1777-1778 [Ref: N-86/105, M-225].

PORTER, Jonathan. Private, Militia, Hearts of Oak Company, 38th Battalion, 1780-1781 [Ref: N-86/105, M-234]. Private, Militia, Hearts of Oak Company, 38th Battalion, 1777-1778 [Ref: N-86/105, M-226]. Took the Oath of Allegiance and Fidelity on or about March 1, 1778 [Ref: J-1814, N-106/114].

PORTER, Joseph. Private, Militia, Bayside Company, 38th Battalion, 1777-1778 [Ref: N-86/105, M-228]. Private, Militia, Bayside Company, 38th Battalion,

1777-1778 [Ref: N-86/105, M-228]. Took the Oath of Allegiance and Fidelity on or about March 1, 1778 [Ref: J-1814, N-106/114].
PORTER, Joseph (of Joseph). Private, Militia, Bayside Company, 38th Battalion, 1780-1781 [Ref: N-86/105, M-233].
PORTER, Nathan. Private, Militia, 2nd Volunteer Company, 4th Battalion, 1777-1778 [Ref: N-86/105, M-224]. Took the Oath of Allegiance and Fidelity on or about March 1, 1778 [Ref: J-1814, N-106/114]. Private, Militia, Volunteer Company, 4th Battalion, 1780-1781 [Ref: N-86/105, M-229].
PORTER, Nathan. Private, Militia, Broad Creek Company, 38th Battalion, 1777-1778 [Ref: N-86/105, M-227]. Private, Militia, Broad Creek Company, 38th Battalion, 1780-1781 [Ref: N-86/105, M-234]. Gunner on the barge *Terable* in 1781 [Ref: D-610]. He placed on the pension rolls on March 5, 1833, aged 78, as a private in the Maryland State Troops with an annual allowance of $52 effective March 4, 1831 [Ref: X-51/514]. In his pension claim (S8970) on November 20, 1832, Nathan stated he was born in Talbot County on October 12, 1755 and served in both the Maryland and Pennsylvania Lines, plus sea service in Maryland. John Dorgan, aged 72, made affidavit that he had known Nathan since he was a boy [Ref: W-2735]. See "John Dorgin," q.v.
PORTER, Philemon. Private, 4th Independent Company of Maryland Regular Troops, Capt. James Hindman's Company, September, 1776 muster roll; enlisted January 25, 1776 [Ref: D-24].
PORTER, Thomas. Private, Militia, Wye Company, 4th Battalion, 1780-1781 [Ref: N-86/105, M-228]. Private, Militia, Wye Company, 4th Battalion, 1777-1778 [Ref: N-86/105, M-222].
PORTER, William. Private, Militia, Wye Company, 4th Battalion, 1777-1778 [Ref: N-86/105, M-222]. Private, Militia, Wye Company, 4th Battalion, 1780-1781 [Ref: N-86/105, M-229].
PORTER, William. Private, Militia, Miles River Company, 38th Battalion, 1777-1778 [Ref: N-86/105, M-227]. Private, Militia, Miles River Company, 38th Battalion, 1780-1781 [Ref: N-86/105, M-235].
PORTER, William. Private, Militia, Sword in Hand Company, 4th Battalion, 1777-1778 [Ref: N-86/105, M-224]. Private, Militia, Sword in Hand Company, 4th Battalion, 1780-1781 [Ref: N-86/105, M-231].
POTTS, Philip. Private, Militia, Miles River Company, 38th Battalion, 1777-1778 [Ref: N-86/105, M-227].
POTTS, Thomas. Private, 4th Maryland Line, 1778 [Ref: D-153]. He applied for a pension (S7326) at Sneedesborough in Anson County, North Carolina on October 8, 1832, aged 71, stating he was born and raised in Talbot County, Maryland where he lived at the time of his enlistment [Ref: W-2746].
POTTS, William. Private, Militia, Third Haven Company, 4th Battalion, 1777-1778 [Ref: N-86/105, M-225].
POUNDER, Richard. Private, Militia, 4th Battalion, Capt. Greenbury Goldsborough's Company, reviewed and passed July 27, 1776 [Ref: D-68].

Corporal, 5th Maryland Line, December 10, 1776; private, April 1, 1777; corporal, April 1, 1779; reported missing after the Battle of Camden, S. C. on August 16, 1780 [Ref: D-237].

POWELL, Henry. Waterman on the barge *Intrepid* in 1781 [Ref: D-610].

POWELL, Howell. Private, Militia, Hand & Hand Company, 4th Battalion, 1777-1778 [Ref: N-86/105, M-226]. Private, Militia, Hand in Hand Company, 4th Battalion, 1780-1781 [Ref: N-86/105, M-233, which listed the name as "Howel Powel"].

POWELL, Howell. Private, Militia, Volunteer Company, 4th Battalion, 1777-1778 [Ref: N-86/105, M-223]. Private, Militia, Volunteer Company, 4th Battalion, 1780-1781 [Ref: N-86/105, M-230, which listed the name as "Howel Powel"].

POWELL, William. Private, Militia, 4th Battalion, Capt. Greenbury Goldsborough's Company, reviewed and passed July 27, 1776 [Ref: D-68].

PRATT, Nathaniel. Private, Militia, Wye Company, 4th Battalion, 1780-1781 [Ref: N-86/105, M-229].

PRICE, Andrew. Private, Militia, Sword in Hand Company, 4th Battalion, 1780-1781 [Ref: N-86/105, M-231]. Private, Militia, Sword in Hand Company, 4th Battalion, 1777-1778 [Ref: N-86/105, M-224]. Took the Oath of Allegiance and Fidelity on or about March 1, 1778; name listed twice [Ref: J-1814, N-106/114].

PRICE, Charles. Waterman on the barge *Intrepid* in 1781 [Ref: D-610]. Private aboard the barge *Fearnought* under Capt. Levin Spedden; enlisted May 29, 1782; 5'10" tall; fair complexion; born in Talbot County [Ref: D-611].

PRICE, Foster. Private, Militia, Capt. Thomas Bullen's Company; no date was given; possibly late 1775 or early 1776 [Ref: Z-3]. Took the Oath of Allegiance and Fidelity on or about March 1, 1778 [Ref: J-1814, N-106/114]. See "Joseph Price," q.v.

PRICE, Foster Jr. Took the Oath of Allegiance and Fidelity on or after March 1, 1778 [Ref: J-1814, N-106/114]. Private, Militia, Third Haven Company, 4th Battalion, 1777-1778 [Ref: N-86/105, M-225]. Private, Militia, Third Haven Company, 4th Battalion, 1780-1781 [Ref: N-86/105, M-232].

PRICE, Francis. Private, Militia, Capt. Thomas Bullen's Company; no date was given; possibly late 1775 or early 1776 [Ref: Z-3].

PRICE, George. Private, Militia, Capt. Thomas Bullen's Company; no date was given; possibly late 1775 or early 1776 [Ref: Z-3]. Took the Oath of Allegiance and Fidelity on or after March 1, 1778 [Ref: J-1814, N-106/114]. Private, Militia, Bullinbrook Company, 4th Battalion, 1780-1781 [Ref: N-86/105, M-231]. Private aboard the barge *Fearnought* under Capt. Levin Spedden; enlisted June 1, 1782; 5'5" tall; fair complexion; born in Talbot County [Ref: D-612].

PRICE, Gilbert. Private, Militia, Hand in Hand Company, 4th Battalion, 1780-1781 [Ref: N-86/105, M-232].

PRICE, Hugh. Private, Militia, Hand & Hand Company, 4th Battalion, 1777-1778 [Ref: N-86/105, M-225]. Rendered patriotic service by supplying wheat for the use of the Army in March, 1780 [Ref: P-277].

PRICE, James. Private, Militia, 1st Class, Sword in Hand Company, 4th Battalion, 1777-1778 [Ref: N-86/105, M-224]. Took the Oath of Allegiance and Fidelity on or after March 1, 1778 [Ref: J-1814, N-106/114].

PRICE, James. Private, Militia, 7th Class, Sword in Hand Company, 4th Battalion, 1777-1778 [Ref: N-86/105, M-224]. Took the Oath of Allegiance and Fidelity on or about March 1, 1778 [Ref: J-1814, N-106/114].

PRICE, James. Private, Militia, Miles River Company, 38th Battalion, 1780-1781 [Ref: N-86/105, M-235]. Took the Oath of Allegiance and Fidelity on or about March 1, 1778 [Ref: J-1814, N-106/114].

PRICE, James Sr. Private, Militia, Sword in Hand Company, 4th Battalion, 1780-1781 [Ref: N-86/105, M-231]. Draughted on May 1, 1781 to serve until December 10, 1781 in the Maryland Continental Troops [Ref: D-371].

PRICE, John. Private, Militia, Volunteer Company, 4th Battalion, 1777-1778 [Ref: N-86/105, M-223]. Private, Militia, Volunteer Company, 4th Battalion, 1780-1781 [Ref: N-86/105, M-230].

PRICE, John. Private, Militia, Hand & Hand Company, 4th Battalion, 1777-1778 [Ref: N-86/105, M-225]. Private, 5th Maryland Line, enlisted June 1, 1778 and discharged in May, 1779 [Ref: D-237].

PRICE, Joseph (1757-   ). Born in St. Peter's Parish, Talbot County, on May 31, 1757, son of Foster and Mary Price [Ref: K-56]. Private, Militia, Third Haven Company, 4th Battalion, 1777-1778 [Ref: N-86/105, M-225]. Took the Oath of Allegiance and Fidelity on or after March 1, 1778 [Ref: J-1814, N-106/114]. Sergeant, Militia, Third Haven Company, 4th Battalion, 1780-1781 [Ref: N-100, M-232].

PRICE, Mary. See "Joseph Price," q.v.

PRICE, Nathan. Private, Militia, Sword in Hand Company, 4th Battalion, 1780-1781 [Ref: N-86/105, M-231]. Private, Militia, Sword in Hand Company, 4th Battalion, 1777-1778 [Ref: N-86/105, M-224].

PRICE, Samuel. Private, Militia, Hand in Hand Company, 4th Battalion, 1780-1781 [Ref: N-86/105, M-232]. Took the Oath of Allegiance and Fidelity on or about March 1, 1778 [Ref: J-1814, N-106/114].

PRICE, Solomon. Took the Oath of Allegiance and Fidelity on or about March 1, 1778 [Ref: J-1814, N-106/114].

PRICE, Thomas. Private, Militia, Capt. Thomas Bullen's Company; no date was given; possibly late 1775 or early 1776 [Ref: Z-3]. Private, Militia, Volunteer Company, 4th Battalion, 1777-1778 [Ref: N-86/105, M-223]. Took the Oath of Allegiance and Fidelity on or after March 1, 1778 [Ref: J-1814, N-106/114]. Private, Militia, Volunteer Company, 4th Battalion, 1780-1781 [Ref: N-86/105, M-230].

PRICE, Thomas Jr. Took the Oath of Allegiance and Fidelity on or after March 1, 1778 [Ref: J-1814, N-106/114].

PRICE, Thomas Lane. Ensign, Militia, Hand in Hand Company, 4th Battalion, April 9, 1778 [Ref: M-112, E-24].

PRICE, Timothy Lane. Second Lieutenant, Militia, Hand in Hand Company, 4th Battalion, June 17, 1777 through 1781 [Ref: N-91, M-232, M-112, and N-101, which listed the name only as "Timothy Lane"]. Took the Oath of Allegiance and Fidelity on or about March 1, 1778 [Ref: J-1814, N-106/114].

PRICE, Vincent. Private, Militia, 2nd Volunteer Company, 4th Battalion, 1777-1778 [Ref: N-86/105, M-225]. Took the Oath of Allegiance and Fidelity on or about March 1, 1778 [Ref: J-1814, N-106/114]. Ensign, Militia, Volunteer Company, 4th Battalion, 1781 to at least November 4, 1782 [Ref: N-96, M-229, M-113, I-298].

PRICE, William. Private, Militia, Hand & Hand Company, 4th Battalion, 1777-1778 [Ref: N-86/105, M-225]. Private, Militia, Hand in Hand Company, 4th Battalion, 1780-1781 [Ref: N-86/105, M-232]. Took the Oath of Allegiance and Fidelity on or about March 1, 1778 [Ref: J-1814, N-106/114].

PRICE, William. Private, Militia, Union Company, 4th Battalion, 1777-1778 [Ref: N-86/105, M-223]. Took the Oath of Allegiance and Fidelity on or about March 1, 1778 [Ref: J-1814, N-106/114].

PRICE, William. Took the Oath of Allegiance and Fidelity on or about March 1, 1778 [Ref: J-1814, N-106/114].

PRICHARD (PRITCHARD), John (1745-   ). Born in St. Peter's Parish, Talbot County, on August 27, 1745, son of Samuel and Margaret Prichard [Ref: V-90]. Private, Militia, Capt. Thomas Bullen's Company; no date was given; possibly late 1775 or early 1776 [Ref: Z-3]. Private, Militia, Volunteer Company, 4th Battalion, 1777-1778 [Ref: N-86/105, M-223]. Private, Militia, Volunteer Company, 4th Battalion, 1780-1781 [Ref: N-86/105, M-230]. Took the Oath of Allegiance and Fidelity on or after March 1, 1778 [Ref: J-1814, N-106/114].

PRICHARD, Margaret. See "John Prichard," q.v.

PRICHARD, Peter. Private, Militia, Capt. Thomas Bullen's Company; no date was given; possibly late 1775 or early 1776 [Ref: Z-3].

PRICHARD (PRITCHARD, PRITCHET), Samuel. Private, Militia, Capt. Thomas Bullen's Company; no date was given; possibly late 1775 or early 1776 [Ref: Z-3]. Private, Militia, 4th Battalion, Capt. Greenbury Goldsborough's Company, reviewed and passed July 27, 1776 [Ref: D-67]. Private, Militia, Volunteer Company, 4th Battalion, 1777-1778 [Ref: N-86/105, M-223]. Private, Militia, Volunteer Company, 4th Battalion, 1780-1781 [Ref: N-86/105, M-230]. See "John Prichard," q.v.

PRICHARD, Samuel Jr. Private, Militia, Capt. Thomas Bullen's Company; no date was given; possibly late 1775 or early 1776 [Ref: Z-3].

PRICHARD (PRITCHARD), Walter. Private, Militia, Bullin Brook Company, 4th Battalion, 1777-1778 [Ref: N-86/105, M-224]. Took the Oath of Allegiance and Fidelity on or about March 1, 1778 [Ref: J-1814, N-106/114]. Corporal, Militia, Bullinbrook Company, 4th Battalion, 1780-1781 [Ref: N-99, M-231].

PRICHARD, William. Private, Militia, Volunteer Company, 4th Battalion, 1777-1778 [Ref: N-86/105, M-223]. Private, Militia, Volunteer Company, 4th Battalion, 1780-1781 [Ref: N-86/105, M-230].

PRIESTLEY, David. Private, 4th Independent Company of Maryland Regular Troops, Capt. James Hindman's Company, September, 1776 muster roll; enlisted January 23, 1776 [Ref: D-24].

PRIESTLY, James. Private, Militia, Volunteer Company, 4th Battalion, 1780-1781 [Ref: N-86/105, M-230]. Private, Militia, Volunteer Company, 4th Battalion, 1777-1778 [Ref: N-86/105, M-223].

PRIESTLY, Perry. Private, Militia, Union Company, 4th Battalion, 1780-1781 [Ref: N-86/105, M-229]. Private, Militia, Union Company, 4th Battalion, 1777-1778 [Ref: N-86/105, M-223].

PRITCHARD, John. Took the Oath of Allegiance and Fidelity on or about March 1, 1778 [Ref: J-1814, N-106/114].

PRITCHARD, Walter. See "Walter Prichard," q.v.

PRITCHETT, Susan. See "Solomon Barrett," q.v.

PROCTOR, Daniel. Took the Oath of Allegiance and Fidelity on or about March 1, 1778 [Ref: J-1814, N-106/114].

PROUCE, George. Sergeant, Militia, Capt. Thomas Bullen's Company; no date was given; possibly late 1775 or early 1776 [Ref: Z-3]. See "Philip Prouce," q.v.

PROUCE, George Jr. Private, Militia, Capt. Thomas Bullen's Company; no date was given; possibly late 1775 or early 1776 [Ref: Z-3].

PROUCE, Jane. See "Philip Prouce," q.v.

PROUCE, Philip (1742-   ). Born in St. Peter's Parish, Talbot County, on November 6, 1742, a son of George and Jane Prouce [Ref: V-82]. Private, Militia, Union Company, 4th Battalion, 1777-1778 [Ref: N-86/105, M-223, which listed the name as "Phil. Pronce"].

PURNAL, Thomas. Private, Militia, United Company, 38th Battalion, 1780-1781 [Ref: N-86/105, M-233].

PURSE, John. Private, Militia, Hearts of Oak Company, 38th Battalion, 1780-1781 [Ref: N-86/105, M-234]. Private, Militia, Hearts of Oak Company, 38th Battalion, 1777-1778 [Ref: N-86/105, M-226].

QUINTON, Joseph. Private, Militia, Third Haven Company, 4th Battalion, 1777-1778 [Ref: N-86/105, M-225].

RAKES, Fisher. Private, Militia, Volunteer Company, 4th Battalion, 1780-1781 [Ref: N-86/105, M-229].

RAKES, William. Private, Militia, Volunteer Company, 4th Battalion, 1777-1778 [Ref: N-86/105, M-223]. Private, Militia, Volunteer Company, 4th Battalion, 1780-1781 [Ref: N-86/105, M-230]. Private, Militia, 2nd Volunteer Company,

who was draughted on May 1, 1781 to serve until December 10, 1781 in the Maryland Continental Troops [Ref: D-371].
RAKES, William Jr. Private, Militia, Capt. Thomas Bullen's Company; no date was given; possibly late 1775 or early 1776 [Ref: Z-3].
RATCLIFFE, Hannah. See "James Benson," q.v.
RATHELL, David. Private, Militia, Capt. Thomas Bullen's Company; no date was given; possibly late 1775 or early 1776 [Ref: Z-3].
RATHELL (RATHALL), Elizabeth. See "Richard Oxenham," q.v.
RATHELL (RATHEL), John. Private, Militia, Capt. Thomas Bullen's Company; no date was given; possibly late 1775 or early 1776 [Ref: Z-3]. Private, Militia, Bullin Brook Company, 4th Battalion, 1777-1778 [Ref: N-86/105, M-224]. Took the Oath of Allegiance and Fidelity on or about March 1, 1778 [Ref: J-1814, N-106/114]. Private, Militia, Bullinbrook Company, 4th Battalion, 1780-1781 [Ref: N-86/105, M-231].
RATHELL (RATHEL), Joseph. Private, Militia, Sword in Hand Company, 4th Battalion, 1780-1781 [Ref: N-86/105, M-231]. Private, Militia, Sword in Hand Company, 4th Battalion, 1777-1778 [Ref: N-86/105, M-224]. Took the Oath of Allegiance and Fidelity on or abour March 1, 1778; name listed twice [Ref: J-1814, N-106/114].
RATHELL (RATHEL), William. Private, Militia, Sword in Hand Company, 4th Battalion, 1780-1781 [Ref: N-86/105, M-231]. Private, Militia, Sword in Hand Company, 4th Battalion, 1777-1778 [Ref: N-86/105, M-224].
RATLIFF, John. Private, Militia, Wye Company, 4th Battalion, 1777-1778 [Ref: N-86/105, M-222].
RAY, Frances. See "John Ray," q.v.
RAY, James. Private, 4th Independent Company of Maryland Regular Troops, Capt. James Hindman's Company, September, 1776 muster roll; enlisted January 22, 1776 [Ref: D-24].
RAY, John (1750-1812). Private, Militia, 4th Battalion, Capt. Greenbury Goldsborough's Company, reviewed and passed July 27, 1776 [Ref: D-68]. Private, Militia, Miles River Company, 38th Battalion, 1777-1778 [Ref: N-86/105, M-227]. Took the Oath of Allegiance and Fidelity on or about March 1, 1778 [Ref: J-1814, N-106/114]. Sergeant, Militia, Miles River Company, 38th Battalion, 1780-1781 [Ref: N-105, M-235]. Ensign, Militia, 38th Battalion, November 4, 1782 [Ref: M-114, I-298]. John Ray was born in Maryland in 1750, married Frances ----, served as an ensign in the revolution, and died on September 14, 1812 [Ref: Y-2411].
RAY, Thomas (1720-1795). Took the Oath of Allegiance and Fidelity on or about March 1, 1778 [Ref: J-1814, N-106/114]. Rendered patriotic service by supplying bacon for the use of the Army in May, 1778 [Ref: P-164]. Appointed a Justice of the Peace on July 22, 1778 [Ref: E-163, which listed the name as "Thos. Ray, Senr."]. Appointed an Inspector of Tobacco on August 30, 1780 [Ref: F-271]. Thomas Ray, Sr. was born in Maryland on December 23, 1720,

married Sarah Edmondson, rendered patriotic and civil service during the revolution, and died on January 21, 1795 [Ref: Y-2412].

RAY, William. Private, Militia, 4th Battalion, Capt. Greenbury Goldsborough's Company, reviewed and passed July 27, 1776 [Ref: D-68].

READER, John. Private, Militia, Union Company, 4th Battalion, 1777-1778 [Ref: N-86/105, M-223]. Took the Oath of Allegiance and Fidelity on or about March 1, 1778 [Ref: J-1814, N-106/114].

REDDISH, Joseph. Seaman on the barge *Terable* in 1781 [Ref: D-610]. Joseph Riddish appears on "a list of men blown up in the barges" in 1782 [Ref: D-615].

REDDISH, Robert. Private, Militia, Bayside Company, 38th Battalion, 1780-1781 [Ref: N-86/105, M-233].

REGISTER, James. Private, Militia, Hand in Hand Company, 4th Battalion, 1780-1781 [Ref: N-86/105, M-232]. Private, Militia, Hand & Hand Company, 4th Battalion, 1777-1778 [Ref: N-86/105, M-226].

REGISTER, Jane. See "John Register," q.v.

REGISTER, John (1743-1802). Private, Militia, Sword in Hand Company, 4th Battalion, 1777-1778 [Ref: N-86/105, M-224]. Private, Militia, Sword in Hand Company, 4th Battalion, 1780-1781 [Ref: N-86/105, M-231]. John Register was born in Maryland on September 23, 1743, married first to Esther Wilson and second to Jane ----, served as a private in the revolution, and died in Delaware in February, 1802 [Ref: Y-2431].

REGISTER, Samuel. Private, Militia, Sword in Hand Company, 4th Battalion, 1780-1781 [Ref: N-86/105, M-231]. Private, Militia, Sword in Hand Company, 4th Battalion, 1777-1778 [Ref: N-86/105, M-224]. Took the Oath of Allegiance and Fidelity on or about March 1, 1778 [Ref: J-1814, N-106/114]. Appointed as Inspector of Tobacco at Kingston Warehouse on October 9, 1780 [Ref: F-320].

REOUGH (REAUGH), John. Private, Militia, Bayside Company, 38th Battalion, 1777-1778 [Ref: N-86/105, M-228]. Took the Oath of Allegiance and Fidelity on or about March 1, 1778 [Ref: J-1814, N-106/114].

REYNOLDS, Frances. See "Woolman Gibson (of John)," q.v.

RIBINSON, John. See "John Robinson," q.v.

RICE, Hugh. Took the Oath of Allegiance and Fidelity on or about March 1, 1778 [Ref: J-1814, N-106/114].

RICE, Hugh Jr. Took the Oath of Allegiance and Fidelity on or about March 1, 1778 [Ref: J-1814, N-106/114].

RICE, John. Private, Militia, Hand in Hand Company, 4th Battalion, 1780-1781 [Ref: N-86/105, M-232]. Took the Oath of Allegiance and Fidelity on or about March 1, 1778 [Ref: J-1814, N-106/114].

RICE, William. Private, Militia, Miles River Company, 38th Battalion, 1777-1778 [Ref: N-86/105, M-227]. Took the Oath of Allegiance and Fidelity on or about March 1, 1778 [Ref: J-1814, N-106/114].

RICHARDS, Robert. Took the Oath of Allegiance and Fidelity on or about March 1, 1778 [Ref: J-1814, N-106/114].
RICHARDSON, Daniel. Private, 4th Independent Company of Maryland Regular Troops, Capt. James Hindman's Company, September, 1776 muster roll; enlisted February 12, 1776 [Ref: D-24]. Private, 2nd Maryland Line, enlisted January 27, 1777; honorably discharged on June 10, 1780 [Ref: D-156]. Placed on the pension rolls on January 15, 1819, aged 77, with an annual allowance of $96 effective May 19, 1818 [Ref: X-41/514]. However, in his pension application (S35047) filed on May 19, 1818, he stated he was aged 65 and then on June 5, 1820 he stated he was aged 63 and upwards. He lived in Talbot County in 1820 and had been blind nearly 8 years. His wife, two "grown up" daughters and a son (no names given) lived with him [Ref: W-2874].
RICHARDSON, Daniel. Private, Militia, United Company, 38th Battalion, 1777-1778 [Ref: N-86/105, M-227]. Private, Militia, United Company, 38th Battalion, 1780-1781 [Ref: N-86/105, M-233].
RICHARDSON, Daniel. Corporal, Militia, Hearts of Oak Company, 38th Battalion, 1780-1781 [Ref: N-104, M-234].
RICHARDSON, Daniel. Took the Oath of Allegiance and Fidelity on or about March 1, 1778 [Ref: J-1814, N-106/114].
RICHARDSON, Henry. Private, Militia, Union Company, 4th Battalion, 1780-1781 [Ref: N-86/105, M-229].
RICHARDSON, Joshua. Private, Militia, United Company, 38th Battalion, 1780-1781 [Ref: N-86/105, M-233]. Private, Militia, Broad Creek Company, 38th Battalion, 1777-1778 [Ref: N-86/105, M-226].
RICHARDSON, Margaret. See "Thomas Richardson," q.v.
RICHARDSON, Peter. Private, Militia, Broad Creek Company, 38th Battalion, 1777-1778 [Ref: N-86/105, M-227].
RICHARDSON, Peter. Private, Militia, Third Haven Company, 4th Battalion, 1780-1781 [Ref: N-86/105, M-232]. Private, Militia, Third Haven Company, 4th Battalion, 1777-1778 [Ref: N-86/105, M-225]. Took the Oath of Allegiance and Fidelity on or after March 1, 1778 [Ref: J-1814, N-106/114].
RICHARDSON, Peter (Bay Hundred). Took the Oath of Allegiance and Fidelity on or after March 1, 1778 [Ref: J-1814, N-106/114].
RICHARDSON, Robert. Private, Militia, United Company, 38th Battalion, 1780-1781 [Ref: N-86/105, M-233]. Private, Militia, Bayside Company, 38th Battalion, 1777-1778 [Ref: N-86/105, M-228].
RICHARDSON, Thomas. Private, Militia, Broad Creek Company, 38th Battalion, 1777-1778 [Ref: N-86/105, M-226]. Private, Militia, Broad Creek Company, 38th Battalion, 1780-1781 [Ref: N-86/105, M-234]. Private aboard the barge *Fearnought* under Capt. Levin Spedden; enlisted June 2, 1782; 5'10" tall; fair complexion; born in Talbot County [Ref: D-612]. Margaret Richardson, widow, applied for a pension (W2698) in Baltimore City on January 2, 1852, aged 74, based on her husband's sea serrvice. She stated she was born Margaret Sands

in Talbot County and married Thomas on January 25, 1796. He died on March 9, 1823. Rachael Shields, aged 85, made an affidavit in Baltimore City in 1852, but no relationship was given. The widow also applied for bounty land (#1972-160-55) on March 22, 1855 in Baltimore City [Ref: W-2879].

RICHARDSON, Thomas (Mill Hundred). Took the Oath of Allegiance and Fidelity on or after March 1, 1778 [Ref: J-1814, N-106/114].

RICHARDSON, Thomas Jr. Private, Militia, Hearts of Oak Company, 38th Battalion, 1780-1781 [Ref: N-86/105, M-234].

RICHARDSON, William. Corporal, Militia, Capt. Thomas Bullen's Company; no date was given; possibly late 1775 or early 1776 [Ref: Z-3].

RIDGWAY, Charles. Private, Militia, Hand in Hand Company, 4th Battalion, 1780-1781 [Ref: N-86/105, M-232]. Took the Oath of Allegiance and Fidelity on or about March 1, 1778 [Ref: J-1814, N-106/114].

RIDGWAY, James. Private, Militia, Hearts of Oak Company, 38th Battalion, 1777-1778 [Ref: N-86/105, M-226]. Private, Militia, Hand in Hand Company, 4th Battalion, 1780-1781 [Ref: N-86/105, M-232].

RIDGWAY, John. Private, Militia, Third Haven Company, 4th Battalion, 1777-1778 [Ref: N-86/105, M-225]. Private, Militia, Third Haven Company, 4th Battalion, 1780-1781 [Ref: N-86/105, M-232].

RIDGWAY, John. Private, Militia, Hearts of Oak Company, 38th Battalion, 1777-1778 [Ref: N-86/105, M-226]. Private, Militia, Hand in Hand Company, 4th Battalion, 1780-1781 [Ref: N-86/105, M-232].

RIDGWAY, John. Took the Oath of Allegiance and Fidelity on or about March 1, 1778 [Ref: J-1814, N-106/114].

RIDGWAY, Joseph. Took the Oath of Allegiance and Fidelity on or about March 1, 1778 [Ref: J-1814, N-106/114].

RIDGWAY, William. Took the Oath of Allegiance and Fidelity on or about March 1, 1778 [Ref: J-1814, N-106/114].

RIDGWAY, William (of Charles). Private, Militia, Hand in Hand Company, 4th Battalion, 1780-1781 [Ref: N-86/105, M-233].

RIGBY, Jonathan. Took the Oath of Allegiance and Fidelity on or about March 1, 1778 [Ref: J-1814, N-106/114].

RIGBY, Moses. Private, Militia, Oxford Company, 38th Battalion, 1780-1781 [Ref: N-86/105, M-235]. Private, Militia, Oxford Company, 38th Battalion, 1777-1778 [Ref: N-86/105, M-227]. Took the Oath of Allegiance and Fidelity on or about March 1, 1778 [Ref: J-1814, N-106/114].

RIGBY, Philemon. Took the Oath of Allegiance and Fidelity on or about March 1, 1778 [Ref: J-1814, N-106/114].

RIGBY, Thomas. Took the Oath of Allegiance and Fidelity on or about March 1, 1778 [Ref: J-1814, N-106/114].

RIMMER, James. Took the Oath of Allegiance and Fidelity on or about March 1, 1778 [Ref: J-1814, N-106/114].

RIMMER, Lambert. Private, Militia, Broad Creek Company, 38th Battalion, 1777-1778 [Ref: N-86/105, M-227]. Private, Militia, Broad Creek Company, 38th Battalion, 1780-1781 [Ref: N-86/105, M-234, which listed the name as "Lambert Rimer"].

RINGROSE, Aaron. Private, Militia, Bayside Company, 38th Battalion, 1777-1778 [Ref: N-86/105, M-228]. Private, Militia, Bayside Company, 38th Battalion, 1780-1781 [Ref: N-86/105, M-233].

RINGROSE, Moses. Private, Militia, Miles River Company, 38th Battalion, 1780-1781 [Ref: N-86/105, M-235]. Private, Militia, Miles River Company, 38th Battalion, 1777-1778 [Ref: N-86/105, M-227]. Took the Oath of Allegiance and Fidelity on or about March 1, 1778 [Ref: J-1814, N-106/114].

ROACH, Thomas. Private, Militia, Sword in Hand Company, 4th Battalion, 1777-1778 [Ref: N-86/105, M-224]. Private, Militia, Sword in Hand Company, 4th Battalion, 1780-1781 [Ref: N-86/105, M-231].

ROBERTS, Andrew. Took the Oath of Allegiance and Fidelity on or about March 1, 1778 [Ref: J-1814, N-106/114].

ROBERTS, Benjamin. Private, Militia, Miles River Company, 38th Battalion, 1777-1778 [Ref: N-86/105, M-227]. Took the Oath of Allegiance and Fidelity on or about March 1, 1778 [Ref: J-1814, N-106/114]. Rendered patriotic service by supplying bacon for the use of the Army in May, 1778 and also by hauling provisions [Ref: P-164].

ROBERTS, Benjamin Jr. Private, Militia, Miles River Company, 38th Battalion, 1780-1781 [Ref: N-86/105, M-235]. Took the Oath of Allegiance and Fidelity on or about March 1, 1778 [Ref: J-1814, N-106/114].

ROBERTS, Edward. Private, Militia, Wye Company, 4th Battalion, 1780-1781 [Ref: N-86/105, M-228]. Private, Militia, Wye Company, 4th Battalion, 1777-1778 [Ref: N-86/105, M-222]. Took the Oath of Allegiance and Fidelity on or about March 1, 1778 [Ref: J-1814, N-106/114].

ROBERTS, George. See "John Roberts, Jr.," q.v.

ROBERTS, John. Private, Militia, Wye Company, 4th Battalion, 1780-1781 [Ref: N-86/105, M-229]. Private, Militia, Wye Company, 4th Battalion, 1777-1778 [Ref: N-86/105, M-222]. Took the Oath of Allegiance and Fidelity on or about March 1, 1778 [Ref: J-1814, N-106/114].

ROBERTS, John. Private, Militia, Union Company, 4th Battalion, 1780-1781 [Ref: N-86/105, M-230].

ROBERTS, John. Sergeant, Militia, Bullinbrook Company, 4th Battalion, 1780-1781 [Ref: N-99, M-231].

ROBERTS, John Jr. (1754-1801). Son of Thomas and Rebeckah Roberts, he married first to Mary ---- by 1785 and second to Sarah Turner (widow) by 1798. His known children were George (died in 1806) and William. John served in these capacities: Maryland Lower House, 1782-1788; Court Justice, 1785-1787, 1791-1795; Sheriff, 1788-1791; Collector of the Tax, 1790; Associate Justice, 1798-1801; Trustee of Easton Academy, 1800; Maryland

Senate Elector in 1796; and, Presidential Elector in 1796. He died before December 24, 1801 (date of bond). [Ref: R-698, R-87, R-88, R-89, R-90, R-91, which latter five sources listed the name without the "Jr."]. Took the Oath of Allegiance and Fidelity on or about March 1, 1778 [Ref: J-1814, N-106/114, which listed the name without the "Jr."]. He may have also served in the Revolutionary War since there were at least three men named John Roberts in the militia of Talbot County [Ref: M-229, M-230, M-231].

ROBERTS, Mary. See "John Roberts, Jr.," q.v.

ROBERTS, Perry. Took the Oath of Allegiance and Fidelity on or about March 1, 1778 [Ref: J-1814, N-106/114]. Corporal, Militia, Miles River Company, 38th Battalion, 1780-1781 [Ref: N-105, M-235].

ROBERTS, Rebeckah. See "John Roberts, Jr.," q.v.

ROBERTS, Thomas. Sergeant, Militia, Wye Company, 4th Battalion, 1780-1781 [Ref: N-96, M-228]. Took the Oath of Allegiance and Fidelity on or about March 1, 1778 [Ref: J-1814, N-106/114]. See "John Roberts, Jr.," q.v.

ROBERTS, Thomas Jr. Corporal, Militia, Wye Company, 4th Battalion, 1780-1781 [Ref: N-96, M-228]. Took the Oath of Allegiance and Fidelity on or about March 1, 1778 [Ref: J-1814, N-106/114, which listed the name without the "Jr."].

ROBERTS, William. See "John Roberts, Jr.," q.v.

ROBERTSON, Robert. Private, Militia, Miles River Company, 38th Battalion, 1780-1781 [Ref: N-86/105, M-235].

ROBERTSON, William. Rendered patriotic service by supplying a horse for the use of the Army in July, 1780 [Ref: P-301].

ROBINS, Henrietta. See "James Lloyd Chamberlaine," q.v.

ROBINS, John. See "Howes Goldsborough" and "William Goldsborough," q.v.

ROBINS, Margaret. See "William Hayward," q.v.

ROBINSON, David. Private, Militia, Hand & Hand Company, 4th Battalion, 1777-1778 [Ref: N-86/105, M-226]. Took the Oath of Allegiance and Fidelity on or about March 1, 1778 [Ref: J-1814, N-106/114]. Waterman on the barge *Intrepid* in 1781; name listed twice [Ref: D-610].

ROBINSON, David Jr. Ensign, Militia, 38th Battalion, May 16, 1776 [Ref: M-117, A-428, which listed the name without the "Jr."]. First Lieutenant, Militia, Oxford Company, 38th Battalion, 1778-1781 [Ref: N-93, N-105, M-235].

ROBINSON, David 3rd. Private, Militia, Oxford Company, 38th Battalion, 1777-1778 [Ref: N-86/105, M-227].

ROBINSON, Ellinor. See "Edward Stevens," q.v.

ROBINSON, James. Private, 4th Independent Company of Maryland Regular Troops, Capt. James Hindman's Company, September, 1776 muster roll; enlisted February 6, 1776 [Ref: D-24]. Private, Militia, Union Company, 4th Battalion, 1780-1781 [Ref: N-86/105, M-229]. One James Robinson, son of John and Mary, was born in St. Peter's Parish, Talbot County, on July 14, 1730 [Ref: V-67].

ROBINSON, Jane. See "Solomon Robinson," q.v.

ROBINSON, John. Private, Militia, Hearts of Oak Company, 38th Battalion, 1780-1781 [Ref: N-86/105, M-234]. Took the Oath of Allegiance and Fidelity on or about March 1, 1778 [Ref: J-1814, N-106/114]. Rendered patriotic service by hauling provisions for the use of the Army in April, 1778 [Ref: P-162].

ROBINSON, John. Took the Oath of Allegiance and Fidelity on or about March 1, 1778 [Ref: J-1814, N-106/114, which listed the name as "John Ribinson"]. Rendered patriotic service by supplying bacon for the use of the Army in April, 1778 [Ref: P-163]. See "James Robinson," q.v.

ROBINSON, John 3rd. Private, Militia, Hearts of Oak Company, 38th Battalion, 1780-1781 [Ref: N-86/105, M-235].

ROBINSON, Joseph. Private in the militia who was draughted on August 30, 1781 to reinforce the American Army and to serve in the Maryland Continental Troops until December 10, 1781 [Ref: D-387].

ROBINSON, Judith. See "Edward Stevens," q.v.

ROBINSON, Lambert. Private, 4th Independent Company of Maryland Regular Troops, Capt. James Hindman's Company, September, 1776 muster roll; enlisted January 20, 1776 [Ref: D-24].

ROBINSON, Mary. See "James Robinson," q.v.

ROBINSON, Richard. Private, Militia, Capt. Thomas Bullen's Company; no date was given; possibly late 1775 or early 1776 [Ref: Z-3]. Rendered patriotic service by hauling provisions for the use of the Army in June, 1778 [Ref: P-175]. See "Edward Stevens," q.v.

ROBINSON, Richard Gurlin. Took the Oath of Allegiance and Fidelity on or about March 1, 1778 [Ref: J-1814, N-106/114].

ROBINSON, Robert. Private in the militia who was draughted on August 30, 1781 to reinforce the American Army and to serve in the Maryland Continental Troops until December 10, 1781 [Ref: D-387]. Took the Oath of Allegiance and Fidelity on or about March 1, 1778 [Ref: J-1814, N-106/114].

ROBINSON, Solomon. Ensign, Militia, 4th Battalion, April 9, 1778 [Ref: M-117, E-24]. Second Lieutenant, Militia, Bullinbrook Company, 4th Battalion, December 3, 1779 [Ref: N-99, M-231, M-117, F-28]. Rendered patriotic service by supplying bacon for the use of the Army in May, 1778 and also by hauling provisions [Ref: P-135, P-164]. One Solomon Robinson, son of Solomon and Jane Robinson, was born in St. Peter's Parish on January 31, 1730 [Ref: V-68].

ROBINSON, Standley. Private, Militia, Capt. Thomas Bullen's Company; no date was given; possibly late 1775 or early 1776 [Ref: Z-3]. Private, Militia, Oxford Company, 38th Battalion, 1777-1778 [Ref: N-86/105, M-227].

ROBINSON, Thomas. Private, Militia, 2nd Volunteer Company, 4th Battalion, 1777-1778 [Ref: N-86/105, M-225]. Ensign, Militia, Oxford Company, 38th Battalion, 1780-1781 [Ref: N-105, M-235].

ROBINSON, Thomas. Private, Militia, Volunteer Company, 4th Battalion, 1777-1778 [Ref: N-86/105, M-223]. Private, Militia, Volunteer Company, 4th Battalion, 1780-1781 [Ref: N-86/105, M-230].

ROBINSON, Thomas. Private, Militia, 2nd Class, Hearts of Oak Company, 38th Battalion, 1780-1781 [Ref: N-86/105, M-234].

ROBINSON, Thomas. Private, Militia, 8th Class, Hearts of Oak Company, 38th Battalion, 1780-1781 [Ref: N-86/105, M-235].

ROBINSON, Thomas. Took the Oath of Allegiance and Fidelity on or about March 1, 1778; name listed twice [Ref: J-1814, N-106/114].

ROBSON, Andrew. Sergeant, Militia, Hearts of Oak Company, 38th Battalion, 1780-1781 [Ref: N-104, M-234]. Took the Oath of Allegiance and Fidelity on or about March 1, 1778 [Ref: J-1814, N-106/114].

ROBSON, Henry. Private, Militia, Hearts of Oak Company, 38th Battalion, 1780-1781 [Ref: N-86/105, M-234]. Private, Militia, Hearts of Oak Company, 38th Battalion, 1777-1778 [Ref: N-86/105, M-226].

ROBSON, James. Private, Militia, Capt. Thomas Bullen's Company; no date was given; possibly late 1775 or early 1776 [Ref: Z-3]. Private, Militia, Union Company, 4th Battalion, 1777-1778 [Ref: N-86/105, M-223].

ROBSON, John. Private, Militia, Hearts of Oak Company, 38th Battalion, 1777-1778 [Ref: N-86/105, M-226]. Sergeant, Militia, Hearts of Oak Company, 38th Battalion, 1780-1781 [Ref: N-104, M-234]. Took the Oath of Allegiance and Fidelity on or about March 1, 1778 [Ref: J-1814, N-106/114]. Rendered patriotic service by supplying bacon for the use of the Army in May, 1778 [Ref: P-172].

ROBSON, Robert. Private, Militia, Hearts of Oak Company, 38th Battalion, 1777-1778 [Ref: N-86/105, M-226].

ROBSON, Thomas. Sergeant, Militia, Hearts of Oak Company, 38th Battalion, 1780-1781 [Ref: N-104, M-234]. Took the Oath of Allegiance and Fidelity on or about March 1, 1778 [Ref: J-1814, N-106/114]. Rendered patriotic service by supplying bacon for the use of the Army in May, 1778 [Ref: P-172].

ROCHESTER, Francis. See "John Stevens," q.v.

ROGERS, Joseph. Private, Militia, Volunteer Company, 4th Battalion, 1780-1781 [Ref: N-86/105, M-230]. Private, Militia, Volunteer Company, 4th Battalion, 1777-1778 [Ref: N-86/105, M-223].

ROGERS, Michael. Private, Militia, Volunteer Company, 4th Battalion, 1780-1781 [Ref: N-86/105, M-230]. Private, Militia, Volunteer Company, 4th Battalion, 1777-1778 [Ref: N-86/105, M-223].

ROLE (ROLLE), John. Captain, Militia, 38th Battalion, May 13, 1776 [Ref: M-117]. Took the Oath of Allegiance and Fidelity on or about March 1, 1778 [Ref: J-1814, N-106/114]. Major, Militia, 38th Battalion, April 9, 1778 [Ref: M-117, E-24].

ROLE (ROLLE), Robert. Private, Militia, Bayside Company, 38th Battalion, 1777-1778 [Ref: N-86/105, M-228]. Private, Militia, Bayside Company, 38th Battalion, 1780-1781 [Ref: N-86/105, M-233].

ROLLINSON (ROLINGSON), Thomas. Private, Militia, 4th Battalion, Capt. Greenbury Goldsborough's Company, reviewed and passed July 27, 1776 [Ref: D-68].

ROLISON, John 3rd. Private, Militia, Hearts of Oak Company, 38th Battalion, 1777-1778 [Ref: N-86/105, M-226].

ROSE, William. Private, Militia, Union Company, 4th Battalion, 1777-1778 [Ref: N-86/105, M-223]. Took the Oath of Allegiance and Fidelity on or about March 1, 1778 [Ref: J-1814, N-106/114]. Paid 12s. 8p. for services rendered on March 11, 1779, by Col. Christopher Birkhead [Ref: E-319]. Sergeant, Militia, Union Company, 4th Battalion, 1780-1781 [Ref: N-97, M-229]. Second Lieutenant, Militia, 4th Battalion, November 4, 1782 [Ref: M-117, I-298].

ROTHE, John. Captain, Militia, 38th Battalion, May 16, 1776 [Ref: M-117, A-428].

ROUSBY, Anne. See "Edward Lloyd," q.v.

ROWLINSON, Thomas. Took the Oath of Allegiance and Fidelity on or about March 1, 1778 [Ref: J-1814, N-106/114].

ROYALL (RYALL), James. Private, Militia, United Company, 38th Battalion, 1777-1778 [Ref: N-86/105, M-227, which listed the name as "James Ryall"]. Private, Militia, United Company, 38th Battalion, 1780-1781 [Ref: N-86/105, M-233].

ROYALL, Joseph. Took the Oath of Allegiance and Fidelity on or about March 1, 1778 [Ref: J-1814, N-106/114].

ROYALL (ROYAL), Thomas. Private, Militia, United Company, 38th Battalion, 1780-1781 [Ref: N-86/105, M-233].

RUSSELL, Daniel. Private, Militia, Bullin Brook Company, 4th Battalion, 1777-1778 [Ref: N-86/105, M-224]. Took the Oath of Allegiance and Fidelity on or about March 1, 1778 [Ref: J-1814, N-106/114].

RUSSELL (RUSSEL), James. Took the Oath of Allegiance and Fidelity on or about March 1, 1778 [Ref: J-1814, N-106/114]. Private, Militia, Hand in Hand Company, 4th Battalion, 1780-1781 [Ref: N-86/105, M-232].

RUSSELL, Mary. See "Thomas Sherwood," q.v.

RUTH, Mary. See "James Lloyd," q.v.

RUX, Mark. Private, Militia, Wye Company, 4th Battalion, 1777-1778 [Ref: N-86/105, M-222].

RYALL, James. See "James Royall," q.v.

RYALL, John. Private, 5th Maryland Line, enlisted June 6, 1778 and honorably discharged on March 20, 1779 [Ref: D-241].

RYAN, John. Private, 4th Independent Company of Maryland Regular Troops, Capt. James Hindman's Company, September, 1776 muster roll; enlisted February 6, 1776 [Ref: D-24].

SAILE, Gabriel Jr. Private, Militia, Capt. Thomas Bullen's Company; no date was given; possibly late 1775 or early 1776 [Ref: Z-3].

SAILE, George. Private, Militia, Capt. Thomas Bullen's Company; no date was given; possibly late 1775 or early 1776 [Ref: Z-3].

SAMPSON, Richard. Private, 4th Independent Company of Maryland Regular Troops, Capt. James Hindman's Company, September, 1776 muster roll; enlisted February 8, 1776 [Ref: D-24].

SAMUELS, John. Private, Militia, 4th Battalion, Capt. Greenbury Goldsborough's Company, reviewed and passed July 27, 1776 [Ref: D-68].

SANDERS, Richard. Private, Militia, Capt. Thomas Bullen's Company; no date was given; possibly late 1775 or early 1776 [Ref: Z-3].

SANDS, Benjamin. Took the Oath of Allegiance and Fidelity on or about March 1, 1778 [Ref: J-1814, N-106/114].

SANDS, Judith. See "Robert Lambdin," q.v.

SANDS, Margaret. See "Thomas Richardson," q.v.

SANDS, Robert. Private, Militia, Bayside Company, 38th Battalion, 1780-1781 [Ref: N-86/105, M-233].

SANDS, Thomas. Private, Militia, Bayside Company, 38th Battalion, 1777-1778 [Ref: N-86/105, M-228]. Private, Militia, Bayside Company, 38th Battalion, 1780-1781 [Ref: N-86/105, M-233]. Took the Oath of Allegiance and Fidelity on or about March 1, 1778 [Ref: J-1814, N-106/114].

SANGSTER, John. Took the Oath of Allegiance and Fidelity on or about March 1, 1778 [Ref: J-1814, N-106/114].

SANSBURY, John. Private, Militia, Capt. Thomas Bullen's Company; no date was given; possibly late 1775 or early 1776 [Ref: Z-3].

SANXTON, George. Private, Militia, 4th Battalion, Capt. Greenbury Goldsborough's Company, reviewed and passed July 27, 1776 [Ref: D-68].

SANXTON, Isaac. Private, Militia, Third Haven Company, 4th Battalion, 1777-1778 [Ref: N-86/105, M-225]. Took the Oath of Allegiance and Fidelity on or after March 1, 1778 [Ref: J-1814, N-106/114]. See "Isaac Langston (Sangston)," q.v.

SANXTON (SANGSTON), James. Private, Militia, Third Haven Company, 4th Battalion, 1777-1778 [Ref: N-86/105, M-225]. Private, Militia, Third Haven Company, 4th Battalion, 1780-1781 [Ref: N-86/105, M-232]. Took the Oath of Allegiance and Fidelity on or after March 1, 1778 [Ref: J-1814, N-106/114]. See "James Langston (Sangston)," q.v.

SANXTON (SANGSTON), John. Private, Militia, Wye Company, 4th Battalion, 1777-1778 [Ref: N-86/105, M-222]. Took the Oath of Allegiance and Fidelity on or about March 1, 1778 [Ref: J-1814, N-106/114]. Private, Militia, Wye Company, 4th Battalion, 1780-1781 [Ref: N-86/105, M-228].

SANXTON, John Atton. Private, Militia, Third Haven Company, 4th Battalion, 1777-1778 [Ref: N-86/105, M-225].

SATCHEL, James. Private, Militia, Bullin Brook Company, 4th Battalion, 1777-1778 [Ref: N-86/105, M-224].
SAVIER (SEVERE), Abraham. Took the Oath of Allegiance and Fidelity on or after March 1, 1778 [Ref: J-1814, N-106/114]. Private, Militia, Third Haven Company, 4th Battalion, 1780-1781 [Ref: N-86/105, M-232, which listed the name as "Abraham Severe"].
SAVIER (SAVERE, SWERE), Vachel. Private, Militia, 4th Battalion, Capt. Greenbury Goldsborough's Company, reviewed and passed July 27, 1776 [Ref: D-68, which listed the name as "Vachel Savere"]. Private, Militia, Sword in Hand Company, 4th Battalion, 1777-1778 [Ref: N-86/105, M-224, which listed the name s "Vachal Sweer"]. Took the Oath of Allegiance and Fidelity on or about March 1, 1778 [Ref: J-1814, N-106/114, which listed the name as "Vachel Swere"]. Private, Militia, Sword in Hand Company, 4th Battalion, 1780-1781 [Ref: N-86/105, M-231, which listed the name as "Vachel Severs"].
SAWYER, William. Took the Oath of Allegiance and Fidelity on or about March 1, 1778 [Ref: J-1814, N-106/114].
SEALE (SCALE?), George. Private, Militia, Capt. Thomas Bullen's Company; no date was given; possibly late 1775 or early 1776 [Ref: Z-3].
SEAMORE, Henry. Private, Militia, Hearts of Oak Company, 38th Battalion, 1777-1778 [Ref: N-86/105, M-226, which listed the name as "Henry Seamour"].
SEAMORE, Henry. Private, Militia, Hearts of Oak Company, 38th Battalion, 1780-1781 [Ref: N-86/105, M-234]. Took the Oath of Allegiance and Fidelity on or about March 1, 1778 [Ref: J-1814, N-106/114].
SEAMORE, John. Private, Militia, Hearts of Oak Company, 38th Battalion, 1777-1778 [Ref: N-86/105, M-226]. Private, Militia, Hearts of Oak Company, 38th Battalion, 1780-1781 [Ref: N-86/105, M-234]. Took the Oath of Allegiance and Fidelity on or about March 1, 1778 [Ref: J-1814, N-106/114].
SEAMORE, John Jr. Took the Oath of Allegiance and Fidelity on or about March 1, 1778 [Ref: J-1814, N-106/114].
SEAMORE, Joseph. Private, Militia, Hearts of Oak Company, 38th Battalion, 1780-1781 [Ref: N-86/105, M-234]. Private, Militia, Hearts of Oak Company, 38th Battalion, 1777-1778 [Ref: N-86/105, M-226]. Took the Oath of Allegiance and Fidelity on or about March 1, 1778 [Ref: J-1814, N-106/114].
SEARS, Ruth. See "John Lowe," q.v.
SEARS, William. Private, Militia, Bayside Company, 38th Battalion, 1777-1778 [Ref: N-86/105, M-228]. Second Lieutenant, Militia, 38th Battalion, November 4, 1782 [Ref: M-119, I-298].
SENEY, Samuel. See "Woolman Gibson," q.v.
SETH, Jacob. Sergeant, 5th Maryland Line, enlisted August 15, 1777; private, July 1, 1778; honorably discharged on August 20, 1780 [Ref: D-244].
SETH, James. Private, Militia, Union Company, 4th Battalion, 1780-1781 [Ref: N-86/105, M-230]. Private, Militia, Union Company, 4th Battalion, 1777-1778

[Ref: N-86/105, M-223]. Took the Oath of Allegiance and Fidelity on or about March 1, 1778 [Ref: J-1814, N-106/114].

SETH, William C. (1757-1815). Born in Maryland in 1757, William married Martha Chamberlaine, served as a cavalry sergeant during the revolution, and died on December 27, 1825 [Ref: Y-2613].

SETH, William E. See "John Gibson," q.v.

SEWELL (SEWEL, SOWEL), Anthony. Private, Militia, Volunteer Company, 4th Battalion, 1777-1778 [Ref: N-86/105, M-223, which listed the name as "Anthony Sewel"]. Took the Oath of Allegiance and Fidelity on or after March 1, 1778 [Ref: J-1814, N-106/114]. Private, Militia, Volunteer Company, 4th Battalion, 1780-1781 [Ref: N-86/105, M-230, which listed the name as "Anthony Sowel"].

SEWELL (SEWEL), Basil. Second Lieutenant, Militia, Bayside Company, 38th Battalion, April 9, 1778 [Ref: N-95, N-102, M-233, M-119, E-24]. Took the Oath of Allegiance and Fidelity on or about March 1, 1778 [Ref: J-1814, N-106/114].

SEWELL, Charlotte. See "Thomas Barnett Sewell," q.v.

SEWELL, James. Private, Militia, Miles River Company, 38th Battalion, 1777-1778 [Ref: N-86/105, M-227]. In December, 1817, the Treasurer of the Western Shore was directed to pay to James Sewell, an old revolutionary soldier, quarterly, the half pay of a private, as a further remuneration for his services during the American war. [Ref: T-390].

SEWELL, John. Private, Militia, 4th Battalion, Capt. Greenbury Goldsborough's Company, reviewed and passed July 27, 1776 [Ref: D-67]. Private, 7th Maryland Line, enlisted June 8, 1778; corporal, August 25, 1778; sergeant, December 27, 1779; reported missing at the Battle of Camden, S. C. on August 16, 1780 [Ref: D-249].

SEWELL (SEWEL), John. Private, Militia, Hearts of Oak Company, 38th Battalion, 1777-1778 [Ref: N-86/105, M-226]. Took the Oath of Allegiance and Fidelity on or about March 1, 1778 [Ref: J-1814, N-106/114]. Private, Militia, Hearts of Oak Company, 38th Battalion, 1780-1781 [Ref: N-86/105, M-235]. Private in the militia who was draughted on August 30, 1781 to reinforce the American Army and to serve in the Maryland Continental Troops until December 10, 1781 [Ref: D-387].

SEWELL (SEWEL), Joseph. Private, Militia, Hearts of Oak Company, 38th Battalion, 1777-1778 [Ref: N-86/105, M-226]. Private, Militia, Hearts of Oak Company, 38th Battalion, 1780-1781 [Ref: N-86/105, M-235].

SEWELL, Joseph. Private, Militia, 4th Battalion, Capt. Greenbury Goldsborough's Company, reviewed and passed July 27, 1776 [Ref: D-68]. Private, Militia, Wye Company, 4th Battalion, 1780-1781 [Ref: N-86/105, M-229].

SEWELL (SEWULL), Joseph. Private whose name appears on "a list of men blown up in the barges" in 1782 [Ref: D-615].

SEWELL (SEWEL), Mark. Private, Militia, Broad Creek Company, 38th Battalion, 1777-1778 [Ref: N-86/105, M-227]. Took the Oath of Allegiance and Fidelity on or about March 1, 1778 [Ref: J-1814, N-106/114]. Private, Militia, Broad Creek Company, 38th Battalion, 1780-1781 [Ref: N-86/105, M-234].

SEWELL, Mary. See "Anthony Lecompte," q.v.

SEWELL (SEWEL), Nathan. Private, Militia, Third Haven Company, 4th Battalion, 1777-1778 [Ref: N-86/105, M-225]. Took the Oath of Allegiance and Fidelity on or after March 1, 1778 [Ref: J-1814, N-106/114].

SEWELL, Nathan. Took the Oath of Allegiance and Fidelity sometime between May and September, 1780 [Ref: L-119].

SEWELL (SEWEL), Samuel. Private, Militia, Hearts of Oak Company, 38th Battalion, 1777-1778 [Ref: N-86/105, M-226]. Took the Oath of Allegiance and Fidelity on or about March 1, 1778 [Ref: J-1814, N-106/114]. Private, Militia, Wye Company, 4th Battalion, 1780-1781 [Ref: N-86/105, M-228].

SEWELL (SEWEL), Thomas. Private, Militia, Third Haven Company, 4th Battalion, 1777-1778 [Ref: N-86/105, M-225]. Took the Oath of Allegiance and Fidelity on or after March 1, 1778 [Ref: J-1814, N-106/114].

SEWELL, Thomas. Took the Oath of Allegiance and Fidelity on or about March 1, 1778 [Ref: J-1814, N-106/114].

SEWELL, Thomas. Took the Oath of Allegiance and Fidelity sometime between May and September, 1780 [Ref: L-119].

SEWELL (SEWEL), Thomas Barnett. Private, Militia, Hearts of Oak Company, 38th Battalion, 1777-1778 [Ref: N-86/105, M-226]. Private, Militia, Hearts of Oak Company, 38th Battalion, 1780-1781 [Ref: N-86/105, M-234, which listed the name as "Thomas B. Sewel"]. In pension file R8070 it states that Charlotte Coleman married Thomas B. Sewell, a soldier in Maryland Sea Service, on November 13, 1828 in Baltimore County. He died there January 14, 1830 and she next married Leon Pecor on September 30, 1830 in Baltimore City. On August 10, 1858, aged 77, she stated she thought Thomas, her first husband, deceased, was born in Talbot County on the Eastern Shore of Maryland. Affidavits were filed by Mary Ann Beverage and Rachel McCanly, but no relationship to the soldier, if any, was given. The widow also applied for bounty land (#84056-160-55) on June 26, 1856; however, her pension application was rejected [Ref: W-3074].

SEWELL (SEWEL), William. Private, Militia, Hearts of Oak Company, 38th Battalion, 1777-1778 [Ref: N-86/105, M-226]. Took the Oath of Allegiance and Fidelity on or about March 1, 1778 [Ref: J-1814, N-106/114]. William Sewell appears on "a list of men blown up in the barges" in 1782 [Ref: D-615]. On February 22, 1822 the Treasurer of the Western Shore was directed to pay to William Sewell, of Talbot County, half pay of a private, for his Revolutionary War service. On February 6, 1832 the Treasurer was directed to pay to Rebecca Sewell, widow of William, a soldier of the Revolutionary War, during life, half yearly, the half pay of a private, for the services rendered by her said husband. [Ref: T-390].

SEWILL(?), William. Private, Militia, Union Company, 4th Battalion, 1777-1778 [Ref: N-86/105, M-223].

SHANNAHAN (SHANAHAN), Elliott. Private, Militia, Hearts of Oak Company, 38th Battalion, 1780-1781 [Ref: N-86/105, M-234]. Second Lieutenant on the barge *Intrepid* in 1781 [Ref: D-610].

SHANNAHAN (SHANAHAN), Elizabeth. See "John Shannahan," q.v.

SHANNAHAN (SHANAHAN), John (c1740-1806). First Lieutenant, Militia, Hearts of Oak Company, 38th Battalion, April 9, 1778 [Ref: N-94, M-119, E-25]. Took the Oath of Allegiance and Fidelity on or about March 1, 1778 [Ref: J-1814, N-106/114]. John Shannahan was born in Maryland circa 1740, married Elizabeth ----, served as a first lieutenant in the revolution, and died on June 17, 1806 [Ref: Y-2624].

SHANNAHAN (SHANAHAN), John. Private, Militia, Hearts of Oak Company, 38th Battalion, 1780-1781 [Ref: N-86/105, M-234].

SHANNAHAN (SHANAHAN), Jonathan. Private, Militia, Hand in Hand Company, 4th Battalion, 1780-1781 [Ref: N-86/105, M-232]. Private, Militia, Hand & Hand Company, 4th Battalion, 1777-1778 [Ref: N-86/105, M-225].

SHANNAHAN, Peter. Private, Militia, Capt. Thoma Bullen's Company; no date was given; possibly late 1775 or early 1776 [Ref: Z-3].

SHARP, Samuel. Private, Militia, Union Company, 4th Battalion, 1777-1778 [Ref: N-86/105, M-223]. Private (substitute), Militia, Union Company, 4th Battalion, 1780-1781 [Ref: N-86/105, M-230].

SHARP (SHARPE), Samuel. Appointed by the Maryland Council as Agent for Purchasing Provisions in Talbot County on April 4, 1778 [Ref: E-8, P-167, P-180]. Took the Oath of Allegiance and Fidelity on or about March 1, 1778 [Ref: J-1814, N-106/114]. One Samuel Sharp or Sharpe was born in Maryland on May 2, 1736, married Sophia ----, rendered patriotic service during the revolution, and died on December 29, 1804 [Ref: Y-2626].

SHARP (SHARPE), Sophia. See "Samuel Sharp," q.v.

SHAW, Matthew (Mathew). Private, Militia, Union Company, 4th Battalion, 1780-1781 [Ref: N-86/105, M-230]. Private, Militia, Union Company, 4th Battalion, 1777-1778 [Ref: N-86/105, M-223].

SHAW, William. Private, Militia, Volunteer Company, 4th Battalion, 1780-1781 [Ref: N-86/105, M-229].

SHAWHANE, John. Private, Militia, 4th Battalion, Capt. Greenbury Goldsborough's Company, reviewed and passed July 27, 1776 [Ref: D-68].

SHEAVES, Robert. Private, Militia, Hearts of Oak Company, 38th Battalion, 1777-1778 [Ref: N-86/105, M-226].

SHENIN, Thomas. Private aboard the barge *Fearnought* under Capt. Levin Spedden; enlisted May 28, 1782; 5'8" tall; fair complexion; born in Talbot County [Ref: D-611].

SHEPHERD (SHIPPARD), John. Private (substitute), Maryland Line; honorably discharged on December 3, 1781 [Ref: I-11]. Private aboard the barge *Fearnought* under Capt. Levin Spedden; enlisted May 28, 1782; 5'6" tall; fair complexion; born in Talbot County [Ref: D-611, which listed the name as "John Shippard"].

SHERWIN, Abraham. Private, Militia, Capt. Thomas Bullen's Company; no date was given; possibly late 1775 or early 1776 [Ref: Z-3]. Private, Militia, Sword in Hand Company, 4th Battalion, 1777-1778 [Ref: N-86/105, M-224]. Took the Oath of Allegiance and Fidelity on or about March 1, 1778; name listed twice [Ref: J-1814, N-106/114]. Private, Militia, Sword in Hand Company, 4th Battalion, 1780-1781 [Ref: N-86/105, M-231].

SHERWIN, Thomas. Private, Militia, Third Haven Company, 4th Battalion, 1780-1781 [Ref: N-86/105, M-232]. Private, Militia, Third Haven Company, 4th Battalion, 1777-1778 [Ref: N-86/105, M-225].

SHERWOOD, Charles. Private, Militia, Miles River Company, 38th Battalion, 1777-1778 [Ref: N-86/105, M-227]. Took the Oath of Allegiance and Fidelity on or about March 1, 1778 [Ref: J-1814, N-106/114]. Private, Militia, Miles River Company, 38th Battalion, 1780-1781 [Ref: N-86/105, M-235]. Private, Miles River Company, draughted on May 1, 1781 to serve until December 10, 1781 in the Maryland Continental Troops [Ref: D-371].

SHERWOOD, Daniel. Private, Militia, Oxford Company, 38th Battalion, 1777-1778 [Ref: N-86/105, M-228].

SHERWOOD, Edward Man (Mann). Private, Militia, Capt. Thomas Bullen's Company; no date was given; possibly late 1775 or early 1776 [Ref: Z-3]. Private, Militia, Oxford Company, 38th Battalion, 1777-1778 [Ref: N-86/105, M-228].

SHERWOOD, Edward Man (Mann). Captain, Militia, Oxford Company, 38th Battalion, April 9, 1778 [Ref: N-93, N-105, M-235, M-120, E-25, which listed the name only as "Edward Sherwood"]. Took the Oath of Allegiance and Fidelity on or about March 1, 1778 [Ref: J-1814, N-106/114]. "Edward Man Sherwood, son of Edward Man Sherwood by Mary his wife, born August 15, 1729." [Ref: V-86]. See "John Sherwood," q.v.

SHERWOOD, Elizabeth. See "Hugh Sherwood, of Huntington," q.v.

SHERWOOD, Hugh. Private, Militia, 4th Battalion, Capt. Greenbury Goldsborough's Company, reviewed and passed July 27, 1776 [Ref: D-68]. Private, Militia, United Company, 38th Battalion, 1777-1778 [Ref: N-86/105, M-227]. Took the Oath of Allegiance and Fidelity on or about March 1, 1778 [Ref: J-1814, N-106/114]. Private, 5th Maryland Line, enlisted June 6, 1778 and discharged in July, 1778 [Ref: D-245].

SHERWOOD, Hugh. Private, Militia, Oxford Company, 38th Battalion, 1777-1778 [Ref: N-86/105, M-227]. Took the Oath of Allegiance and Fidelity on or about March 1, 1778 [Ref: J-1814, N-106/114]. Fifer, Militia, Broad Creek Company, 38th Battalion, 1780-1781 [Ref: N-103, M-234].

SHERWOOD, Hugh, of Huntington (c1752-1807). Only known child of Thomas and Mary Sherwood, he married Elizabeth ---- and their children were: Hugh; Elizabeth T. (1799-1831, married Dr. Edward Speddin); Mary (married ---- Hambleton); and, Susan (married ---- Banning). Hugh served in these capacities: Maryland Lower House between 1781 and 1792; Court Justice between 1779 and 1801; Justice of the Orphans Court, 1796; Commissioner of the Tax, 1798; Trustee of Easton Academy, 1800; Sheriff, 1802-1803; and, held the rank of major at the time of his death [Ref: R-733, R-86, R-87, R-92]. He may have served in the Revolutionary War since there were at least three men named Hugh Sherwood in the militia of Talbot County [Ref: M-227]. He was undoubtedly one of those who took the Oath of Allegiance and Fidelity on or about March 1, 1778 [Ref: J-1814]. Hugh Sherwood died at his plantation "Huntington" in the Second District of Talbot County on September 21, 1807, after an illness of two weeks' duration [Ref: R-733]. See "Thomas Sherwood," q.v.

SHERWOOD, Hugh Jr. Appointed a Justice of the Peace on December 4, 1779 and January 17, 1782 [Ref: F-31, I-46].

SHERWOOD, James. Private, Militia, Oxford Company, 38th Battalion, 1780-1781 [Ref: N-86/105, M-235].

SHERWOOD, John. Private, Militia, Capt. Thomas Bullen's Company; no date was given; possibly late 1775 or early 1776 [Ref: Z-3]. Private, Militia, Volunteer Company, 4th Battalion, 1780-1781 [Ref: N-86/105, M-229].

SHERWOOD, John (1726-   ). Took the Oath of Allegiance and Fidelity on or about March 1, 1778 [Ref: J-1814, N-106/114]. "John Sherwood, son of Edward Man Sherwood and Mary his wife, born July 9, 1726." [Ref: V-86].

SHERWOOD, Jonathan. Private, Militia, Miles River Company, 38th Battalion, 1780-1781 [Ref: N-86/105, M-235].

SHERWOOD, Mary. See "Hugh Sherwood, of Huntington" and "Edward Man Sherwood" and "John Sherwood" and "John Auld" and "Daniel Auld" and "Hugh Auld" and "Philemon Auld," q.v.

SHERWOOD, Nicholas. Private, Militia, 2nd Volunteer Company, 4th Battalion, 1777-1778 [Ref: N-86/105, M-225]. Private, Militia, Third Haven Company, 4th Battalion, 1780-1781 [Ref: N-86/105, M-232].

SHERWOOD, Nicholas. Private, Militia, Bayside Company, 38th Battalion, 1777-1778 [Ref: N-86/105, M-228]. Private, Militia, Bayside Company, 38th Battalion, 1780-1781 [Ref: N-86/105, M-233]. Waterman on the barge *Intrepid* in 1781 [Ref: D-610].

SHERWOOD, Philimon. Private, Militia, Miles River Company, 38th Battalion, 1780-1781 [Ref: N-86/105, M-235].

SHERWOOD, Philip. Took the Oath of Allegiance and Fidelity on or about March 1, 1778 [Ref: J-1814, N-106/114].

SHERWOOD, Robert. Private, Militia, Oxford Company, 38th Battalion, 1777-1778 [Ref: N-86/105, M-227]. Took the Oath of Allegiance and Fidelity on or about March 1, 1778 [Ref: J-1814, N-106/114].
SHERWOOD, Samuel. Private, Militia, Oxford Company, 38th Battalion, 1777-1778 [Ref: N-86/105, M-228].
SHERWOOD, Susan. See "Hugh Sherwood, of Huntington," q.v.
SHERWOOD, Thomas (c1732-c1798). Son of Hugh Sherwood and Mary Russell, he married Mary Money by 1753 and their only known child was Hugh Sherwood (of Huntington). Thomas served in these capacities: Maryland Lower House in 1778; Sheriff, 1768-1771; Court Justice, 1777-1779; Justice of the Peace (appointed 1778); Commissioner of the Tax, 1777-1792; Judge, Court of Appeals for Tax Assessments (appointed 1778); Trustee of the Alms and Work House, 1782; Trustee of the Poor (appointed 1786); and, Organizer of the Charity School, 1787 [Ref: R-734, R-80, E-112, E-163, E-250, Y-2649]. Took the Oath of Allegiance and Fidelity on or about March 1, 1778 [Ref: J-1814, N-106/114]. See "Hugh Sherwood, of Huntington," q.v.
SHERWOOD, Thomas. Private, Militia, United Company, 38th Battalion, 1777-1778 [Ref: N-86/105, M-227]. Private, Militia, Volunteer Company, 4th Battalion, 1780-1781 [Ref: N-86/105, M-229].
SHERWOOD, William. Private, Militia, Miles River Company, 38th Battalion, 1777-1778 [Ref: N-86/105, M-227]. Took the Oath of Allegiance and Fidelity on or about March 1, 1778 [Ref: J-1814, N-106/114]. Private, Militia, Third Haven Company, 4th Battalion, 1780-1781 [Ref: N-86/105, M-232]. Rendered patriotic service by storing bacon for the use of the Army in June, 1778 [Ref: P-177].
SHIELD, Rebecca. See "Levin Stacy," q.v.
SHIELDS (SHIELD), Benjamin. Took the Oath of Allegiance and Fidelity on or about March 1, 1778 [Ref: J-1814, N-106/114]. Private, Militia, Miles River Company, 38th Battalion, 1777-1778 [Ref: N-86/105, M-227, which listed the name as "Benjamin Sheald"]. Private, Militia, Miles River Company, 38th Battalion, 1780-1781 [Ref: N-86/105, M-235, which listed the name as "Benjamin Shields"].
SHIELDS (SHIELD), Griffin. Private, Militia, Wye Company, 4th Battalion, 1777-1778 [Ref: N-86/105, M-222]. Private, Militia, Wye Company, 4th Battalion, 1780-1781 [Ref: N-86/105, M-228]. Took the Oath of Allegiance and Fidelity on or about March 1, 1778 [Ref: J-1814, N-106/114, which listed the name as "Griffin Shield"].
SHIELDS, James. Private, Militia, 4th Battalion, Capt. Greenbury Goldsborough's Company, reviewed and passed July 27, 1776 [Ref: D-68].
SHIELDS, Rachael. See "Thomas Richardson," q.v.
SHIELDS, William. Private, Militia, 4th Battalion, Capt. Greenbury Goldsborough's Company, reviewed and passed July 27, 1776 [Ref: D-68]. Private, Militia, 2nd Volunteer Company, 4th Battalion, 1777-1778 [Ref: N-

86/105, M-225]. Private, Militia, Volunteer Company, 4th Battalion, 1780-1781 [Ref: N-86/105, M-229].

SHIELDS (SHIELD), William. Private, Militia, Miles River Company, 38th Battalion, 1777-1778 [Ref: N-86/105, M-227]. Took the Oath of Allegiance and Fidelity on or about March 1, 1778 [Ref: J-1814, N-106/114].

SHORT, Samuel. Private, Militia, Third Haven Company, 4th Battalion, 1780-1781 [Ref: N-86/105, M-232]. Private, Militia, Hearts of Oak Company, 38th Battalion, 1777-1778 [Ref: N-86/105, M-226].

SHRY, John. See "John Spry," q.v.

SILVESTER (SYLVESTER), Bradbury. Private, Militia, Hand & Hand Company, 4th Battalion, 1777-1778 [Ref: N-86/105, M-226].

SILVESTER (SYLVESTER), David. Private, Militia, Wye Company, 4th Battalion, 1777-1778 [Ref: N-86/105, M-222].

SILVESTER, Isaac. Private, Militia, Union Company, 4th Battalion, 1780-1781 [Ref: N-86/105, M-229].

SILVESTER (SYLVESTER), John. Took the Oath of Allegiance and Fidelity on or about March 1, 1778 [Ref: J-1814, N-106/114]. Private, Militia, Hand & Hand Company, 4th Battalion, 1777-1778 [Ref: N-86/105, M-226].

SILVESTER, Thomas. Private, Militia, Wye Company, 4th Battalion, 1777-1778 [Ref: N-86/105, M-222].

SIMMONS, Thomas. Private, Militia, 4th Battalion, Capt. Greenbury Goldsborough's Company, reviewed and passed July 27, 1776 [Ref: D-67].

SINCLAIRE (SINGCLARE), Alexander. Private, Militia, Broad Creek Company, 38th Battalion, 1777-1778 [Ref: N-86/105, M-226]. Private, Militia, Broad Creek Company, 38th Battalion, 1780-1781 [Ref: N-86/105, M-234].

SINCLAIRE (SINKLAIR), Edward. Private, Militia, Capt. Thomas Bullen's Company; no date was given; possibly late 1775 or early 1776 [Ref: Z-3].

SINCLAIRE (SINGCLARE), John. Private, Militia, Broad Creek Company, 38th Battalion, 1777-1778 [Ref: N-86/105, M-226]. Private, Militia, Broad Creek Company, 38th Battalion, 1780-1781 [Ref: N-86/105, M-234].

SINCLAIRE, Jonathan. Private, Militia, Bayside Company, 38th Battalion, 1780-1781 [Ref: N-86/105, M-233].

SINCLAIRE (SINGCLARE), Peregrine. Corporal, Militia, Bayside Company, 38th Battalion, 1780-1781 [Ref: N-102, M-233].

SINCLAIRE, William. Private, Militia, Broad Creek Company, 38th Battalion, 1780-1781 [Ref: N-86/105, M-234].

SINGLETON, John. First Lieutenant, Militia, 38th Battalion, May 16, 1776 [Ref: M-121, A-428]. One John Singleton was born December 28, 1750 in Whitehaven, England, and married Bridgett Goldsborough (born October 29, 1744, daughter of Nicholas and Sarah) on February 14, 1774 in St. Peter's Parish, Talbot County [Ref: K-57].

SINGLETON, John. Private, Militia, Oxford Company, 38th Battalion, 1777-1778 [Ref: N-86/105, M-227]. Private, Militia, Oxford Company, 38th Battalion, 1780-1781 [Ref: N-86/105, M-235].
SINNETT, Bryan. Private, 4th Independent Company of Maryland Regular Troops, Capt. James Hindman's Company, September, 1776 muster roll; enlisted January 26, 1776 [Ref: D-23].
SISK, James. Private, Militia, Capt. Thomas Bullen's Company; no date was given; possibly late 1775 or early 1776 [Ref: Z-3].
SISK, John. Private, Militia, Capt. Thomas Bullen's Company; no date was given; possibly late 1775 or early 1776 [Ref: Z-3].
SKINNER, Andrew. Corporal, Militia, Miles River Company, 38th Battalion, 1780-1781 [Ref: N-105, M-235].
SKINNER, John. Private, Militia, Bullin Brook Company, 4th Battalion, 1777-1778 [Ref: N-86/105, M-224]. Private, Militia, Bullinbrook Company, 4th Battalion, 1780-1781 [Ref: N-86/105, M-231].
SKINNER, John. Private, Militia, Miles River Company, 38th Battalion, 1777-1778 [Ref: N-86/105, M-227]. Private, Militia, Hearts of Oak Company, 38th Battalion, 1780-1781 [Ref: N-86/105, M-234]. Took the Oath of Allegiance and Fidelity on or about March 1, 1778 [Ref: J-1814, N-106/114].
SKINNER, Joseph. Took the Oath of Allegiance and Fidelity on or about March 1, 1778 [Ref: J-1814, N-106/114, which listed the name as "Josef(?) Skinner"]. Private, Militia, Oxford Company, 38th Battalion, 1777-1778 [Ref: N-86/105, M-228].
SKINNER, Mary. See "John Goldsborough," q.v.
SKINNER, Mordecai (Mordicai, Mordica). Second Lieutenant, Militia, 38th Battalion, April 9, 1778. First Lieutenant, Militia, Hearts of Oak Company, 38th Battalion, December 3, 1779 [Ref: N-94, N-104, M-234, M-121, E-25, F-28]. Took the Oath of Allegiance and Fidelity on or about March 1, 1778 [Ref: J-1814, N-106/114]. Rendered patriotic service by supplying bacon for the use of the Army in May, 1778 [Ref: P-172].
SKINNER, Philimon (Phill.). Took the Oath of Allegiance and Fidelity on or about March 1, 1778 [Ref: J-1814, N-106/114]. Private, Militia, United Company, 38th Battalion, 1777-1778 [Ref: N-86/105, M-227].
SKINNER, Richard. Private, Militia, Miles River Company, 38th Battalion, 1780-1781 [Ref: N-86/105, M-235]. Private, Militia, Miles River Company, 38th Battalion, 1777-1778 [Ref: N-86/105, M-227]. See "John Goldsborough," q.v.
SKINNER, Thomas. Private, Militia, 4th Battalion, Capt. Greenbury Goldsborough's Company, reviewed and passed July 27, 1776 [Ref: D-67]. Lieutenant, 5th Maryland Line, commissioned February 20, 1777 and resigned December 10, 1777 [Ref: D-244]. Took the Oath of Allegiance and Fidelity on or about March 1, 1778 [Ref: J-1814, N-106/114]. Returned to service as a recruiting office and was paid for his services in Talbot County by the Collector of the Tax on June 17, 1780 [Ref: F-198].

SKINNER, Thomas. Private, Militia, Union Company, 4th Battalion, 1780-1781 [Ref: N-86/105, M-229].
SKINNER, William. Private, Militia, Union Company, 4th Battalion, 1780-1781 [Ref: N-86/105, M-230].
SKINNER, Zebulon. Private, Militia, United Company, 38th Battalion, 1780-1781 [Ref: N-86/105, M-234].
SLACK, William. Private, Militia, Third Haven Company, 4th Battalion, 1777-1778 [Ref: N-86/105, M-225]. Took the Oath of Allegiance and Fidelity on or after March 1, 1778 [Ref: J-1814, N-106/114].
SMALL, Ephraim. Private, Militia, 4th Battalion, Capt. Greenbury Goldsborough's Company, reviewed and passed July 27, 1776 [Ref: D-67].
SMALL, James. Private, Militia, Bullin Brook Company, 4th Battalion, 1777-1778 [Ref: N-86/105, M-224]. Took the Oath of Allegiance and Fidelity on or about March 1, 1778; name listed twice [Ref: J-1814, N-106/114].
SMALL, Jonathan. Private, Militia, 4th Battalion, Capt. Greenbury Goldsborough's Company, reviewed and passed July 27, 1776 [Ref: D-67]. Private, 5th Maryland Line, enlisted February 10, 1777; honorably discharged on February 14, 1780 [Ref: D-245].
SMALL, Samuel. Took the Oath of Allegiance and Fidelity on or about March 1, 1778 [Ref: J-1814, N-106/114].
SMALL, Theophilus (Theofilus). Private, Militia, Bullin Brook Company, 4th Battalion, 1777-1778 [Ref: N-86/105, M-224]. Private, Militia, Bullinbrook Company, 4th Battalion, 1780-1781 [Ref: N-86/105, M-231].
SMITH, Archibald. Private, Militia, Union Company, 4th Battalion, 1777-1778 [Ref: N-86/105, M-223]. Took the Oath of Allegiance and Fidelity on or about March 1, 1778 [Ref: J-1814, N-106/114]. Private, Militia, Union Company, 4th Battalion, 1780-1781 [Ref: N-86/105, M-230].
SMITH, Charles. Private, Militia, Bayside Company, 38th Battalion, 1780-1781 [Ref: N-86/105, M-233]. On March 5, 1835 the Treasurer of the Western Shore was directed to pay to Charles Smith, of Talbot County, quarterly, during his life, half pay of a private, in consideration of his services in the war of the revolution. [Ref: T-393]. Charles applied for a federal pension (R9703) on July 27, 1838, based on his Maryland Sea Service, stating he was born in Talbot County on May 19, 1763 and lived there at the time of his enlistment; however, the record indicates he was rejected [Ref: W-3174].
SMITH, Edward. Private, Militia, Oxford Company, 38th Battalion, 1777-1778 [Ref: N-86/105, M-228]. Took the Oath of Allegiance and Fidelity on or after March 1, 1778 [Ref: J-1814, N-106/114]. Private, Militia, Oxford Company, 38th Battalion, 1780-1781 [Ref: N-86/105, M-235].
SMITH, Elijah. Private, Militia, Hearts of Oak Company, 38th Battalion, 1777-1778 [Ref: N-86/105, M-226].
SMITH, Elisha. Private, Militia, Hearts of Oak Company, 38th Battalion, 1780-1781 [Ref: N-86/105, M-234].

SMITH, Francis. Private, Militia, Capt. Thomas Bullen's Company; no date was given; possibly late 1775 or early 1776 [Ref: Z-3].

SMITH, Henry. Private, Militia, Oxford Company, 38th Battalion, 1777-1778 [Ref: N-86/105, M-228]. Took the Oath of Allegiance and Fidelity on or after March 1, 1778 [Ref: J-1814, N-106/114]. Private, Militia, Oxford Company, 38th Battalion, 1780-1781 [Ref: N-86/105, M-235].

SMITH, James. Took the Oath of Allegiance and Fidelity on or about March 1, 1778 [Ref: J-1814, N-106/114].

SMITH, John. Private, 4th Independent Company of Maryland Regular Troops, Capt. James Hindman's Company, September, 1776 muster roll; enlisted January 28, 1776 [Ref: D-24].

SMITH, John. Private, Militia, Wye Company, 4th Battalion, 1780-1781 [Ref: N-86/105, M-229].

SMITH, Katherine. See "James Parrott," q.v.

SMITH, Richard. Private in the militia who was draughted on August 30, 1781 to reinforce the American Army and to serve in the Maryland Continental Troops until December 10, 1781 [Ref: D-387].

SMITH, Thomas. Private, Militia, Bayside Company, 38th Battalion, 1777-1778 [Ref: N-86/105, M-228].

SMITH, Thomas. Took the Oath of Allegiance and Fidelity on or about March 1, 1778; name listed twice [Ref: J-1814, N-106/114].

SMITH, William. Private, 4th Independent Company of Maryland Regular Troops, Capt. James Hindman's Company, September, 1776 muster roll; enlisted January 29, 1776 [Ref: D-24].

SMITH, William. Private, Militia, Union Company, 4th Battalion, 1780-1781 [Ref: N-86/105, M-230].

SNELLING, Henry. Private, Militia, Volunteer Company, 4th Battalion, 1780-1781 [Ref: N-86/105, M-229].

SNELLING, William. Private, Militia, 2nd Volunteer Company, 4th Battalion, 1777-1778 [Ref: N-86/105, M-225]. Took the Oath of Allegiance and Fidelity on or about March 1, 1778 [Ref: J-1814, N-106/114].

SNOOK, Richard. Private, 4th Independent Company of Maryland Regular Troops, Capt. James Hindman's Company, September, 1776 muster roll; enlisted February 3, 1776 [Ref: D-23].

SOWEL, Anthony. See "Anthony Sewell," q.v.

SPEDDEN, Ann or Nancy. See "Edward Spedden," q.v.

SPEDDEN (SPEDDING), Edward (c1750-1823). Second Lieutenant on the barge *Fearnought* under Capt. Levin Spedden in 1782 [Ref: D-611, D-613]. Edward Spedden was born in Maryland (no date given), married Ann or Nancy ----, served as a naval lieutenant, and died before February 22, 1823 [Ref: Y-2752]. See "Hugh Sherwood, of Huntington," q.v.

SPEDDEN (SPEDDING), Levin. Second Lieutenant, Militia, 4th Battalion, May 16, 1776 [Ref: M-124, A_428, which listed the name as "Levin Spreden"].

Took the Oath of Allegiance and Fidelity on or about March 1, 1778 [Ref: J-1814, N-106/114]. First Lieutenant, Militia, 4th Battalion, April 9, 1778. Captain, Militia, Third Haven Company, 4th Battalion, May 11, 1778 [Ref: N-91, N-100, M-232, M-124, E-24, E-73]. Paid for his recruiting services in Talbot County by the Collector of the Tax on January 13, 1780 [Ref: F-57]. Captain of the barge *Fearnought* in 1782 [Ref: D-611, D-612, D-613].

SPEDDEN (SPEDDING), Robert (1760-1834). Private, Militia, Third Haven Company, 4th Battalion, 1780-1781 [Ref: N-86/105, M-232]. Seaman (waterman) on the barge *Intrepid* in 1781 [Ref: D-610]. "Robert Brannock Spedden" was born in April, 1760, served as a sailor during the revolution, married Elizabeth Taylor, and died on August 10, 1834 [Ref: Y-2752].

SPENCER, Humphry. Private, 4th Independent Company of Maryland Regular Troops, Capt. James Hindman's Company, September, 1776 muster roll; enlisted February 2, 1776 [Ref: D-24].

SPENCER, Jonathan. Private, Militia, United Company, 38th Battalion, 1780-1781 [Ref: N-86/105, M-234].

SPENCER, Marmaduke. Private, Militia, United Company, 38th Battalion, 1780-1781 [Ref: N-86/105, M-233]. Private, Militia, United Company, 38th Battalion, 1777-1778 [Ref: N-86/105, M-227].

SPENCER, Perry. Private, Militia, Hearts of Oak Company, 38th Battalion, 1780-1781 [Ref: N-86/105, M-235]. Took the Oath of Allegiance and Fidelity on or after March 1, 1778 [Ref: J-1814, N-106/114].

SPENCER, Philimon. Took the Oath of Allegiance and Fidelity on or about March 1, 1778 [Ref: J-1814, N-106/114].

SPENCER, Richard. Private, Militia, Hearts of Oak Company, 38th Battalion, 1780-1781 [Ref: N-86/105, M-234]. Private in the militia who was draughted on August 30, 1781 to reinforce the American Army and to serve in the Maryland Continental Troops until December 10, 1781 [Ref: D-387].

SPINDILOW, Negro (a free man). Private in the militia who was draughted on August 30, 1781 to reinforce the American Army and to serve in the Maryland Continental Troops until December 10, 1781 [Ref: D-387].

SPROUSE, Philip. Took the Oath of Allegiance and Fidelity on or about March 1, 1778 [Ref: J-1814, N-106/114].

SPRY, Christopher. Private, Militia, Bayside Company, 38th Battalion, 1777-1778 [Ref: N-86/105, M-228]. Took the Oath of Allegiance and Fidelity on or after March 1, 1778 [Ref: J-1814, N-106/114, which listed the name as "Shry"]. Private, Militia, Bayside Company, 38th Battalion, 1780-1781 [Ref: N-86/105, M-233].

SPRY, Francis. Fifer, Militia, Hearts of Oak Company, 38th Battalion, 1780-1781 [Ref: N-104, M-234].

SPRY, John. Private, Militia, Hearts of Oak Company, 38th Battalion, 1777-1778 [Ref: N-86/105, M-226]. Took the Oath of Allegiance and Fidelity on or after March 1, 1778 [Ref: J-1814, N-106/114, which listed the name as "Shry"].

Private, Militia, Hearts of Oak Company, 38th Battalion, 1780-1781 [Ref: N-86/105, M-235]. Rendered patriotic service by supplying bacon for the use of the Armt in June, 1778 [Ref: P-173].

SPRY, Mary. See "Daniel Lambdin," q.v.

SRAKAN(?), William. Private, Militia, 2nd Volunteer Company, 4th Battalion, 1777-1778 [Ref: N-86/105, M-225].

STACK(?), William. Private, Militia, Third Haven Company, 4th Battalion, 1777-1778 [Ref: N-86/105, M-225].

STACY, Levin (1735-   ). Born in St. Peter's Parish, Talbot County, on October 12, 1735, son of William Stacy (died 1742) and Rebecca Shield [Ref: V-88]. Private, Militia, Wye Company, 4th Battalion, 1777-1778 [Ref: N-86/105, M-222]. Took the Oath of Allegiance and Fidelity on or about March 1, 1778 [Ref: J-1814, N-106/114]. Private, Militia, Wye Company, 4th Battalion, 1780-1781 [Ref: N-86/105, M-228].

STACY, William. See "Levin Stacy," q.v.

STAINS, Moses. Private, Militia, Hearts of Oak Company, 38th Battalion, 1777-1778 [Ref: N-86/105, M-226].

STANDFIELD, Richard. Private, Militia, Miles River Company, 38th Battalion, 1777-1778 [Ref: N-86/105, M-227]. Took the Oath of Allegiance and Fidelity on or about March 1, 1778 [Ref: J-1814, N-106/114, which listed the name as "Richard Stanfield"]. Private, Militia, Miles River Company, 38th Battalion, 1780-1781 [Ref: N-86/105, M-235]. Draughted on May 1, 1781 to serve until December 10, 1781 in the Maryland Continental Troops [Ref: D-371].

STANDLEY, Elizabeth. See "James Standley," q.v.

STANDLEY, James (1744-   ). Born in St. Peter's Parish, Talbot County, on January 10, 1744, a son of John and Elizabeth Standley [Ref: V-90]. Private, Militia, Bullin Brook Company, 4th Battalion, 1777-1778 [Ref: N-86/105, M-224]. Took the Oath of Allegiance and Fidelity on or after March 1, 1778 [Ref: J-1814, N-106/114]. Private, Militia, Bullinbrook Company, 4th Battalion, 1780-1781 [Ref: N-86/105, M-231].

STANDLEY, John. See "James Standley," q.v.

STANT, James. Private, Militia, Wye Company, 4th Battalion, 1777-1778 [Ref: N-86/105, M-222]. Private, Militia, Wye Company, 4th Battalion, 1780-1781 [Ref: N-86/105, M-229].

STAPLEFORD, Daniel. Private, Militia, Capt. Thomas Bullen's Company; no date was given; possibly late 1775 or early 1776 [Ref: Z-3].

STAPLEFORD, Henry (1737-   ). Born in St. Peter's Parish, Talbot County, on October 8, 1737, son of John and Rebecca Stapleford [Ref: V-78]. Private, 4th Independent Company of Maryland Regular Troops, Capt. James Hindman's Company, September, 1776 muster roll; enlisted February 15, 1776 [Ref: D-24].

STAPLEFORD, John Jr. Private, Militia, Capt. Thomas Bullen's Company; no date was given; possibly late 1775 or early 1776 [Ref: Z-3]. See "Henry Stapleford," q.v.

STAPLEFORD, Joseph. Private, Militia, Capt. Thomas Bullen's Company; no date was given; possibly late 1775 or early 1776 [Ref: Z-3].

STAPLEFORD, Rebecca. See "Henry Stapleford," q.v.

STAPLEFORD, Robert. Private, Militia, Capt. Thomas Bullen's Company; no date was given; possibly late 1775 or early 1776 [Ref: Z-3].

START, John. Private, Militia, 4th Battalion, Capt. Greenbury Goldsborough's Company, reviewed and passed July 27, 1776 [Ref: D-68]. Private, Militia, Volunteer Company, 4th Battalion, 1777-1778 [Ref: N-86/105, M-223].

START, Moses. Private, 5th Maryland Line, enlisted January 18, 1777 and reported missing after the Battle of Camden, S. C. on August 16, 1780; mustered as a sergeant in October, 1780 [Ref: D-244].

START, Richard. Second Lieutenant, Militia, Miles River Company, 38th Battalion, 1780-1781 [Ref: N-105, M-235]. Draughted on August 30, 1781 to reinforce the American Army and to serve in the Maryland Continental Troops until December 10, 1781; honorably discharged from the Maryland Line on November 27, 1781 [Ref: D-387, and I-5, which listed the name as "Richard Stark"]. Second Lieutenant, Militia, 38th Battalion, November 4, 1782 [Ref: M-124, I-298].

START, Thomas. Private, 4th Independent Company of Maryland Regular Troops, Capt. James Hindman's Company, September, 1776 muster roll; enlisted January 25, 1776 [Ref: D-24].

START, William. Took the Oath of Allegiance and Fidelity on or about March 1, 1778 [Ref: J-1814, N-106/114]. First Lieutenant, Militia, 38th Battalion, April 12, 1780 [Ref: M-124, F-140].

STENGER, Wilbur Jackson Jr. See "Matthew Tilghman," q.v.

STEPHENS, Edward. Took the Oath of Allegiance and Fidelity on or about March 1, 1778 [Ref: J-1814, N-106/114, which listed the name as "Edward Stepens(?)"]. See "Edward Stevens," q.v.

STEPHENS, George. Took the Oath of Allegiance and Fidelity on or about March 1, 1778 [Ref: J-1814, N-106/114].

STEPHENS, John. Took the Oath of Allegiance and Fidelity on or about March 1, 1778; name listed twice [Ref: J-1814, N-106/114]. See "John Stevens," q.v.

STEPHENS, Samuel. Took the Oath of Allegiance and Fidelity on or about March 1, 1778 [Ref: J-1814, N-106/114].

STEUART (STUART), Andrew. Private, Militia, 4th Battalion, Capt. Greenbury Goldsborough's Company, reviewed and passed July 27, 1776 [Ref: D-68].

STEUART (STUART), Isaac. Private, Militia, 4th Battalion, Capt. Greenbury Goldsborough's Company, reviewed and passed July 27, 1776 [Ref: D-67].

STEUART (STUART), Robert. Private, Militia, 4th Battalion, Capt. Greenbury Goldsborough's Company, reviewed and passed July 27, 1776 [Ref: D-68].

STEUART (STEWART), Susannah. See "James Tilghman," q.v.
STEVENS, Benjamin. See "John Stevens," q.v.
STEVENS, Edward (1753-   ). Born in St. Peter's Parish, Talbot County, on October 30, 1753, son of William and Sarah Stevens, he married Ellinor Robinson (born May 23, 1756, daughter of Richard and Judith) on June 22, 1783 [Ref: K-57]. Private, Militia, Third Haven Company, 4th Battalion, 1777-1778 [Ref: N-86/105, M-225]. Ensign, Militia, 4th Battalion, April 9, 1778. First Lieutenant, Militia, Third Haven Company, 4th Battalion, May 11, 1778 through 1780 [Ref: N-91, N-100, M-232, M-125, E-24, E-73, T-397]. See "Edward Stephens," q.v.
STEVENS, Eliza. See "John Stevens," q.v.
STEVENS, George. Private, Militia, Sword in Hand Company, 4th Battalion, 1777-1778 [Ref: N-86/105, M-224]. Private, Militia, Sword in Hand Company, 4th Battalion, 1780-1781 [Ref: N-86/105, M-231]. See "George Stephens," q.v.
STEVENS, George. Private, Militia, Volunteer Company, 4th Battalion, 1780-1781 [Ref: N-86/105, M-229].
STEVENS, Henrietta. See "John Stevens," q.v.
STEVENS, John (c1735-1794). Son of Thomas Stevens and Juliana Thomas (widow of William Stevens and daughter of William Thomas), he married Elizabeth Connolly(?) by 1765 and their children were: Samuel (1778-1860, married Eliza May, and became Governor of Maryland in 1822); Benjamin (died 1794); Thomas (died 1796); Juliana (married Joseph Martin); Mary (married first to Nathaniel Manning and second to Rev. James Thomas); Eliza (married first to John R. Downes and second to Francis Rochester); Sarah (married James Nabb); and, Henrietta (married John Thomas, Jr.). John served in these capacities: Maryland Lower House, 1778, 1786-1787; Court Justice, 1770-1774, 1777; Sheriff, 1774-1775; Court Justice, 1777; Committee of Observation, 1775; Judge, Court of Appeals, 1778; Commissioner to Establish the Town of Easton, 1786; Constitution Ratification Convention, 1788; and, Associate Justice, 1792 [Ref: R-775, R-776, R-80, R-91, E-112]. Took the Oath of Allegiance and Fidelity on or after March 1, 1778 [Ref: J-1814, N-106/114].
STEVENS, John (1728-1797). Private, Maryland Line. John was born in Maryland in 1728, married Ann Burton, served as a private in the revolution, and died in 1797 [Ref: Y-2799]. Since there were several men named John Stevens or Stephens who served in Maryland during the revolution, there is an identification problem as to the service of this particular John Stevens [Ref: D-168, D-248, D-346, D-383, D-404]. Additional research will be necessary before drawing conclusions.
STEVENS, John Jr. Private, Militia, Oxford Company, 38th Battalion, 1780-1781 [Ref: N-86/105, M-235]. Took the Oath of Allegiance and Fidelity on or after March 1, 1778 [Ref: J-1814].
STEVENS, Juliana. See "John Stevens," q.v.
STEVENS, Mary. See "John Stevens," q.v.

STEVENS, Samuel. See "John Stevens," q.v.

STEVENS, Sarah. See "Edward Stevens" and "John Stevens," q.v.

STEVENS, Thomas. Took the Oath of Allegiance and Fidelity on or about March 1, 1778 [Ref: J-1814, N-106/114]. Rendered patriotic service by supplying bacon for the use of the Army in May, 1778 and also by hauling meat [Ref: P-164]. See "John Stevens," q.v.

STEVENS, William. Captain, Militia, 4th Battalion, April 9, 1778 [Ref: M-125, E-24]. Took the Oath of Allegiance and Fidelity on or about March 1, 1778 [Ref: J-1814, N-106/114]. Rendered patriotic service by supplying bacon for the use of the Army in June, 1778 [Ref: P-175]. See "John Stevens" and "Edward Stevens," q.v.

STEVENS, William. Private, Militia, Capt. Thomas Bullen's Company; no date was given; possibly late 1775 or early 1776 [Ref: Z-3]. Private (substitute), Militia, Volunteer Company, 4th Battalion, 1780-1781 [Ref: N-86/105, M-230].

STEVENS, William Jr. Corporal, Militia, Bullinbrook Company, 4th Battalion, 1780-1781 [Ref: M-231].

STEVENS, William Jr. Private, Militia, Volunteer Company, 4th Battalion, 1780-1781 [Ref: N-86/105, M-230].

STEWARD, Stephen. See "Nicholas Martin," q.v.

STEWART, Andrew. Private, Militia, 2nd Volunteer Company, 4th Battalion, 1777-1778 [Ref: N-86/105, M-225]. Took the Oath of Allegiance and Fidelity on or about March 1, 1778 [Ref: J-1814, N-106/114].

STEWART, Charles. Private, Militia, Sword in Hand Company, 4th Battalion, 1780-1781 [Ref: N-86/105, M-231]. Took the Oath of Allegiance and Fidelity on or about March 1, 1778 [Ref: J-1814, N-106/114].

STEWART, Elisha. Private, Militia, Sword in Hand Company, 4th Battalion. Recommended to be Second Lieutenant, Militia, 4th Battalion, June 17, 1777. Commissioned First Lieutenant, Militia, November 4, 1782 [Ref: M-231, M-125, I-298]. Took the Oath of Allegiance and Fidelity on or about March 1, 1778 [Ref: J-1814, N-106/114].

STEWART, Elizabeth. See "John Gibson," q.v.

STEWART, James. Private, Militia, 2nd Volunteer Company, 4th Battalion, 1777-1778 [Ref: N-86/105, M-225]. Took the Oath of Allegiance and Fidelity on or about March 1, 1778 [Ref: J-1814, N-106/114]. Second Lieutenant, Militia, Volunteer Company, 4th Battalion, 1780-1781 [Ref: N-96, M-229].

STEWART, John. Took the Oath of Allegiance and Fidelity on or about March 1, 1778 [Ref: J-1814, N-106/114].

STEWART, Thomas. Private, Militia, Sword in Hand Company, 4th Battalion, 1780-1781 [Ref: N-86/105, M-231]. Private, Militia, Sword in Hand Company, 4th Battalion, 1777-1778 [Ref: N-86/105, M-224]. Took the Oath of Allegiance and Fidelity on or about March 1, 1778 [Ref: J-1814, N-106/114].

STEWART, Susannah. See "James Tilghman," q.v.

STEWART, William. Took the Oath of Allegiance and Fidelity on or about March 1, 1778 [Ref: J-1814, N-106/114].
STOKER, Benjamin. Private, Militia, Third Haven Company, 4th Battalion, 1780-1781 [Ref: N-86/105, M-232].
STOKER, Elijah. Private, Militia, Hearts of Oak Company, 38th Battalion, 1780-1781 [Ref: N-86/105, M-234].
STOKER, James. Private, Militia, Capt. Thomas Bullen's Company; no date was given; possibly late 1775 or early 1776 [Ref: Z-3].
STOKER, John. Private, Militia, Hearts of Oak Company, 38th Battalion, 1777-1778 [Ref: N-86/105, M-226]. Corporal, Militia, Hearts of Oak Company, 38th Battalion, 1780-1781 [Ref: N-104, M-234]. Took the Oath of Allegiance and Fidelity on or about March 1, 1778 [Ref: J-1814, N-106/114].
STOKER, Joshua. Private, Militia, Third Haven Company, 4th Battalion, 1777-1778 [Ref: N-86/105, M-225]. Private, Militia, Third Haven Company, 4th Battalion, 1780-1781 [Ref: N-86/105, M-232]. Took the Oath of Allegiance and Fidelity on or after March 1, 1778 [Ref: J-1814, N-106/114].
STOW, Matthew. Took the Oath of Allegiance and Fidelity on or after March 1, 1778 [Ref: J-1814, N-106/114].
STRAWHAWN, William. Took the Oath of Allegiance and Fidelity on or about March 1, 1778 [Ref: J-1814, N-106/114].
STREET, Richard. Private, Militia, Third Haven Company, 4th Battalion, 1780-1781 [Ref: N-86/105, M-232]. Private, Militia, Third Haven Company, 4th Battalion, 1777-1778 [Ref: N-86/105, M-225].
STREET, William. Private, Militia, Third Haven Company, 4th Battalion, 1780-1781 [Ref: N-86/105, M-232].
STUART, John. Private aboard the barge *Fearnought* under Capt. Levin Spedden; enlisted May 28, 1782; 5'6" tall; dark complexion; born in Talbot County [Ref: D-611].
SUDLER, Elizabeth. See "John L. Elbert," q.v.
SULLIVAN, Patrick. Took the Oath of Allegiance and Fidelity on or about March 1, 1778 [Ref: J-1814, N-106/114].
SUMMERS (SOMMERS), John. Waterman on the barge *Intrepid* in 1781 [Ref: D-610].
SUMMERS, Solomon. Private, 5th Maryland Line, enlisted May 6, 1778 and still in the service on November 1, 1780 [Ref: D-245]. Placed on the pension rolls in Talbot County on July 19, 1819, aged 73, with an annual allowance of $96 effective June 8, 1819; died on February 13, 1823 [Ref: X-41/514].
SUMMERS, Thomas. Private, Militia, Volunteer Company, 4th Battalion, 1780-1781 [Ref: N-86/105, M-230].
SUTERS, Charles. Private, Militia, Hand in Hand Company, 4th Battalion, 1780-1781 [Ref: N-86/105, M-232].
SUTTON, James. Private, Militia, Capt. Thomas Bullen's Company; no date was given; possibly late 1775 or early 1776 [Ref: Z-3].

SWAN, James. Private, Militia, Miles River Company, 38th Battalion, 1777-1778 [Ref: N-86/105, M-227]. Took the Oath of Allegiance and Fidelity on or about March 1, 1778 [Ref: J-1814, N-106/114]. Private, Militia, Miles River Company, 38th Battalion, 1780-1781 [Ref: N-86/105, M-235].

SWAN, John. Private, Militia, Miles River Company, 38th Battalion, 1777-1778 [Ref: N-86/105, M-227]. Sergeant, Militia, Miles River Company, 38th Battalion, 1780-1781 [Ref: N-105, M-235]. Took the Oath of Allegiance and Fidelity on or about March 1, 1778 [Ref: J-1814, N-106/114].

SWEAT, Aaron. Private, Militia, Wye Company, 4th Battalion, 1780-1781 [Ref: N-86/105, M-229].

SWEAT, Edward. Private, Militia, Wye Company, 4th Battalion, 1777-1778 [Ref: N-86/105, M-222, which listed the name as "Edward Swett"]. Private, Militia, Wye Company, 4th Battalion, 1780-1781 [Ref: N-86/105, M-229]. Took the Oath of Allegiance and Fidelity on or about March 1, 1778 [Ref: J-1814, N-106/114, which listed the name as "Edward Sweatt"].

SWEAT, William. Private, Militia, Wye Company, 4th Battalion, 1780-1781 [Ref: N-86/105, M-228].

SWEATING, Richard. Took the Oath of Allegiance and Fidelity on or after March 1, 1778 [Ref: J-1814, N-106/114].

SWEENEY, John. Private, 4th Independent Company of Maryland Regular Troops, Capt. James Hindman's Company, September, 1776 muster roll; enlisted February 1, 1776 [Ref: D-25].

SWEER (SWERE), Vachel. See "Vachel Savier," q.v.

SYLVESTER, John. See "John Silvester," q.v.

TARR, Jonathan. Private, Militia, Hearts of Oak Company, 38th Battalion, 1780-1781 [Ref: N-86/105, M-234].

TARR, Richard. Private, Militia, Hearts of Oak Company, 38th Battalion, 1780-1781 [Ref: N-86/105, M-234]. Private, Militia, Hearts of Oak Company, 38th Battalion, 1777-1778 [Ref: N-86/105, M-226].

TARR, William. Private, 4th Independent Company of Maryland Regular Troops, Capt. James Hindman's Company, September, 1776 muster roll; enlisted February 2, 1776 [Ref: D-24].

TARRING, John. Private, Militia, Wye Company, 4th Battalion, 1780-1781 [Ref: N-86/105, M-229]. Took the Oath of Allegiance and Fidelity on or about March 1, 1778 [Ref: J-1814, N-106/114].

TAYLOR, Elizabeth. See "Edward Lloyd" and "Robert Spedden," q.v.

TAYLOR, Cornelius (Cornelious). Private, Militia, Hand & Hand Company, 4th Battalion, 1777-1778 [Ref: N-86/105, M-225]. Private, Militia, Hand in Hand Company, 4th Battalion, 1780-1781 [Ref: N-86/105, M-232].

TAYLOR, Robert Preston. See "Joseph Dawson," q.v.

TAYLOR, William. Private, Militia, Sword in Hand Company, 4th Battalion, 1777-1778 [Ref: N-86/105, M-224]. Private, Militia, Sword in Hand Company, 4th Battalion, 1780-1781 [Ref: N-86/105, M-231].

TAYLOR, William. Private, Militia, Wye Company, 4th Battalion, 1780-1781 [Ref: N-86/105, M-228].
TAYLOR, William. Took the Oath of Allegiance and Fidelity on or about March 1, 1778 [Ref: J-1814, N-106/114].
TENNANT, James. Took the Oath of Allegiance and Fidelity on or about March 1, 1778 [Ref: J-1814, N-106/114].
TENNANT, Samuel. Private, Militia, United Company, 38th Battalion, 1780-1781 [Ref: N-86/105, M-233].
THARP, Matilda. See "James Parrott," q.v.
THATCHER, David. Private, 4th Independent Company of Maryland Regular Troops, Capt. James Hindman's Company, September, 1776 muster roll; enlisted January 28, 1776 [Ref: D-24].
THATCHER, Susannah. See "John Bartlett," q.v.
THOMAS, Allen. Private, 5th Maryland Line, enlisted July 22, 1777 and still in service on January 1, 1780 [Ref: D-251].
THOMAS, James. Private, Militia, Sword in Hand Company, 4th Battalion, 1777-1778 [Ref: N-86/105, M-224]. Took the Oath of Allegiance and Fidelity on or about March 1, 1778 [Ref: J-1814, N-106/114]. Private, Militia, Sword in Hand Company, 4th Battalion, 1780-1781 [Ref: N-86/105, M-231].
THOMAS, James. Private, Militia, Oxford Company, 38th Battalion, 1777-1778 [Ref: N-86/105, M-227]. Took the Oath of Allegiance and Fidelity on or about March 1, 1778 [Ref: J-1814, N-106/114]. Private, Militia, Oxford Company, 38th Battalion, 1780-1781 [Ref: N-86/105, M-235].
THOMAS, James. Appointed a Justice of the Peace on November 20, 1779 and January 17, 1782 [Ref: F-22, I-46]. Since there were two men with this name who served in the war, additional research will be necessary before drawing conclusions as to which one (or possibly even a third James) was the Justice of the Peace. See "John Stevens" and "Nicholas Thomas," q.v.
THOMAS, John. Took the Oath of Allegiance and Fidelity on or about March 1, 1778 [Ref: J-1814, N-106/114]. Private, Militia, Union Company, 4th Battalion, 1780-1781 [Ref: N-86/105, M-230].
THOMAS, John Jr. Ensign, Militia, Wye Company, 4th Battalion, January 3, 1776. Second Lieutenant, Militia, July 1, 1776. Captain, Militia, Sword in Hand Company, 4th Battalion, April 9, 1778 to November 4, 1782; succeeded [Ref: N-86, N-99, M-230, M-128, A-539, E-24, I-298, and D-67, which listed the name without the "Jr."]. Took the Oath of Allegiance and Fidelity on or about March 1, 1778 [Ref: J-1814, N-106/114]. Appointed a Justice of the Peace on July 22, 1778 and November 21, 1778 [Ref: E-163, and E-250, which listed the name as "John Thomas, son of John"]. See "John Stevens" and "John Gibson," q.v.
THOMAS, John Allen. See "Nicholas Thomas," q.v.
THOMAS, Juliana. See "John Stevens," q.v.

THOMAS, Nicholas (c1735-1783/1784). A son of William Thomas and Elizabeth Allen, he never married, became a lawyer, and was admitted to practice law in Queen Anne's County in 1759, Talbot County in 1759, Provincial Court in 1760, Cecil County in 1760, Somerset County in 1765 and Dorchester County in 1773. His brother John Allen Thomas moved to St. Mary's County and his brother James Thomas moved to Annapolis. Both were very prominent in governmental affairs. Nicholas also devoted his life to public service: Maryland Lower House, 1768-1778 (Speaker, 1778); Maryland Conventions, 1774-1776; Chairman, Talbot County Committee of Safety, 1776; Maryland Council of Safety, 1776-1777; and, Judge, General Court, from 1778 until his death in late 1783 or early 1784 [Ref: A-3, A-202, O-1, O-4, O-28, R-809, R-70, R-72, R-76, R-78]. Quartermaster, Militia, 4th Battalion, from January 12, 1776 to August 8, 1776; resigned [Ref: M-128, B-188].

THOMAS, Nicholas. Private, Militia, Oxford Company, 38th Battalion, 1777-1778 [Ref: N-86/105, M-228].

THOMAS, Samuel. First Lieutenant, Militia, Sword in Hand Company, 4th Battalion, April 9, 1778. Captain, Militia, November 4, 1782 [Ref: N-86, N-99, M-230, M-128, E-24, I-298]. Rendered patriotic service by hiring a wagon and hauling bacon for the use of the Army in May, 1778 [Ref: P-165, P-168]. Justice of the Peace and Judge of the Orphans Court, appointed on November 21, 1778 and November 20, 1779 [Ref: E-250, F-22]. Elected Sheriff of Talbot County; received his commission on October 30, 1782 [Ref: I-294].

THOMAS, Tristram. See "John L. Elbert," q.v.

THOMAS, William. Private, Militia, Union Company, 4th Battalion, 1777-1778 [Ref: N-86/105, M-223]. Private, Militia, Union Company, 4th Battalion, 1780-1781 [Ref: N-86/105, M-230]. See "John Stevens" and "Nicholas Thomas," q.v.

THOMAS, William Dawson. Private, Militia, Union Company, 4th Battalion, 1777-1778 [Ref: N-86/105, M-223]. Private, Militia, Union Company, 4th Battalion, 1780-1781 [Ref: N-86/105, M-230].

THOMPSON, Daniel. Private, Militia, Capt. Thomas Bullen's Company; no date was given; possibly late 1775 or early 1776 [Ref: Z-3].

THOMPSON, George. Private, Militia, Bullinbrook Company, 4th Battalion, 1780-1781 [Ref: N-86/105, M-231].

THOMPSON, John. Private, Militia, United Company, 38th Battalion, 1777-1778 [Ref: N-86/105, M-227]. Took the Oath of Allegiance and Fidelity on or about March 1, 1778 [Ref: J-1814, N-106/114].

THORNTON, Brooks. Private, Militia, Wye Company, 4th Battalion, 1777-1778 [Ref: N-86/105, M-222]. Private, Militia, Wye Company, 4th Battalion, 1780-1781 [Ref: N-86/105, M-228].

THORNTON, John Vickers. Private, Militia, Wye Company, 4th Battalion, 1777-1778 [Ref: N-86/105, M-222].

THORNTON, Nathaniel. Private, Militia, Wye Company, 4th Battalion, 1777-1778 [Ref: N-86/105, M-223].

THORNTON, Richard. Private, Militia, 2nd Volunteer Company, 4th Battalion, 1777-1778 [Ref: N-86/105, M-225].
TIBBLES (TIBBALS), Henry. Private, Militia, Union Company, 4th Battalion, 1777-1778 [Ref: N-86/105, M-223]. Sergeant, Militia, Union Company, 4th Battalion, 1780-1781 [Ref: N-97, M-229]. Took the Oath of Allegiance and Fidelity on or about March 1, 1778 [Ref: J-1814, N-106/114].
TIBBLES (TIBBALS), John. Private, Militia, Union Company, 4th Battalion, 1777-1778 [Ref: N-86/105, M-223]. Private, Militia, Union Company, 4th Battalion, 1780-1781 [Ref: N-86/105, M-229]. Took the Oath of Allegiance and Fidelity on or about March 1, 1778 [Ref: J-1814, N-106/114].
TIBBLES (TIBBELS), Thomas. Paid £7 by the Maryland Council of Safety on October 12, 1776, "for collecting & ascertaining the number of souls in Talbot County." [Ref: B-337]. Ensign, Militia, Union Company, 4th Battalion, June 17, 1777. Second Lieutenant, Militia, April 12, 1780 [Ref: N-88, M-129, E-24, E-73, F-139].
TIBBLES (TIBBELS), William. Took the Oath of Allegiance and Fidelity on or after March 1, 1778 [Ref: J-1814, N-106/114].
TIBBY, John. Private, Militia, 4th Battalion, Capt. Greenbury Goldsborough's Company, reviewed and passed July 27, 1776 [Ref: D-68].
TILGHMAN, Ann. See "Peregrine Tilghman" and "James Tilghman, Jr.," q.v.
TILGHMAN, Anna. See "Tench Tilghman" and "Peregrine Tilghman" and "Lloyd Tilghman," q.v.
TILGHMAN, Edward, Esq. (Certificate from Queen Anne's County). Took the Oath of Allegiance and Fidelity on or about March 1, 1778 [Ref: J-1814, N-106/114]. See "Matthew Tilghman," q.v.
TILGHMAN, Elizabeth. See "James Tilghman, Jr." and "Peregrine Tilghman" and "Tench Tilghman" and "Lloyd Tilghman," q.v.
TILGHMAN, Henrietta. See "Lloyd Tilghman" and James Tilghman, Jr.," q.v.
TILGHMAN, James. Private in the militia who was draughted on August 30, 1781 to reinforce the American Army and to serve in the Maryland Continental Troops until December 10, 1781 [Ref: D-387]. See "Matthew Tilghman" and "Lloyd Tilghman" and "Richard Tilghman," q.v.
TILGHMAN, James (1743-1809). Born in Queen Anne's County, Maryland on August 2, 1743, James married first to Susanna Stewart [or Steuart] and second to Elizabeth Johns, rendered patriotic service during the revolution, and died on April 9, 1809 [Ref: Y-2941]. The Maryland State Papers indicate "James Tilghman (Queens Town) to Conrad Theodore Wederstrandt, receipt for beef, December 22, 1779." [Ref: P-253]. On August 7, 1777, he was commissioned Attorney General of Maryland and was a member of the Maryland Legislature, 1788-1789. In 1791 he was appointed Chief Judge of the judicial district composed of Cecil, Kent, Queen Anne's and Talbot Counties [Ref: S-II:454, 455].

TILGHMAN, James Jr. (1748-1796). Son of James Tilghman (1716-1793) and Ann Francis, he was born in Talbot County on January 2, 1748, married Elizabeth Buley by 1783, and died on November 24, 1796. Their children were: Elizabeth (1783-1839, married Thomas Hemsley); Maria; Ann (married Robert Browne); Margaret (married first to Henry Goldsborough and second to John Goldsborough); and, James (1792-1824). James and family lived in Philadelphia, Pennsylvania from 1764 to 1779. He returned to Maryland, served in the Lower House between 1787 and 1792, and was an Associate Justice, 2nd District (appointed January 17, 1791). [Ref: S-II:457, R-824, R-825, R-92, P-77]. He also rendered patriotic service in Maryland by supplying wheat for the use of the Army in January, 1780 [Ref: P-266].

TILGHMAN, John. See "Richard Tilghman, Jr.," q.v.

TILGHMAN, Lloyd (1749-1811). Born on July 27, 1749, a son of Matthew Tilghman and Anna Lloyd, he married Henrietta Maria Tilghman (1763-1796) on January 22, 1785. Their children were James, Lloyd, Matthew Ward, Anna, Henrietta Maria, Mary, and Elizabeth [Ref: S-II:459]. Private, Militia, Bayside Company, 38th Battalion, 1777-1778 [Ref: N-86/105, M-228]. Took the Oath of Allegiance and Fidelity on or about March 1, 1778 [Ref: J-1814, N-106/114]. Appointed a Justice of the Peace on December 4, 1779 [Ref: F-31]. See "Matthew Tilghman," q.v.

TILGHMAN, Margaret. See "Matthew Tilghman" and "Tench Tilghman" and "James Tilghman, Jr.," q.v.

TILGHMAN, Maria. See "James Tilghman, Jr.," q.v.

TILGHMAN, Mary. See "Matthew Tilghman" and "Lloyd Tilghman," q.v.

TILGHMAN, Matthew (1718-1790). Son of Richard Tilghman and Anna Maria Lloyd, Matthew was born on February 17, 1718, married Anne Lloyd on April 6, 1741, and their son Richard Tilghman (January 28, 1746/7 - May 28, 1805) married first to Margaret Tilghman (1744-1779, daughter of William Tilghman) on December 22, 1770, and second to Mary Tilghman (daughter of Edward Tilghman). His other children were: Matthew Ward (1743-1753); Lloyd (1749-1811, married Henrietta Maria Tilghman, daughter of James Tilghman); Margaret (1742-1817, married Charles Carroll, Barrister); and, Anna Maria (1755-1843, married Col. Tench Tilghman, son of James Tilghman). Matthew died of a paralytic stroke on May 4, 1790 and his wife Anne died on March 15, 1794 [Ref: S-II:453, R-825, R-826, Y-2941, and Maryland Society, Sons of the American Revolution, Membership Application No. 3048 (National No. 133816), approved on November 9, 1989 for Compatriot Wilbur Jackson Stenger, Jr. of Chestertown, Maryland]. Matthew was captain of a troop of horse in 1741 and had a very distinguished public career. He was a Court Justice between 1741 and 1773, served in the Maryland Lower House between 1751 and 1776, and in the Senate between 1776 and 1783 (President, 1780-1782). He attended the first Maryland Conventions, 1774-1776, served on the First Council of Safety in 1775, was Speaker of the Maryland Assembly, a

Delegate to the Continental Congress, 1774-1776, and Justice of the Peace in 1778. He has been referred to as the "Father of the Revolution" in Maryland [Ref: A-3, R-825, R-826, R-70, R-71, R-72, R-74, R-76, R-78, R-80, R-82, R-84, R-86, R-87, R-88, O-1, O-4, E-163]. He also rendered patriotic service by supplying meat for the use of the Army in May, 1778 [Ref: P-170]. See "Tench Tilghman" and "Lloyd Tilghman," q.v.

TILGHMAN, Peregrine (1741-1807). Son of Richard Tilghman and Susanna Frisby, of Queen Anne's County, Peregrine was born on January 24, 1741, married his first cousin Deborah Lloyd by 1775 and moved to Talbot County. Their children were: Robert Lloyd (1778-1823, married Henrietta Maria Foreman); Anna Maria (married James Earle); Tench (1782-1827, married Ann Margaretta Tilghman), William Hemsley (1784-1863, married Maria Lloyd Hemsley); and, Elizabeth (married John Custis Wilson). Peregrine attended the Maryland Convention in 1775, served in the Maryland Lower House in 1775, and in the Senate between 1786 and 1790. He was a Court Justice, 1777-1778, Justice of the Orphans Court in 1778, and Commissioner of the Tax between 1778 and 1786 [Ref: S-II:177, S-II:454, A-3, R-828, R-829, R-70, R-71, O-1, E-163]. Lieutenant Colonel, Militia, 4th Battalion, January 12, 1776. Colonel, Militia, 4th Battalion, April 9, 1778 [Ref: N-90, M-129, E-24]. Took the Oath of Allegiance and Fidelity on or about March 1, 1778 [Ref: J-1814, N-106/114]. Purchasing Agent for the Continental Army in 1778, later resigned, but appointed and served again in 1780 [Ref: P-267, R-829, C-551, F-475]. See "John Betts" and "Archibald Golder" and "Tench Tilghman," q.v.

TILGHMAN, Richard (1746-1796). Son of James Tilghman and Ann Francis, he was born on December 17, 1746 and died unmarried on November 24, 1796 [Ref: S-II:452]. Private, Militia, Union Company, 4th Battalion, 1777-1778 [Ref: N-86/105, M-223].

TILGHMAN, Richard Jr. (1740-1809). Son of William Tilghman and Margaret Lloyd, Richard was born on April 6, 1740, married Mary Gibson (1766-1790) on August 2, 1784, and died on April 12, 1809. Their children were: William Gibson (1785-1844, married Anna Polk); John Lloyd (born in 1788, married his cousin Maria Gibson); and, Richard (born in 1790, died young). Richard attended the Maryland Convention in 1775 and was a major by 1783 [Ref: R-831, R-71, O-4, and A-3, which listed the name without the "Jr."]. Took the Oath of Allegiance and Fidelity on or about March 1, 1778 [Ref: J-1814, N-106/114]. See "Matthew Tilghman" and "Peregrine Tilghman" and "John Gibson," q.v.

TILGHMAN, Robert. See "Peregrine Tilghman," q.v.

TILGHMAN, Tench (1744-1786). Born on December 25, 1744, eldest son of James Tilghman and Anna Francis (daughter of Tench Francis), Tench married Anna Maria Tilghman (daughter of his uncle Matthew Tilghman) and had two daughters: Margaret Tilghman (born 1784 and married Tench Tilghman, son of Peregrine); and, Elizabeth Tench Tilghman (1786-1852, married Nicholas

Goldsborough). Tench was commissioned in June, 1776, as captain of a Pennsylvania battalion of the Flying Camp, and was on duty at Washington's headquarters as Military Secretary from August 8, 1776. He was commissioned a lieutenant colonel and aide-de-camp to Gen. George Washington on April 1, 1777. A brave and efficient officer, he was selected to bear to Congress the news of the surrender of Cornwallis at Yorktown in 1781 [and as a result has been referred to as the "Paul Revere of Maryland" by some]. Col. Tench Tilghman married in 1783, left the service on December 23, 1783, and died on April 18, 1786 [Ref: S-II:457, Y-2942]. In the 1840 Census of Maryland (Talbot County, 3rd District), Anna Maria Tilghman, age 85, was a Revolutionary War pensioner residing in the household of Tench Tilghman [Ref: Q-445]. She died on January 13, 1843 in Kent County, Maryland at Otwell, the seat of Nicholas Goldsborough [Ref: *Baltimore Sun*, January 18, 1843, and Robert W. Barnes' article "Revolutionary Obituaries" in the *Maryland Genealogical Society Bulletin*, Vol. 10, No. 2 (1969), p. 55]. See "Matthew Tilghman" and "Peregrine Tilghman," q.v.

TILGHMAN, William. See "Peregrine Tilghman" and "Richard Tilghman, Jr.," q.v.

TILLARD, Thomas. Major, Militia, 4th Battalion; resigned December 18, 1776 [Ref: M-129].

TIZZARD, William. Private, Militia, 2nd Volunteer Company, 4th Battalion, 1777-1778 [Ref: N-86/105, M-225]. Private, Militia, Volunteer Company, 4th Battalion, 1780-1781 [Ref: N-86/105, M-229]. Took the Oath of Allegiance and Fidelity on or about March 1, 1778 [Ref: J-1814, N-106/114]. See "Matthew Tilghman," q.v.

TOBIN, James. Private, Militia, Bullin Brook Company, 4th Battalion, 1777-1778 [Ref: N-86/105, M-224]. Private (substitute), Militia, Bullinbrook Company, 4th Battalion, 1780-1781 [Ref: N-86/105, M-231]. Took the Oath of Allegiance and Fidelity on or about March 1, 1778 [Ref: J-1814, N-106/114, which listed the name as "James Tobins"].

TODD, James. Private, 4th Independent Company of Maryland Regular Troops, Capt. James Hindman's Company, September, 1776 muster roll; enlisted February 7, 1776 [Ref: D-24].

TOMLINSON, William. Private, Militia, Hand in Hand Company, 4th Battalion, 1780-1781 [Ref: N-86/105, M-232].

TOOP, Ephraim Chick. Private, Militia, United Company, 38th Battalion, 1777-1778 [Ref: N-86/105, M-227]. Private, Militia, United Company, 38th Battalion, 1780-1781 [Ref: N-86/105, M-234]. "Ephraim Toope" took the Oath of Allegiance and Fidelity on or about March 1, 1778 [Ref: J-1814, N-106/114].

TOWERS, John. Took the Oath of Allegiance and Fidelity on or about March 1, 1778 [Ref: J-1814, N-106/114].

TOWNSEND, Allen (Allin). Private who enlisted on April 11, 1781 to serve 3 years in the Maryland Continental Troops [Ref: D-371].

TOWNSEND, George. Private, Militia, United Company, 38th Battalion, 1780-1781 [Ref: N-86/105, M-233]. Draughted on May 1, 1781 to serve until December 10, 1781 in the Maryland Continental Troops; honorably discharged on December 3, 1781 [Ref: D-370, I-10].

TOWNSEND, James. Private, Militia, Sword in Hand Company, 4th Battalion, 1780-1781 [Ref: N-86/105, M-231].

TOWNSEND, Thomas. Private, Militia, United Company, 38th Battalion, 1777-1778 [Ref: N-86/105, M-227]. Took the Oath of Allegiance and Fidelity on or about March 1, 1778 [Ref: J-1814, N-106/114].

TOWNSEND, Thomas Jr. Private, Militia, United Company, 38th Battalion, 1777-1778 [Ref: N-86/105, M-227]. Private, Militia, United Company, 38th Battalion, 1780-1781 [Ref: N-86/105, M-233]. One Thomas Townsend was placed on the pension rolls on January 27, 1834, aged 77, as a private and marine, with an annual allowance of $48.88 effective March 4, 1831 [Ref: X-51/514].

TOWNSEND, Thomas Ogdin. Private, Militia, Sword in Hand Company, 4th Battalion, 1780-1781 [Ref: N-86/105, M-231].

TRIPPE, Anne. See "John Dickinson," q.v.

TRIPPE, Edward. Took the Oath of Allegiance and Fidelity on or about March 1, 1778 [Ref: J-1814, N-106/114]. Rendered patriotic service by storing and transporting meat for the use of the Army in July, 1778 [Ref: P-180].

TRIPPE, Edward Jr. Private, Militia, Volunteer Company, 4th Battalion, 1780-1781 [Ref: N-86/105, M-230].

TRIPPE, Elizabeth. Rendered patriotic service by supplying bacon for the use of the Army in May, 1778 [Ref: P-167].

TRIPPE, Henrietta. See "Christopher Birckhead," q.v.

TRIPPE, James. Private, Militia, Bayside Company, 38th Battalion, 1777-1778 [Ref: N-86/105, M-228]. Took the Oath of Allegiance and Fidelity on or about March 1, 1778 [Ref: J-1814, N-106/114]. Appointed a Justice of the Peace on July 22, 1778 [Ref: E-163].

TRIPPE, John. Took the Oath of Allegiance and Fidelity on or about March 1, 1778 [Ref: J-1814, N-106/114]. Rendered patriotic service by supplying bacon for the use of the Army in April, 1778 [Ref: P-162].

TRIPPE, Mary. See "James Hindman" and "William Hindman," q.v.

TRIPPE, William. Private, Militia, Union Company, 4th Battalion, 1777-1778 [Ref: N-86/105, M-223]. Private, Militia, Union Company, 4th Battalion, 1780-1781 [Ref: N-86/105, M-229].

TROTH, Elizabeth. See "James Fairbanks," q.v.

TROTH, George (1735-   ). Born in St. Peter's Parish, Talbot County, on March 25, 1735, son of Sarah Troth [Ref: V-89]. Private, Militia, Bullin Brook Company, 4th Battalion, 1777-1778 [Ref: N-86/105, M-224]. Took the Oath of Allegiance and Fidelity on or after March 1, 1778 [Ref: J-1814, N-106/114]. Private, Militia, Bullinbrook Company, 4th Battalion, 1780-1781 [Ref: N-86/105, M-231].

TROTH, Henry. Private, Militia, Third Haven Company, 4th Battalion, 1777-1778 [Ref: N-86/105, M-225].

TROTH, Henry (of Henry). Private, Militia, Third Haven Company, 4th Battalion, 1780-1781 [Ref: N-86/105, M-232].

TROTH, Sarah. See "George Troth," q.v.

TROTH, William. Took the Oath of Allegiance and Fidelity on or about March 1, 1778 [Ref: J-1814, N-106/114].

TROTH, William Jr. Private, Militia, Union Company, 4th Battalion, 1780-1781 [Ref: N-86/105, M-229]. Private in the militia who was draughted on August 30, 1781 to reinforce the American Army and to serve in the Maryland Continental Troops until December 10, 1781 [Ref: D-387].

TROUP, Alexander. Private, Militia, Oxford Company, 38th Battalion, 1777-1778 [Ref: N-86/105, M-227].

TROUP, Charles. Took the Oath of Allegiance and Fidelity on or about March 1, 1778 [Ref: J-1814, N-106/114].

TROUP (TROOP), John. Appointed a Justice of the Peace on November 21, 1778 and November 20, 1779 [Ref: E-250, F-22].

TROY, Owen. Private, Militia, Volunteer Company, 4th Battalion, 1780-1781 [Ref: N-86/105, M-230]. Private, Militia, Volunteer Company, 4th Battalion, 1777-1778 [Ref: N-86/105, M-223].

TRUITT, Elizabeth. See "Daniel Lambdin," q.v.

TUCKER, William. Private, Militia, Volunteer Company, 4th Battalion, 1777-1778 [Ref: N-86/105, M-223]. Private, Militia, Volunteer Company, 4th Battalion, 1780-1781 [Ref: N-86/105, M-230]. Took the Oath of Allegiance and Fidelity on or about March 1, 1778 [Ref: J-1814, N-106/114].

TUFFEY(?), Robert. Private, Militia, Hearts of Oak Company, 38th Battalion, 1777-1778 [Ref: N-86/105, M-226].

TURBUTT, Anne. See "John Goldsborough," q.v.

TURBUTT, Foster. See "William Goldsborough" and "Howes Goldsborough," q.v.

TURBUTT, Mary Anne. See "Howes Goldsborough" and "William Goldsborough," q.v.

TURBUTT, Samuel (1760-1821). Private, Militia, Sword in Hand Company, 4th Battalion, 1780-1781 [Ref: N-86/105, M-231, which listed the name as "Samuel Turbott"]. He was born October 3, 1760 and died in 1821 in St. Peter's Parish, Talbot County [Ref: K-58].

TURNER, Abner. Took the Oath of Allegiance and Fidelity on or about March 1, 1778 [Ref: J-1814, N-106/114].

TURNER, Edward. Private, Militia, Sword in Hand Company, 4th Battalion, 1777-1778 [Ref: N-86/105, M-224]. Took the Oath of Allegiance and Fidelity on or about March 1, 1778 [Ref: J-1814, N-106/114]. Private, Militia, Sword in Hand Company, 4th Battalion, 1780-1781 [Ref: N-86/105, M-231].

TURNER, Edward. Private, Militia, Hand & Hand Company, 4th Battalion, 1777-1778 [Ref: N-86/105, M-226]. Private, Militia, Hand in Hand Company, 4th Battalion, 1780-1781 [Ref: N-86/105, M-232]. Took the Oath of Allegiance and Fidelity on or about March 1, 1778 [Ref: J-1814, N-106/114].

TURNER, James. Private, Militia, Miles River Company, 38th Battalion, 1780-1781 [Ref: N-86/105, M-235]. Took the Oath of Allegiance and Fidelity on or after March 1, 1778 [Ref: J-1814, N-106/114].

TURNER, John. Paid £9 for services rendered on March 11, 1779, by Col. Christopher Birkhead [Ref: E-319]. Private, Militia, Volunteer Company, 4th Battalion, 1780-1781 [Ref: N-86/105, M-229].

TURNER, John (Constable). Took the Oath of Allegiance and Fidelity on or about March 1, 1778 [Ref: J-1814, N-106/114].

TURNER, Joseph. Private, Militia, Hand & Hand Company, 4th Battalion, 1777-1778 [Ref: N-86/105, M-226]. Took the Oath of Allegiance and Fidelity on or about March 1, 1778 [Ref: J-1814, N-106/114].

TURNER, Sarah. See "John Roberts, Jr.," q.v.

TURNER, Thomas. Private, Militia, Third Haven Company, 4th Battalion, 1780-1781 [Ref: N-86/105, M-232].

TURNER, Thomas. Private, Militia, Union Company, 4th Battalion, 1777-1778 [Ref: N-86/105, M-223].

TURNER, Thomas. Private, Militia, Sword in Hand Company, 4th Battalion, 1777-1778 [Ref: N-86/105, M-224]. Private, Militia, Sword in Hand Company, 4th Battalion, 1780-1781 [Ref: N-86/105, M-231].

TURNER, Thomas. Took the Oath of Allegiance and Fidelity on or after March 1, 1778 [Ref: J-1814, N-106/114].

TURNER, Valiant. Private, Militia, Volunteer Company, 4th Battalion, 1780-1781 [Ref: N-86/105, M-229].

TUTTLE, William. Private, Militia, Oxford Company, 38th Battalion, 1777-1778 [Ref: N-86/105, M-228]. Private, Militia, Oxford Company, 38th Battalion, 1780-1781 [Ref: N-86/105, M-235]. Took the Oath of Allegiance and Fidelity on or about March 1, 1778 [Ref: J-1814, N-106/114].

VAIN, Henry. Private, Militia, Capt. Thomas Bullen's Company; no date was given; possibly late 1775 or early 1776 [Ref: Z-3].

VALIENT (VALLIANT), James. See "John Valient," q.v.

VALIENT (VALLIANT), John. Private, Militia, Oxford Company, 38th Battalion, 1777-1778 [Ref: N-86/105, M-228]. Private, Militia, Oxford Company, 38th Battalion, 1780-1781 [Ref: N-86/105, M-235]. Took the Oath of Allegiance and Fidelity on or about March 1, 1778 [Ref: J-1814, N-106/114]. "John Vallient" and "James Valliant" were both privates in the 5th Maryland Line who enlisted on March 14, 1777 and were honorably discharged on March 14, 1780 [Ref: D-254].

VALIENT (VALLIANT), Jonathan. Private, 4th Independent Company of Maryland Regular Troops, Capt. James Hindman's Company, September, 1776 muster roll; enlisted February 5, 1776 [Ref: D-24].
VALIENT (VALLIANT), Joseph. Private, Militia, Hearts of Oak Company, 38th Battalion, 1780-1781 [Ref: N-86/105, M-234].
VALIENT (VALLIANT), Nicholas. Took the Oath of Allegiance and Fidelity on or about March 1, 1778 [Ref: J-1814, N-106/114].
VALIENT (VALLIANT), Richard. Took the Oath of Allegiance and Fidelity on or about March 1, 1778 [Ref: J-1814, N-106/114]. Private, Militia, Hearts of Oak Company, 38th Battalion, 1777-1778 [Ref: N-86/105, M-226]. Private, Militia, Hearts of Oak Company, 38th Battalion, 1780-1781 [Ref: N-86/105, M-234].
VALIENT (VALLIANT), William. Private, Militia, Hearts of Oak Company, 38th Battalion, 1777-1778 [Ref: N-86/105, M-226]. Private, Militia, Hearts of Oak Company, 38th Battalion, 1780-1781 [Ref: N-86/105, M-234]. Took the Oath of Allegiance and Fidelity on or about March 1, 1778 [Ref: J-1814, N-106/114].
VANDIKE, John. Private, Militia, Miles River Company, 38th Battalion, 1780-1781 [Ref: N-86/105, M-235]. Private, Militia, Hearts of Oak Company, 38th Battalion, 1777-1778 [Ref: N-86/105, M-226].
VICKERS, Charles. Private, Militia, Miles River Company, 38th Battalion, 1780-1781 [Ref: N-86/105, M-235]. Private, Militia, Miles River Company, 38th Battalion, 1777-1778 [Ref: N-86/105, M-227].
VICKERS, Richard. Private, Militia, Hand & Hand Company, 4th Battalion, 1777-1778 [Ref: N-86/105, M-225].
VICKERS, William. Private, Militia, Hand in Hand Company, 4th Battalion, 1780-1781 [Ref: N-86/105, M-232].
VINING, John. Private, Militia, Union Company, 4th Battalion, 1777-1778 [Ref: N-86/105, M-223]. Private, Militia, Miles River Company, 38th Battalion, 1780-1781 [Ref: N-86/105, M-235].
VINTON, Samuel. Private, Militia, United Company, 38th Battalion, 1780-1781 [Ref: N-86/105, M-233]. Private, Militia, United Company, 38th Battalion, 1777-1778 [Ref: N-86/105, M-227].
VINTON, Solomon. Private, Militia, United Company, 38th Battalion, 1780-1781 [Ref: N-86/105, M-233]. Private, Militia, United Company, 38th Battalion, 1777-1778 [Ref: N-86/105, M-227]. Took the Oath of Allegiance and Fidelity on or about March 1, 1778 [Ref: J-1814, N-106/114].
WAINWRIGHT, James. Private, Militia, Union Company, 4th Battalion, 1777-1778 [Ref: N-86/105, M-223]. Private, Militia, Union Company, 4th Battalion, 1780-1781 [Ref: N-86/105, M-230, which listed the name as "James Wainright"].
WALES (WAILES), James. Private, Militia, Hearts of Oak Company, 38th Battalion, 1780-1781 [Ref: N-86/105, M-234]. Private, Militia, Hearts of Oak

Company, 38th Battalion, 1777-1778 [Ref: N-86/105, M-226, which listed the name as "James Wiles"].

WALES (WAILES), Robert. Private, Militia, Third Haven Company, 4th Battalion, 1777-1778 [Ref: N-86/105, M-225, which misspelled the name as "Waits"]. Took the Oath of Allegiance and Fidelity on or about March 1, 1778 [Ref: J-1814, N-106/114, which listed the name as "Robert Wale"]. Private, Militia, Third Haven Company, 4th Battalion, 1780-1781 [Ref: N-86/105, M-232, which listed the name as "Robert Wailes"].

WALES, Thomas. Private, Militia, United Company, 38th Battalion, 1780-1781 [Ref: N-86/105, M-234]. Private, Militia, United Company, 38th Battalion, 1777-1778 [Ref: N-86/105, M-227]. Took the Oath of Allegiance and Fidelity on or about March 1, 1778 [Ref: J-1814, N-106/114].

WALES, William. Private, Militia, Bayside Company, 38th Battalion, 1780-1781 [Ref: N-86/105, M-233].

WALKER, Daniel. Private, Militia, Capt. Thomas Bullen's Company; no date was given; possibly late 1775 or early 1776 [Ref: Z-3]. Private, Militia, Volunteer Company, 4th Battalion, 1777-1778 [Ref: N-86/105, M-223]. Private, Militia, Volunteer Company, 4th Battalion, 1780-1781 [Ref: N-86/105, M-230].

WALKER, Francis. Private, Militia, Bullinbrook Company, 4th Battalion, 1780-1781 [Ref: N-86/105, M-231]. Private, Militia, Bullin Brook Company, 4th Battalion, 1777-1778 [Ref: N-86/105, M-224]. Took the Oath of Allegiance and Fidelity on or about March 1, 1778 [Ref: J-1814, N-106/114].

WALKER, James Jr. Took the Oath of Allegiance and Fidelity on or after March 1, 1778 [Ref: J-1814, N-106/114]. Private, Militia, Third Haven Company, 4th Battalion, 1777-1778 [Ref: N-86/105, M-225]. Private, Militia, Third Haven Company, 4th Battalion, 1780-1781 [Ref: N-86/105, M-232].

WALKER, James Sr. Took the Oath of Allegiance and Fidelity on or after March 1, 1778 [Ref: J-1814, N-106/114].

WALKER, John. Private, Militia, Capt. Thomas Bullen's Company; no date was given; possibly late 1775 or early 1776 [Ref: Z-3]. Private, Militia, Third Haven Company, 4th Battalion, 1780-1781 [Ref: N-86/105, M-232].

WALKER, Nathan. Private, Militia, Union Company, 4th Battalion, 1777-1778 [Ref: N-86/105, M-223]. Private, Militia, Union Company, 4th Battalion, 1780-1781 [Ref: N-86/105, M-230].

WALKER, Nathan. Private, Militia, Capt. Thomas Bullen's Company; no date was given; possibly late 1775 or early 1776 [Ref: Z-3]. Private, Militia, Third Haven Company, 4th Battalion, 1777-1778 [Ref: N-86/105, M-225]. Took the Oath of Allegiance and Fidelity on or about March 1, 1778 [Ref: J-1814, N-106/114].

WALKER, Richard. Private, Militia, Third Haven Company, 4th Battalion, 1780-1781 [Ref: N-86/105, M-232]. Took the Oath of Allegiance and Fidelity on or about March 1, 1778 [Ref: J-1814, N-106/114].

WALKER, William. Private, Militia, Capt. Thomas Bullen's Company; no date was given; possibly late 1775 or early 1776 [Ref: Z-3]. Took the Oath of Allegiance and Fidelity on or after March 1, 1778 [Ref: J-1814, N-106/114]. Sergeant, Militia, Third Haven Company, 4th Battalion, 1780-1781 [Ref: N-100, M-232].

WALKER, William Jr. Private, Militia, Third Haven Company, 4th Battalion, 1777-1778 [Ref: N-86/105, M-225]. Took the Oath of Allegiance and Fidelity on or after March 1, 1778 [Ref: J-1814, N-106/114]. Private, Militia, Third Haven Company, 4th Battalion, 1780-1781 [Ref: N-86/105, M-232].

WALKER, William 3rd. Private, Militia, Third Haven Company, 4th Battalion, 1777-1778 [Ref: N-86/105, M-225].

WALLEN, Quinton. Private, Militia, Volunteer Company, 4th Battalion, 1780-1781 [Ref: N-86/105, M-229].

WARD, Philemon. Private, Militia, 4th Battalion, Capt. Greenbury Goldsborough's Company, reviewed and passed July 27, 1776 [Ref: D-68].

WARFIELD, John. Took the Oath of Allegiance and Fidelity on or about March 1, 1778 [Ref: J-1814, N-106/114].

WARNER, Gary. Private, Militia, Hand in Hand Company, 4th Battalion, 1780-1781 [Ref: N-86/105, M-232]. Private, Militia, Union Company, 4th Battalion, 1777-1778 [Ref: N-86/105, M-223].

WARNER, John. Private, Militia, 4th Battalion, Capt. Greenbury Goldsborough's Company, reviewed and passed July 27, 1776 [Ref: D-68]. Private, Militia, Miles River Company, 38th Battalion, 1780-1781 [Ref: N-86/105, M-235].

WARNER, Robert. Private, Militia, Wye Company, 4th Battalion, 1777-1778 [Ref: N-86/105, M-222].

WARNER, Stephen Garey. Took the Oath of Allegiance and Fidelity on or about March 1, 1778 [Ref: J-1814, N-106/114].

WARNER, William. Private, Militia, Miles River Company, 38th Battalion, 1777-1778 [Ref: N-86/105, M-227]. Took the Oath of Allegiance and Fidelity on or about March 1, 1778 [Ref: J-1814, N-106/114].

WARNER, Woolman. Private, Militia, Wye Company, 4th Battalion, 1777-1778 [Ref: N-86/105, M-223].

WARREN, Hambleton. Private, 4th Independent Company of Maryland Regular Troops, Capt. James Hindman's Company, September, 1776 muster roll; enlisted February 19, 1776 [Ref: D-24].

WARREN, John. Private, Militia, 4th Battalion, Capt. Greenbury Goldsborough's Company, reviewed and passed July 27, 1776 [Ref: D-67]. Private, 5th Maryland Line, enlisted April 28, 1777; honorably discharged on October 12, 1779 [Ref: D-254].

WARREN, Sampson. Private, Militia, Volunteer Company, 4th Battalion, 1780-1781 [Ref: N-86/105, M-229].

WARREN (WARRING), William. Private, Militia, 2nd Volunteer Company, 4th Battalion, 1777-1778 [Ref: N-86/105, M-224]. Private, Militia, Volunteer Company, 4th Battalion, 1780-1781 [Ref: N-86/105, M-229].

WARRING, John. Private, Militia, 2nd Volunteer Company, 4th Battalion, 1777-1778 [Ref: N-86/105, M-225]. Private, Militia, Volunteer Company, 4th Battalion, 1780-1781 [Ref: N-86/105, M-229].

WARTON, William. Private, Militia, Union Company, 4th Battalion, 1780-1781 [Ref: N-86/105, M-230].

WASHINGTON, George. See "Tench Tilghman" and "John Dorgin," q.v.

WATSON (WATRON?), Benona (Banoni). Private, Militia, Hand & Hand Company, 4th Battalion, 1777-1778 [Ref: N-86/105, M-226, which listed the name as "Benona Watron"]. Private, Militia, Hand in Hand Company, 4th Battalion, 1780-1781 [Ref: N-86/105, M-232].

WATSON, John (of Benona). Private in the militia who was draughted on August 30, 1781 to reinforce the American Army and to serve in the Maryland Continental Troops until December 10, 1781 [Ref: D-387].

WATTS, George. Private, Militia, Capt. Thomas Bullen's Company; no date was given; possibly late 1775 or early 1776 [Ref: Z-3].

WATTS, Henry. Private, Militia, Hearts of Oak Company, 38th Battalion, 1777-1778 [Ref: N-86/105, M-226].

WATTS, Hugh. Private, Militia, Hearts of Oak Company, 38th Battalion, 1780-1781 [Ref: N-86/105, M-234].

WATTS, James. Private, 4th Independent Company of Maryland Regular Troops, Capt. James Hindman's Company, September, 1776 muster roll; enlisted January 20, 1776 [Ref: D-24].

WATTS, John. See "Thomas Watts," q.v.

WATTS, Perry. Private, Militia, Third Haven Company, 4th Battalion, 1780-1781 [Ref: N-86/105, M-232].

WATTS, Susannah. See "Thomas Watts," q.v.

WATTS, Thomas. Private, Militia, Oxford Company, 38th Battalion, 1777-1778 [Ref: N-86/105, M-228]. One "Thomas Wats" was born on April 5, 1731 in St. Peter's Parish, Talbot County, son of John and Susannah Watts (Wats). [Ref: V-68].

WATTS, William. Private, Militia, Hearts of Oak Company, 38th Battalion, 1780-1781 [Ref: N-86/105, M-234]. Private, Militia, Hearts of Oak Company, 38th Battalion, 1777-1778 [Ref: N-86/105, M-226]. Took the Oath of Allegiance and Fidelity on or about March 1, 1778 [Ref: J-1814, N-106/114].

WEAVER, William. Private, Militia, Union Company, 4th Battalion, 1777-1778 [Ref: N-86/105, M-223]. Private, Militia, Union Company, 4th Battalion, 1780-1781 [Ref: N-86/105, M-230].

WEAVER, William Jr. Took the Oath of Allegiance and Fidelity on or about March 1, 1778 [Ref: J-1814, N-106/114].

WEBB, James. Private, Militia, Hand & Hand Company, 4th Battalion, 1777-1778 [Ref: N-86/105, M-226]. Took the Oath of Allegiance and Fidelity on or about March 1, 1778 [Ref: J-1814, N-106/114].

WEBB, John. Private, Militia, Union Company, 4th Battalion, 1777-1778 [Ref: N-86/105, M-223].
WEBB, John. Private, Militia, Hand & Hand Company, 4th Battalion, 1777-1778 [Ref: N-86/105, M-225].
WEBB, Park. Private, Militia, Hand in Hand Company, 4th Battalion, 1780-1781 [Ref: N-86/105, M-232]. Private, Militia, Hand & Hand Company, 4th Battalion, 1777-1778 [Ref: N-86/105, M-225]. Took the Oath of Allegiance and Fidelity on or about March 1, 1778 [Ref: J-1814, N-106/114].
WEBB, Peter. Took the Oath of Allegiance and Fidelity on or about March 1, 1778 [Ref: J-1814, N-106/114].
WEBB, Peter Jr. Private, Militia, Volunteer Company, 4th Battalion, 1777-1778 [Ref: N-86/105, M-223]. Took the Oath of Allegiance and Fidelity on or about March 1, 1778 [Ref: J-1814, N-106/114]. Private, Militia, Volunteer Company, 4th Battalion, 1780-1781 [Ref: N-86/105, M-230].
WEBB, William. Private, Militia, Wye Company, 4th Battalion, 1777-1778 [Ref: N-86/105, M-222].
WEEDEN, Henry. Private, Militia, Broad Creek Company, 38th Battalion, 1780-1781 [Ref: N-86/105, M-234].
WELCH, Edward. Private, 4th Independent Company of Maryland Regular Troops, Capt. James Hindman's Company, September, 1776 muster roll; enlisted January 30, 1776 [Ref: D-24].
WELCH, James. Sergeant, Militia, Miles River Company, 38th Battalion, 1780-1781 [Ref: N-105, M-235].
WELCH, Thomas. Private, Militia, Volunteer Company, 4th Battalion, 1777-1778 [Ref: N-86/105, M-223]. Private, Militia, Volunteer Company, 4th Battalion, 1780-1781 [Ref: N-86/105, M-230].
WEST, Benjamin. Private, Militia, Hearts of Oak Company, 38th Battalion, 1780-1781 [Ref: N-86/105, M-234].
WEST, Henry. Private, Militia, Bullin Brook Company, 4th Battalion, 1777-1778 [Ref: N-86/105, M-224]. Private, Militia, Bullinbrook Company, 4th Battalion, 1780-1781 [Ref: N-86/105, M-231]. Took the Oath of Allegiance and Fidelity on or about March 1, 1778 [Ref: J-1814, N-106/114].
WEST, Henry. Corporal, Militia, Capt. Thomas Bullen's Company; no date was given; possibly late 1775 or early 1776 [Ref: Z-3]. Took the Oath of Allegiance and Fidelity on or about March 1, 1778 [Ref: J-1814, N-106.114].
WEST, Richard William. See "Edward Lloyd," q.v.
WEST, William. Private, Militia, United Company, 38th Battalion, 1777-1778 [Ref: N-86/105, M-227]. Took the Oath of Allegiance and Fidelity on or about March 1, 1778 [Ref: J-1814, N-106/114].
WEYMAN (WAYMAN, WAYMON), Edmond (Edward). Private, Militia, Broad Creek Company, 38th Battalion, 1780-1781 [Ref: N-86/105, M-234, which listed the name as "Edward Wayman"]. Private, Militia, Broad Creek Company, 38th Battalion, 1777-1778 [Ref: N-86/105, M-226, which listed the name as

"Edmond Waymon"]. Took the Oath of Allegiance and Fidelity on or about March 1, 1778 [Ref: J-1814, N-106/114, which listed the name as "Edmund Weyman"].

WEYMAN, Thomas. Took the Oath of Allegiance and Fidelity on or about March 1, 1778 [Ref: J-1814, N-106/114].

WHEATLY, John. Private, Militia, Hand & Hand Company, 4th Battalion, 1777-1778 [Ref: N-86/105, M-226].

WHITBY, Thomas. Private, Militia, Hand in Hand Company, 4th Battalion, 1780-1781 [Ref: N-86/105, M-232]. Took the Oath of Allegiance and Fidelity on or about March 1, 1778 [Ref: J-1814, N-106/114].

WHITBY, William. Private, Militia, Hand in Hand Company, 4th Battalion, 1780-1781 [Ref: N-86/105, M-232]. Private, Militia, Hand & Hand Company, 4th Battalion, 1777-1778 [Ref: N-86/105, M-226]. Took the Oath of Allegiance and Fidelity on or about March 1, 1778 [Ref: J-1814, N-106/114].

WHITE, Edward. See "James Benson," q.v.

WHITE, James. Private, Militia, Third Haven Company, 4th Battalion, 1780-1781 [Ref: N-86/105, M-232]. Private, Militia, Third Haven Company, 4th Battalion, 1777-1778 [Ref: N-86/105, M-225].

WHITE, Joseph. Private, 5th Maryland Line, enlisted April 6, 1778 and reported missing after the Battle of Camden, S. C. on August 16, 1778 [Ref: D-255].

WHITE, Samuel. Private, Militia, Volunteer Company, 4th Battalion, 1777-1778 [Ref: N-86/105, M-223]. Private, Militia, Volunteer Company, 4th Battalion, 1780-1781 [Ref: N-86/105, M-230]. Private in the militia who was draughted on August 30, 1781 to reinforce the American Army and to serve in the Maryland Continental Troops until December 10, 1781 [Ref: D-387].

WHITE, Thomas. Private, Militia, Third Haven Company, 4th Battalion, 1777-1778 [Ref: N-86/105, M-225].

WHITELY, Thomas. Private, Militia, Hand & Hand Company, 4th Battalion, 1777-1778 [Ref: N-86/105, M-225].

WHITTOCKS, William. Private, Militia, Union Company, 4th Battalion, 1777-1778 [Ref: N-86/105, M-223]. Private, Militia, Union Company, 4th Battalion, 1780-1781 [Ref: N-86/105, M-229]. Private in the militia who was draughted on August 30, 1781 to reinforce the American Army and to serve in the Maryland Continental Troops until December 10, 1781 [Ref: D-387].

WICKERSHAM, Thomas. Private, Militia, Union Company, 4th Battalion, 1780-1781 [Ref: N-86/105, M-230]. Private, Militia, Union Company, 4th Battalion, 1777-1778 [Ref: N-86/105, M-223].

WILES, James. See "James Wales (Wailes)," q.v.

WILKINSON, John. Private, Militia, Bayside Company, 38th Battalion, 1780-1781 [Ref: N-86/105, M-233].

WILLIAM, George. Took the Oath of Allegiance and Fidelity on or about March 1, 1778 [Ref: J-1814, N-106/114].

WILLIAMS, Andrew. Private, Militia, Union Company, 4th Battalion, 1780-1781 [Ref: N-86/105, M-230].
WILLIAMS, Edward. Private, Militia, Hand in Hand Company, 4th Battalion, 1780-1781 [Ref: N-86/105, M-232]. Private, Militia, Hand & Hand Company, 4th Battalion, 1777-1778 [Ref: N-86/105, M-226].
WILLIAMS, George. Corporal, Militia, Wye Company, 4th Battalion, 1780-1781 [Ref: N-96, M-228]. Took the Oath of Allegiance and Fidelity on or about March 1, 1778 [Ref: J-1814, N-106/114].
WILLIAMS, James. Private, Militia, Hand in Hand Company, 4th Battalion, 1780-1781 [Ref: N-86/105, M-232].
WILLIAMS, John. Fifer, 4th Independent Company of Maryland Regular Troops, September, 1776 muster roll; enlisted March 16, 1776 [Ref: D-23]. Private, 5th Maryland Line, March 21, 1777 [Ref: D-254].
WILLIAMS, Samuel. Private, Militia, Hand & Hand Company, 4th Battalion, 1777-1778 [Ref: N-86/105, M-226].
WILLINS, Abraham. Private, Militia, Capt. Thomas Bullen's Company; no date was given; possibly late 1775 or early 1776 [Ref: Z-3].
WILLIS, Andrew. Private, 5th Maryland Line, enlisted February 17, 1777 and honorably discharged on February 14, 1780 [Ref: D-254].
WILLIS, Daniel. Private, Militia, 4th Battalion, Capt. Greenbury Goldsborough's Company, reviewed and passed July 27, 1776 [Ref: D-68]. Drummer, 5th Maryland Line, enlisted February 9, 1777; first muster in April, 1778; reported missing after the Battle of Camden, S. C. on August 16, 1780; joined (no date given). [Ref: D-254].
WILLIS, Richard. Paid 45s. by the Maryland Council of Safety for services rendered on July 26, 1776 [Ref: B-118].
WILLIS, Samuel. Private, Militia, Oxford Company, 38th Battalion, 1777-1778 [Ref: N-86/105, M-228]. Took the Oath of Allegiance and Fidelity on or about March 1, 1778 [Ref: J-1814, N-106/114]. Private, Militia, Oxford Company, 38th Battalion, 1780-1781 [Ref: N-86/105, M-235].
WILLOBY, John. Took the Oath of Allegiance and Fidelity on or about March 1, 1778 [Ref: J-1814, N-106/114].
WILLOBY (WILLABY, WILLIBY), William. Private, Militia, Bayside Company, 38th Battalion, 1777-1778 [Ref: N-86/105, M-228]. Private, Militia, Bayside Company, 38th Battalion, 1780-1781 [Ref: N-86/105, M-233]. Private in the militia who was draughted on August 30, 1781 to reinforce the American Army and to serve in the Maryland Continental Troops until December 10, 1781 [Ref: D-387]. "William Willoughby" was a private in the 5th Maryland Line who enlisted on January 29, 1777 and reportedly "deserted" on March 31, 1779 [Ref: D-254]. Additional research may be necessary before drawing conclusions.

WILLSON, Daniel. Private, Militia, Hand & Hand Company, 4th Battalion, 1777-1778 [Ref: N-86/105, M-225]. Private, Militia, Hand in Hand Company, 4th Battalion, 1780-1781 [Ref: N-86/105, M-232].
WILLSON, George. Private, Militia, Hand & Hand Company, 4th Battalion, 1777-1778 [Ref: N-86/105, M-225]. Private, Militia, Hand in Hand Company, 4th Battalion, 1780-1781 [Ref: N-86/105, M-232].
WILLSON, James. Private, Militia, 2nd Volunteer Company, 4th Battalion, 1777-1778 [Ref: N-86/105, M-225].
WILLSON, James Jr. Private, Militia, 2nd Volunteer Company, 4th Battalion, 1777-1778 [Ref: N-86/105, M-225]. Private, Militia, Wye Company, 4th Battalion, 1780-1781 [Ref: N-86/105, M-228].
WILLSON, John. Private, Militia, Third Haven Company, 4th Battalion, 1777-1778 [Ref: N-86/105, M-225].
WILLSON, John Jr. Private, Militia, Third Haven Company, 4th Battalion, 1780-1781 [Ref: N-86/105, M-232].
WILLSON, Southy. Private, Militia, Hand & Hand Company, 4th Battalion, 1777-1778 [Ref: N-86/105, M-225].
WILLSON, Thomas. Private, Militia, Third Haven Company, 4th Battalion, 1777-1778 [Ref: N-86/105, M-225]. Private, Militia, Third Haven Company, 4th Battalion, 1780-1781 [Ref: N-86/105, M-232].
WILSON, Esther. See "John Register," q.v.
WILSON, George. Boatswain on the barge *Fearnought* under Capt. Levin Spedden in 1782 [Ref: D-613].
WILSON, James. Took the Oath of Allegiance and Fidelity on or about March 1, 1778 [Ref: J-1814, N-106/114].
WILSON, John Jr. Took the Oath of Allegiance and Fidelity on or after March 1, 1778 [Ref: J-1814, N-106/114].
WILSON, John Sr. Took the Oath of Allegiance and Fidelity on or after March 1, 1778 [Ref: J-1814, N-106/114].
WILSON, John Custis. See "Peregrine Tilghman," q.v.
WILSON(?), William. Took the Oath of Allegiance and Fidelity on or after March 1, 1778 [Ref: J-1814, N-106/114].
WINSLOWE, John. Private, Militia, Capt. Thomas Bullen's Company; no date was given; possibly late 1775 or early 1776 [Ref: Z-3].
WINSLOWE, Peter. Private, Militia, Capt. Thomas Bullen's Company; no date was given; possibly late 1775 or early 1776 [Ref: Z-3].
WINSON, John. Private, Militia, Volunteer Company, 4th Battalion, 1780-1781 [Ref: N-86/105, M-230].
WINSTANDLEY (WINSTANDLY, WINSTANLEY), Henry. Private, Militia, 4th Battalion, Capt. Greenbury Goldsborough's Company, reviewed and passed July 27, 1776 [Ref: D-68]. Private, Militia, Miles River Company, 38th Battalion, 1780-1781 [Ref: N-86/105, M-235]. Private, Militia, Miles River Company, 38th Battalion, 1777-1778 [Ref: N-86/105, M-227]. Took the Oath

of Allegiance and Fidelity on or about March 1, 1778 [Ref: J-1814, N-106/114].

WINSTANDLEY (WINSTANLEY), John. Took the Oath of Allegiance and Fidelity on or about March 1, 1778 [Ref: J-1814, N-106/114].

WINSTANDLEY (WINSTANDLY, WINDSTANDLEY, WINSTANLEY), William. Private, Militia, 4th Battalion, Capt. Greenbury Goldsborough's Company, reviewed and passed July 27, 1776 [Ref: D-68]. Private, Militia, Miles River Company, 38th Battalion, 1777-1778 [Ref: N-86/105, M-227]. Private, Militia, United Company, 38th Battalion, 1780-1781 [Ref: N-86/105, M-233]. Took the Oath of Allegiance and Fidelity on or about March 1, 1778 [Ref: J-1814, N-106/114].

WINTERBOTTOM, Daniel. Private, Militia, Broad Creek Company, 38th Battalion, 1780-1781 [Ref: N-86/105, M-234]. Private in the militia who was draughted on August 30, 1781 to reinforce the American Army and to serve in the Maryland Continental Troops until December 10, 1781 [Ref: D-387].

WINTERBOTTOM, John. Private, Militia, Broad Creek Company, 38th Battalion, 1777-1778 [Ref: N-86/105, M-226]. Private, 5th Maryland Line, enlisted on June 6, 1778 and honorably discharged on March 23, 1779 [Ref: D-255]. Private, Militia, Broad Creek Company, 38th Battalion, 1780-1781 [Ref: N-86/105, M-234].

WINTERBOTTOM, Robert. Private, Militia, Broad Creek Company, 38th Battalion, 1777-1778 [Ref: N-86/105, M-226]. Private, Militia, Broad Creek Company, 38th Battalion, 1780-1781 [Ref: N-86/105, M-234].

WINTERBOTTOM, Thomas. Private, Militia, Broad Creek Company, 38th Battalion, 1777-1778 [Ref: N-86/105, M-226]. Private, Militia, Broad Creek Company, 38th Battalion, 1780-1781 [Ref: N-86/105, M-234].

WINTERS, Jonathan. Private, Militia, United Company, 38th Battalion, 1777-1778 [Ref: N-86/105, M-227]. Took the Oath of Allegiance and Fidelity on or about March 1, 1778 [Ref: J-1814, N-106/114, which listed the name as "Jonathan Winter"]. Private, Militia, United Company, 38th Battalion, 1780-1781 [Ref: N-86/105, M-233].

WOLCUTT, Matthias. Took the Oath of Allegiance and Fidelity on or after March 1, 1778 [Ref: J-1814, N-106/114].

WOODS, Henry. See "James Woods," q.v.

WOODS, James (1728-   ). Born in St. Peter's Parish, Talbot County, on November 6, 1728, son of Henry and Sarah Woods [Ref: V-86]. Took the Oath of Allegiance and Fidelity on or about March 1, 1778 [Ref: J-1814, N-106/114].

WOODS, Jonathan. Private, Militia, 4th Battalion, Capt. Greenbury Goldsborough's Company, reviewed and passed July 27, 1776 [Ref: D-67].

WOODS, Samuel. Private, Militia, Union Company, 4th Battalion, 1780-1781 [Ref: N-86/105, M-229].

WOODS, Sarah. See "James Woods," q.v.

WOODS, William. Private, 4th Independent Company of Maryland Regular Troops, Capt. James Hindman's Company, September, 1776 muster roll; enlisted January 28, 1776 [Ref: D-24].

WOOLCUTT (WOOLCOT), James Jr. Private, Militia, Capt. Thomas Bullen's Company; no date was given; possibly late 1775 or early 1776 [Ref: Z-3].

WOOLCUTT, John. Private, Militia, 4th Battalion, Capt. Greenbury Goldsborough's Company, reviewed and passed July 27, 1776 [Ref: D-68].

WOOLCUTT (WOOLCOTT), Matthias. Private, Militia, Capt. Thomas Bullen's Company; no date was given; possibly late 1775 or early 1776 [Ref: Z-3].

WOOLCUTT (WOOLCUT), Woolman. Private, Militia, Oxford Company, 38th Battalion, 1777-1778 [Ref: N-86/105, M-227].

WORKS, Hugh. Private, Militia, Hand in Hand Company, 4th Battalion, 1780-1781 [Ref: N-86/105, M-232].

WORSTER, William. Private, Militia, Capt. Thomas Bullen's Company; no date was given; possibly late 1775 or early 1776 [Ref: Z-3].

WORTHINGTON, Ben. Private, 4th Independent Company of Maryland Regular Troops, Capt. James Hindman's Company, September, 1776 muster roll; enlisted January 22, 1776 [Ref: D-24].

WOULDS, James. Adjutant, 5th Maryland Line, March 16, 1777. Ensign, May 27, 1778; resigned September 23, 1779 [Ref: D-254]. Took the Oath of Allegiance and Fidelity on or about March 1, 1778 [Ref: J-1814, N-106/114].

WRENCH, James. Paid £7 by the Maryland Council of Safety on October 12, 1776, "for collecting & ascertaining the number of souls in Talbot County." [Ref: B-337]. Private, Militia, Wye Company, 4th Battalion, 1777-1778 [Ref: N-86/105, M-223]. Took the Oath of Allegiance and Fidelity on or about March 1, 1778 [Ref: J-1814, N-106/114].

WRIGHT, Turbutt. Born in Maryland before 1744, he married Elizabeth Evans, rendered patriotic service during the revolution, and died in 1783 [Ref: Y-3311]. "Turbutt Wright, Esquire" was appointed on February 3, 1777 to serve on the Maryland Council of Safety "in the room of James Lloyd Chamberlaine, Esquire, who declined to act." [Ref: C-109, C-488].

WRIGHTSON, Catherine. See "Wrightson Lambdin," q.v.

WRIGHTSON, James. Private, Militia, Bayside Company, 38th Battalion, 1777-1778 [Ref: N-86/105, M-228]. Took the Oath of Allegiance and Fidelity on or about March 1, 1778 [Ref: J-1814, N-106/114].

WRIGHTSON, James Jr. Took the Oath of Allegiance and Fidelity on or about March 1, 1778 [Ref: J-1814, N-106/114]. Private, Militia, Bayside Company, 38th Battalion, 1780-1781 [Ref: N-86/105, M-233].

WRIGHTSON, Joshua. Private, Militia, Bayside Company, 38th Battalion, 1777-1778 [Ref: N-86/105, M-228]. Took the Oath of Allegiance and Fidelity on or after March 1, 1778 [Ref: J-1814, N-106/114]. Private, Militia, Bayside Company, 38th Battalion, 1780-1781 [Ref: N-86/105, M-233].

WRIGHTSON, Thomas. Private, Militia, United Company, who was draughted on May 1, 1781 to serve until December 10, 1781 in the Maryland Continental Troops [Ref: D-370].

YATES, Thomas. Private, Militia, Union Company, 4th Battalion, 1780-1781 [Ref: N-86/105, M-230].

YERBURY, Sarah. See "Robert Goldsborough," q.v.

Heritage Books by Henry C. Peden, Jr.:

1890 Reconstructed Census of Harford County, Maryland, Volume 1: A-J

1890 Reconstructed Census of Harford County, Maryland, Volume 2: K-Z

A Closer Look at St. John's Parish Registers [Baltimore County, Md.], 1701–1801

A Collection of Maryland Church Records

A Guide to Genealogical Research in Maryland: 5th Edition, Revised and Enlarged

Abstracts of Marriages and Deaths in Harford County, Md., Newspapers, 1837–1871

Abstracts of the Ledgers and Accounts of the Bush Store and Rock Run Store, 1759–1771

Abstracts of the Orphans Court Proceedings of Harford County, 1778–1800

Abstracts of Wills, Harford County, Maryland, 1800–1805

African American Cemeteries in Harford County, Maryland

Anne Arundel County, Maryland, Marriage References 1658–1800
Henry C. Peden, Jr. and Veronica Clarke Peden

Baltimore City [Maryland] Deaths and Burials, 1834–1840

Baltimore County, Maryland, Overseers of Roads, 1693–1793

Bastardy Cases in Baltimore County, Maryland, 1673–1783

Bastardy Cases in Harford County, Maryland, 1774–1844

More Bastardy Cases in Harford County, Maryland, 1773–1893

Bible and Family Records of Harford County, Maryland, Families: Volume V

*Biographical Dictionary of Harford County, Maryland, 1774–1974:
Over 1,200 Sketches of Prominent Citizens during the First 200 years of the County's
History with Seventeen Appendices Listing Public Officials from 1774 to 2020*
Henry C. Peden, Jr. and William O. Carr

Cecil County, Maryland Marriage References, 1674–1824
Henry C. Peden, Jr. and Veronica Clarke Peden

Children of Harford County: Indentures and Guardianships, 1801–1830

Colonial Delaware Soldiers and Sailors, 1638–1776

*Colonial Families of the Eastern Shore of Maryland
Volumes 5, 6, 7, 8, 9, 11, 12, 13, 14, 16, and 19*
Henry C. Peden, Jr. and F. Edward Wright

Colonial Families of the Eastern Shore of Maryland: Volume 21 and Volume 23

Colonial Maryland Soldiers and Sailors, 1634–1734

Colonial Tavern Keepers of Maryland and Delaware, 1634–1776

Dorchester County, Maryland, Marriage References, 1669–1800
Henry C. Peden, Jr. and Veronica Clarke Peden

Dr. John Archer's First Medical Ledger, 1767–1769, Annotated Abstracts

Early Anglican Records of Cecil County

*Early Harford Countians, Individuals Living in
Harford County, Maryland. in Its Formative Years
Volume 1: A to K, Volume 2: L to Z, and Volume 3: Supplement*

Family Cemeteries and Grave Sites in Harford County, Maryland, (Revised Edition)

Farm Directory, 1774–2024, Harford County, Maryland

First Presbyterian Church Records, Baltimore, Maryland, 1840–1879

Frederick County, Md., Marriage References and Family Relationships, 1748–1800
Henry C. Peden, Jr. and Veronica Clarke Peden

Genealogical Gleanings from Harford County, Md., Medical Records, 1772–1852
Winner of the Norris Harris Prize from MHS for the best genealogical reference book in 2016!

Harford County Taxpayers in 1870, 1872 and 1883

Harford County, Maryland Death Records, 1849–1899

Harford County, Maryland Deponents, 1775–1835

Harford County, Maryland Divorces and Separations, 1823–1923

Harford County, Maryland, Death Certificates, 1898–1918: An Annotated Index

Harford County, Maryland, Divorce Cases, 1827–1912: An Annotated Index

Harford County, Maryland, Inventories, 1774–1804

Harford County, Md., Marriage References and Family Relationships, 1774–1824
Henry C. Peden, Jr. and Veronica Clarke Peden

Harford County, Md., Marriage References and Family Relationships, 1825–1850

Harford County, Md., Marriage References and Family Relationships, 1851–1860
Henry C. Peden, Jr. and Veronica Clarke Peden

Harford County, Md., Marriage References and Family Relationships, 1861–1870
Henry C. Peden, Jr. and Veronica Clarke Peden

Harford County, Md., Marriage References and Family Relationships, 1871–1875

Harford County, Md., Marriage References and Family Relationships, 1876–1880

Harford County, Md., Marriage References and Family Relationships, 1881–1885

Harford County, Md., Marriage References and Family Relationships, 1886–1889

Harford (Maryland) Homicides: Cases of Murder and Attempted Murder: Committed by Men and Women Who Were "Seduced by the Instigation of the Devil" in Harford County, Maryland During the 18th and 19th Centuries

Harford (Maryland) Suicides: Cases of Self-killings and Attempted Suicides Committed by Men and Women Who Suffered from an "Aberration of the Mind" in Harford County, Maryland, 1817–1947

Harford (Old Brick Baptist) Church, Harford County, Maryland, Records and Members (1742–1974), Tombstones, Burials (1775–2009) and Family Relationships

Heirs and Legatees of Harford County, Maryland, 1774–1802

Heirs and Legatees of Harford County, Maryland, 1802–1846

Inhabitants of Baltimore County, Maryland, 1763–1774

Inhabitants of Cecil County, Maryland 1774–1800

Inhabitants of Cecil County, Maryland, 1649–1774

Inhabitants of Harford County, Maryland, 1791–1800

Inhabitants of Kent County, Maryland, 1637–1787

Insolvent Debtors in 19th Century Harford County, Maryland: A Legal and Genealogical Digest

Joseph A. Pennington & Co., Havre De Grace, Maryland, Funeral Home Records: Volume II, 1877–1882, 1893–1900

Kent County, Maryland Marriage References, 1642–1800
Henry C. Peden, Jr. and Veronica Clarke Peden

Marriages and Deaths from Baltimore Newspapers, 1817–1824

Maryland Bible Records, Volume 1: Baltimore and Harford Counties

Maryland Bible Records, Volume 2: Baltimore and Harford Counties

Maryland Bible Records, Volume 3: Carroll County

Maryland Bible Records, Volume 4: Eastern Shore

Maryland Bible Records, Volume 5: Harford, Baltimore and Carroll Counties

Maryland Bible Records, Volume 7: Baltimore, Harford and Frederick Counties

Maryland Deponents, 1634–1799

Maryland Deponents: Volume 3, 1634–1776

Maryland Prisoners Languishing in Goal, Volume 1: 1635–1765

Maryland Prisoners Languishing in Goal, Volume 2: 1766–1800

*Maryland Public Service Records, 1775–1783:
A Compendium of Men and Women of Maryland Who Rendered Aid in Support of the American Cause against Great Britain during the Revolutionary War*

Marylanders and Delawareans in the French and Indian War, 1756–1763

*Marylanders to Carolina: Migration of Marylanders to
North Carolina and South Carolina prior to 1800*

Marylanders to Kentucky, 1775–1825

Marylanders to Ohio and Indiana, Migration Prior to 1835

Marylanders to Tennessee

McComas Funeral Home Interments, 1901–1941, Harford County, Maryland

Methodist Records of Baltimore City, Maryland: Volume 1, 1799–1829

Methodist Records of Baltimore City, Maryland: Volume 2, 1830–1839

*Methodist Records of Baltimore City, Maryland: Volume 3, 1840–1850
(East City Station)*

Ministers Directory, 1774-1924, Harford County, Maryland

More Maryland Deponents, 1716–1799

*More Marylanders to Carolina: Migration of Marylanders to North Carolina and
South Carolina prior to 1800*

More Marylanders to Kentucky, 1778–1828

More Marylanders to Ohio and Indiana: Migrations Prior to 1835

Orphans and Indentured Children of Baltimore County, Maryland, 1777–1797

Outpensioners of Harford County, Maryland, 1856–1896
Presbyterian Records of Baltimore City, Maryland, 1765–1840
Quaker Records of Baltimore and Harford Counties, Maryland, 1801–1825
Quaker Records of Northern Maryland, 1716–1800
Quaker Records of Southern Maryland, 1658–1800
Revolutionary Patriots of Anne Arundel County, Maryland, 1775–1783
Revolutionary Patriots of Baltimore Town and Baltimore County, 1775–1783
Revolutionary Patriots of Calvert and St. Mary's Counties, Maryland, 1775–1783
Revolutionary Patriots of Caroline County, Maryland, 1775–1783
Revolutionary Patriots of Cecil County, Maryland, 1775–1783
Revolutionary Patriots of Charles County, Maryland, 1775–1783
Revolutionary Patriots of Delaware, 1775–1783
Revolutionary Patriots of Dorchester County, Maryland, 1775–1783
Revolutionary Patriots of Frederick County, Maryland, 1775–1783
Revolutionary Patriots of Harford County, Maryland, 1775–1783
Revolutionary Patriots of Kent and Queen Anne's Counties, 1775–1783
Revolutionary Patriots of Lancaster County, Pennsylvania, 1775–1783
Revolutionary Patriots of Maryland, 1775–1783: A Supplement
Revolutionary Patriots of Maryland, 1775–1783: Second Supplement
Revolutionary Patriots of Montgomery County, Maryland, 1776–1783
Revolutionary Patriots of Prince George's County, Maryland, 1775–1783
Revolutionary Patriots of Talbot County, Maryland, 1775–1783
Revolutionary Patriots of Washington County, Maryland, 1776–1783
Revolutionary Patriots of Worcester and Somerset Counties, Maryland, 1775–1783
St. George's (Old Spesutia) Parish Harford County, Maryland Church and Cemetery Records, 1820–1920
St. John's and St. George's Parish Registers, 1696–1851
Slaves and Slave Owners, Harford County, Maryland, 1814: Information Gleaned from 1814 Property Tax Assessments and Supplemented with Data from Subsequent Manumissions, Slave Sales and Runaway Notices
Survey Field Book of David and William Clark in Harford County, Md., 1770–1812
Talbot County, Maryland Marriage References, 1662–1800
Henry C. Peden, Jr. and Veronica Clarke Peden
The Crenshaws of Kentucky, 1800–1995
The Delaware Militia in the War of 1812
Union Chapel United Methodist Church Cemetery Tombstone Inscriptions, Wilna, Harford County, Maryland

www.ingramcontent.com/pod-product-compliance
Lightning Source LLC
Chambersburg PA
CBHW060512090426
42735CB00011B/2191